The Poorer Nations

In love,

In joy

in freedom

V

The Poorer Nations:

A POSSIBLE HISTORY OF THE GLOBAL SOUTH

Vijay Prashad

With a Foreword by
Boutros Boutros-Ghali

VERSO
London • New York

This paperback edition first published by Verso 2014
First published by Verso 2012
© Vijay Prashad 2012, 2014
Foreword © Boutros Boutros-Ghali 2012, 2014

3 5 7 9 10 8 6 4 2

Verso
UK: 6 Meard Street, London W1F 0EG
US: 20 Jay Street, Suite 1010, Brooklyn, NY 11201
www.versobooks.com

Verso is the imprint of New Left Books

ISBN-13: 978-1-78168-158-9 (PBK)
eISBN-13: 978-1-78168-487-0 (UK)
eISBN-13: 978-1-78168-953-9 (US)

British Library Cataloguing in Publication Data
A catalogue record for this book is available from the British Library

Library of Congress Has Cataloged the Hardback Edition as Follows

Prashad, Vijay.
The poorer nations : a possible history of the Global South / Vijay Prashad.
     p. cm.
Includes bibliographical references and index.
  ISBN 978-1-84467-952-2 (hbk. : alk. paper) —
ISBN 978-1-84467-953-9 (ebook)
1. Developing countries—Economic policy.
2. Developing countries—Foreign economic relations.
3. Neoliberalism—Developing countries—History.
4. Developing countries—History. I. Title.
HC59.7.P7145 2012
330.9172'4—dc23
                        2012036260

Typeset in Minion Pro by MJ Gavan, Truro, Cornwall
Printed in the US by Maple Vail

Lisa Armstrong, *just because.*
Zalia and Rosa Maya, *so that.*
Soni Prashad and Rosi Samuel, *as per prior arrangement.*

Contents

Foreword

This very significant, highly readable and interesting book should be welcomed by policy and academic circles, especially in the developing countries but also worldwide, and the author congratulated for having undertaken to write about a critical period in the history of the global South.

He has succeeded in producing a unique, exceptional study that weaves together different events, processes and strands into a comprehensive overview of the struggle of the developing countries to change the world economic order and place their development at the center of global preoccupations. The author also discusses their efforts to organize their own collective action for advancing these goals in the international arena, and offers important insights into the dynamics of the frustrating dialogue and negotiations between the South and the North, with the developed countries all too often resorting to stonewalling tactics.

This volume is a major contribution to the institutional history of the South, made by someone from the South who has the developing countries' situation and cause close to his heart. It highlights the critical need for scholarship on development, South-South and North-South *problematique* to be undertaken by authors from the South. This domain has for too long been dominated by scholars from the North. Also, many of the analyses, in trying to be "objective" and to tread a fine line between the positions of the North and the South, failed to be partisan to the cause of development and the weaker partners in this global tango. The sympathetic approach to the cause and case of the South taken by Vijay Prashad is refreshing and is to be commended.

The author should be thanked for his effort to recall some of the early enthusiasm that characterized the Third World movement. The historical picture needs to be clarified and remembered. Vijay Prashad has helped open the vista on complex interrelated events that have preceded today's global situation and standoff. Many of his observations and conclusions are not necessarily favorable to the South, as they point out missed opportunities or inadequate efforts arising from the subjective and objective weaknesses of developing countries. As such, the study could be useful in future efforts to improve and energize their collective action in the world arena.

It is to be hoped that this kind of analysis will contribute to renewed interest in development and in many of the valuable ideas and objectives that were sidelined or forgotten during the recent multilateral journey, so ably depicted by the author. The book should be made required reading in universities of the

South and for all those entering or working in the civil service in developing countries. Without knowledge of history and of one's own past it is impossible to conceive the path to the future. The North is well equipped, has its version of history and wants it to be universally accepted. It is clear in its mind as to what it wants and what it is protecting. The countries of the South are not properly equipped. They have become quite dependent intellectually on the North, its analyses, information, assessments and solutions, as concerns global issues and their domestic situations and objectives. Professor Prashad's study is a contribution to the intellectual-cum-political emancipation of developing countries and their empowerment through greater self-reliance on their own intellectual and analytical resources, i.e. their intellectual liberation from dominance by the North.

Boutros Boutros-Ghali
Former UN Secretary-General and
Chairman of the South Centre Board

Introduction

The Third World today faces Europe like a colossal mass whose project should be to try to resolve the problem to which Europe has not been able to find the answers.

Frantz Fanon, 1961[2]

The massive wave of anticolonial movements that opened with the Haitian Revolution (1791–1804) and came into its own by the last quarter of the nineteenth century broke the legitimacy of colonial domination. No longer could it be said that a European power had the manifest destiny to govern other peoples. When such colonial adventures were tried out, they were chastised for being immoral.

In 1928, the anticolonial leaders gathered in Brussels for a meeting of the League Against Imperialism. This was the first attempt to create a global platform to unite the visions of the anticolonial movements from Africa, Asia, and Latin America. Considerations of expediency and the convulsions of World War II blocked any progress on such a platform. It would have to wait until 1955, in Bandung, Indonesia, when a smattering of newly independent or almost independent African and Asian countries sent their leaders to confer on a planetary agenda. The Bandung dynamic inaugurated the Third World Project, a seemingly incoherent set of demands that were actually very carefully worked out through the institutions of the United Nations and what would become, in 1961, the Non-Aligned Movement (NAM).

The central concept for the new nations was the Third World. The Third World was not a place; it was a project. Galvanized by the mass movements and by the failures of capitalist mal-development, the leaderships in the darker nations looked to each other for another agenda. Politically they wanted more planetary democracy. No more the serfs of their colonial masters, they wanted to have a voice and power on the world stage. What did that voice say? It spoke of three main themes:

a. *Peace.* It had become apparent by the mid 1950s and early 1960s that the Cold War between the two superpower blocs was catastrophic for

---

1 This section relies upon Vijay Prashad, *The Darker Nations: A People's History of the Third World*, New York: New Press, 2008.

2 Frantz Fanon, *The Wretched of the Earth*, New York: Grove Press, 1963, p. 314.

the planet. Not only might the nuclear-fueled confrontation result in Armageddon, but the sheer waste of social resources on the arms race would distort the possibility of human development. By the early 1950s, the United States was spending 10 percent of its gross domestic product on its defense sector, a development that raised the ire of President Eisenhower, who at the end of the decade bemoaned the growth of the "military-industrial complex." This complex did not end at the borders of the United States. It had ambitions for the planet, wanting to sell arms to every country and to insinuate a security complex over the social agenda of the Third World Project. No wonder that the first concrete task after the formation of the Non-Aligned Movement in Belgrade was to send India's Nehru and Ghana's Nkrumah to Moscow, and Indonesia's Sukarno and Mali's Keita to Washington, carrying the NAM's Appeal for Peace. Kennedy and Khrushchev offered the typical bromides, but did not reverse the tensions that intensified with the building of the Berlin Wall and the tank standoff at Checkpoint Charlie. The Third World Project kept faith with the Bandung communiqué, which called for "the regulation, limitation, control and reduction of all armed forces and armaments, including the prohibition of the production, experimentation and use of all weapons of mass destruction, and to establish effective international controls to this end."[3] The International Atomic Energy Agency of 1957 was a child of Bandung, and a cornerstone of the Third World Project.

b. *Bread.* The new nations of Africa and Asia, and the renewed national agendas of Latin America, explicitly recognized that the countries they had seized were impoverished. Any direction forward would have to confront the legacy of colonial economy—with the advantages seized by the Atlantic powers and the trade rules drawn up to benefit those historical, not comparative, advantages. Economists like Raúl Prebisch of Argentina, who would become the first director-general of the UN Conference on Trade and Development (UNCTAD), challenged the Atlantic institutions such as the General Agreement on Trade and Tariffs (GATT) and the IMF, which Prebisch called "a conspiracy against the laws of the market." When Prebisch took the helm at UNCTAD, the economic arm of the Third World Project, he announced the need for a "new order in the international economy … so that the market functions properly not only for the big countries but the developing countries in their relations with the developed."[4] It was out of this

---

3   George McTuran Kahin, ed., *The Asian-African Conference: Bandung, Indonesia, April 1955*, New York: Cornell University Press, 1956, p. 83.

4   Edgar J. Dosman, *The Life and Times of Raúl Prebisch, 1901–1986*, Montreal:

general framework that the Third World fought for a revision of the "free trade" agenda, for better commodity prices, for primary goods cartels (out of which came OPEC), and for a more generous policy for the transfer of investment and technology from North to South. Fought at each turn by the Atlantic powers, the Third World took refuge in the UN General Assembly with the 1973 New International Economic Order resolution. It was the highest point of the Third World Project.

c. *Justice.* The NAM, created in 1961, was designed as a secretariat of the Third World Project, with the Group of 77 (1964) to act on its behalf in the United Nations. The founders of the NAM (Nehru of India, Nasser of Egypt, Sukarno of Indonesia, and Tito of Yugoslavia) recognized that little of their agenda would be able to move forward without a more democratic international structure. The UN had been hijacked by the five permanent members of the Security Council. The IMF and the World Bank had been captured by the Atlantic powers, and the GATT was designed to undermine any attempt by the new nations to revise the international economic order. It was hoped that the NAM, and the G77, would put pressure on both the West and the East to afford political space to the new nations. It was not to be. Nigeria's foreign minister, Jaja Wachuku, came to the United Nations on September 30, 1963, and put the problem plainly: "Does this Organization want the African States to be just vocal members, with no right to express their views on any particular matter in important organs of the United Nations[?] Are we going to continue to be veranda boys?"[5] The implication was that the NAM states would watch from the balcony while the five permanent members controlled the debate within the UN.

That was the Third World Project: for peace, for bread, and for justice. It came to the world stage on shaky terrain. The houses of the new nations were not in order. They were constrained by a lack of democracy in their own political worlds, combined with mismanagement of economic resources and a very shallow reconstruction of the social landscape. The old social classes hesitated before the anticolonial mass movements, but as these were demobilized the old elites called on the generals or on right-wing populist politicians to sweep up the mess. The Project was hampered by these failings, but it was not these limitations that did it in.

What did it in was the Atlantic project.

McGill-Queens University Press, 2008, p. 393.

5 Thomas Hovet, Jr., "The Role of Africa in the United Nations," *Annals of the American Academy of Political and Social Science* 354: 1 (1964), p. 128.

THE ATLANTIC PROJECT

Nothing important can come from the South. The axis of history starts in Moscow, goes to Bonn, crosses over to Washington, and then goes to Tokyo. What happens in the South is of no importance.

Henry Kissinger, 1969[6]

In 1975, the seven leaders of the major advanced industrial countries met in the Château de Rambouillet to decide the fate of the planet. They were the Group of 7: the United States, the United Kingdom, France, Germany, Italy, Japan, and Canada. The Rambouillet gathering was their first formal meeting. The G7 leaders were detained by four facts. Three of them were encumbrances that they wished to do away with:

1. The *social-democratic agenda* that many of them emerged from had now become expensive (in terms not only of the social wages that had to be paid, but also the wage packets to the restive workers).
2. The *communist agenda*, which had become more accommodating, but was still able to offer those restive workers an alternative.
3. The *Third World Project*, whose most recent instantiations—the Oil Weapon of 1973, accompanied by the demand for a New International Economic Order (NIEO)—had come as a genuine shock.

These three horizons needed to be abandoned. The fourth problem was a more general one, and it ended up being the solution to their other three irritants: the new *geography of production*.

Gerald Ford opened the conversation at Rambouillet with a plea that the main thrust had to be for the leaders "to ensure that the current world economic situation is not seen as a crisis in the democratic or capitalist system."[7] The G7 had to prevent the capitalist crisis from becoming a political one; it had to be handled as a technical economic problem. This was all very well as rhetoric, but it was not a salve from the point of view of the more realistic people in the room.

Helmut Schmidt, who was a socialist and chancellor of West Germany, took the floor:

---

6   Seymour M. Hersh, *The Price of Power: Kissinger in the White House*, New York: Summit Books, 1983, p. 263.

7   "Memorandum of Conversation from the First Session of the Economic Summit at Rambouillet," November 15, 1975, Rambouillet Economic Summit, NSA, Memoranda of Conversations, 1973–1977, Gerald R. Ford Library.

Harold [Wilson] of the UK, you talked of viable industries, and indicated that this excluded lame ducks. You referred to textiles as an example. I am a close friend of the chairman of the textile workers union in Germany. It is a union of a shrinking industry. *I would hope that this would not be repeated outside this room.* Given the high level of wages in Europe, I cannot help but believe that in the long run textile industries here will have to vanish. We cannot ward off cheaper competition from outside. *It is a pity because it is viable*; capital invested in a job in the textile industry in Germany is as high as it is in the German steel mills. But wages in East Asia are very low compared with ours. The German textile industry is viable, but will vanish in ten or twelve years.[8]

Foresight, collusion: it does not matter. What matters is the emergence of the new geography of production, *viz.* the disarticulation of Northern Fordism, the emergence of satellite and undersea cable technology, the containerization of ships, and other technological shifts that enabled firms to take advantage of differential wage rates. In Schmidt's case, the wages of East Asia.

This is familiar stuff. It is often taken as the ground for the emergence of neoliberalism. From David Harvey's useful primer, we get the impression that neoliberalism was experimented with during the New York municipal crisis, and then, via the IMF and its *élèves*, exported to the rest of the planet.[9] This is not the full story. What Harvey does not relate is the necessary demise of the Third World Project, and so the opening up of the countries of the South to the new geography of production. Resistance to transnational corporations had been quite strong until the late 1970s, when the Third World Project went into a tailspin, assassinated by the enforced debt crisis. For example, the United Nations Centre on Transnational Corporations spent its energy for three decades defining a code of conduct for transnational firms. It was substantially dissolved in 1992, and became a fixer for corporations rather than a regulator of their business practices.

Neoliberalism had a polycentric revival—in the G7, of course; but so too in the capitals of the Pacific Rim and in the emergent "locomotives of the South" (Brazil, India, South Africa, and China). The ruling classes in these societies had, like their European and American cousins, long wanted to abandon the cultural strictures of old Nationalism: the requirements of the social-democratic Welfare State in the Atlantic sector; and the requirements of the anticolonial Third World State in the continents of Africa, Asia, and Latin

---

8 "Memorandum of Conversation at the Rambouillet Summit, made for Brent Scowcroft by Robert Hormats," November 15–17, 1975, National Security Adviser's Memoranda of Conversation Collection, Box 16, Gerald Ford Presidential Library. Emphasis added.

9 David Harvey, *A Brief History of Neoliberalism*, New York: Oxford University Press, 2005.

America. Small pockets of elite opinion harbored resentment at the anticolonial heritage. Out of these pockets came new intellectual agendas, including the revival of the Hayek school of liberalism, holding that the state must be excluded from economic activity as much as possible. Cultural ideas of individualism and enterprise were celebrated in the corporate media, at the expense of the national liberation ideas of socialism and the collective good. The impatient elites wanted to set themselves apart from the obligations of the postcolonial state. They wanted to live, as the Indian poet Nissim Ezekiel put it,

> At jazzy picnics,
> Cooking on a smoky stove,
> Shooing beggars from the backdoor wall.[10]

It was fitting for them that the new postcolonial states had failed in so many ways; the failures were used as a measure to push for their own agendas. These elites produced their own neoliberalism in response to the same debt crisis that had opened their countries up to the factories of the North.

By the 1980s the reinvigorated Atlantic bloc was fighting back aggressively against the NAM and all talk of a New International Economic Order. At the Cancún meeting in 1981 to discuss the ill-starred Brandt Report, Ronald Reagan and Margaret Thatcher came to throw down the gauntlet. Reagan mocked the proceedings, particularly those "who mistake compassion for development, and claim massive transfers of wealth somehow, miraculously, will produce new well-being." The North-South dialogue was effectively ended.

The corridors of the IMF and the World Bank were scrubbed clean of old Keynesians and developmentalists. Only marginalists and neoliberal thinkers were welcome into the leadership. Questions of history and of sociology were of no consequence. GDP was the only variable that mattered. At the IMF, H. Johannes Witteveen gave way to Jacques de Larosière, and at the World Bank, Tom Clausen and Anna Krueger washed the stains left by Robert McNamara. Liberalism was shown the door.

The UN too had to be cleansed. When he briefed Daniel Moynihan for his new UN post, Henry Kissinger told him, "We need a strategy. In principle, I think we should move things from the General Assembly to the Security Council. It is important to see that we have our confidence and nerve." He wanted the US to "get hold of the Specialized Agencies," such as UNCTAD and UNESCO, and turn them to the "business civilization" of the North.

Having excised the institutional threats to the Atlantic project, the G7 moved to use the debt crisis of the 1980s to its advantage, pushing through a new intellectual property and trade regime to consolidate the gains of the

---

10   Nissim Ezekiel, "Portrait," *Collected Poems, 1952–1988*, New Delhi: Oxford University Press, 1989, p. 45.

North against the South. By the time the NAM met in New Delhi in 1983, the exhaustion of the Third World Project before the fierce thrust from the North was evident. There was to be no effective political strategy to deal with the debt crisis. The Southern countries were willing out of political necessity to see the Club of Paris and the Club of London one by one, receiving their structural adjustment orders so as to extend their credit lines. More radical voices called for a debtors' strike, but this fell on deaf ears. The problem was not the debt itself. The problem lay with the power asymmetry, the favored countries being able to refinance their debts on favorable rates from the bank cartels, as well as having lower risk premiums than other countries. The North could command the banks.

Rather than a South-led New International Economic Order, the world had to live with a North-led New International Property Order. The Uruguay Round of the GATT changed the intellectual property regime so that reverse engineering or transfer of technology became illegal. The North and its businesses would be able to outsource the production of commodities to the South, but the bulk of the profits for their sale would be preserved as rent for intellectual property (this was the process that produced "jobless growth" in the North and led to the debt-fueled consumerism indulged in by its vast mass—a social imbalance that has now exploded, first through the housing market, and soon after through the personal credit market).

In 1981, the new secretary-general of the UN, Javier Pérez de Cuéllar, called the gap between North and South "a breach of the most fundamental human right," and pledged that the UN would work to bridge it. The UN, now under Atlantic tutelage, did no such thing.

THE SOUTH PROJECT

In Mohammed Lakhdar-Hamina's *Chronique des Années de Braise* (1975), a crazy prophet emerges from the city to greet a horde of bedraggled peasants. He extends his arms and says, "You were poor and free. Now you are only poor!"

In 1989, the poor from the hillside settlements around Caracas, Venezuela, rose in revolt against the rise in bus fares, spurred on by an increase in petrol prices. This was the most spectacular of the IMF riots, or bread riots. More such protests and rebellions shaped the social world on all the continents, now increasingly even in the Atlantic world (as we see with the social convulsions in the southern European countries, and with the Tea Party and the Occupy protests in the United States). These protests were united by at least five processes:

1. Enforced austerity regimes, pushed first in Africa, Asia, and Latin America under the name of structural adjustment, and then more

recently in the Atlantic world under the name of balanced budgets and fiscal responsibility.

2. The dominance of the FIRE (finance, insurance and real estate) sector, whose fire-sale of assets in the name of privatization produced higher unemployment and very great levels of social inequality.

3. Catastrophic unemployment in pockets, particularly in rural areas where factory farming has deskilled work through the use of expensive and unsustainable technological inputs. Global unemployment is at spectacularly high levels, with an "alarming" future for joblessness, according to the International Labour Organization's *World of Work Report 2012*. Young people are nearly three times as likely as adults to be unemployed. An estimated 6.4 million young people have given up hope of finding a job.

4. High unemployment comes in the context of a collapsed state-support network, a weakened social fabric, and criminally high food and fuel prices that have resulted mostly from commodity speculation in these markets. From Rome, the Food and Agriculture Organization reports that the number of the world's hungry has topped one billion. Since 2008, food riots have struck Africa, Asia, and Latin America, with the edges of Europe and the United States now prone to inflation protests. The Social Unrest Index shows that 57 out of 106 countries showed a risk of increased social unrest. The IMF recognized that one of the spurs for the Arab Revolt of this year was the rise in bread prices resulting from the end to the "democracy of bread" (*dimuqratiyyat al-khubz*).[11]

5. Disparity and deprivation do not sit well with the commonplace ideas of fairness and justice. The powerful know this. The way they divide the national budgets of their countries demonstrates their values. More goes to the military, police, and prisons than to schools, to the *Mukhabarat* than to the ministry of health, to guns than to bread. Given the social consequences of neoliberalism, it is far more effective and logical for the 1 percent to build a security apparatus, to cage people into devastated cities or to hold them in congested high-security prisons. There is nothing irrational about the prison-industrial complex; from a neoliberal perspective, it is perfectly reasonable. Neoliberalism was always purchased with an iron fist, and rarely with a velvet glove.

6. It is bad enough if one is reduced to the level of bare existence, but even worse if this condition is not general across the population. Rates of social inequality are at record levels for the modern era. "Some have

11   Vijay Prashad, *Arab Spring/Libyan Winter*, Oakland and London: AK Press, 2012.

predicted convergence," the UNDP had noted in 1999, "but the past decade has shown increasing concentration of income among people, corporations and countries."[12] The gaps have increased exponentially since 1999. A 2008 UN report shows us that the richest 1 percent of adults across the planet own 40 percent of global assets, while the richest 10 percent own 85 percent.[13]

One word unites the variegated protests across the planet: no! From Occupy Wall Street to Tahrir Square, from the Kennedy Road shack settlement in Durban to the rural hamlets of Haryana, the policies of neoliberalism have been resoundingly rejected. What has emerged since the 1990s has been *resistance*, the defusing of the energy of the neoliberal policies that emerge out of international and national institutions. The "global South" has come to refer to this concatenation of protests against the theft of the commons, against the theft of human dignity and rights, against the undermining of democratic institutions and the promises of modernity. The global South is this: a world of protest, a whirlwind of creative activity. These protests have produced an opening that has no easily definable political direction. Some of them turn backwards, taking refuge in imagined unities of the past or in the divine realm. Others are merely defensive, seeking to survive in the present. And yet others find the present intolerable, and nudge us into the future.

How has the NAM reacted to these developments? Has it been able to break out of the defensive posture that has distinguished it since the 1980s? At the 2006 Havana NAM summit, Venezuela's Hugo Chávez called for the creation of a new commission to study the current situation and propose an agenda that "will not be thrown to the wind." He nodded to the South Commission, whose work in the 1980s set in motion the theory of the "locomotives of the South"— although its own report, *The Challenge of the South*, published on the day Iraq invaded Kuwait in 1990, is little read.

The South Commission toiled in the unfavorable climate of the 1980s. Shunned by the North, the Commission made a virtue of necessity: it called for South-South cooperation, its general secretary, Manmohan Singh, offering the view that "the new locomotive forces have to be found within the South itself." It was this thinking that provided the calculations for the creation of the Group of 15 (at the 1989 NAM summit), then the IBSA Group (India, Brazil, South Africa) in 2003, and eventually the BRICS formation (Brazil, Russia, India,

---

12   United Nations Development Programme, *Human Development Report 1999*, New York: UNDP and Oxford University Press, 1999, p. 3.

13   James B. Davies, Susanna Sandström, Anthony Shorrocks, and Edward N. Wolff, "The World Distribution of Household Wealth," Discussion Paper no. 2008/03, United Nations University World Institute Development Economic Research, February 2008, p. 7.

China, South Africa) in 2009. These groups were seen as the locomotives of the South.

The IMF's 2011 report suggests that by 2016 the United States will no longer be the largest economy in the world.[14] This is, as the historian Fernand Braudel put it, the "sign of autumn" for Atlantic hegemony.[15] Signals of decline are visible in the fragile economic fundamentals in the Atlantic states, with the red light of caution burning bright over the dominance of finance in the economy and the increase in military spending. Since 2001, the United States alone has spent $7.6 trillion on its wars and its national security apparatus. This has accompanied massive cuts in social spending and tax breaks for the rich (in 2011, the top 1 percent in the United States earned an average tax cut greater than the average income of the other 99 percent). When, in 1925, it became clear that the United Kingdom's autumn was at hand, Winston Churchill proclaimed, "I would rather see finance less proud and industry more content."[16] These words would apply to the dominance of the stock exchanges of Wall Street, the City of London, and elsewhere over the lifeblood of the social economy.

Though, according to IMF projections, China will be the largest economy in 2016, it does not appear to wish to assert itself alone. China appears content to share the stage with the BRICS states, and to push for multipolarity and economic diversity. But the BRICS platform is limited in several ways:

1. The domestic policies of the BRICS states follow the general tenor of what one might consider Neoliberalism with Southern Characteristics— with sales of commodities and low wages to workers accompanying a recycled surplus turned over as credit to the North, as the livelihood of its own citizens remains flat. For example, the Indian people experience high levels of poverty and hunger, and yet India's growth rate is moderately high. Rather than turn over the social wealth in transfer payments or in the creation of a more robust social wage, the country seems to follow World Bank president Robert Zoellick's advice to turn over its surplus to "help the global economy recover from the crisis." There is something obscene about making the "locomotives from the South" pull the wagons of the North (particularly given the North's own reticence in allowing for a new surplus-recycling mechanism during the debt crisis of the 1980s).

---

14   IMF, *World Economic Outlook: Tensions from the Two-Speed Recovery: Unemployment, Commodities and Capital Flows*, Washington, DC: IMF, April 2011.

15   Fernand Braudel, *The Perspective of the World: Civilization and Capitalism, Fifteenth–Eighteenth Century*, Berkeley: University of California Press, 1992, p. 246.

16   D. E. Moggridge, *The Return to Gold, 1925: The Formulation of Economic Policy and its Critics*, Cambridge: Cambridge University Press, 1969, p. 54.

2. The BRICS alliance has not been able to create a new *institutional* foundation for its emergent authority. It continues to plead for a more democratic United Nations, and for more democracy at the IMF and the World Bank. These pleas have made little headway. During the height of the financial crisis, the G8 promised to disband, ceding its role to the G20; that is now forgotten. Anemic increases in its share of the vote at the IMF were insufficient to enable the South to put forward a joint candidate to become its executive in 2011.

3. The BRICS formation has not endorsed an *ideological* alternative to neoliberalism. There are many proposals for the creation of a more sustainable economic order, but these are left at the margins. The Rio formula for "separate and differential treatment" allows the South to make demands for concessions from universal policies that the North refuses to endorse (not the least of which relates to climate change). This is a defensive stand. There is, as yet, no positive alternative that has been taken forward. It might emerge out of the convulsions from below, where there is no appetite for tinkering with a system that most people see as fundamentally broken.

4. Finally, the BRICS project has no ability to sequester the *military* dominance of the United States and NATO. When the UN votes to allow "members states to use all necessary measures," as it did in Resolution 1973 on Libya, it essentially gives carte blanche to the Atlantic world to act with military force. There are no regional alternatives that have the capacity to operate. The force-projection of the United States remains planetary—with bases on every continent and with the ability of the US to strike almost anywhere. Regional mechanisms for peace and conflict resolution are weakened by this global presence of NATO and the US. Overwhelming military power translates into political power.

If we look into the entrails of the system, we will find that its solutions do not lie within it. Its problems are not technical, nor are they cultural. They are social problems that require political solutions. The social order of property, propriety, and power has to be radically revised. That is without question. The issue is what must be the strategy, the tactics, the way forward to a place that is not what we have now. The global South is a place of great struggle, of various tactics and strategies experimented with on the streets and in the halls of government. It is an unfinished story—one that has to have a good ending.

THE POORER NATIONS

The book before you will tell this story in four chapters. It opens at the high point of the Third World Project, with the New International Economic Order on the table before the global North. To thwart the NIEO, the North Atlantic countries formed the G7, which has been the executive of the North's ambitions. It was from the perch of the G7 that the North Atlantic's politicians swept aside Atlantic liberalism and welcomed the dynamic we know as neoliberalism. To tell this story in Chapter 1, I introduce the Brandt Commission, whose deliberations on the North-South divide take us to the high point of Atlantic liberalism. Its collapse, alongside that of the Third World Project, ushers in neoliberalism as the defining logic of the decades that run from the mid 1970s to the early 2010s.

Confounded by the tsunami of neoliberalism, a group of political intellectuals of the South gathered under the leadership of the former Tanzanian Premier Julius Nyerere to create new intellectual concepts and new policy initiatives to enable the South to escape from what had begun to look like its condition of permanent subservience. As the debt crisis and the GATT round took hold of the world order, Nyerere and his South Commission met to find a way out. Their solution lay in the idea of "South-South cooperation," and in their theory of the "locomotives of the South." This was the intellectual map that would produce the BRICS formation.

A close look at the debates inside the South Commission informs Chapter 2, which is about the theoretical possibilities for the South in a condition of abject economic and political servitude.

Released from the imperatives of the Third World Project, stuck in the doldrums of the debt crisis, and now pushed to become "locomotives of the South," the demographically large countries of Brazil, India, China, and later South Africa developed their own variant of Neoliberalism with Southern Characteristics. Chapter 3 is a concise history of the emergence of the BRICS. The BRICS do not promise any kind of revolutionary transformation of the world order; they are modest in their ambitions. Nevertheless, they are the first formation in thirty years to challenge the settled orthodoxy of the Global North. What the BRICS have enabled is the opening of some space, allowing a breath of air to oxygenate the stagnant world of neoliberal imperialism. The BRICS states have their own commitments to neoliberal policies, but they are no longer willing to bend before imperial power. It is in this gap between neoliberal policy and imperial power that an opportunity presents itself for the bloc of the South. At the UNCTAD XIII meeting in 2012, the opportunity was wielded by the South to stand up to the North. This represents a green shoot in an arid desert.

Transformation will not come through the initiatives of the "South from above." Hope rests in the "South from below," which is the focus of Chapter 4. The chapter investigates the potential of an internationalism of the South among social movements that gather at the World Social Forum, and in issue-based formations (such as Via Campesina). These movements are clear that neoliberal policies have no legitimacy. But neither neoliberalism nor the capitalist logic that governs it has been displaced, for at least two reasons. First, neoliberalism continues to exercise institutional power through the central banks and the multilateral financial institutions. Their preoccupation is inflation—not jobs, not the livelihoods of ordinary people. There is little policy space for the bureaucrats of the BRICS and the political parties of the Left to exert other dreams, other imaginations. Second, one of the long-term trends of the capitalist system is the move by those who control capital to substitute machines for labor. Capitalism is a massive labor-displacing system. The problem with actual workers is that they are restive and expensive. Machines are undemanding, and cheaper. Machines might end up being ecologically devastating, but that is not relevant to capitalism. Machines might also end up being socially wonderful, since they free up time for leisure, but that would only work if the fruits of mechanization were not seized by the select few who own or control social wealth.

What we know for sure is that the time of the neoliberal state, of the governments of the possible, is now over. Even if such states remain, their legitimacy has been eroded. The time of the impossible has presented itself. That is the message of *The Poorer Nations*.

CHAPTER ONE

The Demise of Northern Atlantic Liberalism

Politics today are mainly economics.

Edward Tomkins, British ambassador to France,
November 25, 1975[1]

In 1977, Willy Brandt, the former chancellor of West Germany, assembled a commission of experts to carry out a study of the widening inequality between the world's rich and poor, and between the world's richest states and its poorest. Brandt was a Social Democrat, and a leader in the Socialist International, who had enhanced his reputation with the policy of *Ostpolitik*—a rapprochement between East and West Germany, and of course, more broadly, between the Communist and the advanced capitalist blocs. Brandt's idea of "change through rapprochement" appealed to Robert McNamara, who was at the helm of the World Bank. McNamara came to the World Bank from the Pentagon, and before that, the Ford Motor Company. He had a front-row seat on American corporate and military power. With him came the fog of American liberalism, eager to eradicate poverty without making any commitment to serious structural change. McNamara reached out to Brandt, asking him to put together a commission under the Bank's auspices to deal with the new gap between North and South. Brandt agreed. He did not want the Bank's imprimatur, but he took the idea seriously. Brandt's commissioners met from 1977 to 1979. It was a fraught process; agreement did not come. But in 1980 the Commission published its first report, *North-South: A Programme for Survival*.

The report created a splash. Most of its recommendations had been a feature of the North-South dialogue since the 1960s: revise the terms of trade, consider the power of the multinational corporations, rethink the international monetary system, and puzzle through the barrier created by agricultural subsidies in the North and unstable commodity prices in the South. An emergency program to end poverty in the Least Developed Countries, with $4 billion as the potential fund, was the immediate task proposed by the report. The major powers came to Cancún in 1981 to discuss it. Their deliberations came to nothing. As Brandt put it in his autobiography, "Our proposals received a great deal of attention but little favorable response from the International Monetary Fund and the World Bank."[2] Not only the World Bank and the IMF, but all of

---

1   "Rambouillet: the French View," UK Embassy Paris to FCO, November 25, 1975, PREM no. 16/838, Margaret Thatcher Papers, Margaret Thatcher Foundation.

2   Willy Brandt, *My Life in Politics*, New York: Viking, 1992, p. 344.

the major Atlantic powers rejected the recommendations of the report. It sank before it could swim. Three years later, the Brandt Commission produced a second, little-read report, *Common Crisis North-South: Co-operation for World Recovery*. Here the team wrote, "the North-South Summit at Cancún, Mexico, in the fall of 1981, which we had proposed in our Report, fell far short of our expectations. It produced no new guidelines nor any clear impetus for future negotiations. It did not even come close to launching the idea of a world economic recovery programme."[3] Brandt's was the last in a series of reports of eminences that attempted to offer a humanist approach to planetary welfare.[4] It defined the extent of Atlantic liberalism, and it was its last gasp.

The Brandt Commission formed at a crucial time in the twentieth century. During the 1970s, a battle raged not only between East and West, whose Cold War had become hotter during that decade, but, crucially, between the advanced capitalist states, led by the United States, and the Third World. The latter fight was far more important as a context for the Brandt deliberations. Early in the decade, the United States had decided to delink the dollar from the gold standard. Unwilling to pay its creditors with gold, the US decided that the dollar would be its own standard—those who held dollars would not be able to exchange them for gold, and would hold the dollars for themselves (not as a substitute for gold). This enabled the US to print currency if it needed to pay its creditors and to seek new creditors on the basis of the blue-chip standard of the United States Treasury (instead of its gold holdings). This maneuver shaped the world's economy around the needs of the United States and its Atlantic fiefdom. No wonder that the system is known as "dollar seigniorage"—the ability of the United States government to run vast current-account deficits in the certain knowledge that its creditors cannot exhaust Fort Knox's gold supplies, nor effectively try to collapse the dollar (in which they hold their own wealth).[5]

A few years later, in 1973, the Third World Project mounted its major assault against neo-colonialism, as oil prices quadrupled and its demand for a New International Economic Order (NIEO) came to the UN General Assembly. A

---

3   Brandt Commission, *Common Crisis North-South: Cooperation for World Recovery*, London: Pan Books, 1983, p. 2.

4   There were and continue to be a series of Commissions on development and allied subjects, and each of them has produced a report and many other ancillary studies. The most important of these has been the World Commission on Environment and Development (chaired by Gro Harlem Brundtland, 1984–87, which produced *Our Common Future*, 1987) and the Commission on Human Security (chaired by Sadako Ogato and Amartya Sen, 2001–02, which produced *Human Security Now*, 2003). None of these, however, had the same impact as the Brandt Report. It was truly the last of its kind.

5   Peter Gowan, *The Global Gamble: Washington's Faustian Bid for World Dominance*, London: Verso, 1999, pp. 25–6.

new order was indeed in formation. In the 1970s it was not clear how it would shape up, as the assertive countries of the Third World put forward their coherent agenda despite the many differences between the states that adopted the project as their own. But as the decade wore on, and certainly by the early 1980s, it was clear that the victor was what would later be called the global North. The Third World's NIEO faltered, as did Atlantic liberalism. The space abandoned by them was occupied by a philosophy that descended from the stale air of Mont Pèlerin, Switzerland, where Friedrich Hayek, Milton Friedman, Ludwig von Mises, and their comrades had incubated the theory of neoliberalism in the 1940s. From the ashes of Atlantic liberalism and the Third World project rose global neoliberalism.

PETRODOLLARS

On August 15, 1971, the United States government cut the dollar loose from the gold exchange standard.[6] As with many such important decisions made by the US, the United Kingdom followed suit, and the continental European countries came next. The gold standard ended its long run. The currencies would now float against each other. Aware of the resulting instability in the short run, the various central banks authorized the printing of more money to increase their reserves. The dollar lost some of its value, as did the world's wealthy, who had long parked their wealth in the dollar.[7] Among them were the oil states, whose surpluses found their way into dollars, whether held in New York or London.

---

6 The reason for the action is quite straightforward. From 1970, US oil production peaked, and the country became an oil importer. This was a negative draw on its balance of payments. Further, by the early 1970s the cost of the Vietnam War had escalated, and the national debt ballooned. This was partly for artificial reasons, because of the eurodollar market, which held dollars in European (and later other foreign) banks to cover short-term transactions outside the US. By 1971–72, holders of US debt threatened the Treasury Department's gold reserves. In August 1971, President Nixon cancelled payments in gold and offered paper guarantees instead. This was a prelude to the eventual demise of the gold exchange standard. A critical history of these events can be found in Michael Hudson, *Super Imperialism: The Economic Strategy of American Empire*, London: Pluto Press, 2003, and *Global Fracture: The New International Economic Order*, London: Pluto Press, 2004.

7 The maneuver rattled such people as the scion of a Texas oil fortune, Nelson Bunker Hunt, who wanted to preserve his wealth by converting it into silver. Hunt cornered the silver market, but, unlike other investors, actually wanted to take delivery of the silver. "'Just about anything you buy, rather than paper, is better,' Bunker told *Barrons*. 'You're bound to come out ahead in the long pull. If you don't like gold, use silver. Or diamonds. Or copper. Buy something. Any damn fool can run a printing press.'" Bryan Burrough, *The Big Rich: The Rise and Fall of the Greatest Texas Oil Fortunes*, New York: Penguin, 2009, p. 390.

The states that belonged the Organization of Petroleum Exporting Countries (OPEC) chafed at the depreciation of their wealth. They openly threatened a rise in oil prices. A memorandum from the US Department of State in 1971 put the case clearly: "The world is now experiencing what is very likely its last brief buyers' market for conventional oil. By 1975, and possibly earlier, we will have entered a permanent sellers' market, with any one of several major producers being able to create a supply crisis by cutting off oil supplies."[8]

Currency chaos sent investors in search of safer havens. Within the next two years, commodity prices went up as investors put their capital into tangible assets rather than into the new world of goldless money. Wild swings in exchange rates confused investors. The dollar depreciated against the German Mark by 36 percent from January 1973 to June 1975, but it appreciated by 11 percent in the last quarter of 1973. Currency traders had not yet learned their craft. Investors turned to commodities as a hedge against inflation. Prices began to rise in 1972, with copper, coffee, sugar, beef, and grains hitting their high in May 1974 (a rise of 115 percent in two years), while industrial materials reached their peak in April 1974 (a rise of 127 percent in two years). The price of gold also rose sharply, from $35 per ounce (March 1968) to $200 per ounce (January 1975).[9] These were the peak prices; they would begin to drop gradually thereafter, particularly once confidence in goldless money had begun to develop.

The advanced developed states seized the gains from the commodity boom. The prices of commodities produced and exported from the US, Australia, Canada, and South Africa increased by 85 percent, while those of the commodities from the South rose by a much more modest 30 percent. Only the countries that exported oil were able to see much more robust gains.[10] The massive industrial production of wheat and grain in the US gave it a decisive advantage. In 1972, a desperate USSR bought a quarter of US wheat production (this came to be known as the Great Grain Robbery), inflating the price of wheat. Grain prices quadrupled—a development that struck food-importing countries hard, mainly in Africa, Asia, and Latin America.[11]

As part of this overheated commodities market, the mandarins of OPEC went into their huddle and emerged with a comparable price rise. Between the end of World War II and 1967, the price of oil rose by a moderate 2 percent per

---

8   Giuliano Garavini and Francesco Petrini, "Continuity or Change? The 1973 Oil Crisis Reconsidered," *Europe in the International Arena during the 1970s: Entering a Different World*, Brussels: Peter Lang Euroclio, 2010, p. 9.

9   J. B. Dearman, "World Commodity Prices," *Economic Trends* 247 (May 1974) offers a comparison between the UN price series and that of the *Economist*.

10   OECD *Economic Outlook*, July 1974, p. 36; Joe Stork, "Oil and the International Crisis," *MERIP* 32 (November 1974), p. 18.

11   Harriet Friedmann, "The Political Economy of Food: The Rise and Fall of the Postwar International Food Order," *American Journal of Sociology* 88 (1982).

year. On October 16, 1973, OPEC threw down a gauntlet, raising the price of oil by 70 percent, which quadrupled the price of oil from $3 per barrel to $12 per barrel. The immediate political context for the price rise was the Yom Kippur War between Israel and Egypt, with the other Arab states in tow. The Arab branch of OPEC pushed for an embargo of states that supported Israel—and just such a freeze put Israel's supporters, the United States and the Netherlands particularly, in a tough spot.[12] The issue of Israel was not the reason for the oil-price rise; it had been on the cards anyway, mainly pushed by the break from the gold standard and the general increase in commodity prices that followed. As Algeria's oil minister, Belaid Abdessalam, put it after the June 1974 OPEC meeting, the Yom Kippur War "at the most played the role of a catalyst in taking a decision which was already well prepared and well justified on the economic level."[13] The quadrupled price of grains through the US-dominated food grains market was also a spur, for, as the otherwise pliant Shah of Iran put it in 1973, it was the US and its North Atlantic allies that "increased the price of wheat you sell us by 300 percent, and the same for sugar and cement." Also, since the US and its allies controlled the petroleum industry, the large oil multinationals suffocated the economies of the oil lands ("You buy our crude oil and sell it back to us, refined as petrochemicals, at a hundred times the price you've paid to us").[14]

Saudi Arabia's fumbled attempt to downplay the politics of the embargo and the price rise was mirrored by Libya and Syria's exaggeration of the "oil weapon." Certainly the Arab states tried to grow their political power out of an oil barrel, but they were not alone within OPEC. The Venezuelans had less contentious matters to deal with than the intractable Arab-Israeli conflict. The Yom Kippur War was not decisive for them. The general push to develop effective cartels steered the policy, which was helped along by its utility in the immediate political conjuncture (that is, of using the oil embargo as a way to

---

12 India also faced the embargo:

Saudi Arabia included India in the embargo list because Israel had a consulate in Mumbai, and ordered a halt to oil loadings for India. As the Government of India's petroleum advisor for the Gulf, I was asked to rush to Riyadh from Tehran; I met the oil company executive in charge of exports, explained our position on Israel, persuaded them, in consultation with Jeddah, to lift the embargo, load the two ships nominated by Indian Oil and remove our name from the list of "West." I was then asked to go to all the Gulf capitals to explain our policy on Israel and Palestine so that nobody else would be tempted to embargo oil shipments to India.

Prakash Shah, "Iran issue needs diplomacy, not crude weapon," *The Hindu*, February 16, 2012.

13 Stork, "Oil and the International Crisis," p. 13.

14 William D. Smith, "New Rises are Feared; Price Quadruples for Iranian Crude Oil at Auction," *New York Times*, December 12, 1973, p. 1.

isolate Israel—a ploy that failed in relation to the United States, but succeeded marginally in relation to Japan and Europe).

Structural factors (the need to preserve and grow wealth) played a major role in the rise of oil prices.[15] So too did the Third World Project. At the heart of this project was the renegotiation of the abysmal economic situation in the developing world. Most of the countries that joined the NAM had economies damaged by a colonial history that had rendered producers of single crops (either extracted from under the ground or grown on it). The value-added advantages of the raw material would not come to the "peripheral" countries, who were asked to be satisfied with the rents or prices paid for their resources. Corporations of the core then took charge, processing the raw material into commodities with much greater value. All this irked the new states in the NAM, who wanted to fetch better prices and rents for their resources, and to take advantage of their social wealth to grow their national economies. To do so, their raft of policies included land reform, import-substitution industrialization, producers' cartels, and buffer stocks to stabilize commodity prices. OPEC was the first significant cartel to emerge from this dynamic. It was soon followed by the copper cartel (Conseil Intergouvernemental des Pays Exportateurs de Cuivre) and the bauxite cartel (International Bauxite Association). Neither of these had the scale of influence of the oil cartel. OPEC's politics came from the Third World Project, as did its culture of solidarity in the early years. It was a test of the remarkable discipline among the sellers, with no one willing to undersell for short-term gain.[16]

Taking the measure of the Third World Project in February 1974, Algeria's leader Houari Boumediène put the case for the price rise:

> We do not find oil too expensive. For us it is machinery, technicians, the cost of knowledge, studies and money which are too expensive. The man who goes hungry, who rides a donkey, who wants to learn to read, does not have the same preoccupation as the one who goes for a drive on Sunday, and for him the price of wheat is

---

15 There is, as you would expect, a vast literature that tries to assess the price rise. The neoclassical view is best summarized by Robert Pindyck, who explains the rise using an applied wealth-maximization model in the context of an exhaustible resource; in other words, he shows that it was rational for the suppliers to maximize their selling power by cartelizing the world oil market. "Gains to Producers from the Cartelization of Exhaustible Resources," *Review of Economics and Statistics* 60: 2 (May 1978); and "The Cartelization of World Commodity Prices," *American Economic Review* 69: 2 (May 1979). I am less convinced that this was a strictly rational-choice moment.

16 Neoclassical thinkers dismiss solidarity as an explanatory factor. For Morris Adelman, for example, "the higher the price, the better the financial condition of the sellers, and the less pressure on them to cheat and undersell each other in order to pay their bills." James Griffin and David Teece, eds, "OPEC as Cartel," *OPEC Behavior and World Oil Prices*, London: George Allen & Unwin, 1982, p. 55.

more important than the price of asphalt. The price of wheat has quintupled. For a long time the price of iron has not moved, but by how much has the price of a tractor increased? The problem facing the world is much larger than oil alone or even raw materials: it concerns the relations between the developed countries and the others in every field. This is the heart of the question.[17]

By the logic of the Third World Project, the profits earned by the cartels were to have a social purpose. Certainly, the capital would be used to diversify the various one-crop economies—not only by developing other sectors of production but also by improving the infrastructure to create domestic markets (and not allow the country to be just a platform for extraction and then transport to the core). Apart from that, there was a suggestion to use the extra money to finance some kind of Southern Bank, which would then loan money on favorable, concessionary terms to parts of the South that did not have the advantage of a luxurious commodity.[18] Some platforms to use the surplus profits were indeed created within the Arab world, and did some modest good: the Saudi Arabian Development Fund, the Kuwait Fund for Arab Economic Development, the Islamic Development Bank, the Arab Fund for Economic Social Development, the Special Arab Fund for Africa, the Arab Technical Assistance Fund for Africa, and the Abu Dhabi Development Fund. These did not have the kind of money envisioned by the Project, nor were most of them sustained. The hope for the cartel did not pan out.[19]

The profits were put to other uses. In 1972 OPEC's members registered foreign sales of $24 billion. Two years later, the profits rose to $117 billion, and by 1980 to $257 billion.[20] These vast amounts had two major uses. About half the money bought the OPEC states goods from outside, including luxury goods, food, and arms. The bills of lading became startlingly similar. Attempts to diversify the economic base went by the wayside, as the various regimes, from that of the Iranian Shah to the Venezuelan oligarchy, chose aggrandizement over human security. The rest of the money went towards the purchase of foreign, mainly Atlantic, financial assets. Discussions on this subject had already detained

---

17   Stork, "Oil and the International Crisis," p. 14.

18   Vijay Prashad, *The Darker Nations: A People's History of the Third World*, New York: New Press, 2007, p. 187.

19   Maurice J. Williams, "The Aid Programs of the OPEC Countries," *Foreign Affairs* 54: 2 (January 1976); and Mahmoud Fouad, "Petrodollars and Economic Development in the Middle East," *Middle East Journal* 32: 3 (Summer 1978).

20   For the broad overview, see Daniel Yergin, *The Prize: The Epic Quest for Oil, Money and Power*, New York: Simon & Schuster, 1992; and Fadhel al-Chalabi, *OPEC and the International Oil Industry*, Oxford: OUP and the Organisation of Arab Exporting Countries, 1980. Al-Chalabi was the deputy secretary-general of OPEC from 1978 to 1988 (acting as the secretary-general for the last five of those years).

the main intellectuals of the Atlantic world at the annual Bilderberg meeting in May 1973. It was the theme of the accord drawn up between US Treasury Secretary William Simon and the Saudi Arabian Monetary Authority, and in the creation of the US-Saudi Joint Commission on Economic Cooperation, set up in June 1974.[21] The rise in oil prices induced deficits in Western Europe and in the United States. But the massive oil surplus in the OPEC countries created a problem of glut for them. The pact was sealed, with a military threat from the US against the Saudis on the horizon, as the OPEC countries bought the debt from Western Europe and the US.[22]

Ordinary people in Europe and the United States suffered the consequences of the oil-price rise, paying high prices at the pump. The profits were collected by the oil companies and the OPEC exchequers, who then deposited them in the Northern banks. That capital was now a substantial part of what expanded the Northern financial sectors, at whose heart was this petrodollar industry. A low savings rate in the North prevented its banks from harvesting money from the pocketbooks of the people. High oil prices picked their pockets and, via the oil companies, deposited the people's "savings" into the Northern banks. These petrodollars covered the deficits of the Northern governments, provided banks with capital to invest further to their profit, and protected the dollar from depreciation despite the needs of the US economy. It was a royal flush for the moneyed.

In January 1974, the IMF director, H. Johannes Witteveen, made two proposals. The first was that the IMF should take charge of the petrodollar market, becoming the public agent for its disbursement. The European governments backed Witteveen's idea. Witteveen worried that the vast quantum of floating capital might tempt banks into an unproductive spiral, thereby providing them with unprecedented power over the world system. Better to have the IMF run the operation. The second proposal, made in 1975, stemmed from the first— that is to say, the IMF would now disburse the money, with an eye to the rate of return certainly, but also with a measure of equity. The petrodollar fund would help with development activity.

Witteveen, a lifelong Sufi, had been finance minister in the Dutch government and was himself a member of the laissez-faire–leaning political party the People's Party for Freedom and Democracy. He was not driven to his decision by any kind of liberal guilt for the former colonies or by any fealty to the NIEO position. Witteveen felt that the Atlantic world was suffering from "excess

---

21   John Duke Anthony, "The US–Saudi Arabian Joint Commission on Economic Cooperation," in Willard A. Beling, ed., *King Faisal and the Modernisation of Saudi Arabia*, Boulder: Westview Press, 1980.

22   On the military threat, see David Harvey, *A Brief History of Neoliberalism*, Oxford: Oxford University Press, 2005, p. 27.

demand," which is to say that the workers were taking too much home in their pay packets. They needed to be brought down a peg or two. More liquidity in the Atlantic markets might feed "excess demand" and enhance what he called "inflationary psychology." To contain this "excess demand" in the Atlantic world, Witteveen called for anticipatory austerity: "The sacrifice required to fight inflation becomes greater the more entrenched the inflation has become."[23] Redistribution would not run from the rich to the poor, nor from the North to the South. Witterveen sought to move a modest amount of the income of the Northern workers to the Southern governments. Better that the IMF run the petrodollars and channel them away from the Atlantic states to the NAM states. Witteveen came to his proposal without the ideological undertow of Atlantic primacy, and his idea for the Fund therefore floundered under US pressure.[24]

In December 1974 the US abolished its own controls on the entry and exit of finance capital. On May Day, 1975, the United States lowered the fences around the New York Stock Exchange to create a global market in equities and securities. Rather than allow the European-dominated IMF to take charge of the petrodollar market, the US government preferred to let the Northern Atlantic banks run the show, particularly if this meant that New York City would become the pre-eminent global city. In 1981, the Reagan administration and the Federal Reserve turned Wall Street into its own kind of offshore facility through a provision called the International Banking Facilities.[25] Wall Street became the linchpin of the new order. In its constellation would be the City of London and the Frankfurt Finanzplatz.[26] The new finance market rendered

---

23 *IMF Survey*, May 6, 1974, p. 136.

24 Margaret De Vries, *The International Monetary Fund, 1972–1978*, Washington, DC: IMF, 1985, vol. 1, pp. 314–16; Eric Helleiner, *States and the Reemergence of Global Finance: From Bretton Woods to the 1990s*, Ithaca: Cornell University Press, 1994, pp. 111–12.

25 Sydney J. Key and Henry S. Terrell, "International Banking Facilities," International Finance Discussion Papers, no. 333, September 1988, Federal Reserve.

26 The European capitals also wanted their bourses to get a share of the action. As Jacques Delors, president of the European Commission, put it in 1989, a unitary European financial structure would give "our financial centres the opportunity to be among the most important in the world [so as to give] us our say in the world with the Americans and Japanese on debt, on financial flows." David Buchan and Geoffrey Owen, "Undimmed Ambitions for Unity in Europe," *Financial Times*, March 14, 1989, p. 28. For an entertaining account of London's role, see Philip Augar, *The Death of Gentlemanly Capitalism: The Rise and Fall of London's Investment Banks*, Harmondsworth: Penguin, 2001. The secondary place of Britain comes across in the derision with which Henry Kissinger speaks of it to President Ford: "Britain is a tragedy—it has sunk to begging, borrowing, stealing until North Sea oil comes in … That Britain has become such a scrounger is a disgrace—but Britain will support us." January 8, 1975, NSC, National Security Adviser's Memoranda of Conversation Collection, Box 8, Gerald Ford Memorial Presidential Library.

archaic the textbooks on microeconomics. A few gargantuan players (such as Goldman Sachs) dominated the sell-side, creating what Peter Gowan called a "conscious cartel."[27] The North Atlantic financial cartel made a king's ransom in the decades to come, perpetuating a process of *accumulation by manipulation*.

The US project won out, and the IMF backed off. Eighty percent of the OPEC surplus income in 1974 came to the countries that ringed the North Atlantic, mainly the United States. The banks in this zone became the carriers of the petrodollars into the world system. Nixon's Treasury secretary, John Connolly, put it plainly in 1971: "The dollar may be our currency, but now it's your problem."[28] The dollar standard supplanted the gold standard: countries outside the United States began to hold dollars as an instrument of wealth, buying Treasury Bills and providing the US eventually with the ballast against any concern for its own deficit spending. The inflationary glut of dollars pushed many states into competitive revaluations, making their precious exports increasingly uncompetitive. Flush with petrodollars, the North Atlantic states became the hub around which the rest of the world took their places on the spokes.

NEW INTERNATIONAL ECONOMIC ORDER

In 1949, economist Raúl Prebisch delivered a major paper to the Economic Commission on Latin America at its Havana meeting. Called "The Economic Development of Latin America and Its Principal Problems," or the "Havana Manifesto," the document contained a blistering critique of the world order fashioned in colonial times, and provided a coherent set of alternatives that would be more institutionally democratic and economically egalitarian. Most of the rules of the world order had been set when the majority of humanity struggled under colonial or semi-colonial domination. The representatives of the world's peoples had had no real say at the Bretton Woods conference in 1944. The delegates that came to Bretton Woods, New Hampshire, from afar went into the Gold Room at the magisterial Mount Washington Hotel to put their impressions on the final communiqué. That was their role, and little else. It was no surprise, then, that the two major institutions that came out of Bretton Woods—the International Monetary Fund and the World Bank—had to be run by a European and an American, respectively. No one else would have a turn. John Maynard Keynes, who took the lead at the conference, did not want too many others. Those from the colonies and semi-colonies "clearly have nothing to contribute and will merely encumber the ground," he wrote to the

---

27   Peter Gowan, "The Crisis in the Heartland," in Martijn Konings and Jeffrey Sommers, eds, *The Great Credit Crash*, London: Verso, 2010, p. 63.

28   Barry Eichengreen, *The European Economy Since 1945*, Princeton: Princeton University Press, 2007, p. 244.

British Treasury. To Keynes, Bretton Woods ended up being "the monstrous monkey-house assembled for years."[29] It was hardly the attitude to seed a truly international solution to economic crisis.

Keynes's disdain for those not like himself was shared by others, and it was this that moved them to disenfranchise the world from the governance of the IMF and the World Bank (the main votes on their boards of executive directors were held by Europe and the US). "One of the conspicuous deficiencies of the general economic theory, from the point of view of the periphery," Prebisch wrote, "is its false sense of universality."[30]

Much the same kind of discrimination left most of the world without any control over the UN's Security Council, which, against the spirit of the UN Charter, began to act like the executive of the General Assembly. The silence of the colonized and the semi-colonized meant that the new economic and political policies favored those who had already seized the world's wealth, and these policies now set inequality in stone. Most of them lived in countries not yet independent, and so were discriminated against by their absence in the deliberations. When decolonization came, these countries would place the question of international democracy at the top of their agenda. It is what held together so many of the otherwise politically disparate states that joined hands in the Third World Project of the 1950s and 1960s.

Chastened by the economic warfare of the 1920s and 1930s, which not only brought on the hostilities of World War II but also contributed to the prolongation of the Depression, the Atlantic powers now created a currency regime that would be less volatile and a political regime that would be less confrontational. The World Bank was created to help manage the reconstruction of war-ravaged Europe and Japan (but not the rest of Asia, nor Africa, both also damaged by European ambitions). The IMF emerged as an institution to tide over countries that had a balance-of-payments or short-term liquidity problem. There was only a limited or hesitant mandate for poverty reduction or the elimination of the vast global inequalities that marked the end of the colonial era. The IMF and the World Bank were institutions for the maintenance of colonial domination by other means—or so it seemed from Santiago, Dar es Salaam, Cairo, and New Delhi.

For that reason, the countries that had been shut out of the creation of the IMF and World Bank, and of the architecture of the UN, built their own project and their own institutions. Their Third World Project drew from the rich traditions of egalitarianism, took refuge in the promise of the UN and its Charter, and developed an intellectual tradition within which it articulated

---

29 Prashad, *Darker Nations*, p. 68.

30 Edgar J. Dosman, *The Life and Times of Raúl Prebisch, 1901–1986*, Montreal: McGill-Queens University Press, 2008, pp. 248–9.

a set of coherent policies to take the planet out of the miserable present. A central organization for the Project was the UN Conference on Trade and Development (UNCTAD), created in 1964 with Prebisch as its founding secretary-general. At the various UNCTAD meetings, and in other forums, the countries of Africa, Asia, and Latin America, with allies from the Socialist bloc (occasionally the USSR), Yugoslavia (formerly outside the Socialist bloc, but programmatically in sympathy with it), and some European countries (notably the Scandinavian states), developed an alternative perspective that would sharpen by the early 1970s. The view from UNCTAD settled the agenda for the Non-Aligned Movement—the major bloc that adopted the Third World Project, with varying degrees of enthusiasm.

In the UN, the countries that belonged to the NAM or who had fealty to the Third World Project formed a negotiating bloc in 1964 called the G77 (there are now 132 members of the Group of 77, but the name remains).[31] The G77 took up the agenda devised by UNCTAD and other such UN agencies, where the NAM countries were able to use their demographic strength to their advantage. The power of human bodies had no such influence in the IMF, the World Bank, the UN Security Council, or other agencies where the former colonial powers held sway. The USSR and the Eastern bloc saw the NAM, and the G77, as allies, but since the East was wary of the UN and its bodies, its allegiance was in parallel to the NAM, rather than to it directly.

One of the most notable features of this era is that, despite its demographic majority, the states of the Third World Project *petitioned* the global bodies, whereas the North simply *acted*. There is no better illustration of the uneven geometry of imperialism than the mood of international deliberations. The North's wishes are multiplied; the South's pleas are sometimes added, mainly subtracted.

The oil embargo of 1967 whetted the appetites of OPEC and the NAM. It showed that the countries of the Third World Project had some political heft. At the third conference of the NAM in Lusaka, Zambia, in 1970, the main political leaders attempted to strengthen the group institutionally and to refine its ideological challenge to the Atlantic bloc. Once more they stressed the need to bring democracy to international relations, which meant reducing the power of the five permanent members of the UN Security Council and enhancing the authority of the UN General Assembly. The oil embargo had proved that producers' cartels functioned effectively, and that they would be able to mitigate the asymmetrical power of transnational corporations and their countries. The NAM countries wanted to make sure that their efforts provided "an opportunity to bring about structural changes in the world economic system so as to

---

31   Marc Williams, *Third World Cooperation: The Group of 77 in UNCTAD*, London: St. Martin's Press, 1991.

meet the pressing needs of poor nations, to strengthen their independence, and to provide for a more rapid and better balanced expansion of the world economy." Not only did the nations set out the goals and objectives (international cooperation and equitable development); it also put forward a raft of concrete policies to attain these goals. Here are some of the measures:

1. Finance: to alleviate the problem of debt, to increase the net flow of financial transfers from developed to developing countries, to distinguish between investment for development and investment for commerce.
2. Technology: to transfer technology to deficient countries, to expand research opportunities, and to improve educational systems.
3. Production: to protect the prices of raw materials, to create systems to process raw materials and attain the advantages of value-added sales, to create systems of preference for products from developing countries, to diversify (including the promotion of an industrial sector) the economies of the developing countries.

Bits and pieces of the Lusaka declaration can be found in the various UNCTAD statements and documents, at earlier NAM meetings, in various UN forums, and at such diverse venues as meetings of development economists and revolutionary politicians. By 1970, these ideas had formed a coherent alternative to the dominant liberal order. This liberal order wreaked havoc with the dreams of the new states, whose struggles against colonialism and imperialism had pushed them to seek alternatives. As the Chilean economist Osvaldo Sunkel put it, the liberal order wanted the new states to integrate into the world economy and disintegrate national economies.[32] At Lusaka the new ideas had germinated, but the language remained hesitant. The leaders made their requests tentatively— still with the tone of impetuous inferiors, not sure if their entreaty, however correct, would have any bearing in the drawing rooms of seniority.

Then came the *annus mirabilis*, 1973. OPEC's concerted action provided an object lesson for the NAM states that they were not as miserable as they sometimes felt. At Bandung, in 1955, the leaders comforted themselves with the view that, even if they were not militarily strong, they had moral power. Be that as it may, the oil episode showed that at least a section of the NAM states had economic power. Houari Boumediène, Algeria's president who, with Libya's Muammar al-Qaddafi, had done so much to move OPEC in a radical

---

32   Osvaldo Sunkel, "National Development Policy and External Dependence in Latin America," *Journal of Development Studies* 6: 1 (October 1969); and "Transnational Capitalism and National Disintegration in Latin America," *Social and Economic Studies* 22: 1 (1973).

direction, took the floor of the UN's 6th Special Session in April 1974 to make just this point. "The OPEC action," he said,

> is really the first illustration and at the same time the most concrete and most spectacular illustration, of the importance of raw material prices for our countries, the vital need for the producing countries to operate the levers of price control, and lastly, the great possibilities of a union of raw material producing countries. This action should be viewed by the developing countries as an example and a source of hope.[33]

OPEC's "commodity power" reaffirmed several of the planks of the Third World Project, but now no longer just in theory; OPEC's unilateral action showed the certainty and legitimacy of the entire project (from the nationalization of domestic industries to cartelization between states). OPEC's actions made the idea of begging for foreign aid and acceding to the conditions laid down by the advanced states seem quaint. The Pearson Report (1969), which called for more aid from the developed to the developing countries and had a boundless enthusiasm for development through the benevolence of the Atlantic world, seemed musty.[34] OPEC's actions filled the Third World project with meaning.

Shortly after 1973 another political opening gave a fillip to the NIEO dynamic. A series of national liberation movements won independence against implacable colonial powers (notably the Portuguese) and the proxy agents of imperialism. In southwestern Europe, the Portuguese dictatorship of António de Oliveira Salazar collapsed in 1974, after which its empire lost its hold over Guinea-Bissau, Mozambique, Cape Verde, and Angola. The next year, Cambodia and Laos went to various branches of Communism, and the National Liberation Front removed the United States and its allies from Saigon. A brutal general stole Chile from history's positive column, but the defeat of Salvador Allende's government only strengthened the sense that imperialism had to resort to violence to have its way. Hegemony's velvet glove had become tattered, and the iron hand of domination showed itself plainly. Matters seemed settled from the point of view of the world's poor.

A buoyant NAM called for a special session of the UN General Assembly to consider what would become of the NIEO. Two months after it made the call, the General Assembly gathered in April 1974, in its 6th Special Session. The NAM submitted a draft Declaration on the Establishment of a New

---

33   Tony Smith, "Configurations of Power in North-South Relations since 1945," *Industrial Organization* 31: 1 (Winter 1977), p. 4.

34   Lester Pearson, *Partners in Development: Report of the Commission on International Development*, New York: Praeger, 1969. See also Hans Singer, "The One Per Cent Aid Target (Some Reflections on the Arithmetic of International Targetry)," *IDS Bulletin* 2: 2 (1969) for an engaging history of the Pearson commission and for a critique.

International Economic Order. Boumediène hastily called for the Special Session as a way to outflank a diplomatic maneuver by US Secretary of State Henry Kissinger. Cleverly, Kissinger resorted to an old colonial trick: divide and conquer. When oil prices rose, Kissinger sought out the non-oil-producing states among the NAM who had begun to feel the pinch as oil importers. Calling these states "Less Developed Countries" (LDCs), Kissinger sought to peel them away from their unity with OPEC. He also called in favors from OPEC members such as Saudi Arabia, whose role in OPEC was central. To undercut Kissinger, Boumediène called for the UN Session, to force the entire NAM bloc to go on the record in favor of the NIEO.

The New York meeting did not go by without incident. The Chinese sent their deputy premier, Deng Xiaoping, who attacked the Soviets for being an "imperialist state." The Soviet foreign minister, Andrei Gromyko, dismissed the "empty talk" of the Chinese. The UN secretary-general, Kurt Waldheim, tried to stand above the fray, worrying about the "global emergency," calling on the member nations "to secure the optimum use of the world's natural resources with the basic objective of securing better conditions of social justice throughout the world." His attempt at mediation did not bring together the two sides. Speaking for the NAM, Boumediène saw the struggle as one in which the "raw material production countries insist on being masters in their own houses." The Atlantic world, on the other hand, wished to make the dispute about the need for stability, rather than equity. "Trade relations, currency conditions, the development of countries have been seriously upset," said West Germany's foreign minister, Walter Scheel. "All this together has had the effect of an earthquake leaving nothing unscathed." Kissinger concurred: "The great issue of development can no longer be realistically perceived in terms of confrontation between the haves and have nots." But this was precisely how the NAM states saw the issue.

The NIEO came before the General Assembly, where it was passed without dissent.[35] The United States went along with the NIEO, largely because it was both outflanked and unwilling to engage with the NAM countries in the General Assembly. The tide had seemed to move in the NAM's favor, and several European countries (mainly the Scandinavian states), New Zealand, Australia, and Canada favored much of the NAM agenda. The US sought other avenues to squash the NIEO, particularly when the Declaration went towards implementation in the back rooms of the various agencies. The process is byzantine; the details on how it works are often only clear to old UN hands. The upshot was that the NAM countries had a majority in most of the UN agencies.

---

35 Even the US, which opposed the NIEO, did not vote against it, because its representative saw the NIEO as "a significant political development." General Assembly Official Records, 2,229th Plenary Meeting, May 1, 1974, p. 7.

It tried to slip parts of the NIEO agenda through the various sub-agencies of the UN. But the real show of strength was in the General Assembly. It became clear that the US and its immediate allies were not able to move the General Assembly. It had become an embarrassment. The first test for the US and its allies was when the General Assembly took up the Charter of Economic Rights and Duties of States (a document framed within UNCTAD since 1972) in the autumn of 1974. The document came before the Assembly seventy-nine times before it passed with 120 votes in favor and six against, with ten abstentions. The six who voted against the Charter were Belgium, Denmark, Luxembourg, the United Kingdom, the United States, and West Germany. They had put their feet down.

France joined the abstainers and sought a compromise. In October 1974, France's president, Valéry Giscard d'Estaing, proposed an international conference on energy to deal with the OPEC price war and to seek some common ground on the issue of commodities. Before Giscard's conference could get underway, the NAM states organized a Conference of Developing Countries on Raw Materials in Dakar, Senegal (February 4–8, 1975). Their unity was strengthened by the addition of 110 states. The US bloc sought to divide the OPEC states from the others, dealing with the former over the oil price and the latter through the mechanism of foreign aid (following the suggestions of the Pearson Report of 1969). The Raw Materials Conference was to avert such a split in the ranks. Senegal's president, Leopold Senghor, told the gathered heads of government, "We in the Third World have to use our natural resources to break traditional patterns of world trade."[36] The resolution from Dakar underlined that the Paris process had to deal with all raw materials, not just oil. Dakar's demand was joined when the OPEC countries met in Algiers in March 1975 and released a "Solemn Declaration" to keep discussion of *all* commodities on the table (and find ways to help the non-oil-exporting developing countries to manage the rise in oil prices).[37]

Giscard welcomed several key countries to Paris in April 1975 to begin the Paris process. From the NAM and OPEC came Algeria, Brazil, India, Iran, Saudi Arabia, Venezuela, and Zaire. They were led by Venezuela, which was a member of both OPEC and NAM. The United States, the European Economic Community, Canada, and Japan sat at the other end of the table. Canada joined Venezuela as a co-chair of the meeting and of the process. The divide opened up. The US wanted an exclusive emphasis on oil prices. The NAM-OPEC states wanted to combine discussion of oil prices with those of other commodities.

---

36   Smith, "Configurations of Power," p. 5.

37   Alfons Lemper, "A New Economic Order?" *Intereconomics* 10: 2 (February 1975); and Richard Senti, "A Proposal for a New Order for the Commodity Markets," *Intereconomics* 12: 1–2 (January 1977).

The gap between these two camps seemed unbridgeable. The French and a few other states tried to bring the two camps together, but it seemed a wasted effort. The Paris conference—though it lasted for two years, until mid 1977—was going nowhere.

Henry Kissinger, US secretary of state, came to the UNCTAD IV meeting in Nairobi in May 1976 with hints of conciliation. The G77 states had pushed UNCTAD to a policy innovation, an Integrated Programme for Commodities. Fluctuating commodity prices hurt the producer countries, who could not plan their budgets when their exports either soared or flattened. What they sought was a program that would enable producers to get a better deal in their negotiations with the transnational corporations and Atlantic countries. They also sought a mechanism to ensure that their sales of raw materials would not be subject to the oscillations of market demand. The G77 proposal attempted to shift the power asymmetry in the market for commodities—which is why the G77 wanted to found a Producers' Cartel for at least seventeen core commodities (amounting, minus oil, to three-quarters of the exports from the G77 states). Kissinger's speech overshadowed the work of the UNCTAD Secretariat and the G77. He spoke in generalities of a "new cooperative international arrangement." Some of the language of the UNCTAD Secretariat entered his speech, such as that relating to buffer stocks and funds to avert price fluctuations. But Kissinger avoided the political question. Rather than address the question of power in economic relations, he proposed the creation of a modest International Resources Bank to create a bond market as advances and insurance for commodity sales. The British, the French, and the Canadians welcomed Kissinger's contribution; but the G77 was furious. The NGO paper "Cosmos" provided the best analysis of Kissinger's Machiavellian tactics: "Dr. Kissinger [had] retreated into the ever-tightening laager of free trade, piled up his ammunition, and defied those who thought differently to do their worst."[38] The language of apartheid South Africa was probably used deliberately. Kissinger's real reason for coming to Africa was to play the role of emissary for the recalcitrant apartheid regime in South Africa, at the time embroiled in its wars in Angola and Namibia, and on the fringes of Mozambique.[39] The final communiqué from UNCTAD IV was tepid.

Between May and June 1977, the NAM-OPEC bloc faced off in Paris against what appeared to be the fragile unity of the Atlantic states. The US had cemented its position. It wanted to break OPEC's position of primacy over the NAM states. The Carter administration saw the UNCTAD proposals as "extreme,"

38   John Toye and Richard Toye, *The UN and Global Political Economy*, Bloomington: Indiana University Press, 2004, pp. 246–7.

39   Piero Gleijeses, *Conflicting Missions: Havana, Washington and Africa, 1959–1976*, Chapel Hill: University of North Carolina Press, 2002, Chapter 13.

and complained that it left them "practically no negotiating flexibility."[40] The French were less obdurate. Giscard wanted the Paris round to produce a breakthrough, and so was willing to push for some concessions. The North-South disagreement became entangled in an ongoing fracas between France and the United States around NATO, the role of the dollar, and now energy policy.[41] A confidential UK assessment from 1975 noted that the French thought of the dollar policy "in much the same way as they think of the integrated structure of NATO under supreme American command: the prejudice against both is the same."[42] Giscard was galled by what he felt was US domination.[43] He wanted an open dialogue with the NAM states not only on oil, but also on other commodities. The US was furious about this concession. At a November 1975 summit of the Atlantic states in Rambouillet, Kissinger openly declared the US view: "We agree on the need for cooperation with producers. With cooperation we can separate the moderates from the radicals within OPEC, the LDCs from the OPEC countries, and prevent a lot of other 'PECs' [OPEC-like commodity cartels]."[44] He put Giscard into a sulk.

A fragile unity behind UNCTAD's idea of a commodity program held the various elements of the G77 together. The Latin American states did not want confrontation to disrupt their own hard-won agreements on coffee and other commodities. OPEC's core strength was whittled away. The Saudis and their Gulf Arab satellites were not willing to go along with the Algerians and the Libyans.[45] Furthermore, the oil firms still controlled the upstream of River Oil, from drilling to the pump, and their cartel put pressure on the oil states. The more conservative oil states stood down.[46]

40   Toye and Toye, *The UN and Global Political Economy*, p. 250.

41   Aurélie Élisa Gfeller, "Imagining European Identity: French Elites and the American Challenge in the Pompidou-Nixon Era," *Contemporary European History* 19: 2 (2010).

42   "Rambouillet: The French View," UK Embassy Paris to Foreign Office, PREM 16/838, November 25, 1975, p. 4.

43   Branislav Gosovic and John Gerard Ruggie, "On the Creation of a New International Economic Order: Issue Linkage and the Seventh Special Session of the UN General Assembly," *Industrial Organization* 30: 2 (Spring 1976), p. 317.

44   Henry Kissinger, *Years of Renewal*, New York: Simon & Schuster, 1999, p. 677.

45   Saudi Arabia's reasons for conciliation are well laid out in Ian Skeet, *OPEC: Twenty-Five Years of Price and Politics*, Cambridge: Cambridge University Press, 1988, p. 141. Bear in mind that, in 1976–77, Saudi Arabia and Iran accounted for 48 percent of OPEC oil output. Despite this, it is remarkable that Algeria and Libya were able to push the NAM policy through whenever they could.

46   At the August 1981 OPEC meeting, the Saudis would not allow the price of oil to rise above $32 per barrel, earning the ire of the Libyans, who announced that they would "rather cut production down to zero than reduce prices." The Saudis were joined by the other Gulf states, and stood opposed by the Libyans and the Iranians. The

Paris ended in tatters. The NAM-OPEC states bemoaned its collapse, as the Conference "fell short of the objectives envisaged for a comprehensive and equitable program of action" for a NIEO. "With regret," they pointed out in a joint statement, "most of the proposals for structural changes in the international economic system" and "certain proposals for urgent actions on pressing problems" had been nixed by the Atlantic powers, who in turn were disappointed that "some important areas of the dialogue such as certain aspects of energy cooperation" could not be pursued.[47]

The Paris proceedings were lacklustre. As the Iranian ambassador, Jahangir Amuzegar, put it, "There were no ringing passages; no dramatic declarations; no grand design; not even much pious diplomatic platitude."[48] The conference was not bold enough; the parties had simply strengthened their corners. Commodity Power, the slogan of NAM-OPEC, could not be planted on Parisian soil, and so it fell by the wayside. Whatever "concessions" came to the NAM states had already been announced before the meeting (aid in the Pearson style, and a modest fund and special action program). The special action program was to have an "urgent" $1 billion disbursement, but only a fifth of that was forthcoming.[49] The commodities program was also a façade. The initial proposal for a fund of $6 billion collapsed to $470 million.

The failure of Commodity Power had been forecast before the Paris process by a group of economists from the United States, Japan, and Europe. In October 1974, they wrote, "The crucial point … is that the number of commodities on which collusion would be feasible or effective is small, the economic impact is likely to be limited and isolated rather than pervasive as with oil, and the prospects for sustained success over the medium-term, to say nothing of the long-term, are dim."[50] Paris proved them right. The United States, too, felt vindicated. In March 1975, Daniel Patrick Moynihan had made it clear that "the world's economy is not nearly bad enough to justify the measures proposed by

---

Algerians, reliant upon the oil money, wobbled. It was in such tenuous negotiations that OPEC's own resolve would be worn down. Iran's oil minister, Mohammed Gharazi, complained that failure to agree was the responsibility of "those who really support the interests of the West." That might have been so. Saudi Arabia was also eager to increase its military capacity, and had been eager to buy US arms. Paul Lewis, "OPEC Nations Fail to Heal their Rift Over Price of Oil," *New York Times*, August 22, 1981, p. A1.

47   Jahangir Amuzegar, "A Requiem for the North-South Conference," *Foreign Affairs* 56: 1 (October 1977), p. 136.

48   Ibid., p. 136.

49   Jahangir Amuzegar, "Not Much Aid and Not Enough Trade: Cloudy Prospects for North-South Relations," *Third World Quarterly* 1: 1 (January 1979), p. 51.

50   Brookings Institution, Nihon Keizai Kenkyu Senta, Kenzo Henmi, and Universitat Kiel, *Trade in Primary Commodities, Conflict or Cooperation: A Tripartite Report*, Washington, DC: Brookings Institution, 1974, p. 2.

[the NIEO], and yet it is much worse than it would otherwise be in consequence of measures the [NAM-UNCTAD-OPEC] has already taken."[51] Better to roll back the OPEC thrust and disallow NIEO. In 1976, at the close of the Seventh Special Session of the UN General Assembly, the US representative bluntly said that his country "cannot and does not accept any implication that the world is now embarked on the establishment of something called the 'new international economic order.'"[52] That was the US position—and it became reality.

THE G7

But when the poor start "mau-mauing" their actual or potential benefactors, when they begin vilifying them, insulting them, demanding as of right what is not their right to demand—then one's sense of self-respect may take precedence over one's self-imposed humanitarian obligations.

Irving Kristol, 1975[53]

On August 17, 1974, Henry Kissinger met with President Gerald Ford in the Oval Office. The notes from the meeting open with Kissinger being forthright: "On the energy situation, we have to find a way to break the cartel. We can't do it without cooperation with the other consumers."[54] The Saudis are unreliable allies. They are the "most feckless and gutless of the Arabs," said Kissinger, who bemoaned the Saudis' inability to take on the radicals in the Arab wing of OPEC—the Algerians and the Libyans. Instead, Kissinger praised the Iranian shah ("a tough, mean guy"), who had kept Iran out of the oil embargo, and yet he worried about the shah's lack of authority over OPEC and his own relatively small oil resource base. The strategy could not rely upon the self-destruction of OPEC's unity. That was not going to be easy.

Much easier to cement the unity of the consumers: the North Atlantic powers. "We are organizing the consumers. Then we are organizing bilateral commissions to tie their economies as closely to us as possible. So we have leverage and the Europeans can't just move in a crisis. We want to tie up their capital." In February 1974, the United States had organized the Washington Energy Conference and set up the International Energy Program. It was an attempt to corral the countries of the Atlantic world to reduce their energy dependence

---

51   Daniel Patrick Moynihan, "The United States in Opposition," *Commentary*, March 1975.

52   Gosovic and Ruggie, "On the Creation of a New International Economic Order," p. 343.

53   Irving Kristol, "The 'New Cold War,'" *Wall Street Journal*, July 17, 1975, p. 18.

54   "Memorandum of Conversation," August 17, 1974, Oval Office, White House, National Security Adviser's Memoranda of Conversation Collection, Box 5, Gerald Ford Presidential Library.

(through conservation and new technologies), to share their reserves in a time of emergency, and to build political unity. In November 1974 the European and North American countries formed the International Energy Agency, a platform that would be part of the Organisation for Economic Co-operation and Development (OECD). This was one major plank of Kissinger's plan.

Another was to link a recalcitrant Europe to the United States through the supremacy of the dollar. None of the major Western European states wanted the Dollar Standard as a substitute for the Gold Standard. That would have been intolerable to their sense of independence. The Dollar Standard gave the US an enormous advantage. There was the obvious advantage of *seigniorage*—which is to say that, if it cost the US Treasury $1 to print a $100 bill, and if the $100 went into circulation to cover oil purchases by Mali from Saudi Arabia, the US would make $99 by the simple act of the export of that piece of paper. There were far more important advantages than that—namely that the US exchequer could finance its deficits by putting more money in circulation rather than by raising taxes or by offering bonds.[55] With the dollar emergent as the currency of the planet's wealth, a hunger developed for US Treasury Bills, and new markets emerged outside the US for dollars (such as the euro-dollar market). The dollar became the effective world currency, and this gave the United States "the ability to swing the price of the dollar internationally this way and that, having great economic consequences for the rest of the world while the US remained cushioned from the consequences that would apply to other states."[56] These mechanisms allowed the US Treasury and the Federal Reserve to conduct effective monetary policy for the world, without the rest of the world having any say on the dollar's manipulations. The rest of the world's independent action was constrained by that of Washington.

These mechanisms bound the consumers' interests, but they did not form a political instrument to push the interests of the North Atlantic world. Indeed, there was fear that Europe, the United States, and Japan might lose their unity in the midst of the fracas.[57] Kissinger reminded Ford that he and George Schultz had been active in creating such a forum. "We have to use the Library Group," he pointed out, "an informal finance group which is meeting on 7 September to raise the problem of oil prices and work for a coherent structure to deal with

---

55   There is a further way of doing this: the US government borrows money equivalent to its deficits and offers government bonds near that same amount; these are bought by the Federal Reserve, which prints money to pay for it.

56   Peter Gowan, *The Global Gamble: Washington's Faustian Bid for World Dominance*, London: Verso, 1999, pp. 25–6.

57   A *New York Times* editorial bemoaned the danger of the "possibility of a dissolution of the partnerships between the United States, Europe and Japan." "New Dollar Crisis," *New York Times*, February 7, 1973, p. 38.

it."[58] The Library Group was the brainchild of Schultz as US Treasury secretary. In March 1973, Schultz invited his financial peers from France (Valéry Giscard d'Estaing), West Germany (Helmut Schmidt), and the United Kingdom (Anthony Barber) to the White House Library for a quiet discussion over the new floating-exchange-rate system (and the place of the dollar), and to create a process to coordinate policy among the Atlantic allies. No immediate agreement came out of the Library meeting. In Nairobi, at the sidelines of the annual IMF meeting in September 1973, the Japanese foreign minister, Kiichi Aichi, invited the Library Group to dinner and *sake*, and, by the force of his effort, added Japan to the Group.[59] Within two years, the Group welcomed Italy and Canada. They christened themselves the Group of Seven (G7). Their goal was to create "a certain prophylaxis against purely domestic political pressures," as Paul Volcker put it, to provide a forum to share information candidly, so as to "understand the intentions and probable reaction of others," to ensure that the Atlantic governments "minimize uncomfortable surprises and avoid unnecessary frictions."[60]

Such unity was not to be forged as a bulwark against the Soviet threat. The USSR and its Warsaw allies had not been able effectively to challenge the economic basis of the North Atlantic world. After World War II, the standard of living in the USSR increased quite dramatically, with increased access to foodstuffs and better access to public health and education. The results of these policies allowed the economist Gur Ofer to suggest there was a "radical change in the quality of life in the Soviet Union."[61] The devastation of the war and the deprivation of previous years meant that, even with modest gains in the 1950s and 1960s, Soviet levels of consumption were far lower than those in the North Atlantic world.[62] The USSR posed no economic threat to the Atlantic world. It was not a modular alternative to the shining commodity-laden example of the

58   "Memorandum of Conversation," Oval Office, August 17, 1974.

59   Paul A. Volcker and Toyoo Gyohten, *Changing Fortunes: The World's Money and the Threat to American Leadership*, New York: Crown, 1992, p. 134.

60   Ibid., p. 143. Andrew Baker points out that the G7 process was driven by the US, although, as Gyohten shows, others among the G7 wanted in (including Canada, whose entry had to be forced, over French objections). *The Group of Seven: Finance Ministries, Central Banks and Global Financial Governance*, London: Routledge, 2006, p. 250.

61   Gur Ofer, "Soviet Economic Growth, 1928–1985," *Journal of Economic Literature* 25: 4 (December 1987), p. 1,790.

62   Gertrude Schroeder and Imogene Edwards, *Consumption in the USSR: An International Comparison*, Washington, DC: US Congress, Joint Economic Committee, 1982; and Gertrude Schroeder, "Soviet Living Standards: Achievements and Prospects," *Soviet Economy in the 1980s*, ed. US Congress Joint Economic Committee, Washington, DC, 1983.

United States and northern Europe. The Soviet threat was essentially military, and partly ideological. For that there was NATO, and of course the overwhelming military superiority of US armed forces.

The G7 faced off against OPEC and the NAM states. That a handful of oil-rich states could hold the North Atlantic powers hostage irked the founders of the G7. To them, the NIEO was simply irrational, and it had to be stopped. Some of the intellectual work for the G7's relationship to the OPEC-NAM-NIEO formation was done by the Trilateral Commission.[63] In July 1972, Chase Manhattan Bank's David Rockefeller, as chairman of the Council on Foreign Relations, initiated the Trilateral Commission. Rockefeller wanted to focus the powers of Europe, Japan, and the United States. One of the impetuses of the Trilateral was to secure the faltering hegemony of the United States,[64] but its much more obvious purpose was to ensure the combined strength of the "North" against the "South." Zbigniew Brzezinski, who was the intellectual architect of the Trilateral Commission and later President Jimmy Carter's *consigliere*, proposed this kind of combination against the South precisely to contain the "contagious threat of global anarchy."[65] Rockefeller was incensed by the Third World Project. In 1975, at a lecture in Manchester, Rockefeller went after the "new demonology" that had taken hold of the UN General Assembly. The immediate spur was the NIEO, and the push to regulate offshore corporations, which Rockefeller considered to be "the most important instruments in the unprecedented expansion that has taken place in world trade." Rockefeller went after the NIEO and its authors, the "revolutionary left and radical politicians" who had called "most persistently for punitive taxes and crippling regulation of multinationals."[66] A set of Trilateral intellectuals worried that the NIEO would "degenerate into a rejection of an integrated world economy."[67] From this point of view, even the liberal social-democratic vision of the Club of Rome had to be disdained. The Club, founded in 1968 by an Italian industrialist (Aurelio Peccei) and a

---

63 For a full study of the Trilateral's role, see Stephen Gill, *American Hegemony and the Trilateral Commission*, Cambridge: Cambridge University Press, 1990.

64 Rockefeller points out in his *Memoirs* that he had come to terms in the early 1970s with the fact that "power relationships in the world had fundamentally changed," and that US power had frayed, as had the relationships between the three main poles of world power—Japan, the US, and Europe. The Trilateral was formed to "bridge national differences and bring Japan into the international community." David Rockefeller, *Memoirs*, New York: Random House, 2002, pp. 415–16.

65 Zbigniew Brzezinski, "Half-Past Nixon," *Foreign Policy*, Summer 1971, pp. 10–13; and *Between Two Ages: America's Role in the Technetronic Era*, New York: Viking, 1970.

66 David Rockefeller, "Multinationals Under Siege: A Threat to the World Economy," *Atlantic Community Quarterly* 13 (Fall 1975), pp. 313–22.

67 Richard Cooper, Karl Kaiser, and Masataka Kosaka, *Towards a Renovated International System*, Triangle Papers 14, New York: Trilateral Commission, 1977, p. 17.

Scottish scientist (Alexander King), argued that the gap between the richest and poorest in the world should be reduced from 13:1 to 3:1.[68] The Trilateral found this "beyond the realm of practicality" and hastened to ask the Trilateral states to "assume leadership in the system."[69] The Trilateral wanted to bring "those who matter in the world," as German Social Democratic Chancellor Helmut Schmidt put it in 1975, into line with a combined policy against the chaos from the periphery.[70] The periphery needed to be put in its place.

Under US leadership, the G7 attempted to open up the fissures between NAM and OPEC, and within the NAM states themselves. Kissinger had long regarded the unity between the NAM and OPEC to be fragile; even more fragile were the gaps between the economically more sustainable countries of the NAM and those that were not. It was with this in mind that Kissinger invoked the "fourth world"—those who need "immediate help" and the provision of "long-term assistance" and even "special arrangements"—in his address to the Paris conference in 1975.[71] Peeling off the LDCs from the rest of the NAM by devising a strategy to get them some assistance, *without any fundamental alteration of the international system*, might earn the loyalty of the most wretched countries towards the Atlantic states. That, at least, was the hope. "We should try," Kissinger noted, "to break the unholy alliance between the LDCs and OPEC."[72] The former had to be informed that, if it went with OPEC, its lifeline to the IMF, the World Bank, and commercial banks would be in jeopardy. Kissinger's was a straightforward hustle.

The G7's heads of government planned to meet on November 15–17, 1975, at the French president's summer residence, the Château de Rambouillet. The medieval castle had a poor recommendation from Queen Marie Antoinette, who called it a *gothique crapaudière* ("gothic toadhouse"). The conference itself was cramped. Giscard had no intention of admitting the Italians or the Canadians, but they were forced upon him, *à contre cœur*, as the UK ambassador to France, Sir Edward Tomkins, wrote in his dispatch. Tomkins colorfully described Rambouillet, "which was not big enough for everyone." The "houseparty atmosphere" was "preserved with some difficulty. American security men, all wired for sound, thronged the corridors. Heavily armed gorillas haunted the park among autumn leaves blown off the trees by the helicopters. The mandarins were compressed rather than suppressed. The British delegation worked in Napoleon's bathroom. Jean Sauvagnargues [French minister of foreign affairs],

68   Jan Tinbergen, ed., for the Club of Rome, *ROI: Reshaping the International Order*, New York: Dutton, 1976.

69   Cooper, et al., *Towards a Renovated International System*, pp. 27, 34–8, 41–2.

70   Robert D. Putnam and Nicholas Bayne, *Hanging Together: Cooperation and Conflict in the Seven-Power Summits*, London: Sage, 1987, p. 29.

71   Kissinger, *Years of Renewal*, p. 699.

72   Ibid., p. 678.

who seemed strangely disoriented, was reduced to a table in the corridor."[73] As it happened, Canada did not show up.

Giscard had wanted the Rambouillet meeting to inaugurate a new Bretton Woods system. The French were not happy about the dollar–Wall Street complex. "The French thus think of a monetary system dominated by the dollar," British Ambassador Tomkins wrote, "in much the same way as they think of the integrated structure of NATO under supreme American command: the prejudice against both is the same." The French did not want their franc yoked to the will of the dollar. A more pragmatic arrangement, with freedom for the French monetary authorities to control their own currency, was their main objective. The French Finance Ministry could not get the US Treasury to agree to firmer limits to currency fluctuations. Giscard had to give in. "It was the product of hard and secret negotiations between the French and the American Treasury officials," Tomkins noted, "completed in the corners of the Château throughout the weekend." French Gaullism withered before the new Atlanticism—a polite term for the US government's setting of the North Atlantic's agenda.

Once this tussle was out of the way, the real work of the conference could get going. The agenda was twofold: to protect the capitalist system from political challenge and to thwart the New International Economic Order and OPEC. Monetary discussions hung over the proceedings but did not define it. More worrying yet was the constant interruption during the three days of gloomy economic news from the North Atlantic. On the day that the Rambouillet Declaration was being polished up, news came that the French had crossed what Tomkins called a "traumatic" threshold: 1 million unemployed. "The economy remains fragile," he noted, "here as elsewhere." Britain had already crossed this line, adding tens of thousands to the rolls. Wedded to deflationary policies, the governments at Rambouillet had few policy tools at their disposal to address the avalanche of joblessness and social dislocation. The worry was that this paralysis would open the door to a political challenge to capitalism, and this challenge would be exacerbated by the pressure on the price of energy and other commodities from the South. Both had to be stopped in their tracks.

In the late 1960s, the unrest of workers, students, anti-racists, and feminists disturbed the equilibrium of the political compact in each of the G7 states. Union militancy opened up as the rank and file in the United States and parts of Western Europe ejected many of the icons of business unionism. Wildcat strikes broke out during the "hot autumn" of 1969 in the automobile factories of northern Italy, leading slowly and painfully for the G7 leaders into the

---

73   E. E. Tomkins to James Callaghan, November 25, 1975, Paris, PREM no. 16/838, Margaret Thatcher Papers, Margaret Thatcher Foundation. It is likely that this colorful dispatch was written by Christopher Ewart-Biggs, a spirited writer whose life was cut short by the IRA in 1976.

1979 "winter of discontent."[74] From Tokyo University to the Sorbonne, students indicated a failure to accept the terms set by the establishment. Protests against tuition fees escalated into a call for changes in the civic order, and from denunciations of US imperialism to total condemnation of the system. As the French students put it: *Soyez realistes, demandez l'impossible!* ("Be realistic, demand the impossible!"). The counterculture of the students informed and was deepened by the struggles for dignity by oppressed communities, such as racialized minorities and women. Fights for equal rights offered a shock to the cultural compact of the system. Demands for redistribution and recognition, to use Nancy Fraser's terms, were equally powerful in the era.[75] The settled elite felt seriously threatened by this turbulence. It needed to find a way to buy them off, or to destroy them.

Into this context, President Ford opened the Rambouillet discussion with a plea to the leaders "to ensure that the current world economic situation is not seen as a crisis in the democratic or capitalist system."[76] A British summary after the conference pointed to the finesse needed to hoodwink the public about the fortitude of these leaders and of the system to which they were all equally pledged. "To convince a skeptical public opinion," the conference at Rambouillet "had to succeed on two levels—the cosmetic and the substantive. The participants were conscious that they had to make a convincing and demonstrative gesture of solidarity. On the other hand, this objective could only be achieved if the known differences of the participants were submerged in a community of interest clearly established at the meeting itself."[77] The G7 had to stick together, papering over the differences in the wordy but essentially meaningless Declaration. That was the crucial political task.

Despite the negative pressures on each of the national economies, no one could be permitted to run to the exits, erect trade barriers, and protect as much of their own national economies as possible. To go down that road would embolden those who felt that the emergent "global" economy had serious problems. The only exception was agriculture, because, as President Ford put

---

74   Beverly J. Silver, *Forces of Labor*, Cambridge: Cambridge University Press, 2003. Chapter 4 has the details.

75   Nancy Fraser, "From Redistribution to Recognition? Dilemmas of Justice in a 'post-Socialist' Age," *New Left Review* I/212 (July–August 1995). My sense of the weight of redistribution and recognition is in "The End of Multiculturalism," *Global Dialogue* 113 (2011).

76   "Memorandum of Conversation at the Rambouillet Summit, made for Brent Scowcroft by Robert Hormats," November 15–17, 1975, National Security Adviser's Memoranda of Conversation Collection, Box 16, Gerald Ford Presidential Library. For the following paragraphs I rely upon this very significant transcript.

77   FCO to UK Embassy Paris, "The Economic Summit Conference at Rambouillet," February 12, 1976, p. 10, PREM no. 16/838, Margaret Thatcher Papers.

it, "We in the United States recognize that domestic agriculture programs are a very delicate political problem in other countries, as they are in the United States." There is a chilling tone in the discussions, particularly when Chancellor Helmut Schmidt begins to talk about the deindustrialization process that must occur in each of the G7 states:

> Harold [Wilson, of the UK], you talked of viable industries, and indicated that this excluded lame ducks. You referred to textiles as an example. I am a close friend of the chairman of the textile workers union in Germany. It is a union of a shrinking industry. I would hope that this would not be repeated outside this room. Given the high level of wages in Europe, I cannot help but believe that in the long run textile industries here will have to vanish. We cannot ward off cheaper competition from outside. We will eventually need some hothouse or botanical garden for this indus try. It is a pity because it is viable: capital invested in a job in the textile industry in Germany is as high as it is in the German steel mills. But wages in East Asia are very low compared with ours. The garment industries in France and Italy, which make high fashions, will survive. They are ingenious and creative and will survive. The German textile industry is viable, but will vanish in ten or twelve years.[78]

The fatalism ("It is a pity because it is viable") of these heads of government before the almighty influence of Capital is almost as extraordinary as the cynicism of the leaders ("I would hope that this would not be repeated outside this room"). The leaders would collude to allow deindustrialization, and the consonant increased power for finance over industry. There is little sympathy for the workers in their homelands.[79] No smoke would leave the industrial smokestacks; its place would be taken by the chimney swifts, who mimic smoke as their flock takes flight from their new home.

---

78   "Memorandum of Conversation at the Rambouillet Summit, made for Brent Scowcroft by Robert Hormats."

79   Three years later, Helmut Schmidt and Britain's James Callaghan spoke on the telephone just after Callaghan had been able to push the Ford Motor Company to provide some wage increases at its plant in Dagenham (this factory has a long history of resistance, notably in 1968 and again in 1978). Schmidt asked how Callaghan had managed to get Ford's agreement. Callaghan answered, "Well, I don't think Ford's will be repeated everywhere. There are a number of settlements that are taking place at very much lower levels. Ford's is a very profitable company and therefore they can pay it and they've decided to do so and they are multi-national and they don't want their operations held up throughout Europe. But if I were asked I would say the general level of settlements will be much lower than the Ford settlement." Callaghan was right. Ford would begin to slow down production in the UK and turn to offshore sites. Dagenham is now a wind-turbine farm. "Prime Minister's Conversation with Chancellor Schmidt, at approx. 1605 hrs, Sunday 26 November 1978," PREM no. 16/1638, Margaret Thatcher Papers.

The discussion picked up with some force when the G7 leaders turned to the NIEO, OPEC, and the NAM states. They had to fall on the same sword as the German textile workers. Chancellor Schmidt made the point plainly: "It is desirable to explicitly state, for public opinion, that the present world recession is not a particularly favorable occasion to work out a new economic order along the lines of certain UN documents." Schmidt, who had a reputation for decisive action, was unflagging in his determination to prevent "international *dirigisme*" (*dirigisme* is the doctrine of state-directed economic growth). The NIEO had to be stopped, not only for its economic policies, but also for the presumption among its proponents that they could make decisions for the world. Schmidt felt that to leave decisions about the world economy "to officials somewhere in Africa or some Asian capital is not a good idea." Rather, what was important was that the decisions had to be made, as Harold Wilson put it, by "the sort of people sitting around this table." The G7 had to exercise control; everyone else had to be directed.

The way to break the OPEC dynamic was to split the NAM coalition. That was clear to each leader, as it had been to the Trilateral intellectuals. Harold Wilson, of the British Labour Party, set the agenda here. At the 6th Special Session of the UN, the NAM states were strongly united. By the 7th Session some gaps had begun to emerge within OPEC and between the NAM states. Wilson seized on these, as "we have won ourselves a breathing space. The initiative on these issues has, at least partially, been transferred to the sort of people sitting around this table." Now the question was how to control the initiative. There was no doubt, Wilson suggested, that "[t]he conditions of the developing countries have worsened while the expectations have increased." He repeated this assessment a number of times, adding up the list of burdens, from deterioration of the terms of trade to the high cost of oil and the decline in export prices: "If any of us were importers of oil and other commodities, and faced droughts and the need to import food at existing prices, we would also feel extremely bitter. Led by OPEC and other 'pecs' they will be pressing forward at UNCTAD IV and beforehand in CIEC; the needs of some of them are vitally urgent."

Cosmetic assistance needed to be provided before the Paris meetings came to a conclusion against the interests of the G7, and before the agenda was set for the UNCTAD IV meeting in Nairobi, in May 1976. The easiest symbolic gesture was to boost the miserably low foreign aid schemes. The IMF should be asked to be more flexible, mainly by increasing the quota for borrowing, suggested the Japanese prime minister, Takeo Miki, the rather mirthless leader of the Liberal Democratic Party. The suggestions were hardly impressive. The leaders acknowledged the real problems in Africa, Asia, and Latin America; but what worried them more than the suffering, and therefore headed the agenda, were its adverse political implications for the G7.

Rather than deal with the two pressing questions—commodity prices and unemployment—the leaders of the North spent the most significant part of their conversation on how to break the alliance of the South. OPEC's success in 1973 rattled the North; its model could not be allowed to be replicated. Britain's Wilson noted that the North had to "face the fact that the OPEC syndrome was catching on: there were already phosphate-pecs, bauxite-pecs, banana-pecs and others."[80] The "OPEC syndrome" needed to be disinfected.

"How to get the developing countries away from their alliance with OPEC?" asked Helmut Schmidt. This was the central question. The weak link, as far as these men were concerned, were the LDCs. The concept of the LDC emerged between 1968 (the UN's International Development Strategy) and 1971 (when the UN General Assembly adopted the term). It was produced by the secretariat at UNCTAD to allow them to carry out specific analytical work on development policy for countries with low literacy, low manufacturing, and low per capita GDP. There was nothing political about the definition: it was entirely about making development policy precise. The North now saw in this new distinction a political opportunity. LDCs often relied upon the export of one commodity, but they had to import many commodities (notably including energy). This imbalance worked against the LDCs, who had begun to go hat-in-hand to the oil producers for lower oil prices. It was this that provided the entry for Helmut Schmidt's analysis:

> Many of [the developing countries] have to depend on one single crop. We must find a way to break up the unholy alliance between the LDCs and OPEC. But we cannot say so in so many words. We should do this in the CIEC [the Paris process] by discussing the balance of payments problems of the LDCs and showing how they are being damaged by this situation. We can make the point that the newly rich countries have to take part in new developmental aid in accordance with their new riches. We will also have to convince the LDCs of our genuine interest in their well-being, by helping them in the area of raw materials.

"Our object," Schmidt said, "should be to sever [the LDCs] from OPEC." This is what Schmidt called the "dialogue strategy." The US secretary of state, Henry Kissinger, was in the room. Invited to comment, he provided an equally forth-right statement: "We agree on the need for cooperation with producers. With cooperation we can separate the moderates from the radicals within OPEC, the LDCs from the OPEC countries, and prevent a lot of other 'pecs.'" If the NAM states persisted and did not accept the G7 offerings, then "they will pay a price in terms of cooperation, or military exports."

---

80   "Note on the Third Session of the Heads of Government Conference at the Château de Rambouillet on Sunday 16 November 1975 at 4:15 p.m." PREM no. 16/838, p. 11, Margaret Thatcher Papers.

The stick for the LDCs came alongside the carrot for those who would later be called the "locomotives of the South"—the larger economies that might be pulled into the penumbra of the G7. As a Trilateral publication from 1976 pointedly noted, "History has often shown that the greatest dangers to international stability often arise from those nations whose real power is inadequately reflected in both real involvement in the relevant sets of international arrangements and symbols of status therein." The problem for the Trilateral was in its selection criteria for its allies. On the one hand, there was the question of democracy. In Helsinki, the 1973 Conference of the Organization for Security and Cooperation in Europe rallied around the brand "democracy" as the ideal way to show up the USSR.[81] The most reliable countries, however, were not democratic in any way. The Trilateral publication pointed to Brazil (then under military rule), Mexico (then under endemic one-party rule), Iran, and Saudi Arabia (both under the rule of autocratic monarchies) as countries that should be welcomed out of Third Class into First Class. It hardly seemed to matter that the "democratic" governments in these countries wore either military or feudal uniforms. The contradiction did not bother the Trilateral, nor the G7.

The G7 sought new allies among the South to help undermine the unity that led to the NIEO. "Much of the current call for a new international economic order flows directly from such concerns" of being left out of the system, suggested the Trilateral intellectuals. "Indeed, only through integration into the management of international arrangements are such countries likely to acquire the systematic interests necessary for the constructive formulations of their own foreign economic policies."[82] These were to form the "new international middle class," whose future was that of Japan, which had at one time been one of the darker nations, but since 1962 had been a member of the OECD, and since 1975 of the G7. If Japan could enter the club, then why not Iran, or Saudi Arabia, or even Brazil?

High on the agenda of the G7 was the task of breaking the unity between the NAM and OPEC. Equally, the G7 pushed to undermine the role of the UN, particularly where it had come to act on behalf of the Third World Project. The G77 had been able to move a number of pieces of its agenda through the various UN bodies; the NAM advanced its agenda in a number of important, but not yet central, conclaves to write international law. The G7, with US leadership, sought to do an end run around the various UN bodies, preferring bilateral engagement to the work of these organizations. It had become *de rigueur* for

81   Jacques Andreani, *La Piège: Helsinki et la chute du communisme*, Paris: Odile Jacob, 2005.

82   C. Fred Bergsten, George Berthoin, and Kinhide Mushakoji, *The Reform of International Institutions*, New York: The Trilateral Commission, 1976, p. 9.

US political intellectuals to mock the claims made by the NAM states within the UN system. In March 1975, Daniel Patrick Moynihan published a screed against the role of the Third World states in the UN. "Third World extremists" had taken hold of the UN, Moynihan suggested, largely because the US had withdrawn from the field. It was time to return to the fight. Moynihan had made part of his reputation within the United States in the struggle against welfare for indigent populations, with his focus largely on African-Americans, who had only recently won the right to equal social benefits.[83] Moynihan suggested that the "dysfunctional" black family would do well to send its children into the military to be disciplined. A similarly stern attitude was in order towards the dysfunctional Third World.

Moynihan's celebrated essay against the black family was published in the neoconservative US journal *Commentary*. It was to this venue that he returned with his analysis of the UN. If the black family was unwilling to take "personal responsibility" for its purported failures, the Third World states were similarly culpable. Both the black family and the Third World had sought the status of victimhood, Moynihan argued, and failed to see that their poverty (here referring to the Third World) "is of their own making and no one else's, and no claim on anyone else arises in consequence." The reparations movement and the NIEO were symptoms of this failure on their part to face up to their own limitations. The US, Moynihan argued, must end a policy of "appeasement so profound as to seem wholly normal."[84] The *Commentary* essay impressed the White House. When Kissinger and Ford called Moynihan in to brief him as the next ambassador to the UN (1975–76), Kissinger said, "that *Commentary* article is one of the most important articles in a long time. That is why it is essential to have him at the UN."[85] The Third World was the problem. It threatened Israel and South Africa. For Kissinger it was "an outrage" that the UN General Assembly would suspend South Africa. "We have to keep fighting that, or the Group of 77 will be deciding UN membership."

During Moynihan's tenure at the UN, the G77 states pushed through UN Resolution 3379, which framed Zionism as Racism (November 1975). It was a marginal resolution, not at the heart of the UN's work.[86] Nevertheless, the

---

83   Daniel P. Moynihan, "The Negro Family: The Case for National Action," in Lee Rainwater and William L. Yancey, eds, *The Moynihan Report and the Politics of Controversy*, Cambridge: MIT Press, 1967.

84   Daniel P. Moynihan, "The United States in Opposition," *Commentary*, March 1975, pp. 41–4.

85   "Memorandum of Conversation in The Oval Office: American Strategy at the UN," April 12, 1975, White House, National Security Adviser's Memoranda of Conversation Collection, Box 10, Gerald Ford Presidential Library.

86   The exaggerations went so far as to link political support for the Palestinians from the Third World states to antisemitism. For an example of this kind of argument,

US focused almost exclusive attention on it to show that the UN had been destroyed by the Third World's leadership role within it. Moynihan's role was to crush this dynamic (his 1978 memoir of his years at the UN is called *A Dangerous Place*). None of the other initiatives of the Third World within the UN had any space to breathe.

It was in this period, between 1975 and the early years of the 1980s, that the US ran roughshod over reasonable international treaties. In 1982 the US (with Venezuela, Turkey, and Israel) voted against the new Law of the Seas; in 1984 the US tried to scuttle the International Conference on Population and Development. In both forums, the US pushed against *dirigisme*, advancing the interests of transnational corporations—to open the deep seabed to commercial prospecting and to prevent population-control strategies, since population growth was "neutral," and governments should not intervene to moderate it.[87] Delegates were aghast—but there was little they could do. The exact issues under debate seemed less important to the US State Department officials. They had come to exercise their authority and to scuttle the value of the multilateral institutions. Absent the US, as the leader of the G7, the treaties being negotiated would have little value. They would stand as sentinels of an ancient civilization, like the *moai* of Easter Island, staring at the sea for no apparent purpose.

Kissinger pushed for the consolidation of the G7 as the firewall against the NIEO, with OPEC as its main artillery. He was the main intellectual architect of the new alliances. OPEC had to be neutered. Saudi Arabia and the Gulf Arab states were the obvious levers to undermine OPEC. "Military action would of course be inappropriate," Kissinger said at Rambouillet, "but it might be possible to develop the idea that increases in the price of oil were not 'free' in general

---

see Barry Rubin, "The Non-Arab Third World and Antisemitism," in Robert S. Wistrich, ed., *Anti-Zionism and Antisemitism in the Contemporary World*, New York: NYU Press, 1990. Much of the anger against the Third World Project from the Israeli state and its intellectuals came from the role of NAM in the drafting of UN Security Council Resolution 242. The first draft was put forward by India, Mali, and Nigeria; Washington put forward a second draft. The first draft mentioned the Palestinians by name and championed their right to return to their homelands; the US draft called only for a just settlement in the Middle East, leaving out the important particulars. Such evasions helped Israel in its efforts to change the "facts on the ground" to suit its purpose. The UN General Assembly, supported by the USSR, went for the NAM draft. On the basis of this support, the PLO began to attend the UN as an observer from 1969. This rankled both Washington and Jerusalem.

87   David Larson, "The Reagan Administration and the Law of the Sea," *Ocean Development and International Law* 11: 3–4 (1982); Jason Finkle and Barbara Crane, "Ideology and Politics at Mexico City: The United States at the 1984 International Conference on Population," *Population and Development Review* 11: 1 (March 1985). This is the journal of the Population Council.

economic or political terms."[88] If need be, the North Atlantic would have to raise the costs of confrontation, and in the arsenal of the US and Europe lay only its military superiority. It was not until the Soviet Union had collapsed that this weapon could be unsheathed (in 1991, with the first Gulf War).

Without a military strategy, unity within the G7 was imperative. Any weakness there would allow the Third World Project to slip through. "It would be suicidal to enter the consumer-producer dialogue without a common strategy," Kissinger pointed out. Giscard and Schmidt worried that the kind of confrontation described by Kissinger would be dangerous. Nonetheless, none of them denied the fact, as Schmidt put it, that "if danger occurred it was important that the convoy of consumers should stick together ... Solidarity in bargaining must be achieved."[89] Japan's Miki worried that confrontation between North and South would be counterproductive. "A dialogue was indispensible and was possible to achieve," he said, but this was already a minority view. The G7 was born, ready for combat, with Kissinger's plots at its center, and with caution thrown to the wind.

DEBT AND THE NEW COSMOLOGY

By the early 1980s a new world order had begun to emerge. It was not the NIEO, and it was not run by the Third World states—although it was partly financed by OPEC. The G7 came into its own, showing the world that it could withstand the Second Oil Crisis of 1979 with aplomb. Economic stagnation did not stand in its way. Rather, this stagnation, which had persisted since the late 1960s, became one of the main pretexts for the breakthrough of the new ideology of the G7: neoliberalism. Having staked a claim to run planetary affairs, the G7 now pushed its theory of governance on states from Mexico to Mali. The institutions for this thrust were those founded in Bretton Woods, but whose ambit would dramatically change in these years. The IMF and the World Bank would become sharp rapiers, thrust into the heart of the Third World Project— whose highest expression, the NIEO, lay dead by the wayside.

What went by the name of neoliberalism was less a coherent economic doctrine than a fairly straightforward campaign by the propertied classes to maintain or restore their position of dominance.[90] Pressure mounted on the

---

88   "Note on the Third Session of the Heads of Government Conference at the Château de Rambouillet on Sunday 16 November 1975 at 4:15 p.m." PREM no. 16/838, p. 18, Margaret Thatcher Papers.

89   Ibid., p. 19

90   This was the argument made by Ernest Mandel with regard to the rise of monetarism. "World Crisis and the Monetarist Answer," in Karel Jansen, ed., *Monetarism, Economic Crisis and the Third World*, London: Frank Cass, 1983. It was elaborated by David Harvey in his *A Short History of Neoliberalism*, Oxford: Oxford University Press, 2005.

propertied from two fronts; first, industrial productivity in the North under-
went a gradual slowdown; second, trade union struggles in Europe and the
United States, as well as the push for the NIEO, raised the costs of labor. The
propertied reassessed their situation. Their riches needed to be preserved.
The fine arts of the dollar–Wall Street complex enabled them to hoard their
wealth. Financial markets, once prevented from playing an active role in the
international monetary system, came to be equal partners with the Atlantic
state governments. Private financial institutions operated hand-in-glove with
central banks and treasury departments to ensure the "soundness" of money
against the social demands of the population. This idea of "sound money" provided the necessary economic cover for the political thrust of the dollar–Wall
Street complex. It allowed bankers and politicians to hide their political choice
of protecting the propertied behind a slew of technical arguments.[91]

If the dollar went into a slide, the other Central Banks and the private banks
pledged to throw their reserves behind maintaining its authoritative position.
If restoration of wealth was not sufficient, as it was not, and since productivity in the industrial sector was not what it had once been, the propertied went
after those areas of life that had been partially preserved from the profit motive:
these went by the name of the "public sector" or the "commons," but would
soon become the preserve of the wealthy. Fire-sales of public enterprises would
hastily make the millionaires into billionaires, asset-stripping would enrich the
predatory investor, and the low-rent utilization of common resources (such as
water and energy sources) would create a new energy-sector or common-sector
oligarchy. This "accumulation by dispossession" or "accumulation by encroachment" became one of the central means of the further enrichment of the rich.[92]
For the working class, the peasantry, the small producers and shopkeepers,
and for the government employees, the buzzword was not "short selling" but
"austerity." The word "austerity" would be dispensed like bitter medicine by
hardheaded economists, frazzled politicians, and a new breed of IMF officials.
For them, sacrifice and austerity were concepts to restore "stability," when in
fact the sacrifices of the marginal populations would only result in the restoration of the class power of the propertied, and their enrichment.

In the face of neoliberalism, Third World states would be supine. By the
early 1970s, development within the states of the Third World Project had
reached an impasse; no more could be done without major international transformation. The NIEO was to enable that next stage. The only country within
the Third World orbit that could survive the NIEO's demise was China, and

---

91   Gowan, *Global Gamble*, p. 23.

92   David Harvey, "The 'New' Imperialism: Accumulation by Dispossession,"
Socialist Register 2004, New Delhi: LeftWord Books, 2003; Prabhat Patnaik, "The
Economics of the New Phase of Imperialism," manuscript, August 2005.

that was largely because it had delinked from the world economy in the 1940s. China turned to a form of labor-intensive industrialization, with a part of the surplus turned over to the construction of social capacity (such as free education and healthcare).[93] Such a policy required a radical change in the social relations within the country—an initiative that was not possible within most Third World states, dominated as they were by various fragments of the landlord classes, the industrial bourgeoisie, and a state-reliant petty bourgeoisie. Those classes had benefited from the import-substitution industrialization regimes common across the Third World states: tariffs and subsidies to their private industries and large private farms enabled the economies of the formerly colonial states to grow modestly and to keep out the better-funded and better-equipped firms of the North. Now these classes had made their mark and wanted to "go global." They would not countenance Chinese-level expenditure on basic needs and education. These classes wanted access to global markets, and to the coveted dollars. The NIEO was one way to get to them, but it meant confrontation with the North. The other was conciliation—and that would become the approach of the conflict-wary elites of the South. But that second road would only open up in the 1980s, except along the Pacific Rim, where the newly industrialized countries (NICs) were the exception for their earlier "integration" into the circuits of North America. For the rest, the NIEO was the only option to increase their national income, and thereby inject finances into the construction of social capacity (and into their own coffers). When the NIEO failed, these states went into free-fall.

The now despondent Third World states turned to the private capital markets to finance their various initiatives. The rate of foreign aid had not kept up with inflation, nor with the increasing needs of the Third World states. The Pearson Report had asked the advanced industrial countries to raise their foreign aid contribution to 0.7 percent of their gross national product. No country outside Scandinavia ever came close to this modest target.[94] What aid did cross borders came decidedly with strings attached. Some was conditional on the funds being used to finance construction by firms from the aid-giving country (a form of

---

93 For a good summary, see Minqi Li, *The Rise of China and the Demise of the Capitalist World Economy*, New York: Monthly Review Press, 2008, Chapter 2.

94 President Reagan went so far as to argue that the problems of the LDCs stemmed from too much aid—that is, overextended credit was being used for wasteful consumption. This was the US argument for less foreign aid. *IMF Survey*, October 12, 1981. Pearson's report noted that the OECD's Development Assistance Committee (DAC) accepted the UNCTAD target for aid of 1 percent of national income. But Pearson pointed out that it was "ironic to note that total resource flows actually did exceed 1 percent of combined national income in the five years preceding the adaptation of the target by DAC. Since then the target has never been met." Pearson, *Partners in Development*, p. 144.

subsidy to those firms, in effect). Firms from the advanced industrial countries often had high overheads, and were thus much more expensive than local firms in the aid-receiving countries. All this mattered little, and all giving was counted as aid. It did not always appeal to the South.[95] Better to go to the private markets than to rely upon such tied aid.

The offshore branches of the large Atlantic banks stood ready. They operated without regulations, and with few assets held idle as reserves.[96] They had accumulated vast sums in eurodollars (mainly petroleum profits), huge amounts of which they now put at the service of the countries of Africa, Asia, and Latin America. Banks like Manufacturers Hanover Trust lent money using the London Inter-Bank Offered Rate (LIBOR), a floating interest rate (although current scandals around LIBOR reveal that the private banks controlled the "flotation" to their benefit). LIBOR seemed a reasonable bet in the mid 1970s, when its level appeared manageable. The capital came without the kind of conditions that were already in place for IMF funds. Additionally, the money flowed in without care for the solvency of the borrower. This was the international sub-prime market, which stood at the colossal sum of $1.5 trillion in the 1980s.

These billions of dollars went to cover very tight budgetary gaps. States needed the money to deliver short-term consumption goods to their populations, or else for long-term low-return investment for their infrastructure. They required the money to make payments in "hard currency" to their international creditors—those who delivered oil mainly to the shores of the energy-starved states, but also to arms dealers who helped fatten the militaries that states often poised against the other on contested borders. The development paths of many of these states had come to rely upon a combination of foreign aid and private capital. In October 1977, IMF head H. Johannes Witteveen warned UN officials that many of the Third World states "had over-accelerated their economies and were, as a result, borrowing up to 12 percent of their national income. Such a rate of borrowing was unsustainable, and urgent adjustments were called for in order to avert major debt-servicing difficulties which would have serious repercussions on the entire international financial system."[97] This was a private

---

95   Yash Tandon, *Ending Aid Dependence*, Nairobi: Fahamu Books, 2008, Chapter 2.

96   Jessica P. Einhorn, "International Bank Lending: Expanding the Dialogue," *Columbia Journal of World Business* 13: 3 (Fall 1978). The Bank of International Settlements' Standing Committee on Banking Regulations and Supervisory Practices asked for better-consolidated reporting of banking activities, and of common evaluative standards on bank assets.

97   Administrative Committee on Consultation, United Nations, provisional summary record of the first meeting, October 31, 1977, p. 11. Witteveen was not alone in sounding the alarm privately. In 1992, Volcker recalled the concern in the Federal Reserve:

message. The public message from the IMF, the G7, and the offshore branches of the Atlantic banks was that debt was beneficial if it meant that the countries could cover their imbalances, and that petrodollars were being recycled effectively.[98]

The tripwire was pulled in 1979, when the US central bank raised its interest rates. The proximate cause was the continued sluggishness of the US economy, and the need, as Federal Reserve Bank chair Paul Volcker put it, "to slay the inflationary dragon."[99] Slow growth rates from the mid 1960s had been caused by several factors. Higher oil prices suffocated economic activity for the carbon-reliant civilization. Overproduction in the industrial factories from Kyushu, Japan, to Gary, Indiana, put pressure on firms' bottom lines. Corporate profitability fell from +4.7 percent in 1954–59 to −5.3 percent in 1980–89. Philip O'Hara points out that this decline has to be understood in terms of a crisis of overproduction. "Over-supply of commodities and inadequate demand are the principal corporate anomalies inhibiting performance in the global economy."[100] The anarchy of competition leads to two related outcomes: an increased drive to develop new technologies to produce more, faster, and cheaper, and then a consequent move to displace labor by these machines, and so increase general unemployment. Factories became technologically very efficient. By bringing more machines into the factory, the firms were able to displace human labor at the same time as producing more goods. This increased quantity of goods entered the marketplace, whose consumers had little in their pockets, as a result of unemployment. The "effective demand" was low as a

---

It is a fair question to ask where the supervisory authorities were while all this was going on. Were any alarm bells ringing, and if not, why not? As best as I can recall the atmosphere, the good, gray, cautious Federal Reserve did not share the blithe lack of concern of some in government about what was going on. While I wasn't present to vouch for the story, Arthur Burns once recalled that he summoned a group of leading bankers to Washington in 1976 to warn them about the risk of repeating in foreign lands their recent excesses in real estate lending. What he got for his trouble was a response that they knew more about banking than he did.

Volcker and Gyohten, *Changing Fortunes*, p. 195.

98   Bahram Nowzad and Richard Williams, *External Indebtedness of Developing Countries*, IMF Occasional Paper No. 3, Washington, DC: IMF, 1981, p. 11. These IMF economists wrote that, "[t]hough some countries experienced difficulties, a generalized debt management problem was avoided, and in the aggregate the outlook for the immediate future does not give cause for alarm."

99   Volcker and Gyohten, *Changing Fortunes*, p. 170.

100   Phillip O'Hara, "The Contradictory Dynamics of Globalization," in B. N. Ghosh and Halil M. Guven, eds, *Globalization and the Third World: A Study of Negative Consequences*, New York: Palgrave, 2006, p. 26; and Walden Bello, "The Capitalist Conjuncture: Over-Accumulation, Financial Crises, and the Retreat from Globalization," *Third World Quarterly* 27: 8 (2006), p. 1,348.

result of unemployment and the lack of ready credit for a workforce that looked increasingly redundant. This is the primary contradiction of capitalism, which makes its appearance in the downturns in the "business cycle." The 1970s was a particularly bad downturn.

To restore profitability, the US government authorized a major assault on its own economy, to reshape it, to follow the axiom of the German sociologist Werner Sombart, so that "from destruction a new spirit of creation arises."[101] The general theory was that, once overcapacity plunged industry into contraction, new innovations would spring from the minds of inventive firms and their intellectuals. Drawing from Sombart's work, the economist Joseph Schumpeter called this process "creative destruction."[102] It is this theory that emboldens the kind of monetary policy followed by the US in late 1970s. A sharp contraction of the economy at a time of overcapacity can have the necessary inoculative impact. Volcker engineered the most severe credit tightening in a generation, pushing interest rates upward so that interest on all US loans had risen by 21 percent by the early 1980s. In October 1979, Volcker came before the US Congress with a spectacular announcement: "The standard of living of the average American has to decline. I don't think you can escape that." President Jimmy Carter hastened to the Pay Advisory Committee to call for a "sense of partnership" between business and labor, in the hope that the former would not use this time to "protect their interests first, sometimes at the expense of their neighbor."[103] Such a social bargain was illusory. The old manufacturing sites in the US collapsed, never to recover.[104]

In the early years of the Reagan administration, the government went after the trade unions, keeping wages depressed and putting pressure on social welfare spending. Orthodox monetarism crippled whatever minimal social compact existed in the United States. The attack on labor began with a symbolic fight against the air traffic controllers—the only union to back Reagan in his election. In 1990, Volcker noted that the most important action of the Reagan administration "in helping the anti-inflation fight was defeating the air traffic controllers' strike. [Volcker] thought that this action had had a rather profound, and, from his standpoint, constructive effect on the climate

---

101   This is from Sombart's *Krieg und Kapitalismus*, Leipzig: Duncker & Humblot, 1913, p. 207, translated by Hugo Reinert and Erik Reinert.

102   Joseph Schumpeter, *Capitalism, Socialism and Democracy*, London: Routledge, 1942, pp. 82–3.

103   Steven Rattner, "Volcker Asserts US Must Trim Living Standard," *New York Times*, October 18, 1979, p. A1.

104   The definitive work here is the MIT Commission on Industrial Productivity, Michael L. Dertouzos, Richard Lester, and Robert Solow, *Made in America: Regaining the Productive Edge*, Cambridge: MIT Press, 1989.

of labor-management relations, even though it had not been a wage issue at the time."[105] Asset stripping, arbitrage, the deindustrialization of America—all this was to follow, as was the decline in living standards for a section of the population. Entire sections of the formerly industrialized United States became a "factory desert," as industrial units closed down and abandoned a workforce once disciplined and loyal, but now embittered.[106] Once the process had weeded out the unproductive and productive (but not "viable") firms, at great human cost, "the Reagan administration, which had come to office on a programme of balancing the budget, launched what turned out to be the greatest experiment in Keynesianism in the history of the world. The supply-side programme which accompanied monetarism in the US," historian Robert Brenner argues, "highlighted by record tax cuts, did succeed in transferring enormous sums of money into the hands of capitalists and the rich from the pockets of almost everyone else."[107] Capital that had gone overseas now flooded back into the US to create one asset bubble after another (personal credit debt, as credit cards were scattered like dew into the pockets of now marginally employed consumers; real estate debt, as housing prices began to rise). Wall Street slowly but surely increased its own power over the state and society.

When the US Fed raised interest rates, LIBOR went out of control. The impact on the Third World states was catastrophic. There was little creative about it. Non-OPEC Third World states held external debt amounting to $130 billion in 1973. The early debt might have been ameliorated had the IMF, under Witteveen, gone ahead with its plan to open a temporary oil facility. The IMF's official history notes that Witteveen's action "propelled the Fund into a leadership role in helping its members cope with the new crisis." But it was not to hold. Both the US Treasury and the German central bank opposed the idea. The US Treasury, under George Schultz, wanted the price rise to hurt the non-OPEC Third World states, motivating them to put pressure on OPEC to reduce its price.[108] The prices did not drop, and the oil-induced debts increased. The LIBOR rates would take these debts and throw them into relief. By 1982, that debt had ballooned to $612 billion. The World Bank debt figures rankle. In 1979–80, the combined capital accounts of the Third World states ran a surplus of $85.7 billion. Between 1981 and 1984, the states went into a deficit of $54.8 billion. The current account deficit rose to $233 billion by 1984, and then spiraled beyond imagination. The numbers grew larger and larger. The bottom

105   Robert Brenner, "The Economics of Global Turbulence," *New Left Review* 1/229 (May–June 1998), p. 191.

106   The idea of the "factory desert" comes from Marco Revelli, *Lavorare in FIAT*, Milan: Garzanti, 1989.

107   Brenner, "Economics of Global Turbulence," p. 182.

108   Margaret G. de Vries, *The International Monetary Fund, 1972–1978*, Washington, DC: IMF, 1985, vol. 1, pp. 305–6.

line was that the Third World states had walked into a bear trap when they accepted commercial loans at LIBOR rates; when the US Fed acted, LIBOR went from almost negative interest to usurious rates, and the bear trap tightened. The Third World states had no freedom of movement; they were captives.

Commercial banks did not go into their lending spree without insurance. The loans that went to Mexico, Côte d'Ivoire, and elsewhere came as syndicated loans, with the banks pooling their muscle at the delivery and then, most importantly, at the recovery. If the Paris Club was the cartel for official loanmakers, the London and New York Clubs functioned as the bankers' cartel against those in debt to them. The banks abhorred the Third World Project's idea of an International Debt Commission, largely because they did not want to allow the Third World states to treat the debt as *political*.[109] The banking syndicate wanted to treat each country debt on a case-by-case basis. They did not want to have to face an agency of the South, such as the Debt Commission, which would negotiate the entire portfolio of debt held by the South as one package.[110] The case-by-case approach disabled countries that feared for their long-term creditworthiness.[111] The reproach of "moral hazard" was thrust at the indebted states, who were told that if their debts were forgiven they would never learn. There was no such chastisement of the banks, which were given political cover for their own moral culpability. Debts had to be serviced by the borrowers, and this money flowed in large quantities from the Third World

---

109   The United States government, on the other hand, had no compunction about using debt and credit politically. The Nixon administration organized an embargo of credit to the Chilean government of Salvador Allende (1970–73). Then, when General Pinochet came to power, the US government opposed the European hesitancy in lending to the dictatorship. "We expressed displeasure that, broadly speaking," the US government said unctuously, "some countries put political aspects above technical considerations." Clyde H. Farnsworth, "Club of Paris Expands Role in Helping Debtor Nations," *New York Times*, May 17, 1976, p. 44.

110   The NAM had made its position clear as early as 1973, when Boumédienne told the 4th Summit, "It would be highly desirable to examine the problem of the present indebtedness of the developing countries. In this examination, we should consider the cancellation of the debt in a great number of cases and, in other cases, refinancing on better terms as regards maturity dates, deferrals and rates of interest." *Action Program for Economic Cooperation*, 4th Summit of NAM Countries, Algiers, Algeria, September 1973.

111   The rules that prevented a debt strike had been set long before the actual debt crisis of the late 1970s. A World Bank study pointed this out: "Rules of the game have emerged in the field of international finance. One such rule is that default by a debtor country is now excluded as a means of adjusting financial obligations to debt servicing capacity." IBRD, "Multilateral Debt Renegotiations: 1956–1968," unpublished paper, April 11, 1969, p. 39; Charles Lipson, "The International Organization of Third World Debt," *International Organization* 35: 4 (August 1981), p. 622.

states to the offshore branches of the Atlantic banks, and to their homes in New York, London, and elsewhere. In 1981, the net flow of capital to the Third World states stood at $35.2 billion. Six years later, the direction of capital flow had changed: $30.7 billion left the Third World states for the banks. It was a tribute payment.

The Europeans and the Japanese watched aghast as US interest rates created mayhem first in Latin America and then elsewhere. By 1980, the Japanese reached out to the Reagan administration to relay its concern. "We argued that the high interest rates were certainly exacerbating the Third World debt problem and calculated that if US interest rates declined by 1 percent, Latin America's burden of debt service would be reduced by $4 billion a year," reflected Toyoo Gyohten of the Japanese Ministry of Finance. "We got no response in Washington and felt that we were really talking to deaf ears in those days."[112] Washington's stubbornness seemed to Tokyo like a penalty.

Even sections of the IMF could not countenance the punishment to be meted out to Third World states. The Group of 24—the caucus of IMF member states that were also part of the Third World—held a meeting on March 6, 1979, at which they pointed out that "a clearer distinction needs to be made [by the IMF] between the causal factors attributable to the domestic policies of the developing countries and the external elements beyond their control."[113] The Fund's 1979 Annual Report concurred, noting that the balance-of-payments deficits of the non-OPEC Third World states could not be blamed principally on internal factors (such as *dirigisme* or state-centered development). Rather, the IMF argued that the financial instability was a result of the deteriorating terms of trade (the prices of raw materials declining in relation to those of industrial products) and of the rise in the interest payments against the debt incurred by the NAM states.[114] Sidney Dell, a veteran UN economist, reflected on this IMF analysis: "Both of these developments [identified by the IMF] were the result of forces outside the control of the developing countries concerned, including the mounting export prices of the industrial and oil-exporting countries and the increases in interest rates associated with efforts by the industrial countries to curb inflation by means of monetary restrictions."[115] The Third World states had to ascend to the cross for crimes they hadn't committed.

Absent the NIEO, and now with so little authority on the world stage, the Third World states came with beggar's bowl in hand to the banks and to the IMF.

---

112   Volcker and Gyohten, *Changing Fortunes*, p. 185.

113   Group of 24, "Communiqué of the Ministers Issued Mar. 6, 1979," *IMF Survey*, March 19, 1979, p. 87.

114   IMF, *Annual Report 1979*, Washington, DC: IMF, 1979, p. 23.

115   Sidney Dell, *On Being Grandmotherly: The Evolution of IMF Conditionality*, Essays in International Finance, no. 144, Princeton: International Finance Section, Department of Economics, Princeton University, 1981, p. 22.

The idea that this crisis was exogenous, and not indigenous, found few takers among "those who matter," whether the guardians at the Bank of International Settlements, the IMF, or the cabinets of the G7 countries. Northern unity stared the beggarly South down. Volcker, who had set off the little switch that set the process in motion, saw the opportunity of the moment. "The agony of the debt crisis," he wrote, "provided the jolt necessary for Latin American leaders to rethink their old approaches and set off in fresh and much more promising directions."[116] No longer *desarrollo hacia adentro*—the import-substitution industrialization promoted by Prebisch; now the region would return to *desarrollo hacia afuera*, development through the export of raw materials. The clock had to be reversed, with a small modification, in that growth would also come from the export-led manufacturing that relied principally on cheap labor rather than on technology-derived productivity. In Mexico these factories would be called *maquiladoras*.[117] The only way out of the debt crisis for the South was to earn foreign exchange from higher net exports: sales of raw materials, of labor-intensive manufactured products, and of the public sector to foreign investors. There was no other way.

The timing for this shift was serendipitous.[118] A number of technological developments made the turn to the *maquila*-mode possible. The Japanese "just in time" production system became the order of the day. Telecommunications (satellites and secure undersea cables) linked the archipelago of global cities with the hinterland production sites. Orders from retail outfits in the United States could travel in real time to Asia. Ubiquitous computers allowed inventories to be managed across continents. Containers that could go directly from cargo ships onto long-haul tracks or train-beds allowed goods to travel much faster from point of production to point of sale. All this allowed production for the US and European market to move far afield—to the US-Mexico border, to the Caribbean, or to Asia and Africa. In these places, offshore firms had no interest in being tied down by national labor and workplace safety regulations; such encumbrances had to go. Tom Clausen of BankAmerica pined for "an international corporation that has shed all national identity." Carl Gerstacker of Dow Chemical had the audacity to tell the White House Conference on the

---

116   Volcker and Gyohten, *Changing Fortunes*, p. 188.

117   An early ethnography of these factories can be found in M. Patricia Fernández-Kelly, *For We Are Sold, I and My People: Women and Industry in Mexico's Frontier*, Albany: SUNY Press, 1983.

118   The literature on this shift is illuminating. For example, see M. J. Piore and C. F. Sabel, *The Second Industrial Divide*, New York: Basic Books, 1984; T. Elger and C. Smith, eds, *Global Japanization? The Transnational Transformation of the Labour Process*, London: Routledge, 1994; and Peter F. Drucker, *The Post-Capitalist Society*, New York: HarperBusiness, 1993. Some of the dynamic was picked up by Alain Touraine, *La société post-industrielle*, Paris: Denoël, 1969.

Industrial World Ahead, on February 7, 1972: "I have long dreamed of buying an island owned by no nation and of putting the World Headquarters of the Dow Company on the truly neutral ground of such an island, beholden to no nation or society."[119] Clausen and Gerstacker were not dreamers. They articulated what had already become possible for offshore firms, whose production entities were often subcontracted and whose main business was the transit of electronic pulses that showed them how their money went hither and thither.

The Bretton Woods institutions had to pull their socks up and get to work. Liberal voices had to go. Witteveen did not get a second term at the IMF. His place was taken in 1978 by Jácques de Larosière, a hard-nosed former under secretary for monetary affairs at the Directeur du Tresor and head of the Banque de France. De Larosière had no time for equity and the NIEO. He was given over to the monetarist view that stability was the main order (and to get there, workers' wages had to be cut back).[120] As he put it in 1981, firmly in the IMF saddle, it was time for "sacrifices on the part of all: international financing will serve no purpose if spent on consumption as if there were no tomorrow."[121] The "all" here was questionable: it did not include the wealthy, whose own consumption habits came under no such threat. But the lower orders had to tighten their belts.

The World Bank, too, had to be brought into line. Robert McNamara, with his abhorrent brand of liberalism, left the Bank in 1981. In his place came Tom Clausen, straight from his perch at BankAmerica (the same man who wanted corporations to be freed from national sovereignty). Clausen made the requisite, even clichéd statements about poverty, insisting that the industrialized world had not done enough to end it. But his way ahead was not McNamara's. Clausen wanted private capital to enter the hands of the poor, but neither under any system of regulation nor via development agencies. His preference was a free-for-all—the kind of commercial lending that had already swamped

---

119   Anthony Sampson, *The Money Lenders: Bankers in a Dangerous World*, London: Coronet Books, 1981, p. 246.

120   Here is de Larosière in 1984:

> Over the past four years the rate of return on capital investment in manufacturing in the six largest industrial countries averaged only about half the rate earned during the late 1960s ... Even allowing for cyclical factors, a clear pattern emerges of a substantial and progressive long-term decline in rates of return on capital. There may be many reasons for this. But there is no doubt that an important contributing factor is to be found in the significant increase over the past twenty years or so in the share of income being absorbed by compensation of employees ... This points to the need for a gradual reduction in the rate [of] increase in real wages over the medium term if we are to restore adequate investment incentives.
>
> William I. Robinson, *A Theory of Global Capitalism: Production, Class, and State in a Transnational World*, Baltimore: Johns Hopkins University Press, 2004, p. 108.

121   *IMF Survey*, February 9, 1981.

the NAM states (as he put it in 1976, "Today similar 'risky' loans are helping farmers develop the resources that will feed tomorrow's generations"—the quotes around "risky" suggesting that Clausen did not see them as such).[122] With Clausen came people like Anne Krueger (chief economist of the Bank from 1982 to 1986), who supplanted liberal stalwart Hollis Chenery (editor of the influential 1974 volume *Redistribution with Growth*) and put her own brand of orthodox laissez-faire economics to work.[123]

Having cleaned out the liberals from the IMF and the World Bank, the G7 put pressure on both to change their operations. Until the 1970s, the IMF's work was mainly in the advanced industrial states, where it operated as an emergency cash window to cover balance-of-payments shortfalls. The IMF had limited operations in the rest of the planet, having steered clear of the development brief carried by the World Bank. It was the Bank that involved itself with project-related funding. The Bank was guided by a rather wooden modernization theory, seeking to change society in the formerly colonized world through the creation of enormous infrastructure projects and its support for the Green Revolution (the agricultural policy that relied upon expensive inputs, such as fertilizer and pesticide, but kept far away from such basic changes as land reform). The IMF tended to stay away from social transformation; the Bank threw itself in, but generally as an adjutant to social change rather than its author. Both Bank and Fund would change their attitude in the 1970s and 1980s. Debt-strapped states turned their eyes to Washington, DC, to the headquarters of the two institutions, for short-term assistance in covering their adverse balance-of-payments situation. The Fund smiled and promised the money—but only if the stricken country consented to major changes in its domestic arrangements.

The Fund and the Bank set up a row of new windows to cover short-term and medium-term loans: the Structural Adjustment Facility, Enhanced Structural Adjustment Facility, High Impact Adjustment Lending, the Poverty Reduction and Growth Facility, and the Structural Adjustment Programs. The term of the day was "conditionality," with the Fund's loans, line of credit, and surety forthcoming only if the bereaved country agreed to a set of stringent conditions, such as deflation, privatization of public sector firms, deregulation of utilities, desiccation of social service provision (health and education, and agricultural subsidies), financial liberalization, and civil service reforms. Michel Camdessus, who ran the IMF from 1987 to 2000, candidly told a gathering at

---

122   *Los Angeles Times*, March 14, 1976.

123   In the inaugural issue of the *World Bank Research Observer*, Krueger wrote, "Once it is recognized that individuals respond to incentives, and that 'market failure' is the result of inappropriate incentives rather than of non-responsiveness, the separateness of development economics as a field largely disappears." "Aid in the Development Process," *World Bank Research Observer* 1: 1 (1986), p. 62.

the United Nations in 1990 that his organization had little concern for anything other than growth. "Our prime objective is growth. In my view, there
is no longer any ambiguity about this. It is toward growth that our programs
and their conditionality are aimed. It is with a view toward growth that we
carry out our special responsibility of helping to correct balance of payments
disequilibria."[124] Growth *über alles* was the motto of the IMF in the conditionality years.

"Growth" is a misleading category. It does not mean that a national economy
should be robust, as much as that its exports should be considerable. In other
words, "growth" in the IMF lexicon frequently referred to export-earned value,
and not to the well-being of the population—that is, their social indicators such
as average caloric intake, housing, and education. Raising the "growth" of a
society meant that it would be able to sell its products to markets elsewhere.
The UNCTAD theory was that international trade rules prevented the NAM
countries from being able to take advantage of their resources. For example,
the textile industries of Africa, Asia, and Latin America were shortchanged
by the tariff and subsidy regimes in the Atlantic states. As former World Bank
chief economist Joseph Stiglitz put it, "Without subsidies, it would not pay for
Americans to produce much cotton; with them, the US is the world's largest
cotton exporter. Some 25,000 rich American cotton farmers divide $3 to $4
billion in subsidies among themselves—with most of the money going to a
small fraction of the recipients. The increased supply depresses cotton prices,
hurting some 10 million farmers in sub-Saharan Africa alone."[125]

At Rambouillet in 1975, Helmut Schmidt was quite candid about the trade
restrictions:

> In the US and the EC we should recognize the fact, on a mutual basis, that our agri-
> cultural sectors have certain characteristics which are undesirable. We should be
> mutually prepared to discuss agricultural matters in the industrialized sector. This
> matter cannot be settled today and should not be referred to in public. But the US
> and the EC are important trading partners. It would endanger the credibility of our
> liberal approach to world trade, if, in the agricultural sector, agricultural ministers
> undermine the general atmosphere.

British Prime Minister Harold Wilson concurred, but spoke up for the silent
subsidies that boosted the Atlantic textile trade in particular: "Our textile
industry is revivable; it is not a write-off. But we are going to make efforts to
subsidize textiles in assisted areas, giving them reasonable help." US cotton

---

124 Jacques Polak, *The Changing Nature of IMF Conditionality*, Princeton:
International Finance Section, Department of Economics, Princeton University,
1991, p. 19.

125 Joseph Stiglitz, "The Tyranny of King Cotton," *Guardian*, October 24, 2006.

subsidies, for instance, adversely impacted the West African textile industry.[126] All talk of "comparative advantage" went by the wayside when the Atlantic agricultural subsidy came up for discussion. The matter was not "referred to in public."

In 1973, the states of the world entered the Tokyo Round of the General Agreement on Trade and Tariffs (GATT). When the postwar powers failed to create an International Trade Organization in 1948 as the third leg of the Bretton Woods institutions (finance in the IMF, development in the World Bank, and trade in the ITO), they agreed to consult and negotiate through an institutional framework that they called the GATT. The Tokyo Round was the seventh GATT process and, like the previous rounds, took on the question of tariff reduction. At its opening, the Tokyo Round's objective included that it wished "to secure additional benefits for the international trade of developing countries" and "to take into account the specific trade problems of the developing countries." This was the largest GATT round to date, with 102 countries around the table (previous meetings had between thirteen and sixty-two countries in attendance). It was no surprise that the agenda typified by the NIEO came onto the table. But by the time the GATT completed its work in 1977, the idea of tariff reductions in the Atlantic world had disappeared. Olivier Long, the director-general of GATT at that time, wrote in the resulting report, "As for tariffs facing developing countries, the average Most Favoured Nation (MFN) reduction on industrial products was less deep than the overall cut." The tariffs on textiles, clothing, and footwear remained "quite high," he noted.[127] Not long after, in the Third Multi-Fibre Agreement (1981), the European Community pushed the agenda, bought off certain countries (such as Thailand) with favorable arrangements, and scuttled the attempt to topple the North's tariff regime.[128]

The precise effect of these unfortunate developments has been that agriculture in large parts of Africa, Asia, and Latin America have felt the sharp edge of the margin. Agricultural conglomerates in the United States and Europe swept away the petty producers (the real farmers), which were replaced with factory farms using vastly superior technology (including genetically modified seeds, remarkable fertilizers and pesticides, and of course machines such as the self-propelled combine harvester).[129] Total food-grain production increased, but

126   Elinor Lynn Heinisch, "West Africa versus the United States on Cotton Subsidies: How, Why and What Next?" *Journal of Modern African Studies* 44: 2 (2006).

127   GATT, *The Tokyo Round of Multilateral Trade Negotiations: Supplementary Report by the Director-General*, Geneva: GATT, 1979, vol. 1, pp. 36–41.

128   L. N. Rangarajan, "Commodity Conflict Revisited: From Nairobi to Belgrade," *Third World Quarterly* 5: 3 (1983), p. 594.

129   Sripad Motiram, Vamsi Vakulabharanam, and Vijay Prashad, "Iowa is Not Far From Telengana," *Subcontinental* 2: 1 (Spring 2004); and Sripad Motiram, Vamsi

the diversity of agricultural produce and the number of farmers decreased. Industrial farming was the order of the day. Subsidies to the Atlantic agricultural world (in the prices of water and energy, and in price supports) as well as routine price-fixing by European, US, and Japanese agricultural conglomerates gave them an enormous advantage in this global foodstuffs market.[130] The die was cast on behalf of the agricultural conglomerates. Through free trade agreements (such as the North American Free Trade Agreement that went into effect in 1994), the advantages to the North vanquished the petty producers of places as far flung as Mexico and India, Ghana and Bangladesh.[131] In the rural parts of the Third World states, distress became normal. It is from this point that the large migrations began that ended in the vast slums of an increasingly urbanized world. It is on the edge of these slums, which now house one out of every five people on the planet, that the governments desperate to earn foreign-exchange dollars set up the export processing zones (EPZs) and special economic zones (SEZs), which feed off the calamity in the countryside.

In the era just before the neoliberal one, those who produced the social wealth fashioned themselves quite self-consciously as the working class. In China they were known as the *gongren*—the proletariat—a gender-neutral term that was used in the Maoist era to engender a sense of power and pride in the working class. This term, as sociologist Pun Ngai has pointed out, went by the wayside in the 1980s. Those who came to work in the SEZs in Shenzhen did not come as workers (*gongren*), but as those who work for the boss (*dagongmei* or *dagongzai*), most of them women from rural areas. The long days and very difficult working conditions prevented many of these women from working more than four or five years. They treated it as an opportunity to bring some cash back to their struggling rural families, as well as to accumulate some modest savings as they began to carve out other lives for themselves. Few saw themselves as part of a working class that would strive to reorder its social and economic position in society.[132] Enormous similarities in the workplace

Vakulabharanam, and Vijay Prashad, "The Subsidy-Tariff Tangle," *Hindu*, February 14, 2004.

130   In 1993, the US Justice Department indicted Archer Daniels Midland (ADM), Ajinomoto, a French firm, and a Korean firm for price fixing of lysine. ADM settled the anti-trust suit, paying a $100 million fine. This is the most dramatic example of agricultural price fixing. Kurt Eichenwald, *The Informant*, New York: Broadway, 2001.

131   Raj Patel, *Stuffed and Starved: The Hidden Battle for the World Food System*, Brooklyn: Melville House, 2008, Chapter 3.

132   Pun Ngai, *Made in China: Women Factory Workers in a Global Workplace*, Durham: Duke University Press, 2005. See also Jonathan Unger, *The Transformation of Rural China*, New York: M. E. Sharpe, 2002, Part 2; Dorothy Solinger, "Labour Market Reform and the Plight of the Laid-Off Proletariat," *China Quarterly* 170 (June 2002);

link the workers of Shenzhen, China, and Juarez, Mexico (except perhaps in the overt violence against women in the US-Mexico borderlands).[133] It is these workers—mostly women—who leave the failed countryside for the glittering SEZ, where they throw in their youth for the overproduction machine that then spills out its products into the over-filled shops of the Atlantic world, where the debt-ridden consumer tries to keep up with their manufactured desires. It is a tireless and heartless cycle.

The blinded South began to justify the turn to the EPZ, pointing out how it would provide the engines of growth. In Mexico, however, the *maquila* sector hired far fewer workers than the shuttered Mexican-run factories and undercut Mexican farms (the corn sector in Mexico is now overrun by the factory-farm-produced corn from the US midwest).[134] The precise reason of the popularity of the *maquila* is not its capacity to create jobs. It is popular among the international financiers and the multinational corporations because it is capable of being run beyond the rule of established labor and environmental laws and norms—and violations are easily shrugged off as the responsibility of threadbare local factory owners, rather than of the sophisticated firms that market the products under their shining and well-protected brands.

The newly aggressive IMF appeared as a beacon of hope in the sky, hovering around, taking measurements, then swooping down to scuttle all hope of deliverance, all hope of liberty. If this is how it seemed, it is no surprise that a third of Thai children surveyed by Bangkok's Rajabhat Institute thought that the IMF was an unidentified flying object. A host of acronyms (IMF, GATT, FDI), each more alien than the last, a brood of anonymous bureaucrats and technicians, a tribe called Los Chicago Boys, a specter known as the Sachs Effect, the UFO academies known as Wharton and Harvard: all these aliens converged to create an index of reason, a rationality, that resembles the double-entry account book. IMF reason discounted the well-being of the vast mass of people and the reason for odious debt, instead asking the already marginal populations to bear the

---

and Ching Kwan Lee, *Against the Law: Labor Protests in China's Rustbelt and Sunbelt*, Berkeley: University of California Press, 2007.

133   Leslie Salzinger, *Genders in Production: Making Workers in Mexico's Global Factories*, Berkeley: University of California Press, 2003; and Melissa W. Wright, *Disposable Women and Other Myths of Global Capitalism*, New York: Routledge, 2006.

134   Kathryn Kopinak, *Desert Capitalism: What Are Maquiladoras?*, Montreal: Black Rose Books, 1997. See also the many superb essays in Kathryn Kopinak, ed., *The Social Costs of Industrial Growth in North Mexico*, Boulder: Lynne Rienner, 2005—in particular James Cyper, "Development Diverted: Socio-Economic Characteristics and Impacts of Mature Maquilization," and Cirila Quintero Ramirez, "Unions and Social Benefits in the Maquiladoras." On the problems of unionization to increase these poor wage and work conditions, see Quintero Ramirez's longer work, *La Sindicalización en las maquiladoras tijuanenses, 1970–1988*, México: Consejo Nacional para la Cultura y las Artes, 1990.

full brunt of austerity. Even the *Wall Street Journal* worried that the IMF "has not been fighting financial fires, but dousing them with gasoline."[135] The UNDP studied the effects of the IMF's work and reported: "The IMF has exerted a strong influence over developing countries by setting stiff conditions on the loans it offers. This conditionality has generally been monetarist and deflationary, obliging governments to reduce their demand for imports by curtailing overall demand—cutting back on both private and public spending. These cutbacks have often reduced consumption, investment and employment—and stifled economic growth."[136] A senior economist at the IMF studied the economic record of IMF-enforced stabilization measures from 1973 to 1988 and found that growth rates were "significantly reduced in program countries relative to the change in non-program countries."[137] The working poor had nothing to lose, but they nonetheless lost all of it.

The political consequences of neoliberalism frightened the political elites and their business allies in the US and across Europe. Chancellor Dennis Healey, briefly a Communist in the late 1930s, and then a militant Fabian socialist, nonetheless threw in his lot with "those who matter." At Rambouillet in 1975, Healey warned his new peers of how restive his constituency might become as neoliberal policies unfolded:

> President Ford rightly said that the astonishing thing has been that the political impact of increased unemployment has been less than expected. But the critical problem is the large number of unemployed over a long period of time—especially regional pockets of high unemployment, school leavers and colored. There could be some very serious political consequences. We should not yet feel a sense of relief about this problem ... GNP growth will not help much in dealing with unemployment.

His leader, Harold Wilson, had taken a degree at Oxford and had in the late 1930s worked on the pressing themes of unemployment and the trade cycle. Wilson knew a thing or two about what Healey had mentioned. "Chancellor Healey is right," Wilson acknowledged. "We could get growth with little decrease in unemployment." And so the system might be wracked by unrest and protests.[138]

Riots had already broken out, and these would intensify within the decade. Healey's Britain was wracked by "race riots"—from the St. Paul's riot of 1980

---

135 "The IMF in Action," *Wall Street Journal* (Eastern Edition), May 19, 1998, p. 1.

136 UNDP, *Human Development Report*, New York: UNDP, 1992, p. 75.

137 Mohsin Khan, "The Macroeconomic Effects of Fund-Supported Adjustment Programs," *IMF Staff Papers* 37: 2 (June 1990), p. 215.

138 "Memorandum of Conversation at the Rambouillet Summit, made for Brent Scowcroft by Robert Hormats," November 15–17, 1975.

to the Brixton riot of 1981, with Birmingham and Leeds in between. Schmidt's Germany had its own problems with *Ausländerfeindlichkeit*—the hatred of foreigners, mostly Turkish migrants (*Türken, raus!* went the chant). Migrants took the brunt of working-class anger at the loss of jobs in the deindustrialization of the Atlantic zone. This street anger linked Lima to London. More than half the South American countries had some kind of major social and political unrest. From Lima (1976) to Kingston (1979), from La Paz (1983) to Caracas (1989), the continent was beset by protests. The IMF Riots, as they came to be called, sent a shiver down the spine of the various governments of the NAM states, of the G7 leadership, of the governors of the Bretton Woods institutions, and of the captains of finance. Tom Clausen of BankAmerica and soon of the World Bank recognized the impetus for rebellion and offered a reason for moderate reform: "When people are desperate, you have revolutions. It's in our own evident self-interest to see that they are not forced into that. You must keep the patient alive, because otherwise you can't effect the cure."[139]

The Brandt Commission recognized the dangerous social effects of austerity on the working class and poor and of adjustment policies on the societies of the South. "In many cases," the Commissioners wrote,

> these measures reduce domestic consumption without improving investment; productive capacity sometimes falls even more sharply than consumption. This is because many developing countries with deficits have a shortage of food or of basic needs. Indeed, the Fund's insistence on drastic measures, often within the time framework of only one year, has tended to impose unnecessary and unacceptable political burdens on the poorest, on occasion leading to "IMF riots" and even downfall of governments.[140]

Debt and the new cosmology, neoliberalism, gave shape to the world that the Brandt Commission would seek to fix. The contradictions disturbed them, and they sought to create order out of them.

BRANDT'S SÜDPOLITIK

Most of what we said three years ago is today even more germane to the matter. The international community has made little progress in solving the most difficult issues; in many areas the situation has deteriorated in a way that we ourselves had not anticipated—and back then we were criticized by many as fear mongers.

Willy Brandt, Chairman of the North-South Commission, February 9, 1983[141]

---

139   *Sunday Times*, November 23, 1980; and Sampson, *Money Lenders*, p. 344.

140   Brandt Commission, *Common Crisis North-South*, p. 216.

141   "From the introductory remarks by the Chairman of the North-South Commission, Brandt, at the presentation of the report 'Aid in the World Crisis' before the Federal Press Association in Bonn 9 February 1983," Archives of Social

In September 1972, Robert McNamara delivered his annual address to the board of governors at the World Bank. He did not rest on the laurels of the organization's bulky work, with big dams and vast ambitions for the Green Revolution. Instead, McNamara asked his peers what they thought of the pressing problems that afflicted the poor. Governments around the world, he said, "must be prepared to give greater priority to establishing growth targets in terms of essential human needs: in terms of nutrition, housing, health, literacy, and employment—even if it be at the cost of some privileged sectors whose benefits accrue to the few." According to those in the know, McNamara had been quite taken with the data from China.[142] A society deeply broken by war and famine, by monarchy and colonization, had demonstrated by the early 1970s that the Communist government's emphasis on the "basic needs" of education and housing, food and work, had had a marked social impact. It was hard to say anything positive about China before Nixon's visit there in January 1972. With the Nixon opening, McNamara and others could now speak with measured confidence about its achievement. Redistribution through Communism was a threat. The World Bank needed to encourage policies that produced the same outcomes by more "western" means. No longer could growth stand alone as the marker for the world. The objective should be, as McNamara's deputy Hollis Cherney put it, growth with redistribution.[143]

McNamara warned the governors that the widening gaps between North and South had political consequences that should not be ignored: "When the highly privileged are few and the desperately poor are many—and when the gap between them is worsening rather than improving—it is only a question of time before a decisive choice must be made between the political costs of reform and the political risks of rebellion." It was because of these risks that reforms were "prescriptions not only of principle but of prudence. Social justice is not merely a moral imperative. It is a political imperative as well." McNamara would have known. The impoverished Vietnamese peasantry had taken to the

---

Democracy, North-South Commission, B 81 (*Berliner Ausgabe*, vol. 8 for the English translation by Dwight Langston), Friedrich Ebert Foundation.

142   Mahbub ul Haq, *The Poverty Curtain: Choices for the Third World*, New York: Columbia University Press, 1976, pp. 9–10. Haq was the crucial person in the World Bank for the development of the "basic needs" concept. He was a close colleague of Barbara Ward, who herself worked to advise McNamara. In 1971 Haq gave the keynote address to the 12th World Conference of the Society for International Development, in Ottawa, Canada. In the talk, Haq praised the Chinese reforms, which had increased the population's access to basic needs. *Poverty Curtain*, pp. 36–7.

143   This was the consensus view, Hans Singer describing it as "growth plus structural transformation." Jan Pronk, *Quelques remarques sur les rapports entre nouvel ordre international de l'information et nouvel ordre économique international*, Paris: UNESCO, 1979.

gun and had brought the Americans to their knees. Even more resilience was shown from the slums of Latin America, which had nestled on the edges of the elite's urban haciendas.

McNamara turned to a set of liberal advisers when he came to the World Bank. War had failed; now he wanted to try other, less belligerent methods. He arrived at the Bank in 1968 and left in 1981. This was the decade of the fight over the reconfiguration of the political and economic relations between North and South. The NIEO matured as McNamara took the reins in the massive complex on H Street, and by the time he left the Bank the entire liberal project, and the NIEO, had fallen by the wayside. When McNamara came to the Bank, he asked a former Canadian prime minister to lead a commission of inquiry into the state of affairs in the world of development. Lester Pearson chose his commissioners carefully. All had their feet firmly rooted in the Atlantic world (including Sir Arthur Lewis of St. Lucia and Roberto de Oliveira Campos of Brazil). Their 1969 report, *Partners in Development*, recommended that total aid from the advanced industrial states should amount to 1 percent of GNP, with at least 0.7 percent from the official coffers. The report was instantly deposited in the archives. Its recommendation was not taken seriously. Eight years later, McNamara felt the need to call for another Grand Assize. The futile negotiations in Paris around commodities formed the background for McNamara's call. At a World Affairs Council meeting in Boston, McNamara named former West German chancellor Willy Brandt as the chair. A few weeks later, on September 28, Brandt accepted the role in New York City.

Unlike Pearson, Brandt drew many of his commissioners from what Lord Oliver Franks had called the "South," namely, Algeria, Chile, Colombia, Guyana, India, Indonesia, Kuwait, Malaysia, Tanzania, and Upper Volta. The commissioners from these areas were well schooled in the arts of the NIEO, especially people like Shridath Ramphal, Amir Jamal, and Layachi Yaker. Not all of them were radicals; some were plainly of the far right, such as Chile's Christian Democratic leader Eduardo Frei Montalva, who had collaborated in the coup against the socialist president Salvador Allende. The commissioners of the North were also a mixed bag, from the Social Democratic former premier of Sweden, Olaf Palme, to McNamara's close friend, the publisher of the *Washington Post*, Katherine Graham. The main staff person chosen for the Commission was the only person from Eastern Europe, and the entire East, Dragoslav Avramovic. Avramovic came to his new job from the World Bank, where he was the section chief of Latin America and the Caribbean.[144] He had

---

144   For some details, see Dragoslav Avramovic, "Oral History Project," World Bank, 1996. In 1963, W. W. Rostow came to the Bank and spoke about the need for more careful attention to the class realities in the rural world of the developing countries. He was pooh-poohed by the Bank's economists, who were, as Avramovic wrote to his

warned about the debt crisis forthrightly and had the clearest vision of what was to come. Avramovic was helped along by another important staff person, the socialist Dutchman Jan Pronk. Pronk came to Brandt after a stint as the research associate for Jan Tinbergen of the Club of Rome, and as the minister of development cooperation of the Dutch government. Avramovic and Pronk played a crucial role, providing the conceptual framework for Brandt's work.

The terms of reference for the Commission were by now familiar. It was tasked to "study the grave global issues arising from the economic and social disparities of the world community and to suggest ways of promoting adequate solutions to the problems involved in development and in attacking absolute poverty."[145] This was a similar brief to that of the Club of Rome's *Reshaping the International Order* (1976), the UN's *The Future of the World Economy* (1977), and tens of other studies of this ilk. These terms of reference were adopted in Gymnich, Germany, on December 11, 1977. The Commission met at least ten more times (in such diverse places as Mali and the United States), and its staff and a few commissioners met several times in different places, whether China or Jordan. It was a vast enterprise. The money came from a number of countries, with the World Bank giving the Commission only its blessing.

The final meeting was held in mid December 1979—a full two years after the deliberations had begun. It was a curious process, with much discussion and little agreement. Brandt had a free-flowing style that did not demand conclusions.[146] A final draft looked impossible. There was too much disagreement along the lines of what had prevented agreement at the Paris conference. Brandt's final deadline loomed. Two days before it, he dispatched four of his commissioners (Peter Peterson of the United States, Abdlatif al-Hamad of Kuwait, Shridath Ramphal of Guyana, and Olof Palme of Sweden) to make a deal. They returned with a draft, whose upshot was as follows: the North would transfer considerable funds to the South and adopt a new means for power-sharing, whereas the South would promise to secure oil supplies for the North and ensure that price rises would be orderly. But, as the editorial advisor to the Commission, Anthony Sampson, recollected, "others could not agree: the speeches went on, the deadline was passed and the meeting dissolved gloomily

---

boss, "fairly critical of Dr Rostow's idea." Not so Avramovic, who "came in defense" and, even in a minority, tried to argue from the standpoint of the small farmer. "It is the bitter truth that many, perhaps most rural areas … after 15 years of development efforts, have remained as miserable as they have always been." Devesh Kapur, John P. Lewis, and Richard Webb, *The World Bank: Its First Half Century*, Washington, DC: Brookings Institution, 1997, vol. 1, pp. 207–8.

145   Brandt Commission, *Common Crisis North-South*, p. 296.

146   Edward Heath was driven to distraction by what he saw as Brandt's indecision. *The Course of My Life: My Autobiography*, London: Hodder & Stoughton, 1998, pp. 608–10.

without a consensus."[147] Edward Heath (former Conservative prime minister of Britain) and Ramphal, who agreed on almost nothing, hunkered down in Marlborough House, the headquarters of the Commonwealth Secretariat, where Ramphal was the secretary-general. Two months later they had the text, and a deal had been reached. "The forbidden subject of oil was at the center," wrote Sampson, but so too was much of the apparatus of the NIEO. It had found its way into the Commission's report, published in February 1980. The report did not shy away from a frank acknowledgement of the problems that bedeviled the world:

> Current trends point to a somber future for the world economy and international relations. A painful outlook for the poorer countries with no end to poverty and hunger; continuing world stagnation combined with inflation; monetary disorder; mounting debts and deficits; protectionism; major tensions between countries competing for energy, food and raw materials; growing world population and more unemployment in North and South; increasing threats to the environment and the international commons through deforestation and desertification, overfishing and over-grazing, the pollution of air and water. And overshadowing everything the menacing arms race.[148]

Very little is missing from this catalogue of woes. One can almost hear the hoof-beats of the apocalyptic horses. The dangers are sharply outlined, in a way that makes clear that neither the North nor the South will be immune to the catastrophe that will come if the crises are ignored. Brandt had made it clear that he was not interested in arguments from either morality or self-interest. The Bandung tradition, or Third World Project, rooted itself in morality. The years from 1955 to 1980 had rubbed the sheen off the Bandung idea that the institutions of the Third World should be taken seriously because they took a moral position on the issues. "Where has the moral imperative got us in the post-war period," Sonny Ramphal asked the Pakistani journalist Altaf Gauhar in 1980, "and in particular in the period during which we have been negotiating NIEO?"[149] The argument from self-interest had also failed, since it had brought the world to an impasse with the G7 on one side and the South on the other. There was no space for a dialogue. Arguments from self-interest, the Brandt Report noted, prevent both an awareness of the "equal danger" of the catastrophe facing the North and South and an opportunity for North and South to take seriously their respective views.[150]

---

147   Sampson, *Money Lenders*, p. 321.
148   Brandt Commisison, *Common Crisis North-South*, p. 47.
149   "A Choice the World Must Face: Altaf Gauhar interviews Sonny Ramphal," *Guardian*, February 13, 1980, p. 19.
150   On the idea of "equal danger" or "great danger," see Brandt Commission,

If neither morality nor self-interest were useful frameworks to ground the dialogue, the new terms would be mutual regard and mutual interests: "The South cannot grow without the North. The North cannot prosper or improve its situation unless there is greater progress in the South."[151] This was a position that one occasionally heard from within the G7, as in Harold Wilson's comment at Rambouillet: "To help [the LDCs] is not mere charity; a recovery in their buying power will serve as a fillip to world economic recovery from which we will all benefit."[152] Brandt's commissioners tried to appeal to the self-interest of the North, wracked as it was by stagflation and malaise. The aggressive posture of the NAM states in the NIEO process and at Paris was not to the taste of North Atlantic liberalism.

The posture of the Brandt Report was hastily named Global Keynesianism.[153] Brandt drew much of his thinking from Keynes's theory that diminished aggregate demand among the working class would create a major crisis. The appropriate tonic for this problem was to stimulate demand among the masses through various forms of government intervention. Brandt wanted to bring the insights of Keynesian policy out of the framework of the nation-state and into the international arena. Now the quest was to find a way of providing massive transfers of wealth to the South, which would then be used to buy goods from the North and bring the Northern economies back to life: "The industrial capacity of the North is underused, causing unemployment unprecedented in recent years, while the South is in urgent need of goods that the North could provide."[154] Theoretically, it was all quite straightforward.

To transfer that wealth, the Brandt Commission recommended that aid levels rise, that the IMF undo some of its own shackles (sell more of its gold, for instance), and that a World Development Fund be set up. The first two recommendations had become mantras and represented nothing new. The third—the brainchild of Avramovic[155]—conjured a welfare state on a planetary scale. There would be a progressive tax on the Gross National Products of different states, a tax on international trade, a tax on military expenditure, and a tax on mining

Common Crisis North-South, pp. 13, 30. It is true that the report frequently notes that there is a need to develop "worldwide moral values" (p. 7) and to cultivate the "great moral imperative" (p. 77), but the report itself does not rest on the moral argument.

151 Ibid., p. 33.

152 "Memorandum of Conversation at the Rambouillet Summit, made for Brent Scowcroft by Robert Hormats," November 15–17, 1975.

153 My assessment of the Brandt report is greatly influenced by Diane Elson, "The Brandt Report: A Programme for Survival," *Capital and Class* 6: 1 (1982); and André Gunder Frank, "North-South and East-West Keynesian Paradoxes in the Brandt Report," *Third World Quarterly* 2: 4 (October 1980).

154 Brandt Commission, *Common Crisis North-South*, p. 267.

155 Brandt Commission, Secretariat Paper no. 21, February 1979.

the international sea-bed: this was where the World Development Fund would get its capital. The money would then be released without conditions. To sweeten this deal for the North, the South was asked to disarm the Oil Weapon: oil prices were to be stabilized. It was a huge concession, coming as it did after the second oil-price rise that took place in 1979.

Brandt's Global Keynesianism had a wounded aspect. The framework itself was predicated on what might be considered a faulty history. Stimulation of demand did not succeed in the advanced industrial countries until World War II, when military expenditure pulled the countries out of deep depression and recession.[156] The New Deal in the United States, for instance, conducted a "salvage operation" to fix a major problem in the Atlantic sector of the world economy. New Deal spending was unable to act as a full stimulus; powerful interests refused to allow a pliant Roosevelt administration to increase government civilian consumption and investment beyond around 15 percent of the gross domestic product. That was a political decision. Any higher spending on those sectors would have provided the social basis for solidarity among the population. It was far safer to run the stimulus through military expenditure— the same kind of Keynesian pump-priming expenditure occurred, but this time without the political threat. Brandt's faith in Global Keynesianism did not sit well with his disdain for military spending. In other words, his program spoke in the language of "mutual interests," but if it were to work, it would have to reorganize power relations between and within nation-states. That had been part of the spirit of the NIEO, which is why Brandt offered it his backing;[157] but it was not to be revived with the Brandt Report—which, if it had come on as strong as that, would have been stillborn.

Not only did Brandt have an excessively charitable view of Keynesianism, his Commission might also have misread the major changes afoot in the 1970s. There was indeed a problem of insufficient demand, but that might have been only the symptom of a deeper cause. Over the previous fifty years, at least, industrial plant in the Atlantic core had grown in leaps and bounds: there was far too much productive capacity, producing far too many high-value goods. Old sectors had been worn down,[158] while new ones had not emerged, largely

---

156   Paul Sweezy and Paul Baran, *Monopoly Capital*, New York: Monthly Review Press, 1966.

157   To Altaf Gauhar, Brandt said of the NIEO, "I sympathise with the general idea." "Willy Brandt and Altaf Gauhar," *Third World Quarterly* 1: 2 (1979), p. 19. Brandt also felt that the NIEO would bring about "major changes in international and national development efforts." Sonny Ramphal told Gauhar, "The Commission's Report could be a positive contribution toward the development causes and indeed the goals of the NIEO generally." Also see Brandt Commission, *Common Crisis North-South*, p. 51.

158   Gunder Frank, "North-South and East-West Keynesian Paradoxes," p. 675; Elson, "Brandt Report," p. 116–17.

for lack of investment. Finance was chary of being bound for the long-term to retrofit older factories, or to take risks in the construction of new factories with new technology, and governments lacked the ready capital to sponsor the transition. Nor was capital ready to risk investment with labor restive and able to command a decent wage. Financiers thought it far better to enter the stock market and the world of finance, where returns could be expected on a much shorter timescale. The asset bubbles opened up by neoliberal policies in the world of finance sucked away investable capital. "The rich will not make progress in a world economy characterized by uncertainty, disorder and low rates of growth," the Brandt Report pointed out; "it is equally true that the rich cannot prosper without progress by the poor."[159] This was indeed not the case, as it turned out. Even by 1980 it had become clear that social uncertainty and political chaos abetted the machinations of finance, which thrived on turbulence in its currency speculations and gains through short-selling. The devastation wrought by financial tumult impoverished rural smallholders and landless workers, as well as industrial workers, who were often in unions. The rural displaced would migrate to the *maquila* industrial sector, the sunbelt of the global South, whose rate of return came close to but did not equal those of the asset bubbles in the stock exchanges. Retrenched industrial workers would remain in the rustbelt of the global South, to turn to social ideologies of resentment and bitterness.

Brandt's report seemed out of date, even when it first appeared, and yet it was one of the only statements from Atlantic liberalism that put the well-being of the emergent global poor into the conversation. Brandt adopted McNamara's idea of "basic needs." The World Bank, in turn, had adopted this idea from a *samizdat* literature within the UN community. The International Labour Organization's 1976 World Employment Conference articulated the principal elements of basic needs (clothing, education, food, housing, and public transportation) and urged that these be funded not simply by higher growth rates, or by immediate redistribution of wealth, but through the formula of redistribution through growth—i.e. to ensure that future income from higher growth rates be more equitably distributed.[160] The "basic needs" framework

---

159   Brandt Commission, *Common Crisis North-South*, p. 270.

160   International Labour Organization, *Employment, Growth and Basic Needs: A One World Problem*, Geneva: ILO, 1976. These ideas emerged in a series of forums, including the Bariloche group (Amilcar Herrera, with Hugo Scolnik, Graciela Chichilnisky, Gilberto Gallopin, Jorge Hardoy, Diana Mosovich, Enrique Oteiza, Jorge Romero Brest, Carlos Suárez, and Luis Talavera, *Catastrofe o Nueva Sociedad? Modelo Mundial Latinoamericano*, Ottawa: Fundación Bariloche, International Development Research Centre, 1977) and in the Dag Hammarskjöld Foundation ("What Now? Another Development," *Development Dialogue*, vol. ½, Uppsala: Dag Hammarskjöld Foundation, 1975). The ideas had been put into motion by Pitambar Pant of the Indian

would only work if it were part of a macroeconomic framework for structural change. The *politics* of disparity had to be part of the equation. No such insistence was in Brandt, which leaned a little towards the kind of apolitical charity that would paralyze the Millennium Development Goals (MDGs) twenty years later. Countries were obliged to hit a series of individual targets in such areas as literacy and nutrition, but each of these was atomized—treated as if it were an individual test that could be administered to gauge the health of a nation. There was no consideration of the constraints on people's lives, or on management by government, nor any concern for a holistic approach to development instead of stage-managed, piecemeal reforms. The concept of basic needs also provided a way to cast attention away from the old illiberal order and the emergent neo-liberal order, and towards the domestic problems within states. This was what the South considered "incremental gadgetry"—new policy techniques that appeared to be for the benefit of the people of the South, but which casually diverted attention away from the international inequities of power and wealth towards indefensible mismanagement by the governments of the South.[161] Brandt could not directly criticize the domestic arrangements of governments; that was not in its terms of reference. This limited his Commission's range of tactics, so Brandt had to make do with innuendo.[162]

Brandt did not mince his words on the issues of war and agriculture. War provided the scaffolding for the report: it was the massive expenditure on real and on potential wars that crippled the ability of humanity to take full advantage of its advances towards civilization. War leads to hunger, Brandt wrote in his preface, but also: "[W]e are less aware that mass poverty can lead to war or end in chaos."[163] For these ideas, Brandt drew from the intellectual work of the 1979 World Conference on Agrarian Reform and Rural Development, as well as the many declarations by the UN World Food Council and the UN's Food and Agricultural Organization. This was the era of the Green Revolution, when the hope was that expensive technical inputs, such as high-yield seeds, fertilizer, pesticide, and piped water would be able to increase productivity without recourse to land reform. A Green Revolution, the theory went, would undercut the Red Revolution. The Brandt Report, in a typical formulation, expressed a

---

Planning Commission in 1951. See Pitambar Pant, *Perspectives of Development: 1961–1976: Implications for Planning for a Minimum Level*, New Delhi: Planning Commission of India, 1962. Here Pant and his team wrote, "The central concern of our planning has to be the removal of poverty as early as possible. The stage has now come when we should sharply focus our effort on providing an assured minimum income to every citizen of the country within a reasonable period of time. Progressively, this minimum itself should be raised as development goes apace."

161   Amuzegar, "Requiem for the North-South Conference," p. 147.

162   *Guardian*, "A Choice the World Must Face," p. 19.

163   Brandt Commission, *Common Crisis North-South*, p. 16.

desire to take the best from both, and, even as they might be incommensurable, to champion both simultaneously. Brandt demanded the redistribution of the Green Revolution's worldly goods and "agrarian reform and the promotion of farmers' and workers' organizations." In addition, Brandt sought immediate poverty alleviation in the rural areas through "special programmes of employment creation through public works," such as schemes of soil conservation, reforestation, drainage and flood control, and road-building.[164] Agricultural reconstruction would be a "task of the South" that would be the bedrock upon which a sane international trade policy might be constructed.[165] There was no sense in fair trade if agricultural lands remained infeudated, and no sense in land reform if there was no socially just market that would pay fair prices for the goods of petty producers. Here Brandt spoke to the South, but only for 1 percent (three pages) of his text.

In its quest to champion the mutuality of interests, the Brandt report went back and forth between the interests of the masses of the South and of the dominant classes of the South (who are sometimes, but not always, in full control of the governments of the South). Debate during the framing and drafting of the report survived into the finished product. Unable to find a consensus, Brandt's final document reflected all of the contradictions. The Commissioners could not settle the main problem: whose interests should set the agenda. The idea of "mutual interest" implied that the divergence of interests in different regions could be set aside. This problem came up in every meeting of the Brandt Commission, and it remains in the published report.

The impoverished in the South would require low-wage goods that they could afford to buy, which would themselves not be produced in the high-wage factories of the North. Insufficient industrial capacity in the South would mean that it could not yet churn out enough low-wage goods for the masses. Funds to stimulate demand would be welcome, but initially by the dominant classes in the South, who would absorb them into their ambitions to modernize their states. This would not necessarily encompass the liberal dream of creating Scandinavia in the tropics. The dominant classes in the South might divert the funds towards the creation of an America instead, with a vastly well-off sector living in protected zones, separated from the rest of the population by well-crafted *cordons sanitaires*. There was nothing to bind the South to democratic socialism, particularly since that vision had already faltered in Europe, been set aside in the United States, and begun to fall apart in the Eastern bloc. There was no incentive for egalitarianism, and so little hope that the investment might regenerate the rustbelt of the Ruhr and the American midwest. The poor of the South could not afford the products of the industrial North.

---

164   Ibid., pp. 130–1.
165   Ibid., p. 126.

The Brandt report took acute notice of the geography of poverty. Certainly the entire report drew from the axial division between North and South. But, more than that, it recognized that there were a series of "poverty belts" that stretched from Northern Mexico down the backbone of South America to the slums of Santiago, from the massive townships of Southern Africa to the graveyard town of Cairo, from the miserable hovels of Mumbai to the perennially flooded shacks in Dacca.[166] The disparities between North and South were extreme. In 1979 the World Bank reported that 700 million people lived in absolute poverty—a wretched condition unimaginable to those of us reading Brandt's report in our armchairs.[167] Foreign investment, even foreign aid, did little for these hundreds of millions. In 1975 three-quarters of foreign direct investment went to the North; it was uninterested in the South and its potential. Of the quarter that did go South, the lion's share went to the zones known as the newly industrialized countries, or NICs (Hong Kong, Singapore, South Korea, and Taiwan).[168] The NICs and countries such as Mexico and the Philippines are the homelands of the *maquila*-type factories, the places where offshore production is overseen by US, European, and Japanese multinational companies. Its products are not for the markets of the South, but for those of the North, where former workers become consumers who fuel their consumption through the massive personal debts induced to keep the maladjusted system going. Brandt tentatively recommended a slowdown of the consumption-oriented growth in the North, enabled by low-wage NIC production. This model ignored the vast bulk of the planet, whose billions were left as passive onlookers. The radiance of rapid development among the NICs fed a false hope that others could follow. There was little acknowledgement that the symbiotic path of NIC *maquila*-squeezed production and Northern debt-fueled consumption was neither sustainable nor equitable. The report's idea that growth was a "political necessity" foreclosed the opportunity to question the problems with the growth-driven symbiotic model of the North-NIC. To promote growth within this new cosmology made it hard for Brandt to call for an adjustment of planetary relations.[169] It was far easier to ask the South to adjust towards the NIC model.

In October 1979 the world commemorated the fiftieth anniversary of the 1929 Wall Street Crash. Fears of inflation and financial collapse remained alive.

---

166   Ibid., p. 78.

167   World Bank, *World Development Report 1979*, Washington, DC: World Bank, 1979, pp. 16–19.

168   Brandt Commission, *Common Crisis North-South*, pp. 187–8.

169   Brandt Commission, *Common Crisis North-South*, p. 34. In a later passage, the report points out that the values of the North require adjustment, for the North "must not pursue selfish policies depleting the world of precious resources; it too must find new patterns of growth, more sensitive to the world's needs." Ibid., p. 270.

With the rise in LIBOR, the debt-to-service ratio for the commercial loans taken out by the South in the 1970s escalated. Defaults were inevitable. The Brandt Report did not contribute much to the debate over the short-term debt crisis.[170] The South would have to take out new loans to make the interest payments on its old loans, but money was not available. No new concessionary window opened at the IMF. The Committee of 20, representing the South within the IMF, tried to push for more liquidity, but they were thwarted by the G7.[171] There was nothing inevitable about the terms of the debt or the obstinacy of the IMF and the banks to ease up on the payment schedule, or indeed to ameliorate the social consequences of the debt. All of this was on the table. Active choices in the G7 condemned the South to suffer the aftershock of fiscal contraction to deal with the debt.

Looking back at the Commission and its report, Brandt conceded, "The Commission did not identify itself with maximalist, comprehensive demand for a 'new world economy,' ideas such as those considered by the United Nations in 1974–75—as if the resolutions passed in its glass palace in New York could have revolutionary consequences world-wide."[172] The Commission had a limited ambit: to push for a reconsideration of the neoliberal agenda that had already made its presence felt through the deliberations of the G7, in the domestic agenda of the United Kingdom, in the election campaign of Ronald Reagan, and indeed in the framework proposed by the North for the reorganization of development—now through the growth of offshore production facilitated by the creation of new pools of labor, freed from the apparent disincentives of social welfare. At a maximum for Brandt, development could be driven by aid, charity, and private foreign direct investment; but it would certainly not take the form envisaged by the NIEO. Brandt wanted to put liberalism back on the table, here in the guise of Global Keynesianism. "The recommendations of the Commission," he wrote, "were not conspicuous for radicalism, particularly not in matters of money and finance."[173] Indeed not.

170   Gunder Frank, "North-South and East-West Keynesian Paradoxes," p. 677.

171   The Report of the Committee of 20 called for an increased role in the IMF's currency, the special drawing rights (SDRs), even calling for the SDRs to be made "the principle reserve asset in the international monetary system." And moreover, "whereas reserve creation has in the past involved resource transfers to gold producers and reserve centers, it would be appropriate in a reformed system that a greater part of the benefit derived from the switch to reserve creation in the form of SDRs should be channeled on an agreed basis to developing countries." IMF, *International Monetary Reform: Document of the Committee of 20*, Washington, DC: IMF, 1979, p. 96. On the failure of the Committee of 20 to move an agenda from 1972 to 1979, see Toye and Toye, *The UN and Global Political Economy*, p. 238.

172   Brandt, *My Life in Politics*, p. 345.

173   Ibid., p. 347.

What is remarkable about the report, and about Atlantic liberalism in general, is the failure to acknowledge the role of power behind ideas. Correct ideas are never sufficient; they are not believed or enacted simply because they are right. They become the ideas of the time only when they are wielded by those who have a united belief in their own power, using it in ideological and institutional struggles that, in turn, consolidate their social authority. The representatives of the unwashed, the Third World states, had little authority, even as they came to the UN with an overstuffed portmanteau of the best ideas. They came with the power of mass anticolonial movements behind them; but by the 1970s these movements had dissolved. The NIEO was the high point of the Third World dynamic. Brandt tried to salvage some of its ideas, but without the political context. His vision was to bring people together, to appeal to the best of human nature; but it was not enough. Indeed, it represented an illusion that the world would be reformed without a sharp kick from below—the grassroots struggles that build power against the entrenched and seize a new world for themselves.[174]

CANCÚN AND THE ORIGIN OF NEOLIBERALISM

Despite the limitations of the Brandt Report, it was well received both by social democrats in the North and in the political corridors of the South. The South called for "global negotiations" based on the Report, and initially got very little response.[175] Nothing else should have been expected. In 1978 Brandt commented, "There is some parallel between the way industrialized countries are behaving now and the way old-fashioned capitalists in the West handled their relationship with labour. I say this with regard to attempts at splitting up developing countries, but also often waiting too long and making concessions only when there is no way out."[176] It seemed unlikely that much would come out of the initiative. The report called for a meeting to discuss the agenda. That call might

---

174 Elson, "Brandt Report," p. 119. In fact, Brandt worried about the consequences of "international class warfare," and wished to ameliorate it rather than harness it towards social change. "Willy Brandt and Altaf Gauhar," p. 9.

175 The Havana NAM meeting of 1979 had made this call as the Brandt Report was being completed. Brandt Commission, *Common Crisis North-South*, p. 265.

176 "Willy Brandt and Altaf Gauhar," p. 13. There is ample evidence for this. A report from 1975 shows that the North prefers not to interrupt or offer new proposals, but to "talk them to death." Ann Crittenden, "Doubt is Voiced on Impact of US Plan on Poor Lands," *New York Times*, September 19, 1975, p. 4. Roger Hansen pointed out, in the Summer of 1980, that "Northern responses to Southern initiatives in the dialogue of the late 1970s remained fundamentally negative. Led by the United States, the North continued to reject almost all Southern proposals without engaging in serious negotiation, and seldom, if ever, presented alternative proposals on its own initiative." Roger Hansen, "North-South Policy: What is the Problem?" *Foreign Affairs* 58: 5 (1980), p. 1,105.

have gone unheeded, had not the outgoing UN chief, Kurt Waldheim, put pressure on the Austrian prime minister, Bruno Kreisky, who in turn joined with Mexico's Jose López Portillo to invite the countries of the world to a meeting in Mexico. Waldheim, Kreisky, and López Portillo shared little in the way of ideological affinity. By late 1981 it had become clear that Waldheim's bid for a second term at the UN had foundered on the threat of a Chinese veto. Kreisky, a friend of both Waldheim and Brandt, was willing to accommodate them.[177] López Portillo had been stung by the *sexenio*—the financial crisis of 1976 that had opened his presidency—and was, by 1981, in the midst of a financial maelstrom that would culminate in Mexico's bankruptcy in 1982. He was eager for an international Grand Assize to bail out Mexico, and the South in general.[178]

The G7 grumbled, through the medium of the OECD. Reagan, newly elected as president of the US, did not want to be a part of the process. Thatcher called him and urged him to attend. "I felt that whatever our misgivings about the occasion, we should be present both to argue our positions and to forestall criticism that we were uninterested in the developing world," Thatcher reflected. "The whole concept of 'North-South' dialogue, which the Brandt Commission had made the fashionable talk of the international community, was in my view wrong-headed."[179] Thatcher had to hold the G7 together. A Commonwealth meeting preceded Cancún. "Our Australian colleagues are rather keen to have a grand declaration about the rights of the Third World countries," she wrote to Reagan in August 1981. "We are trying to tone it down because it would be wrong to raise false hopes."[180] Thatcher was the chief whip of the G7, bringing the straying Australians into the fold, and stiffening the resolve of Reagan to stand and fight rather than scoff from afar.

---

177 Bruno Kreisky, *The Struggle for a Democratic Austria*, New York: Berghahn Books, 2000, Chapters 12 (on Brandt) and 25 (on the Third World, and, briefly, on Cancún).

178 The CIA did not agree, in a retrospective analysis in 1984: "Pressures on former President López Portillo to increase public spending became irresistible after Mexico became a net oil exporter, but the former President's tendency toward grandiose scheming contributed significantly to the disastrous boom and bust cycle that followed." It is remarkable how much neoliberal thinking had infected the intelligence agencies. "The Outlook for Mexico," *National Intelligence Estimate*, pp. 81–4, April 25, 1984, *CIA Electronic Reading Room*.

179 Margaret Thatcher, *The Downing Street Years*, London: HarperCollins, pp. 168–9. On June 16, 1980, Thatcher told the House of Commons, "We did not agree that there should be what is called a Brandt summit. As the hon. Gentleman will gather from what I have said, we discussed a number of things that concerned the Brandt report." It was inconceivable to allow Brandt to set the agenda.

180 Thatcher to Reagan, August 20, 1981. NSA Head of State File, Box no. 35, Ronald Reagan Presidential Library.

Reagan acceded to Thatcher's request, but he had his own demands. Cuba was not to be permitted to be at the conference; that was non-negotiable. Reagan had his own games afoot in Central America and the Caribbean, and he did not want to have to sit at the same table as Fidel, whom he regarded as beneath contempt.[181] In addition, the conference was to have no agenda and produce no joint communiqué.[182] After decades of negotiation over the terms of development, Reagan had now made it clear that deliberation was not to be the main procedure—decisions would be made privately, by fiat.

In August, two US F-14 jets shot down two Libyan SU-22s near the Gulf of Sidra. The provocation was a US military exercise in contested waters.[183] Qaddafi fulminated, but he had no recourse. Its raw military power and political authority over the G7 gave the United States inordinate sway over the process. The Libyan episode foreshadowed the new US attitude to world affairs.

In September 1981, a month before Cancún, Brandt and Ramphal wrote a letter to the heads of government who were to come to the meeting, laying out the main points of the Brandt Report. The letter called for a new Global Round of negotiations to take place within a Special Session of the UN General Assembly. The agenda for this Special Session would include emergency action in some critical areas, notably to alleviate the hunger epidemic and to set limits on the authority of international finance. Their letter ended with a mixed emotion, despondent hopefulness—an awareness that this was not going to go anywhere, and yet a lingering desire to see something come of it. "Cancún is in one sense a measure of last resort in the face of serious failures in the development dialogue," they wrote. But because the fate of the planet rested in the balance, "Cancún is not an end but a beginning."[184] In fact, it was more an end than a beginning: the closure of an epoch of Atlantic liberalism.

Twenty-two states came to Cancún in late October 1981 for the International Meeting for Cooperation and Development. The USSR stayed away, in accordance with its own view that the problems of the South were a result of colonialism, and it was up to the West to answer for its history before the Third World. When Waldheim asked the Soviet foreign minister to consider Cancún as a special meeting, Andrei Gromyko answered, "It is up to them to make up for what they have done to the countries of the Third World. We shall not attend

181   Louis A. Pérez, Jr., "Fear and Loathing of Fidel Castro: Sources of US Policy toward Cuba," *Journal of Latin American Studies*, vol. 34, no. 2, May 2002, pp. 245–6.

182   Jha, p. 61.

183   Bernard Gwertzman, "US Reports Shooting Down 2 Libya Jets that Attacked F-14's Over Mediterranean," *New York Times*, August 20, 1981, p. A1.

184   "Joint Letter by the Chairman and the Member of the North-South Commission, Brandt and Ramphal, to the participants of the Cancún Summit 11 September 1981," Archives of Social Democracy, Nord-Süd Kommission, 3 (*Berliner Ausgabe*, vol. 8), Friedrich Ebert Foundation.

because we do not wish to be placed in the same category with the Western powers." What help the Soviets would give would be on a bilateral basis, and not as part of a Grand Assize.[185] That was its official view. The unofficial view was that the USSR had its own economic difficulties, and, apart from substantial commitments to Cuba and Vietnam, it was hard-pressed to discharge any planetary duties. Afghanistan was another thorn in its side, compromising its freedom to maneuver. The Asian Tigers (Hong Kong, Singapore, South Korea, and Taiwan) also stayed away, which was not a surprise. They had liberated themselves from the world of development, now constituting the leading edge of the NICs. The Brandt Commission's report celebrated their achievements, but did not offer them anything tangible beyond that. They had no reason to be at the table.

Reagan said that the conference should have no agenda, but at every opportunity he articulated a very strong position—a neoliberal capture of the space once held by the NIEO. Standing in the South Portico of the White House on the day of his departure for Cancún, Reagan told the press that the problems of hunger and poverty "cannot be solved overnight, nor can massive transfers of wealth somehow miraculously produce well-being." In other words, the entire edifice of the Brandt agenda was swept aside. In its place, Reagan offered the idea that "the road to prosperity and human fulfillment is lighted by economic freedom and individual incentive." In the Cancún Sheraton the next day, Reagan pointed out that the US "will suggest an agenda composed of trade liberalization, energy and food resource development, and improvement in the investment climate." A few months later—at the Organization of American States meeting of February 24, 1982—Reagan fleshed out this agenda much more clearly. The US program of free trade, aid to the private sector and not to governments, and technical assistance and investment would create conditions under which "creativity, private entrepreneurship and self-help can flourish." "Others mistake compassion for development, and claim massive transfers of wealth somehow, miraculously, will produce new well-being," he said, repeating the line he had used often at Cancún. With his customary smile, Reagan pointed out that this "misses the real essence of development." The private sector had to be favored, aid had to be thrown back to the charity industry, and free trade and liberalized financial systems had to be the engine for development. That was the neoliberal development agenda.

It meant, of course, that the NIEO (driven by the South's perceived notion of its strength) and the Brandt agenda (driven by idea of Northern self-interest in development) would be cast aside. Little from Brandt came up for

---

185 Bernard D. Nossiter, "Parley in Cancún: Next Step By World's Leaders in Doubt," *New York Times*, October 25, 1981, p. 12; and Kurt Waldheim, "The United Nations: The Tarnished Image," *Foreign Affairs*, vol. 63, no. 1, Fall 1984, p. 99.

discussion, and almost nothing from the NIEO; both were harshly scoffed at. At Andrews Air Force Base, upon his return from Cancún, Reagan told reporters, "We didn't waste time on unrealistic rhetoric or unattainable objectives." Reagan and his team hit the message hard: the NIEO was the platform of rabble-rousers, and the Brandt agenda was, as Alexander Haig put it, "simply unrealistic." Better to be "pragmatic" and "realistic."[186]

A major thrust of the pragmatism was to allow the IMF and the World Bank to be untouched by the NAM, and by the clamor of the UN General Assembly. One of the reasons Thatcher had urged Reagan to come to Cancún was so that the two of them, together, could resist "the pressure to place the IMF and the World Bank directly under United Nations control."[187] This idea had been on the table—but it was abhorrent to the G7 and to the financiers to have the IMF and the World Bank answer to the South. A South-directed IMF might be pressured to increase the global money supply, remove the dollar from its dominant position, and bring back the dreaded inflation. In July 1981, at the Ottawa OECD summit, the G7 pledged to "maintain a strong commitment to the international finance institutions." Reagan picked this up at his opening plenary at Cancún, insisting that the talks should "respect the competence, functions and powers of the specialized international agencies, upon which we all depend, with the understanding that the decisions reached by these agencies within respective areas of competence are final. We should not seek to create new institutions."[188] No World Development Fund, in other words, to muddy the money supply with increased emoluments of gold sales and Special Drawing Rights offerings. When asked about this at a press conference, Reagan mumbled, "Well, we think in some of the organizations that are already existing in the United Nations, that we direct our efforts and their efforts more specifically to doing things that need doing—for example, such things as the World Bank and the International Monetary Fund, other UN organizations that are being directed toward being helpful—and from out of this to learn the specifics, that we can go and work with them to make them more effective." It

---

186   Howell Raines, "President Asserts Meeting in Cancún was Constructive," *New York Times*, October 25, 1981, p. A1.

187   Thatcher, *Downing Street Years*, p. 169. It was not just Reagan and Thatcher: the West Germans and the other G7 states were all in agreement. Reagan would have learned this from a CIA memorandum prior to Cancún which informed him that the West Germans and the British "opposed the text favored by the Group of 77 (the Developing Countries' UN caucus) because it could have reduced the autonomy of such UN agencies as the World Bank and the International Monetary Fund." CIA, "Prospects for a North-South Summit on International Economic Development and Cooperation," January 12, 1981, CIA National Foreign Assessment Center.

188   Alan Riding, "Reagan Supports Talks on Poverty in Cancún Speech," *New York Times*, October 23, 1981, p. A12.

was vintage Reagan. He did not want the "gigantic international bureaucracy to be in charge." Better to let the financiers, the G7, and the captains of the vast international corporations take charge of things. They were so much better at the pursuit of making money.

When the "old order" tried to assert itself, Reagan brushed it off. India's Indira Gandhi spoke of the need for agricultural subsidies; but her heart was not fully in it. Gandhi had vacillated between the road to socialism and the IMF's road since the early 1970s.[189] It was her vote bank in rural India that won her the election in 1980, and it was this vote bank—mainly large and middling farmers—whose well-being was sustained by governmental subsidies. Reagan cut her off. "This is cheating," he said, "Subsidizing agriculture is cheating." Tanzania's Julius Nyerere was in the meeting and was clearly confused. He stopped Reagan, which was itself an unusual occurrence: "But President Reagan, I have the figures here about your subsidies," he said, referring to the considerable US government subsidies to its agribusiness sector. Nyerere read out the numbers. Reagan consulted with his team. After a while, he said, "But the subsidies were established by Carter."[190] No more was allowed of such heresy.

The Brandt team was despondent. The Algerian delegation had come only on the promise that Brandt himself would stay away. It was a curious stipulation, stemming partly from the Algerians' fury that Brandt had stolen the NIEO's thunder, and of course that he had tried to sell out not only Oil Power, but also Commodity Power. Algeria's ambassador to the UN and chair of the Third World Group, Mohammed Bedjaoui, called for a UN conference on global negotiations to begin on May 3, 1982.[191] They wanted to revive the momentum of the NIEO. But this initiative went nowhere—and the Club of Rome symposium, held in March 1982, fared no better.

In his opening address at Cancún, Reagan hoped that whatever happened there, "[t]he dialogue will go on. The bonds of our common resolve will not

---

189 In 1971, Mrs. Gandhi moved a *garibi hatao* ("remove poverty") agenda, with elements such as the Crash Scheme for Rural Employment as crucial parts of it; four years later, during the Emergency period, she pushed for the liberalization of trade rules. It was always a mixed bag with her. Coming back to power after Charan Singh's "kulak budget" of 1979, which increased agrarian subsidies, she could not afford to relinquish them—if she had, the rural landlords would have dampened her prospects for re-election.

190 Julius Nyerere, "The Rabbit and the Elephant: The Challenge to the South," *The North-South Institute*, Ottawa, 1991, p. 13.

191 Mohammed Bedjaoui, who later became a jurist on the International Court, knew what he wanted. He was the author of *Towards a New International Economic Order*, New York: UNESCO, 1979.

disappear with our jet trails."[192] Reagan was pleased with the work at Cancún. All three of his maneuvers had succeeded. Firstly, the Third World states had wanted to move discussion of the dialogue to the one-country, one-vote UN General Assembly rather than the bodies, such as the GATT and IMF, where votes were weighted by financial contribution. As López Portillo put it, the IMF and GATT tended "to become mere sounding boards" for the "countries that dominate the voting."[193] They failed to shift the venue for the dialogue. The US insisted that "competence" was more important than democracy. Secondly, the Third World states wanted to hold a much larger and more focused dialogue on development, with all the countries participating together. Brazil's foreign minister, Ramiro Saraiva Guerreiro, noted, "The IMF, the World Bank and the GATT have never tackled specific problems of the developing countries in a comprehensive and integrated manner." The case-by-case approach was fine for the rich countries, but the "poor nations lose out when supply and demand are given a free rein."[194] The US preferred to hold the talks on a one-to-one basis. Thirdly, The Third World states had sought financial assistance to dig their way out of their debt problems, as well as financial investment to help galvanize a stagnant development agenda. To this, the US replied that aid was off the table. Instead, the US encouraged free markets and private initiative.

Brandt was miserable about Cancún's failure. The Brandt team gathered to be debriefed in Kuwait on January 7 and 8, 1982—and then went to work on the post mortem. The resulting book appeared in 1983 as *Common Crisis North-South: Cooperation for World Recovery*. No one paid any attention. Things had gotten so bad intellectually that when, in that same year, the World Bank published its Berg Report on sub-Saharan African poverty, it laid the blame largely on "the rapid rise of population."[195] This was a miserable collapse of imagination, far from the kind of reflections in the UNCTAD-NIEO documents, and even from the Atlantic liberalism of Brandt.

Brandt would later write: "The North-South summit in Cancún led nowhere."[196] He was wrong. It led to the new dispensation that we now call neoliberalism.

192　Riding, "Reagan Supports Talk on Poverty," p. A1.

193　Bernard D. Nossiter, "Cancún is Cool to Reagan Call for Multiple Talks," *New York Times*, October 23, 1981, p. A12.

194　Ibid.; Bernard D. Nossiter, "Parley in Cancún: Next Step By World's Leaders in Doubt," *New York Times*, October 25, 1981, p. 12.

195　World Bank, *Sub-Saharan Africa: Progress Report on Development Prospects and Programs* (the "Berg Report"), Washington, DC: World Bank, 1983, p. 29. For an alternative perspective, see Esther Boserup, *The Conditions of Agricultural Growth*, London: Allen & Unwin, 1965.

196　Brandt, *My Life*, p. 350.

The need for the North-South bridge did not recede. In December 15, 1981, the new UN secretary-general, the Peruvian Javier Pérez de Cuéllar, made the cautious remark that the income and wealth gaps between North and South were "a breach of the most fundamental human right." If no one else would take up the challenge, the UN would "provide impetus" for the transfer of wealth from the rich to the poor.[197] The UN, now increasingly under US authority, would not do any such thing. The momentum passed back to the South. From there would come the next phase of the conversation, with the formation of the South Commission.

---

197   "Peruvian is Sworn in at UN: Assails Disparities in Wealth," *New York Times*, December 16, 1981, p. A6.

CHAPTER TWO

The Conundrums of the South

The South is essentially a project, an idea in the making.
Working Party on South-South Cooperation, South Commission, 1988[1]

If Zeus had released his eagles to find the exact center of the world in the twentieth century, they might have clashed over Switzerland, above the beautiful town of Mont Pèlerin. For such a small town, with such a humble name (Mount Pilgrim), it has a curious history. Neoliberalism's institutional birth took place there in 1947, with the formation of the Mont Pèlerin Society. Trying to revive Keynesianism in an unfriendly environment, the Brandt Commission held its second meeting there. And, then, in 1987, the last gasp from the Third World project begins its work in this mountain redoubt above the hills of Montreux. Mont Pèlerin was the Delphi of the previous century.

On October 3, 1987, an assembly from Africa, Asia, Europe, and Latin America filled a conference room in a well-appointed hotel in Mont Pèlerin. Their subject was to be the fate of the planet. It was in crisis. Debt in their various countries sealed the destiny of humankind. Economic growth per capita was at a dismal 2.3 percent, down from 2.8 percent the previous year. All the trends were downward. In 1987 alone, the South sent $30 billion more in debt payments to the North than it received in new money. The drain of wealth was atrocious. The participants in this meeting did not need to be told these figures; they were tattooed on their frontal lobes. They were in the middle of the "lost decade," and no exit was visible.

Two weeks after this meeting, the stock market in the Atlantic world went into free-fall. October 19 came to be called Black Monday. The Group of 33—revered economists who meet at the Institute for International Economics in Washington, DC—worried that the "the next few years could be the most troubled since the 1930s."[2] They wanted the "underlying economic fundamentals" to be addressed: a matter taken up by the G7 in February 1987, and by the OECD later in the year. The main issue here was for the United States to reduce its

---

1 Working Party on South-South Cooperation (South Commission), "South-South Cooperation: A Strategic Option," November 7, 1988, p. 28. South Commission Archives (hereafter SCA), South Centre, Geneva, Document South IV/5. The South Commission papers are not organized, so the numbers that I use to refer to them do not appear in a serial form. They are simply the numbers that were printed on the document when it was prepared.

2 "Group of 7, Meet the Group of 33," *New York Times*, December 26, 1987.

budget deficit, and to reduce the government's role in the rest of the Atlantic states (as the Louvre Accord of the G7 put it, their governments were pursuing structural reforms such as "deregulation of business to increase efficiency and privatization of government enterprises to strengthen reliance on private entrepreneurs and market forces"[3]). There was concern for the debt crisis in the South, but the tonic proposed was simple: those countries needed to reorient their economies and pursue more exports to erase their formidable debts. Export your way out of the crisis, in other words.

The Louvre Accord sat well with the Mont Pèlerin Society, the descendants of the 1947 conference organized by Friedrich Hayek. Having been imperiled by the rise of the strong state, Hayek and his friends proposed to gird themselves for a fight to promote the "belief in private property and the competitive market." Four decades later, Hayek was far from the margins. The views of Hayek—a Nobel laureate in 1974—had come firmly to the center of the Atlantic world by 1987. Hayek and his circle held the imagination of policymakers from Washington to Tokyo to London. Their views allowed the G7 to consolidate power, to make the most of the advantages of history—which, in this context, were the advantages of colonial conquest and its effects. For the first three decades after World War II, the advance of socialism, social democracy, and the Third World project had hemmed in Mont Pèlerin's thinkers. They had had few adherents among policymakers around the world. All this changed in the 1970s, as the social, economic, and political crisis furnished the opportunity to leave their exile for power. Hayek and Milton Friedman become the court's intellectuals. They flattered the G7, and were flattered by it.[4]

Over the course of the early 1980s, the countries of the global South seemed flattened by the debt crisis and by the newly aggressive IMF and World Bank. Taking advantage of the debt situation, the North rode roughshod over the development agendas of the Southern states. The South was not able to move an agenda on the world stage. Political division convulsed the Non-Aligned Movement. In the UN, the G77 found the space for its actions limited by the

---

3   "Statement of the G6 Finance Ministers and Central Bank Governors (Louvre Accord). Canada, France, Germany, Japan, United Kingdom, United States. Paris, France, February 22, 1987."

4   For an excellent and informative set of essays on the intellectual project of neoliberalism, see Philip Mirowski and Dieter Plehwe, eds, *The Road from Mont Pèlerin: The Making of the Neoliberal Thought Collective*, Cambridge: Harvard University Press, 2009. The policy prescriptions of neoliberal thought are more ideological than practical, being in direct contradiction to the actual policies enacted in their name (not so much *laissez faire* as managed regulation on behalf of financial capital). Neoliberalism represents the restoration of the dominant classes in the name of Liberty. Martijn Konings, "Rethinking Neo-Liberalism and the Crisis: Beyond the Re-Regulation Agenda," in Konings and Sommers, *Great Credit Crash*.

G7. The various agencies of the UN no longer afforded the G77 or its member-states the platform to discuss the main issues. UNCTAD, which had operated as a secretariat for the South, had been under attack from the North and would soon be tethered. UNCTAD VI, held in Belgrade in June 1983, offered a clear analysis of the problems before the South, but it could put forward no new agenda. It simply reiterated the demands of UNCTAD V (Manila, 1979), which were warmed-over versions of the agenda from the UNCTAD IV (Nairobi, 1976). At Belgrade, the UNCTAD final report called for "an integrated set of policies, encompassing short-term measures in areas of critical importance to developing countries and long-term changes relevant to the attainment of a new international economic order."[5] UNCTAD's general orientation would be transformed in the 1980s, as neoliberal policy frameworks encaged the agenda of the NIEO. Even Atlantic liberalism was no longer of value, as the derailing of the Brandt Commission had shown. Neither UNCTAD nor Brandt were able to provide a new policy direction, given the new realities. The new geography of production that resulted from recent technological developments bewildered those who were familiar with the project of building a national economy. The pressure from the North made anything other than "the market" unintelligible as policy.

The UNCTAD secretariat had played a significant role in producing techni-cal material that benefited the South. Unlike the North, most of the countries of Africa, Asia, and Latin America did not have the vast technical departments required to produce new policy agendas, or even to decipher and negotiate the major trade and other treaties. The North's individual countries had not only large bureaucracies to offer them technical assistance, but also the OECD and the now fully neoliberal IMF, World Bank, and GATT bureaucracies. It had long been the wish of Southern nations to create something like a South Secretariat. It was out of the discussions over the paralysis of the South, the desire to reinvigorate the NIEO dynamic, and the need for something like a South Secretariat that Malaysia's premier, Mahathir Mohamad, announced the formation of a South Commission at the NAM Summit in Harare, Zimbabwe, in September 1986.[6] The main objective, apart from the usual concerns, was "to assess the situation of the South," and to "contribute to the mobilization of public opinion in the countries of the South regarding the challenges facing those countries." Confusion about the new political and economic shifts had lain waste to the program of the Third World. Something new was needed.

---

5 *Proceedings of the United Nations Conference on Trade and Development*, Sixth Session, Belgrade, June 6–July 2, 1983, *Vol. 1: Report and Annexes*, New York: United Nations, 1984, p. 8.

6 For a sense of why Mahathir pushed for the Commission, see Johan Saravanamuttu, "Malaysia's Foreign Policy in the Mahathir Period, 1981–1995: An Iconoclast Come to Rule," *Asian Journal of Political Science* 4:1 (June 1996), p. 6.

The search for something new was evident at the May 1986 Second Summit of Third World Scholars and Statesmen. Held in Kuala Lumpur, the meeting seemed listless. The discussions did not engage with such developments as the breakdown of the factory regimes across the world (post-Fordism), the emergence of the new technological infrastructure (computers, satellites), and the magnetic attraction of all the planet's wealth to the all-powerful financial centers of the North (financialization). It was this lack of engagement with such profound changes that provoked Jamaica's Michael Manley to seek a forum "to develop a new framework of analysis."[7]

Mahathir and Venezuela's Carlos Andrés Perez had discussed the formation of an independent commission of the South. The experiences of the Brandt and Brundtland commissions were mixed. They had been paralyzed by bickering, mainly driven by the North's members, who were often unable to grasp the challenges of the South. They favored a commission made up of members from the South alone. Mahathir and Perez wanted the former Tanzanian President Julius Nyerere to lead the commission. Mahathir flew to Dar es Salaam to talk to Nyerere, who was initially not keen on the idea. Nyerere wanted to travel around and discover whether there was both an interest in and need for such a commission. When the NAM blessed the idea in Harare, Nyerere finally accepted the role.[8]

In Tanzania and in the NAM, Nyerere was known as *Mwalimu*, or "teacher," not only because that was his profession before he had entered politics, but mainly because of his temperament and position. His colleagues revered him, even when they disagreed with him. Nyerere played teacher and doctor, offering his views through a diagnosis of the ailing developing world and the supine Third World project. In 1982 Nyerere received the Third World Prize in Delhi. He threw down the gauntlet for the South: "It is in fact becoming increasingly clear that an unjust and exploitative international economic system is in the process of falling apart, and no arrangements for its orderly replacement are

---

7   "*South-South II*: Charting the Way Forward," *Third World Foundation News: Third World Quarterly* 8: 4 (1986), p. 1,421. The call for something new goes back to the early 1980s. It is precisely one of the reasons for the creation of the Third World Foundation, run by the Pakistani intellectual and bureaucrat Altaf Gauhar—and funded, unfortunately, by the Bank of Credit and Commerce International (BCCI). At its several meetings, and in its journal, *Third World Quarterly*, the Foundation pushed for such a reassessment. In 1982, at one of its meetings, Shridath Ramphal pointed out, "The South must help to lay the intellectual foundations of the new order. Its contribution must go well beyond formulation. In short, the response to the frustrations of the dialogue must be vision and creativity—and persistence." Shridath Ramphal, "South-South: Parameters and Pre-Conditions," *Third World Quarterly* 4: 3 (July 1982), p. 462. The ghost of Brandt's failure lay behind much of this, as well as the death of the NIEO.

8   Note from Branislav Gosovic, January 13, 2012.

in sight. The Law of the Jungle is returning."[9] Nyerere saw the problem and took the bull by the horns. But three years later, when the South Commission returned its verdict, it left much to be desired. The vision in its document, *The Challenge to the South* (1990), did not provide the pathway for a new NAM politics, nor for a new politics for the South. It was an indictment of the new order and its jungle-laws, but it was not clear about what should come in its stead.

The proposals from the Commission were both audacious and modest. This schizophrenia was attributable to a lack of agreement on the strategy for development in the South. The dominant direction proposed by the South Commission was for the larger countries—the locomotives—to pull along the smaller and less endowed states. No longer could the North be relied upon to be the engine; in particular, its obduracy on the debt crisis and on intellectual property made it at best a reluctant ally and at worst the principle adversary. Some method needed to be found to create high enough growth rates in some Southern countries—and if this required neoliberal prescriptions, then so be it. Only growth in these locomotives would be able to fire up the rest of the South from its condition of dormancy.

A minority in the South Commission offered a different approach. It proposed that the South eschew the "growth first" agenda: far better to harness the energy of the people and create a strategy for development that put the interests of the vast mass of the people first. Here the suggestions ranged from people's planning to industrialization for popular consumption—funded not by personal debt but by sufficiently high wages. This popular direction intersected here and there with the socialist agenda, although it was not itself pledged to full-blown socialism.

The document, *The Challenge of the South*, though now largely forgotten, is still worth reading. What is most useful for our purposes is to trace the debates in the Commission, as the various members sought a new paradigm for the South. Indeed, that story might just be the most useful part of the Commission's legacy.[10]

---

9   Julius Nyerere, "South-South Option: Third World Lecture 1982," *Third World Quarterly* 4: 3 (July 1982), p. 433.

10   "I really do think that we should chronicle the evolution of thought within the Commission, the waves of change that it went through and why. I think its historical record would be even more important than its recommendations. Since the world moves more than historical understanding." Devaki Jain to Branislav Gosovic, November 25, 1997, SCA.

THE STUBBORN NAIL

During the years of rapid urbanization in the People's Republic of China, a few people refused to allow their old houses to be knocked down by developers. These houses were called *dingzihu*, or "stubborn nails." Like nails stuck in wood that cannot be easily removed, these houses sat perched on building sites, holding up construction, refusing to give way.

Nyerere was a stubborn nail. As the NIEO floundered and the G7 began its inexorable march, the leaders of the NAM states wore an air of defeat. Their meetings were a shell of what they had once been, their speeches worn out— clichés from the past mixed with pleas for pragmatism and accommodation to the G7. Movements from below germinated into protests against the desiccation of agriculture, rising prices, and cutbacks in social spending. The target was now as much the IMF as it was the NAM governments. People had begun to lose patience with their postcolonial leadership. Even Nyerere, in 1984, had been forced to bind Tanzania's exchequer to the IMF, leaving his post to a bitter struggle between his successors.[11] It was not an inspirational example.

Nyerere was undeterred by the failures of state-construction and social development. He had suffered a major setback in his own Tanzania, where his various experiments with African socialism had not given the country or the continent the breakthrough that they sorely needed. Politics had become bureaucratic, and both popular discontent and political dissent could find no legitimate avenue in an increasingly stifled country.[12] It was heartbreaking for Nyerere. Nevertheless, the teacher continued to teach, to push an agenda for complete freedom and equality that was at odds with the neoliberal dispensation. In London, in 1975, at a meeting on development, Nyerere thundered:

---

11   Issa Shivji, "Electoral Politics, Liberalization and Democracy," and Andrew Kiondo, "Economic Power and Electoral Politics in Tanzania," in Rwekaza Mukundala and Haroub Othman, eds, *Liberalization and Politics: The 1990 Elections in Tanzania*, Dar es Salaam: University of Dar es Salaam Press, 1994. In 1979, Nyerere noted,

> The problems of a Foreign Minister are not the same as the problems of a Finance Minister. The poor Minister of Finance goes to the International Monetary Fund for assistance. He needs money and the Fund requires him to fulfill certain conditions. He is worried because I talk of the ideals all the time. I ask him to reject the conditions. 'But President, how can I fill the *gap*?' I realize I have to acquiesce because I have an objective to achieve. I promise to myself next time I will be tougher!

> Julius Nyerere, "Third World Negotiating Strategy,"
> *Third World Quarterly* 1: 2 (April 1979), p. 22.

12   Prashad, *Darker Nations*, pp. 191–203.

I am saying it is not right that the vast majority of the world's population should be forced into the position of beggars, without dignity. In one world, as in one state, when I am rich because you are poor, and I am poor because you are rich, the transfer of wealth from rich to poor is a matter of right; it is an appropriate matter for charity. The objective must be the eradication of poverty, and the establishment of a minimum standard of living for all people. This involves its converse—a ceiling on wealth for individuals and nations, as well as deliberate action to transfer resources from the rich to the poor within and across national boundaries.[13]

Such a moral position had become decidedly unpopular in the capital cities of the G7, and indeed it had become increasingly unseemly in the drawing rooms of the comfortable elites of the South. Not many people of authority agreed with what increasingly sounded like a harangue from the pulpit.

Nyerere was not as isolated as he may have sounded. The dream of systematic change had not been entirely obliterated among the *éminences* of the South. In early 1979, the G77 once more returned to the UN with an audacious proposal, this one called the New International Development Strategy (NIDS). It inherited the substance of the NIEO, with a call for industrialization (drawing on the ideas in the second United Nations Industrial Development Organization meeting, held in Lima, Peru, in 1975), a call for balanced agricultural growth (drawing on the ideas developed in the UN Food and Agriculture Organization's 1974 World Food Conference), and calls for better terms of trade, transfer of technology, a more responsive monetary system, and so on.[14] By 1981, the NIDS would be folded into the comically named Substantial New Programme of Action (SNPA) of the Third Development Decade. Rather than a proposal for the transformation of North-South relations, the NIDS became a way to target aid towards the Less Developed Countries (LDCs) if these countries conducted economic liberalization, ended corruption, and embraced transparency. It was a menu that had become exhaustingly familiar. "Donor fatigue" in the 1980s sidelined even this entirely co-opted strategy.

Through the 1980s, Nyerere tried to derive a vision from his moral standpoint. Little changed between his 1982 lecture in Delhi, when he won the Third World Prize, and his 1989 address in Belgrade before the NAM Summit Conference. At both meetings, Nyerere began with the premise that the Southern countries had juridical independence, but little real political or economic freedom of maneuver. In Belgrade, Nyerere sketched out the political economy of the planet in stark terms:

---

13   Julius Nyerere, "The Economic Challenge: Dialogue or Confrontation" (England, November 21, 1975), *International Development Review* 18: 1 (1976), p. 242.

14   *Preparation for an International Development Strategy for the Third United Nations Development Decade*, document 33/193, 95th Plenary Meeting, 33rd Session of the UN General Assembly, January 29, 1979.

We cannot pretend that the North does not exist. It does. It is powerful and it makes decisions that affect the South. The market economy countries of the North increase their already great strength by meeting on a regular basis and before any major international conferences; they coordinate their activities and plan their cooperation; they organize themselves in the OECD and in other ways. In their dealings with the South they accept the discipline of solidarity, and use a "divide and rule" strategy to get their way. They therefore dominate the world economy, and use its institutions to promote their own interests.[15]

During the decade, Nyerere's main interest was to promote a "strategy of solidarity" among the countries of the South. He was personally interested in the new social movements, but these did not make their mark on the Commission. The people he picked to join him on the Commission were not so predisposed to these movements—a weakness that would come out starkly in their deliberations. At the NAM meeting, Nyerere pleaded with the delegates to take his prognosis seriously, for "an unsuspecting and disunited South is now finding that the North is using them to put in place a New International Economic Order which serves its interests even more effectively than the present one." In a handwritten addition to his prepared remarks, Nyerere pointed out, "We do not seek unity as an instrument of domination over others. We seek unity as an instrument of liberating ourselves, and resisting those who dominate us. Comrade Chairman, the Non-Aligned Movement cannot afford to forget that imperialism is not dead."

From this assessment of imperialism's presence and the need for Southern solidarity, Nyerere offered two paths for the South. The first path was to mimic the North, but this was impossible economically and unsustainable ecologically. The South, with its vast population, would not be able to emulate the US, for instance, whose capacity to absorb the world's surplus could not be duplicated: 6 percent of the world's population lived in that country, and yet they consumed 40 percent of the world's raw material and energy output. That path was impossible. Also, the Northern road would only create "a 'modern' sector which we point to as a sign of development. But it exists in a sea of poverty, ignorance and disease."[16] Nyerere gave this speech in Delhi, not far from the most exclusive neighborhoods of South Delhi—areas similar to Dar es Salaam suburbs such as Ada Estate, Masaki, and Oyster Bay. Little differentiated these

15   Julius Nyerere, "Address to the Summit Conference of the Non-Aligned Movement," Belgrade, Yugoslavia, September 4, 1989, SCA. Ten years before, in Arusha, Nyerere was more colorful: "The so-called neutrality of the world market turned out to be neutrality between the exploiter and the exploited, between the bird of prey and its victim." Julius Nyerere, "Unity for a New Order," in Khadija Haq, ed., *Dialogue for a New Order*, New York: Pergamon Press, 1980, p. 3.

16   Nyerere, "South-South Option," p. 437.

zones from those in the North; and yet this was cold comfort to the bulk of the population in India and Tanzania.

Nyerere favored the second path—one that was committed to the "basic objectives" of ending destitution, hunger, ignorance, and preventable diseases. A school of thought within the UN world had come to espouse the concept of "basic needs," and so Nyerere made this the cornerstone of his theory of development.

> Development in this sense requires increased consumption—therefore, necessarily increased production—of food, clothing, and shelter. It requires the public availability of clean water, of basic knowledge, and basic health service. And it means that all resources are devoted to expenditure or investment which can be shown to contribute—directly or indirectly—to the provision of these basic needs for everyone.[17]

Both the means and the ends should be this "people-oriented development." What technology and investment should come to the South should not put it on the quixotic path to "catch up with the North"; it must galvanize the population towards the ends of this kind of development. There is something deeply Gandhian about Nyerere's vision, which he said needed "a deliberate commitment." It was not enough merely to nod towards this kind of orientation and not do anything to realize it.[18]

The stubborn nail took his South Commission assignment with aplomb. To assemble his commissioners and his staff, Nyerere went on a world tour. At each stop he talked to people he respected, asking them to suggest names, to nudge him in interesting directions. The reason for his trip was articulated by the Uruguayan economist Enrique V. Iglesias: "The South is aware of the North and the North is aware of the South, but the South is not aware of itself."[19] It was to generate this awareness that Nyerere went on his tour. In March 1987, Nyerere went to the Caribbean and South America. From Cuba to Argentina, Peru to Brazil, Nyerere went to presidential palaces and working-class neighborhoods such as Villa Salvador, one of the *pueblos jóvenes*, in Lima, Peru. In Salvador, 300,000 people had been able to turn a social desert into "a

---

17 Ibid.

18 Much of the program sketched out by Nyerere resembled that of the Pakistani economist Mahbub ul Haq, whose "Beyond the Slogan of South-South Cooperation" (in Haq, *Dialogue for a New Order*) is a good introduction. For more, see his *The Poverty Curtain: Choices for the Third World*, New York: Columbia University Press, 1976. Ul-Haq was the pioneer of the UNDP's *Human Development Report*, and its various human development indicators.

19 *Crónica de un viaje para la historia: La Comisión del Sur: Un reto para el mundo en desarrollo*, Caracas: Oficina del Comisionada en Venezuela, 1987, p. 71; and "A Gleam in the South," *IDFA Dossier*, no. 60 (July–August 1987), p. 2.

habitat vibrating with life."[20] In Lima, and in Salvador especially, the extreme contradictions of the economic, social, and political lives of the South came to life. The disparity of wealth aside, Peru's political crisis held center stage. Its dynamic president, Alan Garcia (then head of the Socialist International), presided over hyperinflation of astronomic proportions, and over a seemingly permanent military campaign against the Sendero Luminoso (Shining Path). Sendero's violence was matched, and then exceeded, by that of the state (in 1986, Garcia sent armed forces into the El Frontón prison, where they executed 200 inmates sympathetic to Sendero).

Nyerere did not speak openly about these matters, but he did take refuge in Salvador, in people such as Maria Elena Moyano, the vice mayor of the shantytown. Moyano would have made an excellent commissioner for the South Commission. She came from the slums, articulated an acute critique of her everyday reality, and would have proposed a unique way forward. Her total commitment to the "basic objectives," such as her pioneering work with the Vaso de Leche (intended to get every child one glass of milk a day), aligned her completely with Nyerere.[21] Nyerere told the press in Lima, "The purpose of the South Commission is essentially to act as an instrument to mobilize ideas for development of the Third World in more imaginative and effective ways."[22] Nyerere turned to more establishment figures to sit on his Commission. He wanted people who were already conversant in the terms of the North-South dialogue. This decision limited its scope. In 1992, Maria Elena Moyano was killed by Sendero, who wanted to muscle into her neighborhood.[23]

Economists, politicians, and scientists filled Nyerere's Commission. There were some obvious people, who seemed to have been on every important international commission of the century. Sonny Ramphal was on the Brandt, Palme, Aga Khan, Hassan Bin Talal, and Brundtland commissions. A prodigy, Ramphal went straight from college to become a very young attorney general of his native Guyana, and later foreign minister. In 1975 Ramphal became the secretary-general of the Commonwealth. He had a strong commitment to non-alignment and the Third World approach, and was angry at the burial of the Brandt agenda. "The tragedy of Cancún," he remarked, "was that the West

---

20   *Crónica*, p. 63; Noël Cannat, *L'honneur des pauvres: Valeurs et strategies des populations dominées à l'heure de la mondialisation*, Paris: Éditions Charles Léopold Mayer, 1997, p. 66.

21   Cecilia Blondet, "El movimiento de mujeres en el Perú," in Julio Cotler, ed., *Peru 1964–1994: Economía, Sociedad y Política*, Lima: Instituto de Estudios Peruanos, 1995, p. 104.

22   *Crónica*, p. 87.

23   For a very brief statement on her life, see Maria Elena Moyano, *The Autobiography of Maria Elena Moyano: The Life and Death of a Peruvian Activist*, Gainesville: University of Florida Press, 2000.

produced Reagan and Thatcher."[24] Reflecting on the decade that led to Cancún, Ramphal noted, "I think we were unwise to over-radicalize NIEO." Cautious about a return to radicalism, he now sought change at a slow pace, at a painful pace, agreeing that there would be "great suffering in the world because of it."[25] Afraid of the radical path, and yet upset with the present conditions, Ramphal took refuge in the view that more education of the elites might encourage them to nudge history along towards the alleviation of suffering. This was not, of course, a rout for neoliberalism, but in fact an orderly retreat towards it.

Ramphal had many allies on the Commission for this view; several of them were far less concerned about the levels of suffering than he was. One of them was Abdlatif al-Hamad, who had been on the Brandt Commission. Al-Hamad came from one of the wealthiest families in Kuwait. He had been the minister of finance in Kuwait before taking on his post as head of the Arab Fund for Economic and Social Development (he held this position from 1985). As for many from his background, al-Hamad's political teeth had been cut in opposition to Arab nationalism and communism. He believed in the power of oil money to undercut these radical tendencies and to offset suffering in the world through the creation of a business civilization. Non-alignment appealed to him, which is why, under his aegis, the Kuwait Fund and the Arab Fund ploughed money into Asia and Africa—including, from the 1970s, the People's Republic of China.[26]

Another close ally was Gamani Corea of Sri Lanka. Corea had been the secretary-general of UNCTAD between 1974 and 1984, presiding over the unraveling of the North-South dialogue. At UNCTAD IV (1976) at Nairobi, Corea had had to settle for the hollow passage of an Integrated Programme for Commodities. One observer said that, at Nairobi, Corea "passed through the melee like a general disbanding his army."[27] Ramphal, al-Hamad, and Corea came to the South Commission with an accommodating frame of mind. Not for them a standoff against the Atlantic world, or a sharp attack on the structures of late-twentieth-century capitalism. Ramphal relied also on people like Ivory Coast's Aboubakar Diaby Ouattara and Malaysia's Ghazali Shafie to push the business civilization view in the Commission. Exhausted politicians who had struggled to grasp the social collapse of their societies (notably Venezuela's Carlos Andrés Perez) gave themselves over to the concessionary framework of Ramphal, if not by instinct then certainly by programmatic defeat.

---

24   Thomas Weiss, Tatiana Carayannis, Louis Emmerij, and Richard Jolly, *UN Voices: The Struggle for Development and Social Justice*, Bloomington: Indiana University Press, 2005, p. 258.

25   Ibid., p. 229.

26   For details, see Michael McKinnon, *Friends in Need: The Kuwait Fund in the Developing World*, London: I.B.Tauris, 1997, p. 67.

27   Toye and Toye, *The UN and Global Political Economy*, p. 248.

Other veterans, such as Jamaica's Michael Manley and Cuba's Carlos Rafael Rodríguez, contested Corea's accommodation of the G7. Economists such as Egypt's Ismail Sabri Abdalla (who had chaired the Third World Forum), Celso Furtado (who had begun his career at Raúl Prebisch's UN Economic Commission for Latin America), and Devaki Jain (founding member of the Development Alternatives with Women for a New Era—DAWN—network) went toe to toe with the more neoliberal-minded economists on the Commission. They were the main allies of the very few representatives on the Commission of the various social movements that had begun to assert themselves in the South, such as Simba Makoni of Zimbabwe (a politician who had an instinct for popular struggles) and Marie-Angélique Savané of Senegal (of the Association of African Women for Research and Development).

Nyerere chose this wide disparity of ideology and instinct deliberately. In 1979, he reflected on the problems of disunity in the South:

> If we now define the economic objective too narrowly the ensuing struggle will only divide the group ... We have to keep them all together. The purists will find that unpalatable. But I have always resisted "purity" during the liberation days. There are levels of purity. At the international level, purity at a certain stage of struggle can be terribly divisive. Each country must advance according to its own lights. If you require everyone to conform to a rigid political prescription, you will be weakening yourself.[28]

There was no doubt that from the ruins of the NIEO new questions and new answers were needed. The powerful thrust from the North that came on the terrain of debt and intellectual property rights squashed the ability of the Southern intellectuals to have a free discussion about their predicament and about possible futures. The dilemmas of the present absorbed the energies of the intellectuals. The kind of vigorous debate needed to discuss the various paths of development could not happen. A false kind of unity against the North's avalanche took hold. This was a defensive unity. It worked to the benefit of the Southern neoliberals in the room, who had substantial differences with the North on debt and intellectual property rights, but who agreed with the neoliberal emphasis on growth over equity. Those intellectuals who disagreed on the "growth first" strategy nonetheless joined hands with the neoliberals to ward off the catastrophes of debt and intellectual property. The South Commission, therefore, spent its three years responding to pressure from the North—and thus was easily able to maintain its Southern unity—and then making a generic call for South-South transactions that appealed to all the strands within the Commission, and within the world of the South in general.[29]

---

28 Julius Nyerere, "Third World Negotiating Strategy," *Third World Quarterly* 1: 2 (April 1979), p. 21.

29 Several of the Commissioners played almost no role in its deliberations. Celso

Nyerere, his assistant Joan Wicken, the Commission's general secretary Manmohan Singh, and its staff (including Branislav Gosovic and Carlos Fortin) played a central role in the creation of the drafts and the reports, pushing against one current or another. Nyerere tried to balance the accommodative standpoint of Ramphal, with Manmohan Singh perched in the middle seeking a position of compromise. Even when Nyerere was in Butiama, in rural Tanzania, he was in close contact with Manmohan Singh. They were the heart of the South Commission.[30]

At Mont Pèlerin, Nyerere addressed his motley crew, setting out the agenda for the Commission: "The South Commission's eventual purpose is to allow the developing countries to appraise their situation in the light of the current development crisis and the greater technological and political changes taking place, with their likely effect on the world economy in the coming years and into the twenty-first century."[31] Illusions had to go out of the window. The G77 was not powerful; UNCTAD had been ground under. "Not only is the South adrift and largely demoralized," Nyerere noted, "the global environment in which it drifts is itself undergoing great changes, some unpropitious for economic development in the accepted sense. There is a need for the South to take stock of where it is now, where it is going, if no action is taken, and where it wants to go." Fulfilling that need was the Commission's task.

SEASON OF ASH[32]

In 1984, a Union Carbide factory exploded in Bhopal, India. The blast and the chemical effluent killed thousands of people. Two years later, reactor no. 4 exploded at the Chernobyl nuclear power plant. Hundreds of thousands of people were affected by the radioactive cloud. These disasters had a tangible origin, and immediate victims. No one admitted blame, and no real compensation came the way of the victims.

A disaster two years before Bhopal inaugurated the long season of ash: Mexico's finance minister, Jesús Silva Herzog, announced that his country could

---

Furtado came to only one meeting, as did Cardinal Paulo Arns; the experience of these two Brazilians was lost. Manley had been ill, but he did send in his responses to the various drafts. Widjojo Nitisastro, a leading Indonesian economist, came only at the very end. His main role was in helping set up the South Centre.

30   One of the limitations of this chapter is that it does not have access to the Joan Wicken papers, including her notes and diary, which are in the Rhodes House, Oxford University.

31   Julius Nyerere, "Discussion Notes," October 1987, SCA.

32   The metaphor that governs this section is drawn from Jorge Volpi's novel, *No será la tierra*, Madrid: Alfaguara, 2006.

not cover its financial obligations. It was a shock to the world system, particularly to the virtually insolvent countries of the South. By 1987 the debt in the South was 47 percent of its gross national product. A full quarter of its export earnings had to be turned over to the banks in the North to service the ballooned debt.[33] Not long after the debt crisis had bankrupted most of the South, the countries of the North pushed an agenda that threatened to condemn the South to perpetual penury. In September 1986, at Punta del Este, Uruguay, the General Agreement on Trade and Tariffs (GATT) launched its eighth round. Some of the issues put forward by the North were much like those in the previous seven rounds (reduction in tariffs on various commodities). Disagreement emerged around three new sets of issues: trade in services, investment liberalization, and intellectual property rights. Rather than extend and protect the scientific commons, corporations of the North sought to protect their proprietary claims over inventions and discoveries. Knowledge transfer and technology transfer in the interest of human development would be suborned to the battle against piracy. The Indian foreign minister, V. P. Singh, found the Round "untenable," inveighing that it reversed the "long struggle against colonial rule."[34] Such fulminations did not deter the North. The G77 had no standing in the GATT, and so there was no bloc of the South. Countries would gather together informally. Singapore and Brazil went into quiet dialogue with the North; others remained on the margins, terrified by the consequences of the decisions being made.[35]

Asking the hard questions is simple; much harder is to focus the mind when crisis is at the door. The Commissioners at Mont Pèlerin could not plunge themselves into the big questions for a new agenda for the South. Far more pressing were the consequences of debt and the devices of Punta del Este. The *idée fixe* of Reality took control of the agenda. Early in the Commission's work, Michael Manley warned of the distraction of crises. "The crisis absorbs the best brains," he wrote in a memorandum of December 1987, "denuding the landscape of strategic planning."[36] This is precisely what happened in the Commission itself. How could it have been otherwise? A considerable amount

---

33   World Bank, *World Development Report 1989: Financial Systems and Development: World Development Indicators*, Oxford: Oxford University Press, 1989, pp. 204–13 (data derived from Tables 21–25).

34   V. P. Singh's opening speech at the Punta Del Este meeting, GATT, MIN (86)/ ST/33, September 17, 1986.

35   An Argentine official put the case for those who wanted this kind of quiet accommodation: "There is also an understanding that the more aggressive you are, the harder it is to get things." Ernest H. Pegg, *Traders in a Brave New World*, Chicago: University of Chicago Press, 1995, pp. 47–8.

36   Michael Manley, "A Programme and Possible Methodology for Stimulating South/South Cooperation," December 1987, p. 2, SCA.

of energy went towards the two main disasters of the decade—the debt crisis and the threat of the new intellectual property regime.

The Debt of Sisyphus

Nyerere had wanted a South Asian economist to be the general secretary of the Commission. Mahbub ul Haq could not come, as the government of Pakistan would not release him from his post as finance minister.[37] Nyerere asked India's Rajiv Gandhi to recommend someone. He offered up Manmohan Singh, the deputy chairperson of the Planning Commission. Gandhi had his differences with Singh; the prime minister found Singh to be old-fashioned, interested in a mode of development that included the poor, of all horrors. Gandhi called Singh and his Planning Commission colleagues a "bunch of jokers," and insisted that they take on board his vision for India, with a plan "for the construction of autobahns, airfields, speedy trains, shopping malls, and entertainment centres of excellence, big housing complexes, modern hospitals and healthcare centres." Gandhi wanted to develop India along the lines of an American suburb.[38] Singh's rectitude and intelligence came along with a sense of obligation to those in power. He has not the temperament of a radical, although his sense of duty towards ideas of justice often interrupted his tendency to please those in authority. Nyerere was pleased to have Singh, who was a recognized economist and an honest and hard-working bureaucrat.[39] But Singh did not share Nyerere's capacity to hope for a socialist outcome.[40] Singh was more sympathetic to Ramphal and his group.

Nevertheless, Nyerere and Singh agreed on the gravity of the debt crisis; it was what brought them together. The debt crisis condemned the South to a

---

37 Author interview with Devaki Jain, New Delhi, January 7, 2010.

38 C. G. Somiah, *The Honest Always Stand Alone*, Delhi: Niyogi Books, 2010, pp. 142–4.

39 Rajiv Gandhi had released "one of his key officials to be Secretary General. I am confident that in this crucial position Dr Manmohan Singh will make a great contribution to the success of our work." Nyerere to Gro Brundtland, August 17, 1987, SCA.

40 In 1972, Indian Ambassador G. J. Malik hosted Manmohan Singh in Lima, Peru. Singh was then chief economic advisor to the Finance Ministry. "Are you a socialist?" Malik asked Singh. "Certainly not," replied the advisor, "I am a civil servant and by law I am not allowed to join any political party. In fact, I am not even allowed to tell anybody how I have voted in an election. As it happens, I have never voted in an election. My political views are my own and I am under no obligation to embrace those of the government in power." "You are a very brave man," Malik said, and then recalled, "We have never discussed politics since then." G. J. Malik, "The Last Days of Salvador Allende," *The Ambassador's Club: The Indian Diplomat at Large*, ed. Krishna V. Rajan, New Delhi: HarperCollins, 2012, p. 136.

lack of resources to extend its growth rate. Neither Singh's nor Nyerere's visions would make sense unless the debt overhang was removed. Singh turned to his friend Chandra Hardy at the World Bank to write a special paper for the South Commission. Hardy's paper set the terms for the discussion, and it shows us how much agreement there was within the Commission on this subject.

Hardy delivered her note in January 1988. Entitled "The Debt Problem in 1988," it covered the basic empirical background. Hardy had already written two papers on the Mexican and African debt landscapes.[41] She knew the material well. The African debt, she said, was "unsustainable," but so too was the debt carried by Latin America. The international institutions and the bankers were reluctant to "publicly acknowledge the unsustainability of the debt burden of Latin America for fear that such an acknowledgement would be enough to provoke an international banking crisis."[42] The debt crisis, Hardy forthrightly noted, could not be blamed on the debtor countries. They had been swindled by the Northern banks, which came at them with "inappropriate terms" and no oversight. The people of the South were now forced to pay back these odious debts. The payments were so high that the countries had to cut away at the basic livelihoods of their populations to pay the interest on the debt, and to abdicate any hope of growth towards development.[43] "The developing countries were forced to bear not only the burden of externally imposed austerity programs," she wrote, "but also the burden of preventing an international banking crisis. No major bank has been allowed to fail; no major bank shareholder has lost a dividend; no major bank chairman has resigned. In fact, no major costs have been imposed on banks."[44] The bankers had the power to avoid the sin peculiar to their discipline: bankruptcy.

For a World Bank or IMF senior economist to heed the painful evidence of Latin American and African reality is unusual. Hardy belonged to that class of World Bank economists who came before the Clausen purges at 19th Street. In her published work she had advocated for the cancellation of Africa's debt, as well as the debts of several Latin American countries.[45] In her South Commission study, Hardy noted that "if a substantial write-off of the debt is

---

41   Chandra Hardy, "Mexico's Development Strategy for the 1980s," *World Development* 10: 6 (June 1982); and "Africa's Debt: Structural Adjustment with Stability," in Robert J. Berg and Jennifer Seymour Whitaker, eds, *Strategies for African Development*, Berkeley: University of California Press, 1986.

42   Chandra Hardy, "The Debt Problem in 1988," January 19, 1988, p. 2, SCA.

43   Alwyn Taylor of the African Centre for Monetary Studies, in his paper for the South Commission, pointed out that the austerity programs "have had the effect of frustrating the long term growth of these economies." "The African Debt Crisis," A Paper Prepared for the South Commission, Dakar, December 1987, p. 6, SCA.

44   Hardy, "Debt Problem in 1988," p. 7.

45   Hardy, "Africa's Debt," pp. 470–1.

not politically feasible, all of the debt should be restructured on concessional terms."[46] She had many suggestions: outright cancellation, lengthening the repayment period of the loans, rescheduling each year, improving the quality of the aid provided so that it was not diverted to debt-servicing, and allocating more IMF standard drawing rights (so that these might substitute for the debt). None of this was on the agenda of the G7, nor of the Paris Club. They had the same preoccupation as ever: to get the bankers a preferred place in the queue for the debt repayment, though all the while talking about incentives and moral hazards. "Old solutions are being given new names," Hardy noted caustically.[47]

On January 23–24, 1988, Manmohan Singh assembled an informal meeting on debt. Towards producing a final draft to present to the Commissioners at their second meeting at Kuala Lumpur, Singh had written "Elements for a South Commission Statement on the Debt Issue." In many ways, Singh's "Elements" follows Hardy's analysis: the debt was debilitating; there was no way to escape from it; the bankers crowded out solutions:

> Given the great weight and influence of creditors in the management of international credit mechanisms and the strong ideological overtones of economic policies in major creditor countries, policy failures of the developing countries were singled out as the most important cause in the deteriorating debt situation and thus emphasis came to be laid on domestic adjustment as the primary corrective route ... Macroeconomic policies were so designed as to reduce domestic spending so that more resources could be made available for servicing the debt.[48]

Bankers win; debtors lose. It was as simple as that—and it was entirely because the bankers held all the political cards, and the debtor states held none. "We are conscious of the fact that international economic relations are in the final analysis power relations," Singh wrote, "and that the creditors are invariably in a stronger position than debtors."[49] The creditors—the banks and the G7—did not simply find themselves in a position of strength: they had earned that position. The creditors "have virtually organized a cartel which has the backing of powerful industrial countries as well as the IMF." Creditors have their cartel, but debtors have none. "The time has come to make a beginning to end this asymmetry," Singh wrote; "Cooperation among debtors and developing countries in general could be an important means of articulating the common concerns of developing countries. The debtors should mutually inform and consult each other on the course of proceedings of debt management operations."[50]

---

46   Hardy, "Debt Problem in 1988," p. 11.

47   Ibid., p. 4.

48   Manmohan Singh, "Elements for a South Commission Statement on the Debt Issue," December 28, 1987, first draft, p. 2, SCA.

49   Ibid., p. 14.

50   Ibid., pp. 14–15. Manmohan Singh announced this idea at a press conference

Such a debtors' forum, however, was not to be. In another paper for the South Commission, Jorge Eduardo Navarrete, Mexico's ambassador to the United Kingdom and an economist, struck a cautious note: "Both the past experience and the present outlook underline the fact that a radical departure from [the basic cooperative approach], however desirable it may look on the paper, is certainly not feasible."[51] Navarrete pointed to Brazil, which, under finance minister Luiz Carlos Bresser-Pereira, had tried to take a hard line against the banks. Between April and December 1987, Bresser-Pereira had pushed the administration of President José Sarney to be creative with the debt. He wanted a moratorium on debt-servicing, and he suggested that the debt be turned into securities and sold in the secondary market. Sarney did not want to antagonize the IMF or the bond markets; solvency was more important than development. The debt was impossible, Bresser-Pereira later reflected, and yet, "the majority of the elites in the debtor countries continue to be willing to try to pay it for a number of reasons." One was that they feared the retaliation of the banks and the bond markets. Another was that, since the elites did not suffer from the debt crisis or the austerity, they had little sympathy for those bearing its social costs (indeed, the debt allowed rentiers and financiers among the elites to make money out of their misery). Finally, the elites in the South wanted to be accepted into the "First World," and wanted their economies "integrated with those of the advanced capitalist countries." But integration with the First World, wrote Bresser-Pereira, was "not accomplished through good manners but rather through economic growth and price stability."[52] These two goals were hindered by the heavy debt.

The hesitancy of the elites identified by Bresser-Pereira held Manmohan Singh's own analysis back. He did not go as far as Hardy. African debt should be cancelled or rescheduled—that was clear. But Africa's debt, in absolute terms, was not very large. The problems in the late 1980s were elsewhere—in Latin America and parts of Asia. For these regions, Singh was not willing to push for cancellation in general. Like Bresser-Pereira, Singh wanted the debt to be made into securities and then traded at a discounted rate. In this way, the debts would

---

in Misurata, Libya, on March 27, 1989. Creditors have cartels, he noted, whereas debtors allow themselves to be "strangulated one by one and case by case." "Debtors' Forum to Avoid Bondage," *South Letter* 1 (April 1989), p. 7.

51   Jorge Eduardo Navarrete, "Debt Management Options for Middle Income Countries: A Working Paper for the South Commission," November 1987, p. 3, SCA.

52   Luiz Carlos Bresser-Pereira, "A Debtor's Approach to the Debt Crisis," in Christine A. Bogdanowicz-Bindert, ed., *Solving the Global Debt Crisis*, New York: Harper & Row, 1989; and for a remarkably candid retrospective on Brazil's debt crisis and the role of the Washington institutions, see Luiz Carlos Bresser-Pereira, "A Turning Point in the Debt Crisis: Brazil, the US Treasury and the World Bank," *Revista de Economia Política* 19: 2 (April–June 1999).

not be annulled, but they would also not be uncollectable.[53] The banks would get some of their money back, and the South would be able to move towards a growth agenda. As part of the bargain, the South would have to move to an austerity regime. This is what Hardy had not wanted, but it is what Singh accepted. "Austerity—even very severe austerity—can be justified as a response to crisis," he wrote. "But there must be light at the end of the tunnel … Developing countries do accept the need for structural reforms. But structural reforms cannot have as their objective the servicing of debts. Their primary focus must be on growth with equity."[54]

Growth with equity was Nyerere's slogan. It would occur several times in the South Commission's final report, *The Challenge to the South* (1990), and in Nyerere's speeches throughout the late 1980s. A clear indication of the divergence of views on the South Commission comes across in Manmohan Singh's interpretation of austerity in the service of growth with equity. His laundry list of "structural reforms" provide an early window into the quiet accommodation of a swath of the South Commission to neoliberal views:

> In principle there can be no objection to conditionality designed to ensure that the funds made available internationally will be used for promoting genuine development … We are also strongly in favor of structural reforms to improve the buoyancy and elasticity of tax systems, strengthen [the] public sector's performance and its resource generating capacity, provide a stable environment for the regulation of [the] private sector enabling it to play its allotted role in line with national priorities and removal of obstacles to increased production of food and agriculture, particularly on the part of small and marginal farmers. We also recognize the need for an efficient policy framework for promoting exports and managing the balance of payment.[55]

Written in a very guarded style, this paragraph nonetheless signals the validation of the neoliberal agenda. Here is my translation:

- Structural adjustment is acceptable if it targets growth, not impoverishment.
- Tax reforms are needed to ensure fewer penalties on the wealthy.
- Productive parts of the public sector should be sold off to earn resources.
- The private sector needs to be encouraged, so any barriers against it should be lowered.
- Food and agricultural subsidies should be removed, so that private

---

53   In September 1987, the G24 noted, "there is a growing sentiment in the market that part of the debt is uncollectable." Navarrete, "Debt Management," p. 5.

54   Singh, "Elements," pp. 4, 8.

55   Ibid., p. 15.

    capital can enter the sector and enhance its output with more capital inputs.

- Import-substitution needs to give way to export-promotion.
- Balance-of-payments solvency is more important than anything else.

This did not go over well with some of the Commissioners. They were loath to bend their knee so quickly to the new orthodoxy of the G7. But Singh's text was hastily discussed at the Commission's second meeting at Kuala Lumpur, and adopted. Disagreements over the way forward were papered over by agreement on the diagnosis.[56] Singh's razor-sharp attack on the banks and the call for a debtors' cartel mollified those who were discomfited by the superstructure of neoliberalism that seemed to surround these radical gestures.[57] This was a foreshadowing of much of the work of the Commission—and indeed of the paralysis that afflicted Southern intellectuals during the decade.

    On June 24, 1989, Nyerere wrote a letter to President George H. W. Bush. It began with a cutting paragraph, and ended with a painful question: "I am writing to you on a subject which you have doubtless discussed *ad nauseum*. It is the problem of debt." During the course of the 1980s, the United States had done as much as possible to prevent the cancellation of the debt. Neither the Baker Plan (1985) nor the Brady Plan (1989) had provided any space for the kind of ideas entertained by the South Commission. Baker essentially asked the Japanese to unload some of their budget surplus to help the highly indebted middle-income countries; Brady went with the grain of the IMF's Structural Adjustment Program, suggesting that debt relief could come to countries that implemented major "reforms" of their economic systems.[58] In 1988, at the G7's Toronto Economic Summit, there was again a discussion of debt relief through its refinancing and re-engineering. There was no word of debt

---

56   Devaki Jain, "South Commission's First Meet: A Participant's View," October 29, 1987, SCA, offers a sense of how at the first meeting disagreements over some of the substantial issues held the Commission back ("Thus a statement on debt was not issued ..."), and how the limited mandate prevented the Commission from intervention in "national, even international conflicts—it had neither the clout nor was [that its] role."

57   On "moral hazard" and the banks, Singh wrote that if there is no relief the "governments of the creditor countries enforce bad loans. They thus encourage poor lending policies on the part of commercial banks who now expect their governments to help collect even the poorest sovereign loans." Singh, "Elements," p. 13. On the debtors' cartel, the minutes of the Kuala Lumpur meeting underscored "the proposal to set up a debtors' forum" and "called for an active and catalytic role on the part of the Commission." "Chairman's Report on the Second Meeting of the South Commission," 1988, SCA, South II/12, Confidential.

58   For a sympathetic account of the Brady Plan, see Jeffrey Sachs, "Making the Brady Plan Work," *Foreign Affairs* 68: 3 (Summer 1989).

cancellation—even for the poorest states. "The Toronto agreement," Nyerere wrote, "like other plans for other groups of debtors, was a menu of technical proposals. But the solution to this tragedy cannot be found at a technical level: it has to be the outcome of bold political action." The G7 did not have the stomach for such action, and it did not extend its arms to the South. This was why Nyerere ended his letter with a moral question: "How can there be peace without justice?"[59]

A New International Property Order

In Punta del Este, Uruguay, the GATT member-states gathered in September 1986 to launch the eighth round of discussions on trade issues. The previous seven rounds had mostly preoccupied the Atlantic states and Japan, since these were the major producers of industrial goods, and GATT had until then been the forum for discussing reductions of tariff barriers. Agriculture remained outside GATT, and the countries of the South produced too few industrial goods to be major players at the GATT rounds. The Uruguay Round had much bolder ambitions. The Quad (the United States, Europe, Canada, and Japan) came to the Round to push the comparative advantage of their economic zone: to preserve as much as possible of their agricultural protections, to protect their technological and scientific advantages (through an intellectual property regime), and to safeguard the well-being of Northern service-providers who wanted to extend their reach into the rest of the world. In exchange for its agenda being adopted into the GATT, the Quad indicated that it would allow for some modest opening of its markets to agriculture and labor-intensive manufactured goods from the South. The Quad, as an arm of the G7 and the OECD, teased the South that if concessions were made to its agenda then the Multi-Fiber Arrangement (MFA), which imposed quotas on such imports into the North from the South, might be allowed to lapse. It was a very poor bargain.

India and Brazil hastily formed an agreement against the opening gambit of the North. They formed a group (the G10) that included Argentina, Cuba, Egypt, Nicaragua, Nigeria, Peru, Tanzania, and Yugoslavia. Their response to the GATT was straightforward: they opposed the intellectual property regime, for example, because it would interfere with domestic laws and condemn the South to technological and scientific dependence. Intellectual property had always been a sensitive matter. The regime that governed patents, the Paris Convention of 1883, had been unfairly negotiated and accepted.[60] That was bad

---

59 Nyerere to President George Bush, Dar es Salaam, Tanzania, June 24, 1989, SCA. There is no reply in the archive.

60 Only fifteen countries came to Paris to sign the agreement in 1883. Of them, three (Ecuador, El Salvador, and Guatemala) came along as US protectorates, on the very steamship that brought the US delegation. The French brought along the Tunisians.

enough. The new draft, known as TRIPS (Trade-Related Aspects of Intellectual Property Rights), was worse. The G10 wanted discussion on intellectual property to remain within the ambit of the UN's World Intellectual Property Organization (WIPO), or of UNCTAD.[61] The North was not happy with this. GATT was its territory; WIPO seemed more on the side of the South, and it had few enforcement mechanisms. TRIPS had to be robust and meaningful: it was essential to the plans for the North's new agenda for growth.

When the South Commission turned its attention to the Uruguay Round, the G10 began to wobble. The United States played hardball, enacting a little-known provision (Section 301) of its 1974 Trade Act. In 1988 the US Congress passed a new Trade act with a stronger Section 301, which pointedly called for sanctions against any state with inadequate intellectual property standards. The new Section 301 authorized *mandatory*, not discretionary, retaliation by the United States. This put pressure on the countries with growing industrial sectors that had their eyes on the US and European markets. Even the leaders of the G10 lost their stomach for the fight. This was the context for the South Commission's involvement in the Uruguay Round.

A group within the Commission joined with various Southern ambassadors to the UN in Geneva to furnish the entire Commission with a draft by late June 1988. The draft reiterated the G10 position that the North was using all its power to force a new agenda, and that it was doing so without adequate technical preparation in the South to deal with the massive legal infrastructure being put in place for the new international property order. The Round should be seen by the South "as a very high policy priority," the draft pointed out, since "only a collective response from the South can hope to face the well-organized strategy of the developed countries, which are attempting to put in place, piece by piece, a structure for a new system corresponding essentially to their vision of the world and their interests."[62] The South entered the negotiations without

---

The Netherlands, Serbia, and Switzerland did not have a domestic patent law, and yet they participated to frame an international agreement. *The Paris Convention for the Protection of Industrial Property from 1883 to 1983*, Geneva: International Bureau of Intellectual Property, 1983.

61   As it had been. UNCTAD's International Code of Conduct of the Transfer of Technology group met six times between November 1975 and July 1978. It moved its work to the United Nations Conference on the International Code of Conduct on the Transfer of Technology, which also met six times between 1979 and 1985. A deadlock stopped the deliberations, mainly with pressure from the North on issues of enforcement and dispute settlement. A parallel process went from the UNCTAD group to the WIPO, which held four sessions from February to March 1984. Its work was also stuck on the same issues. These venues, where the South had a larger bargaining position, were abandoned for the GATT, where the North dominated.

62   "Statement on the Uruguay Round. Adopted by the South Commission, at its

adequate technical preparation. A typical problem was that the North had a vast and over-prepared secretariat (in the various treasury departments, legal departments, at the OECD secretariat, at the G7, and so on), while the South was short-staffed.[63] This was the reason why there had long been a need for a South Secretariat. The creation of the South Centre, the Secretariat of the South, would be one of the main positive outcomes of the South Commission.

The South Commission's July draft and August final statement on intellectual property are its most powerful and clear documents. Shifts in the geography of production and in the nature of economic growth sent the governments of the North into a flurry.[64] They worried that shifts in the site of production offshore threatened their own economic strength. What would be the engine for the growth of the North Atlantic core if industrial production set sail for warmer climates? They needed to alter the international system to protect their various growth industries—finance, pharmaceuticals, information technology, agro-chemicals, and entertainment. These were not national industries, of course, but industrial sectors dominated by a handful of very large transnational firms. Based on this view, the Commission noted,

> The motive force for the new development is undoubtedly provided by the unprecedented acceleration of technical progress in such crucial areas as information and communication. The large research and development budgets which form the basis of technical change, the substantial economies of scale associated with new products and processes, and the economies of agglomeration made possible by advances in corporate and financial management technologies, have provided a powerful incentive for the globalization of economic processes. In this setting, host country regulations are seen by the transnational actors as unwarranted interference with their corporate objectives.[65]

In short, what the South Commission pointed out was that the Uruguay Round was a form of structural adjustment of the international order, and of domestic policy. Whereas previous GATT Rounds had simply prevented states from

---

third meeting, Cocoyoc, Mexico, 5–8 August 1988," p. 1, SCA. I use the final statement when there is no difference from the draft. Where there are differences, I rely on the draft.

63   I. William Zartman, "Negotiating from Asymmetry: The North-South Stalemate," *Negotiation Journal* 1: 2 (April 1985); Constantine Michalopoulos, "The Developing Countries in the WTO," *World Economy* 22: 1 (1999); J. Michael Finger, "Implementing the Uruguay Round Agreements: Problems for Developing Countries," *World Economy* 24: 9 (2001).

64   All this was clear by the time the South Commission went to work. The main text on the new economy was M. J. Piore and C. F. Sabel, *The Second Industrial Divide*, New York: Basic Books, 1984, which built on the insights of A. Touraine, *The Post-Industrial Society: Tomorrow's Social History*, New York: Random House, 1971.

65   "Statement on the Uruguay Round," p. 10.

operating in certain ways (mainly lifting tariffs), the new GATT agenda had a more positive aspect: it obliged governments to bring their domestic laws in line with the wishes of the new GATT rules. Since the GATT rules had been framed with an eye to the comparative advantage of the North and of Northern-based transnational corporations, these new domestic laws would facilitate their interests above those of the populations of the South.[66]

The South would find itself at a great disadvantage. By adopting a set of procedures that protected the intellectual monopolies of the North, the new GATT rules would curtail the technological and scientific development of the South. No longer would the patents be on processes (which allowed Southern firms to find new processes to get to the product): they would now be on products themselves. The Intellectual Property Coalition, which included Pfizer, Du Pont, and Monsanto, pushed the G7 to ensure this became a GATT principle.[67] This amounted to technological starvation: no reverse-engineering allowed. The South Commission's Abdus Salam (of Pakistan, and based at the International Centre for Theoretical Physics in Trieste) had produced a series of papers for the Commission on the importance of both scientific and technological training. For a variety of reasons, Salam showed, the South spent insufficient amounts of money on science and technological training and promotion. Only in China was the increase in the scientific workforce remarkable (500 researchers in 1949; over 300,000 by 1988).[68] The South held no more than 1 percent of the 3.5 million patents recognized by the international patent-holding agencies. The Atlantic states and their transnational firms certainly held the bulk of the world's patents, and of the various advanced technologies that had already become fundamental for economic growth; on the other hand, Daniel Querol and others had shown that more than 80 percent of the planet's genetic resources were found in the South.[69] Not only was the South's forty-year history

---

66   Chakravarti Raghavan, *Recolonization: GATT, the Uruguay Round and the Third World*, London: Zed Books, 1990.

67   Deepak Nayar, "The Dunkel Text: An Assessment," *Social Scientist* 20: 1–2 (January–February 1992), p. 112; and S. P. Shukla, "The Emerging International Trading Order: A Story of the Uruguay Round," G. S. Bhalla and Manmohan Agarwal, eds, *World Economy in Transition*, Simla: Indian Institute of Advanced Study, 1992.

68   Abdus Salam, "Notes on Science and High Technology in the Development of the South," prepared for the 3rd Meeting of the South Commission, August 5–8, 1988, Cocoyoc, Mexico, June 28, 1988, SCA, South III/2, Restricted. The numbers might not tell enough of the story. At the same time as China produced more scientists, it turned its back on the popular science tradition that came out of the 1949 revolution. Sigrid Schmalzer, "On the Appropriate Use of Rose-Colored Glasses: Reflections on Science in Socialist China," *Isis* 98 (2007).

69   Daniel Querol, *Genetic Resources: Our Forgotten Treasure, Technical and Socio-Economic Approaches,* Kuala Lumpur: Third World Network, 1988.

of making institutions and building its own technological arsenal lacking—it was already unprepared for the new developments in "communications, micro-electronics and most important for the coming century, biotechnology."[70] Bad as the past might have been, the future would be bleak indeed with the new restrictions on the transfer of science and technology.

The colonial rupture obscured the conjoined history of science—one that linked the Vedic zero to the Persian scholar Musa al-Khwarizmi to Lombardan mathematician Girolamo Cardano to imaginary numbers, as these intellectual goods travelled across a real geography. The "West" emerged as the sole origi-nator, and "globalization" pretended to be the first deep linkage of the planet's social and cultural imaginations. The dismissal of the older linkages reinforced a sense of inferiority imposed by force of colonial arms. It also produced a desire to mimic the fruits of science—the final commodities, not the cultural underpinnings of science.[71] It was in order to purloin this heritage back that many writers in the South uncovered their scientific histories. It was the task of scientists such as Abdus Salam to insist not only upon the transfer of technol-ogy (which is often a passive act), but the transfer or revival of science and the scientific temper. It was this latter act that seemed to be curtailed by the stric-tures of intellectual property and the proprietary treatment of science itself.

The "transfer of technology" model treated technology as culturally neutral, and it saw its entry into the South as consisting of turnkey projects to use Southern (cheap) labor. Technological systems, then, were grafted upon cultural and social contexts in which they would be alien, or at least distinctive. Technology would be instrumentally imported to facilitate faster labor by people who would not be allowed to understand how the machines worked in the first place. They were to be reduced to "hands," their minds kept at rest.

Not only was the South at a disadvantage as far as the distribution of sci-entific knowledge was concerned; it was also greatly at a loss when it came to its attempt to enter the world market for technologically sophisticated goods and services. Attempts to ease this entry through a reconsideration of trade barriers had led to the unfinished discussions around the International Code on Transfer of Technology and the Code on Transnational Corporations. They

---

70   Salam, "Notes on Science," p. 14. See also Abdus Salam to Manmohan Singh, June 5, 1989, with attachments, SCA.

71   In June 1989, Abdus Salam wrote a note for the South Commission, which he hoped would be an appendix to the final report. In it he pointed out that "[v]ery few developing countries, with the exception of the 'Confucian belt' countries—like China or Singapore—or Brazil or India are conscious of the need for or have made progress in 'High' Technology, the general feeling being that this whole area is beyond them. It is this feeling of lack of interest and faith in their own scientists that one must fight against since the future undoubtedly lies here." Abdus Salam's note, June 5, 1989, pp. 5–6, SCA.

went nowhere "because of opposition from developed countries."[72] These codes would have dealt with the question of science and technology transfer; the Uruguay Round seemed keener on blocking access to the new knowledge. Instead of allowing the South the prospect of leapfrogging several stages of technological development, the transnational corporations would have the opportunity to refashion domestic laws and international regulations in their own interests, and not those of the development of the populations of the South.[73]

TRIPS did not stand alone. It came alongside the General Agreement on Trade in Services (GATS) and the Trade Relations Investment Measures (TRIMS). Both of these put pressure on the countries of the South to open up the service sector to private participation, and to give relatively free rein to commercial investment. The latter struck a negative chord among many in the South, largely because of the worry that financial investment no longer seemed to come for long-term development, but only for short-term speculative gain ("hot money").[74] The problem of services also irked the Commission, which wondered why GATT considered the delivery of services to the South, but not the migration of people from the South to the North, as acceptable and as part of TRIMS: "It is essential for developing countries that such asymmetries are removed and that negotiations on services are balanced in coverage to include labour services. Barriers such as immigration laws and consular practices which impede the export of labour services from developing countries should therefore receive the necessary attention in the negotiations."[75] The suggestion might as well have been written in Kamassian.

Between the draft and the final statement not much changed. The only major change was one of emphasis and tone. In the draft, the Commissioners much more directly fingered the role of the United States for discounting the role of the South—both in its initiation of the agenda and in the conduct of its leadership.[76] The South Commission's members did not want to confront the

---

72   "Statement on the Uruguay Round," pp. 12–13.

73   Ibid., pp. 9–10, 13. At the World Health Assembly on May 6, 1981, India's prime minister, Indira Gandhi, put the case for free transfer: "My idea of a better ordered world is one in which medical discoveries would be free of patents and there would be no profiting from life or death." A superb position, but one that was not followed by her during her long tenure as prime minister; she did not insist that Indian medicine be universal and free.

74   As the influential business writer Peter Drucker put it in 1989, "90 percent or more of the transnational economy's financial transactions do not serve what economists would consider an economic function." Peter Drucker, *The New Realities*, London: Heinemann, 1989, p. 121.

75   "Statement on the Uruguay Round," p. 12.

76   For instance, "As early as the beginning of the 1980s, US government officials

powerhouse behind the OECD directly, particularly as the Southern countries began to bow their heads in the various negotiations of the Round. There was no stomach for a fight. There was an objective basis for a resource-strike, but there was no political will for one.

GLOBAL PERESTROIKA

On July 18, 1988, Manmohan Singh held a press conference in Geneva. The principal issue was the failure of the negotiations on debt. Old ways had "exhausted their utility," he pointed out, and there was "no pressure" on the North and its institutions to do "something different." "This is the harsh reality, and unless you organize publically, unless the collective views of the Third World can be articulated in meaningful dialogue, no amount of mere technical solutions will solve the problem of debt." This was run-of-the-mill stuff, already articulated in many press conferences held by the South Commission. But then Singh put down a different marker: "What we in the Third World need is global perestroika, restructuring of international economic relations which would take into account the legitimate aspirations of the four-fifths of humanity that lives in the Third World, for better life for their peoples."[77] The call for a "global perestroika" was bold, even cheeky. In June 1987, Soviet leader Mikhail Gorbachev had presented the idea of perestroika to the Central Committee of the Communist Party. The term means "restructuring," and it referred to the transformation of the political and economic systems within the Soviet Union. If such a momentous occurrence could happen in the USSR, one of the two superpowers, it was not inconceivable that it could happen in inter-state relations, particularly those between the North and the South.

---

and Congressional leaders began floating the idea of a new round of trade negotiations that would bring into the fold of GATT some areas of special concern to the international expansion of US business, notably services, direct foreign investment and intellectual property rights." "Draft: Statement on the Uruguay Round," June 1988, p. 2, SCA. Other emphases, such as "led by the US" (p. 30), disappeared. The finger pointed at the North generally, not directly at the United States, which was leading the fight for the OECD in the 8th GATT Round and fending off European pressure on agriculture.

77 Chakravarti Raghavan, "South Commission Official Calls for Global Perestroika," *SUNS* 1,983 (July 20, 1988). This phrase would be picked up, but then forgotten. Gro Harlem Brundtland used it in her Third World Prize lecture, given at Harare, Zimbabwe, on April 24, 1989. It was time, she said, to "revive the process that stopped halfway in Cancún … [We need] global perestroika." "Brundtland Calls for World Consensus for Growth," *South Letter* 2 (June 1989), p. 11. In 1992, political scientist Robert W. Cox wrote an essay on "Global Perestroika," in *Socialist Register* 28 (1992), but did not give the full context of the term's emergence—*viz.* the South Commission, as a critique of the North's power and intransigence.

By the late 1970s, discussions at the UNCTAD and in the UN had become secondary to the might of arms. Four left-wing revolutions had moved the US to a much more aggressive military posture: Angola (1975), Afghanistan (1978), Iran (1979), and Nicaragua (1979). In Central America, the United States joined with the most reactionary elements among the landowners and the military to suppress the flowering of a second wave of revolutionary movements. Using Honduras as its base, the United States provided arms, logistical support and inspiration to the right-wing paramilitaries of El Salvador and Nicaragua, at the same time turning Honduras and Guatemala into its military encampments.[78] The US-aided violence in the Caribbean would culminate in the invasion of Grenada in 1983 and the invasion of Panama in 1989. Grossly unable to come to terms with a revision in the power equation in the Middle East (notably after the Iranian Revolution), the United States, with Israel, fell back on a militaristic approach, with its attacks on Libya (1981, 1986), the deployment of troops in the Sinai (1982), the Israeli invasion of Lebanon that resulted in a US marine force invasion of the country (1982), and the arming of the *mujahideen* (with Saudi and Pakistani backing) in the mountains of southern Afghanistan. The US provided backing to the most reactionary elements in the Hindu Kush, who were sent to destabilize the already brambled Marxist government in Kabul.[79] In southern Africa, apartheid South Africa's wars against Marxist-inflected national liberation organizations in Angola, South-West Africa, and Mozambique were fierce. The CIA and the Pentagon worked closely with Pretoria's generals. It was part of the new strategy emanating from Washington, DC, called "rollback," abandoning the idea of the mere "containment" of communism in favor of using military force to push back against its exertions—even when these were met with massive popular support. Camouflaged as freedom fighters, and funded by the long arm of Washington, the Contras, UNITA, and the *mujahideen* tried to wreak havoc in areas of the world where reform and revolution had emerged on the table after long periods of suppression.

From the lonely and level snows of Moscow, the faltering Politburo of the Soviet Communist Party sought to extend its reach into events that were running out of its control. In February 1981, the Soviet Foreign Ministry gave voice to the paralysis: "If the Americans invaded Nicaragua, what would

---

78   As the Honduran politician Jorge Arturo Reina put it in 1985, "the US has put its eyes on Nicaragua, its hands on El Salvador, and its feet in Honduras, flattening us." James Dunkerley, *Power in the Isthmus: A Political History of Modern Central America*, London: Verso, 1988, p. 517.

79   The rogues' gallery includes such venerable activists of the Sazman-i Jawanan-i Musulman (Muslim Youth) as Gulbuddin Hekmatyar (who made his name in Kabul University for throwing acid in the faces of women students) and Ahmed Shah Massoud (who would later be lionized in Europe as the Afghan Che Guevara, but whose roots were firmly in the ground of a deeply reactionary fraternity).

we do? What could we do? Nothing."[80] In southern Africa, it was Cuba that took the lead—sometimes with Soviet backing (as with its intervention in Ethiopia), but mostly without Soviet involvement (as with the Cuban entry into Angola, about which the Soviets were not even informed in advance).[81] In March 1979 the Politburo's key members spent days in discussion over the Afghan fiasco. The Marxist leaders in Kabul were at each other's throats, and their hard line against their liberal and radical opponents had turned potential allies into enemies. When the US- and Iranian-backed reactionaries took the field in southern Afghanistan and Herat, the Kabul Marxists were at their wits' end. They wanted Soviet intervention. The Soviet leadership was stuck, unsure of what the Red Army might be called upon to accomplish.[82] They were aware that any intervention would be illegal (since, as Andrei Gromyko put it, "Afghanistan has not been subject to any aggression. This is its internal affair, a revolutionary internal conflict, a battle of one group of the population against another. Incidentally, the Afghans haven't officially addressed us on bringing in troops").[83] Gromyko highlighted one of the principle reasons not to intervene: "all the nonaligned countries will be against us." Already isolated politically and struggling economically, the USSR's leadership did not want to break the ties that still held between the East and the South. By the late summer of 1979, a group within the Politburo decided to up the ante, and in December the Red Army crossed the Amu Darya into Afghanistan.[84] It was a fatal move.

The Soviet entry into Afghanistan divided the NAM states. It weakened their bloc in the UN, where eighteen countries (led by Algeria, India, and Iraq) refused to go along with the US resolution asking for the Soviet withdrawal. In the NAM, the Soviets pushed their allies to seek Pakistan's ouster, since it was an active part of the US project in Afghanistan. Fidel Castro, as the head of NAM from 1979 to 1983, could not find any way to use his influence in Moscow and in the NAM capitals to mediate (the Soviets feared that Fidel might seek a rapprochement between Islamabad and Kabul, cutting Moscow out of the

80   Dunkerley, *Power in the Isthmus*, p. 267.

81   Piero Gleijeses, *The Cuban Drumbeat*, Calcutta: Seagull Books, 2009, p. 37.

82   Andrei Kirilenko put it plainly on March 17, 1979: "The question arises, whom will our troops be fighting against if we send them there? Against the insurgents? Or have they been joined by a large number of religious fundamentalists, that is, Muslims and among them large numbers of ordinary people? Thus, we will be required to wage war in significant part against the people." "Meeting of the Politburo of the Central Committee of the Communist Party of the Soviet Union," March 17, 1979, National Security Archives (NSA), Washington, DC. Translated by Svetlana Savranskaya.

83   "Meeting of the Politburo," March 18, 1979, NSA.

84   "Gromyko-Andropov-Ustinov-Ponomarev Report to CPSU CC on the Situation in Afghanistan, June 28, 1979. Top Secret. Special File," *Cold War International History Project Bulletin* 8–9 (Winter 1996–97), pp. 152–3.

picture[85]). Out of such misery, the very shallow political unity in the NAM, and in the South in general, became clearly apparent. The fruits of such chaos favored the US and its Atlantic partners. They tightened their embrace of the Islamist Right in Afghanistan and Pakistan, of the military landlords in Central America, and of the South African apartheid regime. (In 1986, Congressman Dick Cheney voted against a resolution calling for the release of Nelson Mandela, whom Cheney called a "terrorist." This is the proud boast that can be made by today's Republican Party: that it supported apartheid South Africa right up to its demise.)

The emboldened North pushed against the UN institutions, rendering them close to irrelevant. In April 1975, Ford, Kissinger, and Daniel Patrick Moynihan, the US ambassador to the UN, met in the White House. Moynihan complained: "One mistake we make is acting like the General Assembly has semi-legislative powers."[86] Kissinger concurred: "We need a strategy. In principle, I think we should move things from the General Assembly to the Security Council. It is important to see that we have our confidence and nerve." A decade later, that is what happened. In 1987, when the South Commission first met, the majority of its 159 states voted in the General Assembly with the United States only 18.5 percent of the time.[87] This foreshadowed the shift of power in the UN from the General Assembly (where the G77 held sway) to the Security Council (where the Permanent Five—the United States, the USSR, the United Kingdom, France, and China—held the power of veto). UN Secretary-General Javier Pérez de Cuéllar was pushed against the wall by the Reagan administration. Not wanting to alienate the US, Cuéllar tried to move many important decisions to the Security Council, and, unwittingly perhaps, performed the task, envisaged by Kissinger, of shrouding the General Assembly.[88] By the time Boutros Boutros-Ghali had taken over as secretary-general at the United Nations, the US promised to make up for its lapses. For political reasons it had failed to pay its dues (set at a quarter of the UN budget). It now said it would do so (it should be pointed out that a full 50 percent of the UN staff were US citizens, so this is not US payment for the salaries of foreign nationals).[89]

85   Roy Allison, *The Soviet Union and the Strategy of Non-Alignment in the Third World*, Cambridge: Cambridge University Press, 1988, p. 91.

86   "Memorandum of Conversation in The Oval Office: American Strategy at the UN," April 12, 1975, White House, National Security Adviser's Memoranda of Conversation Collection, Box 10, Gerald Ford Presidential Library.

87   Paul Lewis, "UN Support for US Hits New Low," *New York Times*, May 16, 1989, p. A10.

88   Javier Pérez de Cuéllar, *Pilgrimage for Peace*, New York: St. Martin's Press, 1997, p. 10.

89   Boutros Boutros-Ghali, *Unvanquished: A US-UN Saga*, New York: Random House, 1999, p. 67.

Kissinger also wanted the US to "get hold of the Specialized Agencies." First among them were those UN agencies that had development as their primary agenda. UNCTAD, badly bruised, was his chief target. In September 1984, the US pushed for UNCTAD to become a clearing-house rather than a place to negotiate agreements (a role that would move to the G7-dominated GATT).[90] The pressure wore on the organization. At its 1987 meeting in Geneva, the South came without any prepared drafts. No resolutions were adopted—only a toothless Final Act. By 1989, UNCTAD's new head, Kenneth Dadzie, urged the South "to get to grips with the hard realities of the international market place."[91] By February 1992, UNCTAD would blur its mission into that of the GATT and the "business civilization" of the North.[92] The secretariat of the South capitulated. In this miserable context, the South Commission conducted its deliberations.

In 1988 the Commission convened its second meeting, in Kuala Lumpur. "The role of raw economic power, and its unabashed application in combination with military power," the Commission found, had "raised doubts about the validity of some of the fundamental premises on which the whole edifice of the United Nations and post–World War II cooperation has been built."[93] It was not only the Commissioners who understood that "the spirit of multilateralism has

---

90   The pressure on UNCTAD began at its origin, in the early 1960s. By the mid 1960s, after UNCTAD I, with Raúl Prebisch in charge, the US put pressure on UNCTAD to merge some of its operations under GATT. According to Prebisch's deputy, R. Krishnamurti, this "would have hampered the dynamic evolution of UNCTAD." "UNCTAD-GATT Relationship (1965–68)," p. 1, R. Krishnamurti Papers (in the author's possession). Prebisch went along with the move for some kind of relationship, only because he was well aware of the politics of alienating the US. UNCTAD was open to being a partner, and went to the GATT Trade and Development Committee meeting at Punta del Este in January 1968. Here the US finally put its foot down, insisting that if UNCTAD did not bow down before GATT it would not allow a joint programming committee. A sense of the hardball being played here is visible in the "Note on Conversation with GATT Officials on Friday, 20 May 1966," and in the letter from Wyndham White (GATT director-general) to Prebisch (UNCTAD director-general) on March 9, 1967. Both documents in the Krishnamurti Papers.

91   "UNCTAD Says Trade Curbs Have Increased," *South Letter* 1 (April 1989), p. 8.

92   "Strengthening National and International Action and Multilateral Cooperation for a Healthy, Secure and Equitable World Economy," the 8th Session of UNCTAD, produced documents that might just have come from the GATT. The idea of "business civilization" is developed in Susan Strange, *States and Markets*, New York: Blackwell, 1988. It is no surprise that the head of UNCTAD from 2005 has been Dr. Supachai Panitchpakdi, who was previously the head of the World Trade Organization (2002–2005).

93   "Draft Work Programme of the South Commission and a Programme of Studies," February 1, 1988, p. 4, SCA, South II/3, Restricted.

been weakened and the UN system has been deliberately undermined."[94] The Oval Office echoed the shrill noises emanating from the Heritage Foundation. The South wanted to revive the UN organizations and to move decision-making to the venues where the South acted with as much influence as the North. The tone of the discussions suggested that this reasonable suggestion would find no takers among those with real power in the world.

The World Bank and the IMF needed a major overhaul, but "it seems unlikely that significant change can be achieved in the foreseeable future." Nevertheless, the Commission felt it imperative that "the critique of the existing structures should be reiterated at some point."[95] The catalog of the North's mendacity grew longer and longer: "The Group of Seven regard the management of the world economy as their province; bilateral initiatives and decisions are increasingly replacing multilateral ones, even superseding fora in which the North holds control, such as GATT, the IMF and the World Bank. United Nations structures tend to be ignored altogether. The North-South dialogue has been totally abandoned by the North."[96] The tragedy was compounded when the very language of "reform" was hijacked by the project of the American right wing: "in part, the 'reform' has been inspired by the general trend for less government and therefore less international organization in international relations."[97]

Given the Commission's bleak portrait of the situation, reflected in their final report in 1990, it is remarkable that one of the great distractions of the Commission's work was over the question of imperialism and neo-colonialism. At the fifth meeting of the Commission—in Maputo, Mozambique—the members were informed of a disagreement among them on the tone to be taken. "Caution was advised by some members about the use of terms like 'neo-colonialism' in describing the state of North-South relations."[98] The Commonwealth Secretariat had the most problems. Dr. B. Persaud of its Economic Affairs Division wrote to Manmohan Singh after reading the first draft of Chapter 1 of the Commission's report, "The Chapter sees the problems of the South too much in terms of domination and oppression from the North. This material needs to have a better balance and could be written more convincingly and persuasively."[99] A few days later, Commissioner Ramphal, also

94   Ibid., p. 9.
95   "Issues in South-North Relations and the Management of the International System," November 7, 1988, p. 16, SCA, South IV/7.
96   Ibid., p. 2.
97   "The Future of the United Nations System from the Perspective of the Economic South," November 7, 1988, p. 4, SCA, South IV/10.
98   "Chairman's Report on the Fifth Meeting of the South Commission," p. 5, SCA, South V/12, Confidential.
99   B. Persaud to Manmohan Singh, June 1, 1989, SCA.

head of the Commonwealth Secretariat, wrote a longer and more pointed note. He accepted that the term "neo-colonialism" is a good "analogy," but said that its use was not "prudent." "As to prudence, I believe it gives the Chapter the appearance of yesterday's thinking expressed in yesterday's language. It could, therefore, be a 'turn-off'—and not only for readers in the North."[100] What Ramphal wanted was the South Commission to "get away from the NIEO type of presentation."[101]

Nyerere, on the other hand, caviled at the expunged text.[102] Carlos Rafael Rodríguez, Ismail Abdalla, Devaki Jain, and others provided a fuller sense of why it was important to have a sharper final report. Not for them the unthreatening language that would be palatable to the North. They wanted spicier fare. Both Rafael Rodríguez and Abdalla wrote long notes on the first draft, and their analyses were similar. Both felt that the report needed to be frank. In Abdalla's rarefied terminology, "We should not therefore endeavour to edulcorate words" (edulcorate = sweeten).[103] Absent the concept of imperialism, how would the Commission explain the debt crisis other than by blaming the South for poor financial management and a bloated state sector? This was indeed the position of Commissioner Ghazali Shafie, who pointed out that the countries of the South "should not always for the sake of convenience blame the countries of the North for all the ills in the present state of their economies."[104] With such major disagreements was the Commission filled in its last years, as the Commissioners struggled to come to terms with their stance towards the North and to produce some kind of program from their deliberations. In short, the North was united and the South was divided.

---

100   S. Ramphal to Manmohan Singh, June 12, 1989, pp. 1–2, SCA.

101   Ibid., p. 3.

102   Nyerere's assistant, Joan Wicken, wrote to Manmohan Singh:

The Chairman, in talking to me, said he couldn't put his finger on what it was that was worrying him about the draft now, but somehow has the feeling that the tone has been changed so that it no longer gives leadership, or makes people want to *do* something. He is not sure whether this is still because he doesn't like pretending that there is no neo-colonialism or need for liberation, or whether it is more than leaving out those words. If you could 'beef it up' a bit, and make it more exciting and challenging it would be good. But I don't know whether that is possible while still leaving it acceptable to the 'opposition' [namely, Ramphal and Correa].

Joan Wicken to Manmohan Singh, December 2, 1989, "Chapter 1: Comments of Chairman and J. E. Wicken," SCA.

103   Ismail Sabri Abdalla, "Some Reflections on the Draft Report," June 29, 1989, p. 5, SCA. Rafael Rodríguez was clearer, complaining that the "concept of imperialism is missing completely" and that "references to the New International Economic Order have been avoided." Carlos Rafael Rodríguez to Manmohan Singh, July 10, 1989, p. 10, SCA. Carlos Rafael Rodríguez, "Opinions," 1989, p. 1, SCA.

104   Ghazali Shafie to Manmohan Singh, August 18, 1989, p. 1, SCA.

THE CHALLENGE OF THE SOUTH

As was the practice in such commissions, the Commissioners formed various working groups to tackle different aspects of the problem. They hired outside consultants to assist them and produced working papers for discussion at their various meetings. In preparing a draft of the final report, towards the end of 1988, the Commission farmed out the working papers to various individuals. Nyerere and Joan Wicken wrote the first draft of Chapter 1. It was the most contentious chapter, with Ramphal and Nyerere having gone toe to toe during the Delhi meeting of the Commission. This is when Ramphal was angry about the "NIEO type of presentation." Chapter 2 was drafted by Manmohan Singh and Carlos Fortin, with input from the UNCTAD secretariat (notably its statisticians). The Mexican economist Jamie Ros drafted Chapter 3, on national development, and Chapter 4, on South-South cooperation, was put together by Branislav Gosovic and the Bangladeshi economist Rehman Sobhan. Carlos Fortin wrote Chapter 5, on North-South relations, and Manmohan Singh was responsible for Chapter 6. Towards the end of the process, Nyerere was confined to his hotel room, convalescing from prostate surgery. Manmohan Singh was in London, resting after a heart-bypass operation. This did not stop them. From his bed, Manmohan Singh wrote a draft out by hand (his favorite method of work, according to many in the Commission's secretariat).

In early 1989, versions of the draft went out to the Commissioners. Not long after, reports came in from them with their views. Cuba's Carlos Rafael Rodríguez wrote a hard-hitting note in mid 1989: "In our Objectives and Terms of Reference, we offered to seek 'to fashion a well-founded, realistic and practical strategy and programme of action for the Third World.' I believe that the reader will find a well-founded, realistic and practical strategy for the South, but not the programme he is looking for. We owe the drafting of such a programme."[105] There was certainly not much of a well-elaborated program in the draft; whether there was a strategy or not was another matter. The draft tried to bridge a major ideological divide between the Commissioners, and in doing so it had to sacrifice a clear strategy and definitive program. The divisions in the Commission represented clear-cut divisions in the governmental corridors of the South, if not also on some in its streets. The Left put its shoulder against the door to neoliberalism, but the "pragmatists" tried their best to open it wide.

---

105   Rafael Rodríguez, "Opinions," p. 10.

THE SOCIAL CONSEQUENCES OF THE ECONOMICS

Early into the Commission's work, it became clear that a broad line divided the Commissioners. One day at Mont Pèlerin, Devaki Jain asked Sonny Ramphal what paper he read in the morning. "The London *Times*," he replied. She read the *Hindustan Times*. "That's the problem, you see," Jain remembers saying, "The view of the South is very different for you."[106] Jain, with Rodríguez, Abdalla, Savané, Makoni, and a few others, shared a vision for the South that was both censorious of nostalgia for what had been and eager to frame a new developmental path that was grounded in the participation of the people. Bureaucratic politics and instrumental economics, with no concern for social and cultural consequences, were of no interest to them.[107] They had other visions for the South.

Devaki Jain distinguished between these two lines, and the two kinds of people who advanced them. There were the doves, who favored people-centered development, and there were the hawks, who wanted growth-led development. The doves "propose a more dispersed form of growth, a growth which may not show itself in the trade statistics." They "would emphasize the production of health and food, and provision of basic education as necessary preconditions of economic growth and the growth of human capabilities." The hawks, on the other hand, "push and pull the economies and societies of the poor countries towards high rates of growth accompanied by the manufacture of industrial products and their exports."[108] The god of the hawks was the market in the

---

106   Devaki Jain, author interview. At an informal gathering in Cancún in 1981, Nyerere reported that the first thing he did each morning was listen to the BBC. The Canadian prime minister, Pierre Trudeau, joked that Nyerere thought of the British prime minister each morning. Thatcher replied, "Julius, I too think of you every morning." Alan Riding, "Cancún Meeting Fails to Resolve Key Differences," *New York Times*, October 24, 1981, p. 5.

107   One example was Rodríguez's critique of the public sector, a holy cow in some sections of the South:

In dealing with the problem of privatization, I believe that it is important to mention the mistakes in the management of the public sector. Public sector is a recent phenomenon. Privatization and external investment in private hands was common during the first fifty years of this century, not only in Latin America but also in Asia. It has not worked. It has led to deformations in the structure of production. We don't deny that certain parts of the public sector that were unduly nationalized must be privatized, but *the tendency to privatize* is wrong.

Rodríguez to Manmohan Singh, July 10, 1989, p. 18.

108   Devaki Jain, "Can We Have a Women's Agenda for Global Development?" *Development* 1 (1991), pp. 74–8.

north Atlantic. The doves placed their faith in the voices and activity of the grassroots.

At the center of the doves' vision was popular participation. Social movements had flooded the South, and Third World networks of various kinds had tried to forge linkages among these movements, as well as between the movements and their less receptive governments.[109] What does the South have? Abdalla asked in 1988. "The answer is obvious, but too often overlooked: *the energy of the people*. Hence, self-reliance is, before everything else, reliance on the people."[110] The South was rich with physical resources, but its real strength was in its people. The people referred to here were the masses, of course—but not just the masses as an undifferentiated block. New sociopolitical formations emerged as the older forms, such as industrial workers, were displaced by the new geography of production. Trade unions of the Fordist period had a much harder time marshaling the strength of their workers, and were thus less able to put pressure on the much more mobile transnational firms; subcontracting made it hard to influence the behemoths, who hid behind disposable contractors who hired equally disposable workers. The informal sector eclipsed the formal sector not only numerically, but also in importance. The proletariat of the earlier epoch gave way to the precarious proletariat, the "precariat," whose lives were governed by an unsecured social landscape: temporary and part-time jobs, unregulated and non-unionized jobs—and of course the jobless populations who lived off the books, earning when they could, living by their wits. This precariousness, as Guy Standing puts it, "implies a lack of a secure work-based identity."[111] New sociopolitical formations have become meaningful as the historically powerful idea of the "worker" have given way to that of the precarious earner. Important examples include the women's movement, the movement of the indigenous, and the movement of the slums—among others.

Women. Capital's increasing reliance on women workers, whether in the industrial or rural sectors, put pressure on the women's networks to take the new developments seriously and to organize this new international working class. Such discussions made a fleeting appearance at the 1975 World Conference on the International Women's Year (Mexico City) and at the 1980 Mid-Decade Conference for Women (Copenhagen). After Mexico City, in 1976, the UN set up UNIFEM, the UN Development Fund for Women, to take charge of the outlay of funds in the area of gender and development ("special consideration should

---

109   Jain, "South Commission's First Meet," p. 5.

110   Ismail-Sabri Abdalla, "What Development?" 1988, p. 10, SCA, South III/3, Annex 5.

111   Guy Standing, *The Precariat: The New Dangerous Class*, London: Bloomsbury, 2011, p. 9.

be given to those [projects] which benefit rural women, poor women in urban areas and other marginal groups of women, especially the disadvantaged").[112]

Solidarity was not going to be easy. In 1982 the Association of African Women for Research and Development (with the Dag Hammarskjöld Foundation) held a seminar in Dakar, Senegal. It was led by the Association's president, Marie-Angélique Savané, who would later become a member of the South Commission. She brought together leading thinkers from across the South to discuss the idea of "another development for women." In her remarks, Savané noted the gaps that had widened between women of the North and the South: "The drift of industries such as textiles and electronics toward the South aggravates the conflicts between women of the North and South, and creates a formidable obstacle to attempts to form a policy of solidarity between workers of the North and South."[113] The seminar was occupied by a "lively debate" on solidarity along the North-South axis. The terms of the debate were straightforward, even if Savané tends to draw the lines too firmly and without nuance:

> In Europe, women have mainly concentrated their efforts on such problems as the equality between the sexes, the organization of household work and child care and the right to have or not to have children. In the Third World, women's demands have been more explicitly political, with work, education and health as major issues per se, and not necessarily so linked to their specific impact on women. In addition, women of the Third World perceive imperialism as the main enemy of their continents and especially of women—something which is rarely fully understood in the North.[114]

From 1985 to 1995, the UN process foundered on the rocks of these broken bridges. Nonetheless, it allowed activist women from the South to gather together and attempt to build a platform against the new dispensation—often, though not always, with allies from the North.

At the 1985 End of Decade Conference in Nairobi, a strong sentiment emerged that women should not be seen as adjutants in the sociopolitical response to the new conditions, but as central to it. Secretary-general of the Nairobi conference, Leticia Shahani, from the Philippines, pointed to the "paradox between the international commitment to the advancement of women and the increasing structural imbalance in the global economy."[115] "Women's rights" had taken

---

112   UN General Assembly Resolution 31/133, "Voluntary Fund for the United Nations Decade for Women," 1: vi (December 16, 1976).

113   Marie-Angélique Savané, "The Dakar Seminar on 'Another Development' with Women,'" *Development Dialogue* 1–2 (1982), p. 8.

114   Ibid., p. 9.

115   Judith Zinsser, "From Mexico to Copenhagen to Nairobi: The United Nations Decade for Women, 1975–1985," *Journal of World History* 13: 1 (2002), p. 162. Shahani

on a sacred aura; everyone was in favor of them. But not everyone was willing to admit how the planetary shifts in economic and social relations dispro-portionately and negatively affected the lives of women. The new economic and social realities pushed the national delegations of women and the various non-governmental organizations from the global South (at what was known as Forum '85) to explore the crisis in the lives of women in their countries. Both the structural transformation of the world economy, which put special pres-sure on women as workers and as social and familial actors, and the political developments of the decade deepened and radicalized women's organizations.

The decade's activities allowed women from the South the "right to speak out and the right to be heard" (*le droit à parole*), as Senegalese sociologist Fatou Sow put it.[116] In recognition of this development, Gita Sen and Caren Grown of DAWN (Development Alternatives with Women for a New era) noted in September 1986 that women across the world had managed to "forge grassroots women's movements and worldwide networks such as never existed before."[117] Devaki Jain, as one of the initiators of DAWN, and Savané brought their rela-tionship to this new movement into the Commission. Jain reported to DAWN at its several meetings, and was even referred to in a DAWN publication as its "representative to the South Commission."[118] Women, as producers and

---

came from a remarkable family. Her mother, Angela Valdez-Ramos, was a prominent Filipino campaigner for women's rights, and her father Narciso Ramos was a well-regarded journalist and liberal politician. Her brother, Fidel Ramos, was a military man who executed martial law on behalf of Ferdinand Marcos, but then broke with him. He was the president of the Philippines from 1992 to 1998. Leticia Shahani was a high-level UN official who returned to domestic politics when she realized that "[a]t the UN, despite all the talk about 'one world' and 'the global village,' unless your own country is strong and has developed its own stance, it doesn't have much say in international affairs." Steven Erlanger, "From a Life of Privilege a Woman of Substance," *New York Times*, November 9, 1989.

116   Zinsser, "From Mexico," p. 166; and Nilüfer Çagatay, Caren Grown, and Aida Santiago, "The Nairobi Women's Conference: Toward a Global Feminism?" *Feminist Studies* 12: 2 (Summer 1986), pp. 405–6.

117   Gita Sen and Caren Grown, *Women, Crises and Alternative Visions: Third World Women's Perspectives*, New York: Monthly Review Press, 1987, p. 22.

118   Devaki Jain, "South Commission," *Dawn*, April–June 1989, p. 3. See also, more significantly, her paper "Defining Development," delivered at DAWN's African Regional Meeting on Food, Energy and Debt Crises in Relation to Women, at the Institute for African Studies, University of Ibadan, September 27–29, 1988. Jain pointed to the "vital role" played by women that was being "reduced, sometimes totally displaced without providing an alternative" (p. 8). It was essential for DAWN and the women's movement to take the fight to the center of things and redefine development with women's interests at their heart. Much the same point was made by Savané in her 1989 note to the South Commission, "The Gender Dimension of Development," SCA.

citizens, needed to be at the heart of the new pathway envisaged by the South Commission.[119] That was one of Jain and Savané's objectives, but it was not to be fully realized. As the Finnish feminist and UN advisor Hilkka Pietilä put it in her note on the Commission's report, there remained a tendency that aimed "only at equality of women and men on existing, that is, male terms." It failed to shake the foundations of development and offer an alternative, people-centered framework.[120]

The Fourth World. In 1974, indigenous leaders from the Americas, Australia, and New Zealand held a conference to form the World Council of Indigenous Peoples (WCIP). One of the founders of the WCIP was Chief George Manuel, who had just authored a book entitled *The Fourth World: An Indian Reality.*[121] One of Manuel's comrades, Marie Smallface, had been in Zambia for a few years, where she had met and married ANC activist Jake Marule. At a gathering organized by them in Ottawa, Manuel had a conversation with the Tanzanian diplomat Mbuto Milando, who first uttered the electric phrase, the "fourth world." It enabled Manuel to gather indigenous or the native people under a concept: "When Native people come into their own, on the basis of their own cultures and traditions, that will be the Fourth World."[122] The WPIC spent its first decade building alliances with indigenous people across the planet.[123] It was a quick sell, as groups hastily found the WPIC a receptive home. The moral claims made by the WPIC pushed the UN to host a conference in 1977 entitled "Discrimination Against Indigenous Populations in the Americas," out of which was created the process that led in 1982 to the UN Working Group on Indigenous Populations. Rather quickly, in response to struggles against land acquisition and resource theft, the WCIP and the UN Working Group began to articulate a politics of resource preservation and use, rather than the older

---

119   In 1994, the UN secretary-general appointed Noeleen Heyzer to run UNIFEM. Dr. Heyzer, a member of DAWN, led the work on women in the informal sector in the global South with her path-breaking book, *Working Women in South-East Asia: Development, Subordination and Emancipation*, Milton Keynes: Open University Press, 1986, and then later in her book (co-edited with Gita Sen), *Gender, Economic Growth and Poverty: Market Growth and State Planning in Asia and the Pacific*, New Delhi: Kali for Women, 1994.

120   Hilkka Pietilä, "Women: The Missing Element," in South Centre, ed., *Facing the Challenge: Responses to the Report of the South Commission*, London: Zed Books, 1993, pp. 92–3.

121   George Manuel and Michael Posluns, *The Fourth World: An Indian Reality*, New York: Free Press, 1974.

122   Ibid., p. 236.

123   Ronald Niezen, *The Origins of Indigenism*, Berkeley: University of California Press, 2003.

politics of morality.[124] Mining and timber concessions began to make their way into regions held by indigenous peoples, often without their consent and certainly without much benefit to them. This became the central theme of unrest, from Ecuador to Indonesia. It would be the basis for the indigenous peoples' coming into their own, as Chief Manuel put it. In July 1989 the movement went further, with indigenous women taking center stage in the First International Indigenous Women's Conference. Here the activists recognized that women in their communities led and participated in the bulk of the struggles against the invasion of their lands.

Native people and indigenousness did not enter the lexicon of the South Commission, but the general themes of the Fourth World movement did come up in the discussion. Abdalla's note from 1989 gestured in that direction, with his assessment of the virulent destructiveness of capital towards the environment.[125] But even there the gesture did not point to the indigenous movements that were fighting against big dam construction, iron ore mines, clear-cutting of forests, and so on. Tragically, the actions of the indigenous faced as much resistance from the national governments of the South as from the transnational firms that treated their land as *terra nullius*. Chief Manuel came to Tanzania in 1971, met with Nyerere, and discussed the idea of *ujamaa* (family-hood), which he later said influenced his own ideas of the Fourth World. But Nyerere's consideration for this Canadian Native leader did not extend to the Barabaig, a cattle-herding clan of the Datoga community, who moved across Tanzania at will. In 1968 Nyerere's regime removed the Barabaig from their homelands.[126] It was the kind of displacement that had become commonplace in the South, and it is precisely what had spurred the independent political organizing among those who would seize on the category of the indigenous, join the WCIP, and work through the channels opened up by the UN. The South Commission, aware of the issues raised both by these struggles and by the new social actors produced within them, nevertheless did not see them as essential to the new project.

Slum dwellers. In the 1970s a series of IMF riots broke out in the cities of Africa and Latin America. These were often called "bread riots" as well, because the

---

124   Andrea Muehlebach, "'Making Place' at the United Nations: Indigenous Cultural Politics at the UN Working Group on Indigenous Populations," *Cultural Anthropology* 1: 3 (2001), p. 416.

125   Ismail Sabri Abdalla, "Reflections on Maputo Draft Report," June 29, 1989, pp. 6–7, SCA.

126   Jim Igoe, "Becoming Indigenous Peoples: Difference, Inequality and the Globalization of East African Identity Politics," *African Affairs* 420 (2006), p. 413; and Moringe Parkipuny, "The Human Rights Situation of Indigenous Peoples in Africa," *Fourth World Journal* 4: 1 (1989).

people who took to the streets were angry about the failure of their states to control the prices of basic foodstuffs. At least 150 such riots took place between 1976 and 1982. These "riots" have been described as "large-scale collective actions including political demonstrations, general strikes, and riots, which are animated by grievances over state policies of economic liberalization, implemented in response to debt crisis and market reforms urged by international agencies."[127] They were directed not only at IMF-led policies, but also at the urban planning policies of the now more confident domestic elites. Slum-clearance programs were commonplace, either to reclaim the city for the expansion of the domestic elite or for mega-events (expos, sporting events, international summits). Bulldozers and guns came to demolish worker housing and to eject workers to the outskirts of cities. The combination of slum-clearance and the rise in prices of basic foods created the conditions for the emergence of the politics of the slum, in which workers from the informal and formal sectors found common cause and forged new social identities of protest.

In 1978, as a direct consequence of the crisis of urban life, the UN created HABITAT, an intergovernmental agency, to come to terms with the explosion of cities and mega-cities, the centrality of the poor in the cities, and the instability occasioned by the lack of a social-democratic urban policy. Two years before this, the UN hosted a conference in Vancouver, Canada, on "Human Settlements," at which Barbara Ward convened a group that included the architect Richard Buckminster Fuller. Reflecting on their work, Buckminster Fuller pointed to the explosion of squatter settlements, or slums, and to the way in which "people coming to squat are very ingenious in the way they employ the limited available materials to provide shelter." Based on this analysis, and rejecting the fear of the slums and their inhabitants, the Ward committee called upon the governments of the world to "decree that all the land which these squatters occupy be made public lands, on which the people are allowed to remain."[128]

---

127   John Walton and David Seddon, *Free Markets and Food Riots: The Politics of Global Adjustment*, Oxford: Blackwell, 1994, p. 39.

128   Richard Buckminster Fuller, "Accommodating Human Unsettlement," *Town Planning Review* 49: 1 (January 1978), p. 55. The Ward Committee came at this problem a decade before the Peruvian economist Hernando de Soto Polar wrote *The Other Path: The Invisible Revolution in the Third World*, New York: HarperCollins, 1989. De Soto argued that the government should give the squatters property rights as individual titles, so that this would provide equity to the new owners that could be used as collateral for bank loans towards economic activity. In Spanish, the title is *El Otro Sendero* (1986)—a reference to Peru's guerrillas, the Sendero Luminoso. Jan Breman, using Indian material, makes the opposite argument, pointing out that it is not so much rights in land (property) that are lacking among squatters who are also informal workers, but rights in the workplace. Jan Breman, *The Labouring Poor in India: Patterns of Exploitation, Subordination and Exclusion*, New Delhi: Oxford University Press, 2003, p. 201. For more

Squatters had entered world history as political actors, but no one seemed willing to greet them.

In late February 1989 the government of Venezuela, led by Carlos Andres Pérez, raised the price of petrol by 100 percent. Buses of course had to raise their fares. This came a week after the government announced that it had been taken in hand by the IMF. Students in the city began a sit-down strike on February 27, and were quickly joined by the general public. Caracas was the chief locus, but protests took place simultaneously in other cities. The *marginales* streamed into the city and took charge of public space.[129] At 6 p.m. on February 28, President Pérez took over the television and radio networks and, standing with his cabinet, announced the suspension of constitutional guarantees and imposed martial law. The president looked tired, and old.

The police went out and blood flowed on the streets. As Margarita Lopez Maya argues, the "repressive overreaction, with substantial human rights violations, was in fact part of [a general] institutional weakness." An inability to deal with the broader political and economic crisis produced a state unable to deal with its social consequences: "The lack of action at the beginning of the protest has led to the brutal repression of the days following, revealing the incompetence of the public institutions in general."[130] Pérez, one of Nyerere's key partners in the South Commission, had been utterly discredited by the *Caracazo*. He had no plan to get Venezuela out of its predicament. From his sick-bed in a military encampment, Lieutenant Hugo Chávez heard of the uprising. When he went back to his duties a few days later, the presidential guard complained that they longer wished to shoot at civilians. They wanted another dispensation.[131] This is not how the president saw the event. Pérez saw the *Caracazo* as the work of hooligans, the formidable *antisociales*. He had no

---

on the slums in the modern age, see Alain Durand-Lasserve, *L'exclusion des pauvres dans les villes du tiers-monde*, Paris: l'Harmattan, 1986.

129   In the 1989 urban uprisings in Argentina, much the same kind of mayhem ensued. One activist told the press, "We are *marginalized*, but not *marginals*. We are hungry, but we are not suicidal." Sergo Serulnikov, "When Looting Becomes a Right: Urban Poverty and Food Riots in Argentina," *Latin American Perspectives* 21: 3 (Summer 1994), pp. 74–5. Frantz Fanon wrote of the slums that "circle the towns tirelessly, hoping that one day or another they will be let in" to their colonial cities. Fanon, *The Wretched of the Earth*, New York: Grove, 1965, p. 103. Fanon wrote of men. In Venezuela's cities of the parasitic oil bourgeoisie, it was women who took the lead, as they did in the *Caracazo*.

130   Margarita Lopez Maya, "The Venezuelan Caracazo of 1989: Popular Protest and Institutional Weakness," *Journal of Latin American Studies* 35: 1 (2003), p. 129; and "Venezuela After the Caracazo: Forms of Protest in a Deinstitutionalized Context," *Bulletin of Latin American Research* 21: 2, 2002.

131   Richard Gott, *Hugo Chávez and the Bolivarian Revolution*, London: Verso, 2005, p. 47.

control of the events of Caracas. He had no understanding of the new social identity, the politics of the urban poor. Others in the Commission had a sense of this development, but it did not frame their discussions. The urban poor were not their allies; they were simply a symptom of the problem.

Women, the Fourth World, and the slum dwellers raised issues of deprivation and environmental collapse, resource disparities, and social maladies. It is because of these upsurges that the South Commission's Abdalla could say that the people must take back their "legitimate place in development, both as agent and as beneficiary." Putting the people at the center must not be simply rhetorical—it had to find a basis in reality. These were the agents, but they were missing from the narrative.

Rather than turn to the activists and organizations in this upsurge, the Commissioners went to Poona Wignaraja, a Sri Lankan scholar at the United Nations University who had previously run the Society for International Development. If one were to remain within the Brandt framework, Wignaraja pointed out, "one does not need to find a great deal of new thinking."[132] The Brandt phrase was simple—"redistribution with growth," a form of international Keynesianism with a program as old as the 1930s. An alternative proposal would go to the "creative energies of the people, local resources and local knowledge." If people formed their own organizations, they would be able to build countervailing power, which "leads to a healthier democracy." Wignaraja offered several concrete examples, of two discrete types. One came in the guise of the land invasions that were the rural cognate of the slum rebellions. In the 1970s, landless peasants captured private land in places such as Anta (Peru) and Attock (Pakistan). The capture of the land was followed by its creative use, and by new experiments in local government. Left-wing parties were part of these struggles, and they had a base in the mass organizing work of affiliated peasant organizations. The other kind of example came from voluntary organizations led by charismatic leaders, such as the Deedar Comprehensive Village Development Cooperative Society, formed in Bangladesh by a remarkable former tea-stall owner, Mohammed Yeasin, in 1960. It was a precursor to Muhammad Yusuf's Grameen Bank, formed in 1976.[133] Wignaraja gestured towards these and other developments, but he did not fully analyze them in terms of their origins (as the products of mass movements, of charismatic leaders, or of spontaneous uprisings). Wignaraja's faith in the "people" as an abstraction overwhelmed his analysis; and yet there was something very pow-

---

132   Poona Wignaraja, "Participatory People-Centered Development," South III/6, Para. 5, Sections B and C, VIII, October 25, 1988, p. 4, SCA.

133   Much of the material came from Poona Wignaraja, "Towards a New Praxis of Rural Development," *Annals of Public and Cooperative Economics* 56: 1–2 (January 1985).

erful about the suggestion that, if one looked closely at these developments, one might see the seeds of a new paradigm. As the dispossessed pressed to get their views onto the agenda, they would run into the limits of the current system and engage those limits politically. In that sense, participation was "a basic need."[134]

One of the reasons that Wignaraja's idea of the "people" hastily went into the abstract mode was that most of the Commissioners were suspicious of the newly promoted non-governmental sector. From the mid 1970s onward, the World Bank offered a populist antidote to its critique of the inefficient Third World state: the sector of the people, which would be harnessed through non-governmental organizations (NGOs). From the mid 1970s to the late 1980s, the NGO sector provided neoliberalism with its community face. The language of empowerment, the grassroots, and people power disguised arguments about the dismemberment of national economies and state-run welfare schemes. NGOs often became conduits of official (government) and unofficial (private donor) foreign aid, which was often canalized through the donor's interests and not the actual needs of the area where the NGO worked.[135] Little wonder that the Commissioners worried about the insinuation of nefarious agendas in the name of the people. If, on the other hand, they had understood the "people" concretely to mean those who were in the midst of crucial struggles in mass movements to protect their livelihoods or to ensure that their everyday lives were not compromised by consumerism and avarice, they would have been able to be much less vague in their formulations. Wignaraja wrote off both the NGOs (Grameen) and mass peasant movements (Anta and Attock). The former sent up the flag of surrender to imperialist motivations, while the latter struck fear in the heart of an essentially bourgeois national development strategy that was loath properly to share the spoils with the peasantry. It was easier to see the "people" as an abstract ideal than in their reality.

The Working Party on National Development took the matters raised by the doves in hand: "Through effective devolution and decentralization, development planning can and should build upon the accumulated reserves of knowledge and experience at the grassroots and local levels."[136] When the people are not brought into the process of development and planning, the state adopts a paternalistic attitude. This situation results "in widespread attitudes of apathy which in the end have weakened the capacity of the state itself to face the

---

134   Poona Wignaraja, "Participatory People-Centered Development," Discussion Note for the South Commission, November 25, 1988, pp. 12–13, SCA.

135   Judo Fernando, *The Political Economy of NGOs*, London: Pluto Press, 2011; and Elisabeth B. Armstrong, "Globalization from Below: AIDWA, Foreign Funding and Gendering Anti-Violence Campaigns," *Journal of Developing Societies* 20: 1–2 (2004).

136   "Working Party on National Development Issues: Summary of the Discussion," November 7, 1988, p. 7, SCA, South IV/2.

tasks of development."[137] A "bottom-up" approach allows for a broad consensus on the various pathways that perhaps have to be taken, even as some of these must necessarily impair the short-term well-being of parts of the population. If new technology enters the rural sector, it will displace people; if large-scale production is needed to absorb the unemployed, it will take land; if small-scale community enterprises develop, they will cut into the profits of independent artisanal production. That is certain to occur. As Manley pointed out, "Unless a consensus is arrived [at] on such a matter particularly in the plural society, the backlash of such modernization could well disrupt the development process."[138] But such popular participation was not only for the purpose of building the consent of the masses. One had to also recognize that the broad masses had to benefit from the transformations underway—and might also want to participate in the design of the policies.

To deal with poverty and unemployment, the default option had become to seek growth in the export sector, which meant linking up with the new geography of production (*maquiladoras*, special economic zones), in which cheapened labor in the South provided the basis for some revenue to the countries to the South, modest gains in technology transfer, and hopes for an industrial take-off that resembled what the World Bank suggested had happened in the newly industrialized countries (Hong Kong, Singapore, South Korea, and Taiwan). In this scenario, the transnational corporations inserted themselves into the South, and the states had to "submit their local development to the global strategy" of the transnational corporations.[139] If the context of industrialization were not taken seriously, then there was a danger that the promotion of industry might simply benefit transnational corporations (and the accumulation of capital), rather than promoting the well-being of the people.

Since the Commission as a whole did not adopt this people-oriented approach, it makes only sporadic appearances in the final document.[140] For that

---

137   "National Development Policies: Past Experience and Lessons for the Future," November 7, 1988, p. 7, SCA, South IV/3.

138   Michael Manley, "Development Redefined," December 1987, annex 2, p. 6, SCA, South III/3.

139   Ismail-Sabri Abdalla, "Heterogeneity and Differentiation: The End of the Third World," *Development Dialogue* 2 (1978), p. 7; and Carlos Rafael Rodríguez, July 1989, p. 8, SCA.

140   After reading the final draft, Dr. H. Ashok Chandra Prasad, who worked in UN circles and later in the government of India, sent in a note to the Commission, which made this clear,

The people-centered strategy does not come out clearly. It includes a lot of elements which were popular in the past—basic needs, redistribution, etc. and so it does not look very innovative. Yet, it could be, if people-centered development is seen less in terms of redistribution and more in terms of mobilizing all, including the poor, women, etc. for development.

reason, the approach itself is not fully developed, though elements of it occur in the various interventions by individual members of the Commission.[141] Even in the general literature on development, this approach is not fully articulated. At times it comes in a form that could be considered to be overly romantic, but mostly it is advanced in only a piecemeal fashion. No major systematic elaboration of this position was available at that time, and none is today. There are four main elements of this position:

Basic needs. With such acute distress in many parts of the South, it was inconceivable for a people-centered strategy to avoid the question of "basic needs."[142] It was imperative to support social and political movements that wanted to alter the class character of the state, so as to create policies that supported the basic needs of the population.[143] The state had to be pushed to deliver social goods, such as healthcare, minimum food allowances, education, and security from male violence. Such goods would not only improve the quality of life of the population, but would also offer a mechanism to create demand from below.[144] This, in turn, would provide a massive and socially beneficial stimulus to the economy.

Production for domestic consumption. The problem for the working class, the peasantry, and those in the informal sector was that the wealth they produced quickly leached out of their localities and headed towards their rich, property-owning countrymen, and eventually to the "global cities" (New York, London,

---

Human resource development and democracy to ensure participation of all could provide unity and innovative themes.

Marginal note, 1989, SCA.

141   They also find themselves in such important documents as the "African Charter for Popular Participation in Development and Transformation" (Arusha, 1990), the fruit of the International Conference on Popular Participation in the Recovery and Development Process in Africa (organized by the UN Economic Commission for Africa and its partner organizations).

142   The basic needs concept, Abdalla wrote, has "been hijacked by the international aid establishment, [and made to sound] almost like a dirty word in the ears of many Third World people." Abdalla, "What Development?" pp. 11-12.

143   "In most cases it was not 'lack of clarity' that kept the underdeveloped countries in backwardness," wrote Rodríguez. "There are classes and groups in our countries that worked together with the exploiters of the North, who were traitors to their own countries, established military dictatorships to contain the protests of the people, and murdered and sent to jail thousands of people. Why excuse them?" Carlos Rafael Rodríguez, July 1989, p. 9, SCA. If this was the nature of the bourgeoisie, it was not predisposed to provide basic needs without pressure from below. In other words, basic needs was a class question.

144   "National Development Policies," p. 21, SCA.

Frankfurt, Singapore, Hong Kong). The project from below had to strive to maintain the poor people's surplus in their own hands. To nudge things in this direction, Devaki Jain proposed that production be engineered for domestic consumption. Rather than support industrial development for export, Jain, Abdalla, and Rodríguez hoped to forge a new production strategy that would promote consumption among the producers themselves. "Small-scale industries (whether urban or rural)," wrote Abdalla in 1989, "are by definition more employment generating (or labour intensive) than very large scale industries because their technologies are linear. Further and because of this, they can be replicated anywhere without much loss in efficiency. Consequently, they do more to widen the base of the technological arts than the giant large scale industries."[145] There was of course room for the very large scale, but all the developmental energy must not be linked to titanic industries. The realm of production for domestic consumption employs large numbers of self-employed and informal women workers, whose well-being is rarely on the radar of development planners.[146]

People-centered planning. There was no sense in providing basic needs or engineering production for domestic consumption if the entire process of development was once more organized from the top down. To craft a bottom-up ethos, it was necessary to encourage the process of participatory or people-centered planning. This would later become central to the local administrations of the Brazilian Worker's Party in São Paulo and Santo André, and in the Left Democratic Front government's experiments with state-level planning in Kerala.[147] It was at this stage an inchoate idea.

Solidarity. The call for popular participation is not a call for a parochial localism. Abdalla proposed that the states of the South forge regional linkages to take advantage of what they could share with each other and to create solidarity blocs that would be able to withstand the pressure from the North. Small states, weakened states, and states with elites who

---

145   Abdallah's note on the Draft Report, September 25, 1989, p. 2, SCA.

146   Devaki Jain, "Note for Dr. Manmohan Singh," 1987, p. 7, SCA; and Marie-Angelique Savané, "Some Ideas for Discussion," May 8, 1988, pp. 2–3, SCA.

147   On the Kerala experiment, see T. M. Thomas Isaac (with Richard W. Franke), *Local Democracy and Development: People's Campaign for Decentralized Planning in Kerala*, New Delhi: LeftWord Books, 2000; and my "The Small Voice of Socialism: Kerala, Once Again," *Critical Asian Studies* 33: 2 (June 2001). On Brazil, see Yves Cabannes, "Participatory Budgeting: A Significant Contribution to Participatory Democracy," *Environment and Urbanization* 16: 1 (April 2004); and Boaventura de Sousa Santos, "Participatory Budgeting in Porto Alegre: Toward a Redistributive Democracy," *Politics & Society* 26: 4 (December 1998).

had no stomach to stand against the G7 would be strengthened by such solidarity.[148]

The doves on the Commission wanted, in Abdalla's words, to let the people take their "legitimate place in development, both as agent and as beneficiary." It was this twin role that distinguished the doves' thrust. But it was not to be: the lack of clarity on this approach allowed the language of "people-centered development" to be hijacked by the hawks. Writing in response to the South Commission's report, IMF chief Michel Camdessus celebrated the idea, and then defined it: "The introduction of better management of the economy, greater transparency in politics, the elimination of complex regulatory procedures, the increased accountability of public institutions, and the dissemination to the public of adequate information about the economic situation."[149] For Camdessus, people were not actors but spectators: looking in at government, but not making it happen. People-centered development had been suborned to the neoliberal agenda, with deregulation and good governance as its main pillars.

SOUTH-SOUTH COOPERATION

Disagreement between the Commissioners at the New Delhi meeting in November 1989 almost derailed the process. Skillful mediation by Nyerere held things together. When the draft of the final report made its rounds, the Commissioners who favored popular participation put forward their objections, while the others sneered. They had no time for such frivolity. Disagreements among the Commissioners had been commonplace, but now, as they worked on the draft, the fissures opened up. Sonny Ramphal had already thrown down his marker at the early meetings. "In considering South-South functional cooperation," he wrote to Manmohan Singh in 1987, "we need to look beyond the traditional concerns. In what ways for instance could private sector and other forms of non-governmental cooperation be assisted?"[150] Ramphal took the draft off to London, where his Commonwealth Secretariat worked on it.[151] Manmohan Singh and his secretariat also worked on it. Occasionally the

---

148   Indeed, the states with ruling classes eager to accommodate the G7 "express doubts about Third World solidarity." It would be the popular classes whose states would be most receptive to genuine solidarity. Abdalla, "What Development?" p. 13 and "Heterogeneity and Differentiation," p. 3.

149   Michel Camdessus, "Effective Development Strategies," in South Centre, *Facing the Challenge*, p. 216.

150   Shridath Ramphal to Manmohan Singh, November 20, 1987, SCA.

151   The Commonwealth Secretariat simultaneously worked on its own book, *International Economic Issues: Contributions by the Commonwealth, 1975-1990*, London: Commonwealth Secretariat, 1990. This was a 270-page mirror of *The Challenge*

final draft evokes the language of popular participation, but the framework is alien to what had been expected by the doves. The report was grounded in a stage theory of development: first the postcolonial state must move from an agrarian-based economy to an industrial one, and only then would questions of equity be genuinely raised. If the debt overhang and intellectual property strictures could be set aside, then the Southern economies would be able to grow. If the economies could grow, then equity might come; not growth *and* equity (Nyerere's slogan), but first growth, then equity.

The centrality of growth emerges in most of the working papers, but nowhere more strongly than in the paper of the Working Party on the Role of the Business Sector. "The report of the Commission," the paper notes, "should not give the impression that we are against growth. Indeed, without strong growth there could be no meaningful solution to the social and economic problems of the Third World." The Commissioners argued that growth must be the primary task, but that it should not come without concern for the social consequences of mal-development.[152] Therefore, "if sufficient care was not taken, growth could be potentially very disruptive. The message we ought to convey is a necessary though not sufficient condition of sustained equitable development."[153] The head of the Working Party was Ghazali Shafie, a former foreign and home minister in Malaysia. His instinct was for growth and business (in 1971 he engineered Malaysia's New Economic Policy, which framed growth-promotion as the path to ethnic and class equality).[154] The call for sustainability and equity seemed disingenuous coming from a magnate in the timber forests of Papua New Guinea.

It was no surprise, then, that the final document would contain a conclusion with a subheading—"Development: First Things First"—signaling that the first priority was to increase the growth rate, with no equity considerations at all. "Most developing countries will need to expand their economies at a

to the South. The Report of the South Commission, New York: Oxford University Press, 1990.

152   This was the view of the much-cited Ignacy Sachs, *Développer: les champs de planification*, Paris: Université coopérative internationale, 1984—as well as, from a Marxist framework, of Charles Bettelheim, *Planification et croissance accélérée*, Paris: F. Maspero, 1967.

153   "Note of the Working Party on the Role of the Business Sector," May 1989, p. 6, SCA.

154   Donald Snodgrass, "Economic Growth and Income Inequality: The Malaysian Experience," in Mukul Asher, David Newman, and Thomas Snyder, eds, *Public Policy in Asia: Implications for Business and Government*, Westport: Quorum Books, 2002, pp. 12–13; Ho Khai Leong, "Dynamics of Policy-Making in Malaysia: The Formulation of the New Economic Policy and the National Development Policy," *Asian Journal of Public Administration* 14: 2 (December 1992).

fairly rapid rate to satisfy the legitimate aspirations of their people," proclaimed *The Challenge of the South*: "The South needs strong economic growth, including advances in both agriculture and industry, to provide a decent livelihood for all those entering the labour market. This process of growth will entail a significant increase in the use of natural resources, to which the international community will have to adjust if the South is to attain its development goals without harming global ecological stability."[155] The point about ecological balance was not to be scoffed at. It came directly from the UN's Brundtland World Commission on Environment and Development (1987). The Brundtland report saw poverty as the major cause of environmental degradation (not capitalist development), so that it called for countries to achieve their "full growth potential" by "high levels of productive activity."[156] Concerns about corporate malfeasance and industrial pollution took a back seat to the survival strategies of the poor. Bhopal was certainly not in the spotlight.[157] There was to be no alternative to Northern Atlantic growth strategies, which the South simply had to mimic. The problem was not the growth strategy itself, but the inability of the South to adopt it.

The South's growth strategy was hampered by the G7, which would neither allow the debt to disappear nor reorient the GATT rules to benefit the South. What Ramphal and his cohort proposed was for the North to remove these barriers so that the South could properly implement the strictures of neoliberalism. It was remarkably naive for these seasoned campaigners and intellectuals to believe that the North would make these concessions when it had reorganized its own accumulation strategy around finance and intellectual property. The broad outlines of the neoliberal agenda infused the final report. Apart from

---

155   *The Challenge of the South*, p. 272. This is a massive—and longstanding—debate in the scholarly literature. Paul Rosenstein-Rodan argued for a "big push" to industrialize and move from backwardness to modernity ("Problems of Industrialization of Eastern and South-Eastern Europe," *Economic Journal* 53: 210–11 [1943]). Rosenstein-Rodan's position was much elaborated by Sir Arthur Lewis ("Economic Development With Unlimited Supplies of Labour," *Manchester School* 22: 2 [May 1954]). Ragnar Nurske worried that this "big push" would not happen because of supply-related challenges (poor infrastructure, inadequate access to technology) and demand-related barriers (protectionism in the North). For that reason, he hoped that the countries of the South would either industrialize for "home markets" or for each other ("Notes on 'Unbalanced Growth,'" *Oxford Economic Papers*, New Series 11: 3 [October 1959]). Nurske's position would become the standard for South-South cooperation, even though none of the economists of the South who advocated it read or referred to him.

156   World Commission on Environment and Development, *Our Common Future*, Oxford: Oxford University Press, 1987, p. 44.

157   Thijis de la Court, *Beyond Brundtland: Green Development in the 1990s*, London: Zed Books, 1990, pp. 24–5.

the gentle suggestion of scaling back the state's role in economic life, there is the strong suggestion that the development path be premised on export-oriented growth, not on the enhancement of domestic consumption: "The importance of export performance to economic recovery and industrialization has become more visible as the scarcity of foreign exchange has become the major obstacle to economic growth."[158] Export as a route out of poverty should have been the final report's watchword, but that would not have enabled a consensus document. The recommendations had to come in a sugar-coated way.[159] Ideology had to be eschewed: enter neoliberalism, disguised as pragmatism.

The narrative on the origins of neoliberalism formulated by scholars like David Harvey leaves out the role of the demise of the Third World Project, and the enthusiastic commitment to the ideology from the emergent elites in the "global cities" of Africa, Asia, and Latin America. The IMF did not force them into these ideas; they came to them willingly. In some cases the elites took refuge behind the IMF, allowing it to take the blame for policies that would otherwise have been politically unappetizing if they had come from the already weakened political parties. The appeal of neoliberalism is that it appears to be a discourse of equal opportunity (innovation and enterprise by anyone against the regimented authority of the state), but which of course has very divergent effects since it has to operate in social conditions that are highly unequal. The elites of the South pushed against the nationalist expectation that they maintain a patriotic and social commitment to the working class and peasantry, whose struggles had won freedom for their countries a generation before. Merit overwhelmed patriotism. For elites in the global South, to echo Margaret Thatcher, the point was: *there was no nation, only families.*[160]

The North would have none of it. It wanted its debts paid and it wanted to protect its hold over technological advances. When Oxford University Press sent *The Challenge of the South* to be reviewed, one scholar took umbrage at the few appearances of the term "neo-colonialism," and at the thrust of the analysis of the debt crisis and the Uruguay Round: "It is too much simplified if the South Report in this connection speaks of 'neo-colonialism.' It is obvious that the development crisis is first of all the result of wrong domestic policies

---

158   *Challenge of the South*, p. 96.

159   The Working Party on the Role of the Business Sector explored this tone: "While an ideological line should not be taken on privatization, emphasis should be given to the importance of management efficiency" ("Note of the Working Party," p. 8).

160   Thatcher felt that there was no society, only individuals. In a large part of the South, the ideology of individualism is as yet subsumed under the capacious family (sometimes clan, caste, or what have you)—as in Harish Damodaran, *India's New Capitalists: Caste, Business and Industry in a Modern Nation*, Delhi: Permanent Black, 2008.

in the South."[161] The reader's views would be amplified once the report came out, and the UN's Economic and Social Council held a discussion on it in July 1991. Switzerland's note is representative. It opposed "the excessively hardened and hostile views with respect to international economic relations," and was unhappy with "the tendency to cite certain flaws in the market economy as justification for proposals for further State intervention, which would undermine the reforms that have been advocated." Like the OUP's reader, the Swiss pointed to "the responsibility of the developing countries themselves for the management of their economies."[162] The United Kingdom wished that the South would work with the North to complete the Uruguay Round, which "will result in increased trade liberalization" and permit "the most competitive to reap their rewards. The North can help the South by investing both money and technology in the area, but before it can do that the countries of the South must first make a commitment to respect intellectual property and streamline their current inefficient economies. The latter point is becoming generally accepted by the least developed countries."[163] Sadly, the North's view was reflected by K. K. S. Dadzie, secretary-general of UNCTAD, the dented shield: "The South should accept primary responsibility for its own destiny."[164]

Dadzie's comment gestured in the direction of the South Commission's main proposal—to increase South-South cooperation. The North would not be an active partner, but the South could take advantage of its own resources and its own mutual interactions. The type of South-South cooperation being called for, however, bore little resemblance to the solidarity economies of the Third World Project—to the barter of discounted oil for consumer goods, or of bauxite for iron ore. "The time has perhaps also come to look beyond traditional forms and mechanisms of South-South co-operation," Dadzie noted. "Several possibilities exist. For example, the mutual co-operation of developing countries could be pursued not in terms of exclusive inward-looking arrangements, but as a means of improving the overall efficiency and competitiveness of productive sectors in individual countries and of raising the level of exports to all destinations."[165] The "synergies" of the South would have to be

---

161   "Oxford University Press Referee's Reports on the First Draft of the Commission's Report," Reader no. 1, p. 11, SCA.

162   "Report on the South Commission: Note by the Secretary General. Addendum." E/1991/90/Add. 1, June 18, 1991, ECOSOC. Switzerland's note, pp. 14–15, SCA.

163   Ibid., United Kingdom's note, p. 16.

164   "Notes for Statement by K. K. S. Dadzie, Secretary General of UNCTAD," July 3, 1991, p. 2, SCA.

165   Ibid., p. 10. Dadzie hoped that the UNCTAD VIII meeting in Cartagena, Colombia, in 1992 would sort things out in this respect. Indeed, it did. UNCTAD's mandate was slashed by the North. It was unhinged from the Third World Project and yoked to neoliberal strategies.

used towards the creation of a domestic export-oriented development strategy. Rather than worry about the needs of its population, the state managers were now being tasked with administering their population to meet the needs of the Great Commodity Chain. That is precisely what the report meant when it championed South-South cooperation.

The South needed to industrialize. The direction that the Commission proposed was towards heavy industry: capital goods, fertilizers, petrochemicals, pharmaceuticals, steel, and energy.[166] Since the state sector was not to be promoted, the report pointed to the existence of "Third World multinationals" that had "shown willingness to accept much lower equity participation compared to multinationals of developed countries. There is thus much less fear of these countries exercising political and economic control over the natural resources of host developing countries."[167] The Commission provided no examples, but many come to mind for the 1980s. There are the explosive South Korean firms that left the peninsula for the rest of Asia: Samsung, Goldstar, and Hyundai. Taiwanese, Singaporean, and Hong Kong–based firms were equally quick to depart from their islands to lands afar, notably Malaysia and Indonesia. Indian firms, such as the Birlas and Tatas, made their mark in Africa and Southeast Asia. Brazil's Embraer and Mexico's Grupo Bimbo and Vitro manufactured and sold aircraft, bread, and glass across Latin America.[168] To enable the activities of these Third World multinationals, the Southern states were asked to create a raft of institutions, including a South Bank, an Association of Central Banks of the Third World, a South Chamber of Commerce (modeled after the ASEAN Chamber of Commerce), a Third World Institute of Development Research, and a South-South Partnership Promotion Center. The Commission also wanted to revitalize the regional economic cooperation blocs (such as the Andean Group, the Bangkok Agreement, the Council for Arab Economic Unity, and CARICOM).[169] To enable the South to circumvent resistance from

---

166 "Draft Programme of the South Commission and a Programme of Studies," 1988, pp. 15–16, SCA; *Challenge of the South*, p. 180.

167 "South-South Cooperation: A Strategic Option," Document South IV/5, November 7, 1988, p. 23, SCA; and *Challenge of the South*, p. 180, which does not use the phrase "Third World multinationals," but simply says "Third World firms."

168 For a sense of their emergence, see Krishna Kumar, "Third World Multinationals: A Growing Force in International Relations," *International Studies Quarterly* 26: 3 (September 1982); and for a critique of the concept, see Henry Wai-Chung Yeung, "Third World Multinationals Revisited: A Research Critique and Future Agenda," *Third World Quarterly* 15: 2 (June 1994). Both essays ask for more research. Not much more has been done in the past twenty years.

169 *Challenge of the South*, Chapter 4, "Mobilizing the South"; Ghazali Shafie to Manmohan Singh, August 18, 1989, SCA; "South-South Cooperation: A Strategic Option," November 7, 1988, pp. 30–1, SCA, Document South IV/5.

the North for this path, and so to make the technical preparations for the South-North dialogue, the Commission underscored the need for the creation of a permanent secretariat—the South Secretariat, which would become the South Centre.

In an early document, those who favored the business route (such as Aldo Ferrer, Diaby Ouattara, Ghazali Shafie, and Papic) wanted the Commission to recognize "that the NICs had the potential to give dynamism to business cooperation, and that the South should draw on their experiences and resources in such fields as human resource development, investment, technology and access to markets."[170] All eyes turned to the "East Asian Miracle." If the Pacific Rim could take off, why not the rest of the Global South? South Korea and Taiwan's route was hard to champion—not because theirs was a state-authoritarian capitalism, but because these countries had moved beneath the US military and political umbrella. It would be hard to sell such a route in the NAM, where suspicion of US power had intensified through the 1980s. When socialist China turned to the same kind of path in the late 1980s, this validated it for people like Nyerere, the conscience of the South.

In 1989, Nyerere visited China. Joan Wicken later wrote to Manmohan Singh, describing Nyerere's fascination:

> During the visit to South China (Senzhen Special Economic Zone and Guangdong Province, i.e. in the region of what used to be known as Canton) we saw very impressive developments, both on the basis of self-reliance and on the "Joint-Ownership" basis. A lot of the latter is confined to production for export—and in a few cases is little more than putting value-added into imported materials before selling them abroad again. In most other cases (the animal feed firm was the only exception they admitted to) they said that the agreements setting up the factory very rarely allowed more than 20 percent of the production to be sold within China, and sometimes not that.[171]

China appears only a few times in the report (the Commissioner from China, Jiadong Qian, a veteran Chinese diplomat, did not ruffle any feathers or

170   "Linking Business to the South," *South Letter* 1 (April 1989), p. 2.

171   Joan Wicken to Manmohan Singh, December 2, 1989. Nyerere's impressions of China should not be seen out of context. He remained enamored of North Korea. "A number of the commissioners are highly impressed by the achievements of South Korea," he said in Canada. "Now I don't know South Korea. I know only North Korea, and I tried to say, 'What about North Korea?' And there was a lot of pooh-poohing about North Korea." Julius Nyerere, "The Rabbit and the Elephant: The Challenge to the South," *North-South Institute* (Ottawa), September 25, 1990, pp. 6–7. At the Havana meeting of the South Commission, Nyerere interrupted the conversation, saying, "We don't need a South Commission report. We don't need an alternative paradigm. It's here. Cuba's model." Ramphal and Manmohan Singh looked at each other, almost in horror.

contribute much to the paperwork of the Commission); but where it does appear, it is in an exemplary way, able to "achieve fast economic growth ... supported by successful reforms in [its] system of development planning."[172] The NICs and China were the models, and what they modeled was this: high growth rates at any cost; and then, once the social wealth had been produced, mechanisms for social redistribution—growth, then equity.

"Microbusiness is mentioned," Devaki Jain wrote to Manmohan Singh, "but not the context in which I put it forward. I am concerned that the perspective I brought of workers, employment, self-employed entrepreneurs for the poor as a ballast and a lift to modify the over-emphasis on networks of Private Business of Chambers of Commerce as a club of the rich has not found adequate mention. The focus on equity is thus weakened."[173] The commitment was so weak, Devaki Jain later admitted, that "we never bothered to read the final draft because there was nothing we could do to change it."[174]

SADDAM HUSSEIN'S GIFT

On August 2, 1990, as the South Commission prepared to release its final report in Caracas, Saddam Hussein's army invaded Kuwait. It was an unexpected occurrence, and its effects were dramatic. It prepared the way for the US to extend itself militarily into the oil lands. As Dasman Palace fell, and as news filtered out about the invasion, Nyerere awoke in his Caracas hotel room. He knew immediately that six years of work would come to nothing. Now the world's media would be preoccupied by Kuwait and Iraq. Two months later, the South Commission's last formal act was to release a statement on the Iraq crisis. It positioned the South as a neglected but essential element in inter-state relations: "The Gulf Crisis also highlights the great importance of durable effective, subregional, regional and interregional arrangements being worked out by the Third World countries to resolve their conflicts in a peaceful manner."[175] This polycentric regionalism would be a crucial part of the South's demands in the years to come. On August 2, this was the furthest thing from Nyerere's mind. Caracas, barely recovered from the *Caracazo*, was of no relevance. No one would pay attention. It was symptomatic of the decline of the South's own agenda. The South would appear—but only as problem, no longer as possibility.

---

172   *Challenge of the South*, p. 66.
173   Devaki Jain to Manmohan Singh, January 27, 1990, SCA.
174   Author interview with Devaki Jain, New Delhi.
175   "South Commission's Statement on the Gulf Crisis," October 7, 1990, Arusha, Tanzania, p. 2. The statement also took a critical view of the hypocrisy of the North: the US and Europe were willing to ignore the UN resolutions directed to Israel, but made a capital offense of resolutions directed to what the North considered rogue states.

The G7 states pilloried the report. The Austrian government's response at the UN was quite straightforward: "It is regrettable that the report does not contain a clear commitment to the market economy, which is obviously the best guarantee of the success of the development strategy it recommends."[176] The European Community acknowledged the debt crisis, but hastily pointed out that the "urgent need for debt alleviation measures does not mean that all efforts have to come from the international community." Rather, the "developing countries themselves must remain at the center of any debt strategy."

Nyerere went to Havana to release the Spanish edition of *The Challenge of the South*. Fidel Castro received a copy the night before. The next morning, Castro came to Nyerere. "I don't accept this," he said angrily. What irked Castro the most was the section that argued for the market as an efficient distributor of resources. The Soviet Union's imminent demise threatened the future of the Cuban Revolution. It would soon have to encourage foreign direct investment to help the agricultural and tourism sectors. These were starved of investment, and, because of the sanctions, of *matériel*. It would have to rely upon the outside world, and on the "market." But what Castro disparaged was the idea that the market was a natural, and not a social, institution. Cuba had fewer resources, so it would be dependent on the outside world for investment; but it could not afford to allow allocation decisions to be left to the "market," which, in the absence of statutory authority, would mean to the whims of plutocrats and financiers. The "market" did not make decisions; powerful institutions, hiding behind the anonymity of the "market," made the choices.[177] If the report had come out fifteen years previously, Nyerere said, "I might have behaved like Fidel on the market. I don't know. But thirty years ago this report would have caused me a little trouble."[178] Times had changed.

It may appear odd that the South Commission would end its search for a new path at the door of neoliberalism—or, to be precise, of Neoliberalism with Southern Characteristics. Certainly there was no mimicry of the agenda that emanated from Washington, London, Frankfurt, or Paris. The questions of debt and of intellectual property, which had taken most of the Commission's attention, remained a barrier between the South and the North. Unwilling to be whipped by the North out of their self-respect, the Commission promoted the idea of South-South cooperation. It was not quite the people-driven development hoped for by the Commission's doves. What it entailed was the belief that the South had to gather together, use its own resources, emulate the NICs and China, and allow its economic growth to lead eventually to equity. Some

---

176   ECOSOC, E/1991/90, June 10, 1991, p. 6, SCA.

177   Fidel Castro and Ignacio Ramonet, *Fidel Castro: My Life*, New York: Scribner, 2006, p. 387.

178   Nyerere, "The Rabbit and the Elephant," pp. 14–16.

commissioners went in this direction by instinct, some by resignation, others for pragmatic reasons. They were not united by a common sense of human failure; what united them was hope that the South also exists:

> *Con su fe veterana*
> *el Sur también existe.*

> With its veteran faith,
> The South also exists.

Mario Benedetti, "El Sur
también existe," 1985

CHAPTER THREE

The Locomotives of the South

> *The South Commission is convinced that the developed countries cannot play the role of the engine of Southern growth. The new locomotive forces have to be found within the South itself. South-South cooperation is therefore crucial.*
>
> Manmohan Singh, May 1989[1]

In March 1989, Manmohan Singh wrote his keynote address for a World Bank conference on development economics. He submitted his forty-four page address to the organizers, who hastily wrote back asking him to prune the speech. Length was a problem. But more than that, they worried about its tone.

> As you can guess, a number of statements in your paper are likely to evince strong responses from the audience. This is entirely welcome and in keeping with the special nature of the conference series which we hope can build bridges between the development research and the development policy communities. For this very reason, we are also hoping that the debate on the issues you raise, and more generally during the rest of the conference, will take place on a factual basis without undue deference being paid to ideology.[2]

Singh went to Washington in April and delivered a shorter, but no less punchy speech.[3] He assailed the Atlantic states for their role in the debt crisis (its origin and prolongation). The debt crisis had hobbled the South. A "sharp deterioration" in the southward export of capital, whether private or public, threatened more fiscal challenges for the global South. To fix this mess, the international agencies, such as the World Bank and the IMF, were not up to the task. Singh pointed his finger at the "one-sided" encroachment of "a strong pro-private sector ideology in the major developed countries" into the international financial institutions. These stale ideas did not recognize two serious problems for the South: first, the increase in protectionist policies in the North, which

---

1   "The South Must Be Its Own Engine," a talk given by Manmohan Singh at the "What is Development?" symposium at Espoo, Finland, May 1989, in *South Letter* 2 (June 1989), p. 6.

2   Dennis de Tray and Shekhar Shah, World Bank, to Manmohan Singh, South Commission, faxed letter, March 9, 1989, SCA.

3   The drafts are in the SCA, and so too was the final version, published as Manmohan Singh, "Keynote Address: Development Policy Research: The Task Ahead," *Proceedings of the World Bank Annual Conference on Development Economics 1989*, Washington, DC: The International Bank for Reconstruction and Development, 1990.

prevented the South's ability to export its way out of the crisis; and second, the technological apartheid that stemmed from the new intellectual property strictures.[4] The answer to every problem studied by the World Bank and the IMF was the same: less state intervention and more private initiative.

Singh's speech was derived almost entirely from the work of the South Commission, and, of course, from his own long career as a government economist (first as director of the Reserve Bank of India, and then as the head of the Indian Planning Commission). Countries like India carried a high debt-to-GDP ratio, with no end in sight to debt-servicing payments. This made a mockery of orthodox neoclassical economics. Alongside the new ferocity about structural adjustment that had wreaked havoc in South America and in the Caribbean, this completed the picture: development policy could not be effective if the levers of power remained in the North Atlantic states. The facts were bitter; it was sufficient to recite them.

Elsewhere, few options remained. Chronic problems with the colonial legacy had left the African states vulnerable to the acute crisis brought on by debt. The gross national product of the continent fell from 17.6 percent of world GNP in 1975 to 10.5 percent by 1999. This was largely due to the catastrophic urgency with which the IMF and the World Bank had implemented the Washington Consensus across the continent, with very little push-back.[5] Latin America crawled through its *década perdida* ("lost decade"), with all the implications of perdition in the phrase. Japan's spectacular economic successes had already begun to unravel, and by 1991 it too would enter its lost decade (*ushinawareta junen*). The only sparkling successes in terms of GDP were the newly industrialized countries (NICs), including the Four Tigers (Hong Kong, Singapore, South Korea, and Taiwan)—and it was to their example that the ruling classes of the South looked.[6]

Manmohan Singh did not dwell on any of this. It was the reality that defined his analysis, and out of it he recommended an agenda for reform, with suggestions "tailored to the specific requirements of each country."[7] No single plan in the manner of the Washington Consensus, foisted on each country regardless of its history and social dynamics.[8] Singh looked inward first,

4   Singh, "Keynote Address," pp. 12–15.

5   Giovanni Arrighi, "The African Crisis: World Systemic and Regional Aspects," *New Left Review* II/15 (May–June 2002).

6   Prashad, *Darker Nations*, pp. 245–59.

7   Singh, "Keynote Address," p. 14.

8   On the Consensus, Moisés Naím, former Venezuelan Minister of Trade and Industry in the Pérez government, noted, "The paradox is that any country capable of meeting such stringent requirements [of the Consensus] is already a developed country." "Washington Consensus or Washington Confusion?" *Foreign Policy* 118 (Spring 2000), p. 96. This paper was originally given at the IMF Conference on Second Generation

towards the need to reform the states of the South. Taking his cue from the NICs, Singh pointed out that the states would still play a "highly intervention-ist role."[9] Nevertheless, the barriers to trade (import controls and industrial licensing) had to be removed or loosened, and the state apparatus needed a dose of modernization (public-sector reform, tax-system reform, the rule of law strengthened, and political reform "designed to promote participatory and people-centered approaches to development").[10] All these reforms would come to naught if there was no agenda for the enhancement of economic growth. The default option was to seek demand in the North, which is what the NICs relied upon, and allow this demand to drive exports from the South, which would lead to growth. "But will markets still be available if all the countries that have pursued inward-looking development strategies switch over to export-oriented strategies based on labor-intensive manufactures?"[11] If it was the North that had to be the buyer of last resort, then the answer to this question was no; if it was the North and the elites of the South, then the answer is still no.[12] In May, in Finland, Manmohan Singh widened the ambit: demand for the newly trans-formed South had to come primarily from the South itself. It is this that the South Commission had called "South-South Cooperation." "The new locomo-tive forces," he said, "have to be found within the South itself."

The Washington Consensus's Structural Adjustment policy had to be shown the door. So too the import-substitution industrialization scheme of the Third World Project. Drawing from the NICs and Japan, as well as the work of the South Commission, intellectuals like Manmohan Singh began to trumpet a new siren: Neoliberalism with Southern Characteristics for domestic policy, and South-South Cooperation for international policy. It was not a capitulation to the North, but the creation of a new approach.

TOKYO'S ROAD TO NOWHERE

The rise of Japan as a major economic power has far reaching implications and devel-oping countries need to pay increasing attention to the possible role of Japanese capital,

---

Reforms, October 26, 1999. Naim elaborated: "The means to attain utopia are themselves utopic goals for most countries. This does not imply, of course, that these are not valid aspirations. They are valid but, mostly, they are overwhelming. The challenge, therefore, is to use the many lessons accumulated throughout decades of development efforts to create agendas that include intermediate stepping stones and more manageable goals."

9   Singh, "Keynote Address," p. 15.

10   Ibid., p. 16.

11   Ibid., p. 19.

12   There is also a social problem: "The widening social gap between the ruling minority and the great mass of people can erode the moral authority of these elites to command willing acceptance of restraint on the growth of consumption," ibid., p. 14.

> *Japanese technology and the Japanese market in widening the developing options*
> *open to them.*
>
> Manmohan Singh, 1989[13]

In 1945, Japan had been devastated. Four years later, under the shadow of the US occupation, the government created the Ministry of International Trade and Industry (MITI), whose 1950 directive, "Policy Concerning Industrial Rationalization," set the path for Japan's recovery.[14] The state directed the large corporations, the *zaibatsu* or *keiretsu* (for example, Mitsui, Mitsubishi, and Sumitomo), to use resources towards a very particular set of ends, notably industrialization to develop an internal market and for export. The prime minister, Hayato Ikeda, pushed the banks to move money into the conglomerates, and eventually, through this massive state action, redeveloped the commanding heights of the economy. Japan's Gross Domestic Product (GDP) skyrocketed, reaching just under $1 trillion in 1965. Creative accounting and administrative guidance from the state enabled the *keiretsu* to draw large profits and create a pact with the workers through reasonable wages and lifelong employment.[15] It was not paradise, but it was not the ruins of Hiroshima.

By the early 1970s, creeping inflation and the oil shocks had disturbed the political class.[16] Japan relied entirely on imported oil and had few reserves of other energy sources. Most of the oil came from the Gulf region. OPEC's 1973 thrust scared Japan. The Japanese government feared that its too-close relationship with the US might narrow its options. In the MITI, the government created an Agency for Energy and Natural Resources. The Agency released a White Paper in September 1973, warning of calamity for Japan. MITI minister Yashuhiro Nakasone, later prime minister, pointed out, "It is inevitable that Japan will competitively follow her own independent direction"—namely, independent of the United States. "The era of blindly following has come to an end." In June 1973, Nakasone wanted his government to forge a new resource policy "standing on the side of the oil producing countries."[17] In November the cabinet secretary, Susumu Nikaido, laid out a "new Arab policy," specifying that the rights of the Palestinians must be recognized. This was as much a threat to Washington as it was to its ally, Israel.

---

13   Manmohan Singh, "Inaugural Remarks at the International Conference on Development and Planning Convened by Indira Gandhi Development Research Institute," Bombay, January 5, 1989, SCA.

14   Chalmers Johnson, *MITI and the Japanese Miracle: The Growth of Industrial Policy, 1925–1975*, Stanford: Stanford University Press, 1982; and Shigeto Tsuru, *Japan's Capitalism*, Cambridge: Cambridge University Press, 1993.

15   Tsuru, *Japan's Capitalism*, p. 96.

16   Ibid., pp. 119–29.

17   Yergin, *The Prize*, p. 581.

Japan had its rebellion, but quickly came back to its best behavior. The ruling political and economic elite feared their dangerous neighborhood. A Soviet reconnaissance plane, the Tokyo Express, flew daily towards Japan. Japanese Communists and the wider left (especially the student left) exerted their pressure after the social uprisings of 1968.[18] With the People's Republic of China and North Korea in the frame, the Japanese ruling elite had a lot to worry about. As much as the occupation, these threats were the basis for the US-Japanese strategic alliance, which was therefore hard to shake. A nudge against Washington here and there was sufficient; it could go no further. For that reason, in September 1973, Japan's foreign minister, Kiichi Aichi, invited the Library Group for a drink in Nairobi and helped earn Japan a seat in what became the G7. The following year, Gerald Ford became the first US president to visit Japan.

The G7 response to the debt crisis distressed sections of the Japanese Ministry of Finance. Elements of the Washington Consensus seemed unrealistic, even sadistic. In the early years of the Reagan administration, the Japanese government requested a revised approach to the debt crisis. "We argued that the high interest rates were certainly exacerbating the Third World debt problem and calculated that if US interest rates declined by 1 percent, Latin America's burden of debt service would be reduced by $4 billion a year," reflected Toyoo Gyohten of the Japanese Ministry of Finance. "We got no response in Washington and felt that we were really talking to deaf ears in those days."[19] The deafness persisted, which frustrated Japan.

Japan had a longstanding suspicion of the World Bank, which appeared to give weight to European and US interests rather than those of Japan. For that reason, in 1966 the Japanese government threw its weight behind the formation of the Asian Development Bank (ADB).[20] The ADB was not hostile to the North Atlantic dispensation. Its first president, Takeshi Watanabe, was the secretary of the Japanese section of the Trilateral Commission, and had previously served at both the IMF and the World Bank, as bank president Eugene

---

18   Ford told former Prime Minister Eisaku Sato in January 1973, "Not just the Communists, but some socialists—the left in general—think that the way to peace is to disarm, disband alliances. A nice dream, if there weren't other nations with other ideas." They were united in their fears of the USSR and the Japanese left upswing. "Memorandum of Conversation in The Oval Office," January 31, 1973, White House, National Security Adviser's Memoranda of Conversation Collection, Box 1, Gerald Ford Presidential Library.

19   Volcker and Gyohten, *Changing Fortunes*, p. 185.

20   The early history of the Asian Development is best told in R. Krishnamurti, *ADB: The Seeding Days*, Tokyo: Asian Development Bank, 1977. Krishnamurti, on behalf of the UN Economic Commission for Asia and the Far East, was one of the pioneers of the ADB in September 1963.

Black's protégé (Watanabe's father was a member of the Privy Council, and his grandfather had been finance minister; he came with impeccable establishment credentials). But even though Japan threw its prestige and surplus capital into the ADB, it was unable to influence the US campaign to locate the headquarters of the new Bank in Manila rather than Tokyo.[21] Japan nonetheless continued to exercise leadership (its presidents are all Japanese), and it used the ADB to push its view of development. This view was encapsulated in the "flying geese" theory developed first in the 1930s by Kaname Akamatsu, and elaborated later by Kiyoshi Kojima.[22] The theory, in its multi-country version, argued that one country—the lead goose—exploits its advantage to direct the skein. As it moves forward and develops new economic activity, it transfers the older production lines to the geese that follow, and so on. Japan was the leading goose, and behind it came the NICs, and then the ASEAN states (Malaysia, Thailand, the Philippines, and Indonesia). Targeted lending by the ADB along the lines of Japan's domestic development and of the "flying geese" theory would enable development to occur along the Pacific Rim. Manmohan Singh hoped that the ADB would "play a vital role" in social development. "It is hoped that Japan," in the context of the work of the ADB, "will use its tremendous influence and position as a major economic power in the world to initiate and concretize some constructive thinking and action among developed countries on the issue of enhanced resource flows to developing countries."[23]

The ADB and Japan's "model" was anathema in Washington. By the early 1980s, Washington wanted to shut down the ADB's Asian Development Fund, and it demanded that loans go out on the condition of privatization and adherence to free-market principles. In other words, Washington wanted the ADB to dress like the IMF and the World Bank. Using its votes in the ADB, Washington pushed hard against the leadership of Masao "Shogun" Fujioka (president since 1981). Against Fujioka was the US executive director at the ADB, Joe Rogers, who many saw as "an inexperienced ideologue with little understanding of Asia, trying to use his 'textbook knowledge' to help develop Asia."[24] Rogers

---

21   Dennis Yasutomo, *Japan and the Asian Development Bank*, New York: Praeger, 1983, pp. 77–82.

22   Kaname Akatmatsu, "Historical Pattern of Economic Growth in Developing Countries," *Developing Economies* 1 (1962); Kiyoshi Kojima, "The 'Flying Geese' Model of Asian Economic Development: Origin, Theoretical Extensions, and Regional Policy Implications," *Journal of Asian Economics* 11 (2000); Satoru Kumagai, "A Journey Through the Secret History of the Flying Geese Model," *IDE Discussion Paper no. 158*, Tokyo: Institute of Developing Economics, 2008. See also Yoshikara Kunio, *The Rise of Ersatz Capitalism in South-East Asia*, Manila: Manila University Press, 1988.

23   Manmohan Singh, "Revitalizing Development Cooperation: Issues and Priorities," *Asian Development Review* 7: 1 (1989), p. 29.

24   Shafiqul Islam, "Foreign Aid and Burdensharing: Is Japan Free Riding to

complained that Fujioka was "an embarrassment."[25] The dispute was ferocious between 1983 and 1984, with an open confrontation at the ADB's 1985 annual meeting. Behind closed doors, Fujioka relented. The United States had too much influence over Japan's existence; Japan had to resort to slyer methods. It appeared to bow to the US with some "highly publicized but token programs," while quietly continuing with its own lending strategies.[26]

By 1989, Japan accounted for 14 percent of the world's GDP, second only to the United States, with 25.4 percent. Japan would soon be the second-largest shareholder in the IMF and the World Bank's affiliate, the International Finance Corporation. The Japanese yen replaced the dollar as the dominant currency to denominate Asian external debt. "Though now a dim memory," Herman Schwartz notes, "1989 saw serious speculation that the yen or European currencies might replace the dollar" on the world stage.[27] Japanese firms had become household names: Canon, Casio, Fuji, Honda, Mazda, Mitsubishi, Nikon, Nintendo, Nissan, Olympus, Pioneer, Sony, Toshiba, and Toyota. By 1991, Japan was the largest exporter of automobiles in the world, and, more ominously for the US, thanks to guided investment from MITI, it was one of the largest exporters of computer equipment.[28]

From a position of relative confidence, the Japanese intelligentsia began to speak tentatively of "Japan Inc." (*kigyo kokka*)—the business state, a model for development elsewhere.[29] In 1981 Malaysia inaugurated its "Look East" policy,

---

a Coprosperity Sphere in Pacific Asia?" in Jeffrey Frankel and Miles Kahler, eds, *Regionalism and Rivalry: Japan and the United States in Pacific Asia*, Chicago: University of Chicago Press, 1993, p. 365.

25   Samantha Sparks, "Cooking the Books in Asia," *Multinational Monitor* 8: 3 (March 1987).

26   Ming Wan, *Japan between Asia and the West: Economic Power and Strategic Balance*, Arnold: M. E. Sharpe, 2001, p. 158.

27   Herman Schwartz, "Structured Finance for Financed Structures," in Konings, *Great Credit Crash*, p. 175; Philipp Hartmann, *Currency Competition and Foreign Exchange Markets: The Dollars, the Yen and the Future International Role of the Euro*, Cambridge: Cambridge University Press, 1998, p. 37; and Nora Field, "Japan is Still No. 1," *Fortune*, June 30, 1990.

28   The computer sector was fashioned by MITI, which ran a "very high speed computer system project" from 1966 to 1972, as a direct challenge to IBM System 360, and then the Mainframe Computer Project (1972–76) and the Pattern Information Processing System Project (1971–80). IBM accounted for 80 percent of Japan's computer market in the 1950s, but this share shrank to 50 percent in the late 1970s. Hitachi, NEC, and Fujitsu began their domination in the domestic market, but were only able to get a handle on peripheral sales (printers, hard drives) in the international market. Wataru Nakayama, William Boulton, and Michael Pecht, *The Japanese Electronics Industry*, Boca Raton: CRC Press, 1990, pp. 44–6.

29   For a full critique of the idea of "Japan Inc.," see Gavan McCormack, *The*

designed to turn away from the old colonial master (Britain) and towards the dynamism apparent in the NICs, under what appeared to be Japanese tutelage. An inflated yen pushed Japanese industrial conglomerates to seek offshore production along the Asian Rim, to create a "capitalist archipelago" with the islands of East and Southeast Asia in a sea of horizontal exchanges.[30] In 1987, MITI published *The New Asian Industries Development Plan*—a blueprint for Japanese capital's initiatives in Southeast Asia. Aid was not to be used as charity; it was tied to the imperatives of Japanese capital. As MITI officials put it, "Japan will increasingly use aid ... as seed money to attract Japanese manufacturers or other industrial concerns with an attractive investment environment."[31] In this period, Japan considered joining the Malaysian-sponsored East Asian Economic Caucus, a direct challenge to the US-sponsored Asia-Pacific Economic Cooperation Forum (EAEC eventually became a part of ASEAN, and was defanged).

In 1988 the Japanese government convened a symposium under the auspices of the Asian and Pacific Development Centre in Tokyo on the role of Japan and the Pacific Rim. Naoyuki Shinohara, of the Ministry and Finance (and later a deputy director at the IMF), proposed the Pacific Rim, under Japanese leadership, as a major dynamic center for the planet. Professor Harry T. Oshima suggested that Japan restrict the Rim to the main islands, and not carry its ambitions into the mainland of China and down to India. Veteran Japanese official and economist Saburo Okita agreed with the general thrust of this triumphalism, but cautioned that the surpluses in the North and the debt in the South had created a dangerous imbalance. It was necessary to transfer

---

Emptiness of Japanese Affluence, New York: M. E. Sharpe, 2001 [1996]. The Japanese model certainly influenced Singapore:

> The Japanese made it without any help. In fact, they made the Meiji transformation despite the West putting obstacles in their way to industrialise. They learnt, they imitated; they were poor imitators at first; they caught up, they surpassed. The Koreans are doing [likewise] and Brazil and Mexico are making the grade. And they could make the grade better and faster if the industrial countries and their governments were not so self-centered and took a longer view in terms of one interdependent, inter-reacting world. But I think it would be a waste of energy and effort to try and wring sympathetic charitable concessions out of the industrial world.
>
> > "North-South Dialogue," Altaf Gauhar interviews Lee Kuan Yew,
> > November 1978, *Third World Quarterly* 1: 2 (1979), p. 3.

30   Bruce Cumings, "The Political Economy of the Pacific Rim," in Ravi Arvind Palat, ed., *Pacific-Asia and the Future of the World System*, Westport: Greenwood Press, 1993, pp. 25–6.

31   Robert Wade, "Japan, the World Bank, and the Art of Paradigm Maintenance: *The East Asian Miracle* in Political Perspective," *New Left Review* I/217 (May–June 1996), p. 7. For what follows, I rely upon this essay and on Wade's *Governing the Market*, Princeton: Princeton University Press, 1990.

the surpluses from North to South. Manmohan Singh agreed with Okita, and hoped that "the tremendous weight and influence that Japan now enjoys as a major economic power of the world will be used to promote some fresh thinking among the developed countries about the problem of resource flows to the developing world." But Singh was not comfortable with Oshima's restricted vision.

> I do wish to point out that in the context of a sluggish world economy, slow growth of the OECD countries and a sharp decline in the rate of growth of world trade since the early eighties compared with 1950–73, the dream of an Asian Pacific age cannot become a living reality unless vigorous efforts are made to raise the productivity of the teeming millions of China and India. I suggest for your consideration that the growth rate of Japan, ASEAN and the NICs will experience a new powerful stimulus by a sharp improvement in the purchasing power and the import capacity of the people of China, India and other countries of South Asia. In a world of growing interdependence, an attitude of "prosperous provincialism" is clearly misplaced and I hope our Japanese friends will realize this.[32]

The highest aspiration for Southern intellectuals, in the late 1980s, was to align themselves with and mimic Japan, Inc. That was the highest hope, even as there was some reticence on Tokyo's part to propose itself for this role.

Japan's cautious eagerness to put its model forward as a rival to the Washington Consensus brought the debate into the offices of the World Bank. In June 1989 the Japanese government sent Masaki Shiratori to be Japan's man at the World Bank. A few months later, in September, Moeen Qureshi, senior vice president of the Bank, wrote a letter to Japan's Overseas Economic Cooperation Fund. Qureshi urged the Japanese to reconsider their subsidized "policy-directed loans to developing countries." Such loans went against the free-market nostrums fashionable in Washington. The Bank worried that such loans "could have an adverse impact on the development of the financial sector," and so "could create unnecessary distortions and set back financial reforms." Shiratori saw the letter and felt that Qureshi's argument "was hardly acceptable to us, both for practical reasons and in light of Japan's postwar experience of economic development."[33] A fight broke out both inside the Bank and between Tokyo and the Bank. "Many Executive Directors from developing countries

---

32   "Tokyo Conference on Global Adjustment and the Future of Asian Pacific Economy. Co-Sponsored by Asian and Pacific Development Centre and Institute of Developing Economies, Tokyo, 10–13 May 1988. Comment by Dr. Manmohan Singh, Secretary-General, The South Commission," SCA.

33   Masaki Shiratori, "Afterword to the Japanese Translation of the World Bank Report *The East Asian Miracle*," in Kenichi Ohno and Izumi Ohno, eds, *Japanese Views on Economic Development: Diverse Paths to the Market*, London: Routledge, 1998, p. 77.

agreed with the Japanese position, but to no avail," reports Robert Wade, who was a World Bank economist from 1984 to 1988.[34]

Like Shiratori, Isao Kubota of the Ministry of Finance was incensed. Both were bureaucrats with a deep commitment to the Japanese model. Kubota had his ministry write a paper on the Japanese view of Structural Adjustment. It appeared in October 1991 as "Issues Related to the World Bank's Approach to Structural Adjustment." The report criticized the Bank's neoliberal analysis and prescriptions, and offered instead the Japanese model—an explicit industrial strategy guided by directed and subsidized credit.[35] Kubota was livid with the United States. "It's really incredible," he pointed out. "They think their economic framework is perfect. I think they're wrong."[36] A highly respected academic, Shimada Haruo, pointed out that it had been "six years since the United States became a net debtor nation. The Americans seem to think that the problem [of US deficits] is like a simple 'temporary virus,' but it may be a case of AIDS."[37] Debt-driven consumerism and regulation on behalf of finance were hardly the answer, Shimada insisted. The Japanese model seemed more prudent. MITI's industrial policy, he noted, "does not take the form of pure government control nor does it function as pure industry self-adjustment. In a sense, it is similar to what takes place in a planned economy of a socialist country. Japanese-type capitalist systems of this nature have heretofore never been subjected to a discussion involving a thorough identification and analysis of advantages and disadvantages."[38]

The "Japanese road" evoked smirks at the Bank, whose new chief economist (from 1991) Lawrence Summers had a very low opinion of Japanese economists, who he called "second-rate."[39] The Bank was comfortable with its prejudices. When Shiratori asked the Bank to prepare a report on the Japanese view of development, the Bank dithered. Japan's economic clout clearly did not confer political heft.

---

34   Wade, "Japan, the World Bank, and the Art of Paradigm Maintenance," p. 9.

35   Ibid., p. 10.

36   "Japan Wants Strings on Aid: At Odds with US, Tokyo Urges Managed Economics," *International Herald Tribune*, March 2, 1992.

37   Chalmers Johnson, *Japan: Who Governs?* New York: W. W. Norton, 1995, pp. 58–9.

38   Johnson, *Japan*, p. 59. Saburo Okita's formula was for "planning *with* market forces rather than planning *against* market forces." "Many Paths to Development," in South Centre, *Facing the Challenge*, p. 273.

39   Wade, "Japan, the World Bank, and the Art of Paradigm Maintenance," p. 10. Such cutting remarks seem commonplace. Joseph Stiglitz, who was the Bank's chief economist, complained that the IMF staff "frequently consists of third-rate students from first-rate universities." "What I Learned at the World Economic Crisis," *New Republic*, April 17–24, 2000, pp. 56–60.

Indeed, in 1991, the Bank already had an internal problem to deal with. One of its most respected senior economists, Sanjay Lall, had written a report on industrialization in Korea, India, and Indonesia that veered dangerously close to the MITI position. It was spiked. The Bank's senior vice president wrote to the chairman of the Joint Audit Committee that Lall's report "is at variance with best practices as we know them, and would therefore be very counter-productive to the country dialogues." If the Bank allowed this report to be published, governments would "point out that the Bank's own evaluation department has concluded that the Bank's current approach is incorrect."[40] Most of the sixty-six-page report was along neoliberal lines, commending the Bank's work in pushing export-oriented industrialization in the South. It contained a modest criticism of the Bank's inadequate attention to institutional support and capacity-building—code words for government intervention in industrial policy. If Japan had not pushed for its publication, it might still sit in an archive. It was published in 1992.[41]

It was into this fight that Manmohan Singh waded in March 1989. Sections within the Bank had begun to lose confidence in the Structural Adjustment approach, and in the Bank's preferred policy of financial "deregulation" (as opposed to the Japanese approach of industrialization via directed credit). When the Bank championed "deregulation," it did not mean no regulation: what it meant was reconfiguring the rules to benefit the financial sector. Governments enhanced the capacity of private banks and investment houses to discipline Southern borrowers and Northern debt-financed borrowers. The financial houses were "too big to fail," but not so the indebted countries of the global South or the indebted families of the global North: their failures had to be reconciled, their liabilities paid up. More than three-quarters of the economists at the World Bank were trained in US economics departments, where the orthodoxy of the 1980s used technical skill (econometrics, for example) to mask their adherence to neoliberal principles.[42] The Bank's reluctance to

---

40   Wade, "Japan, the World Bank, and the Art of Paradigm Maintenance," pp. 11–12.

41   Farrokh Najmabadi, Shyamadas Banerji, and Sanjay Lall (Operations Evaluations Department), *World Bank Support for Industrialization in Korea, India and Indonesia*, Washington, DC: World Bank, 1992. Najmabadi had been a minister in the shah's government before coming to the World Bank.

42   For a broad study, see Jamie Peck, *Constructions of Neoliberal Reason*, Oxford: Oxford University Press, 2010. The literature on how professional economists devastated the South is very rich, including Sarah Babb, *Managing Mexico: Economists from Nationalism to Neoliberalism*, Princeton: Princeton University Press, 2001; Juan Gabriel Valdés, *Pinochet's Economists: The Chicago School in Chile*, Cambridge: Cambridge University Press, 1995; Paul Dragos Aligica and Anthony Evans, *The Neoliberal Revolution in Eastern Europe*, Cheltenham: Edward Elgar, 2009; and the essays in

acknowledge the Japanese argument was a function of this ideological fealty of its economists, but also of more prosaic factors. Like most of the corporate world, it had to bend its knee to the institutional dominance of finance. As Wade put it, "the Bank's ability to borrow at the best rates and to act as a country-rating agency depends on its reputation among financial capitalists, which in turn depends on its manifest commitment to *their* version of 'sound' public policies."[43]

Japanese pressure eventually forced the Bank to begin a study of its model—which it carried out grudgingly. The regional vice president for East Asia, Gautam Kaji (a Wharton graduate), had not been told of the study. When he found out, he was aghast. The chief economist in his division, Vinod Thomas (a University of Chicago economics graduate), was just completing a book that described East Asia's example as a triumph of neoliberal policies and the Washington Consensus.[44] The book was co-authored with Ramgopal Agarwala (a University of Manchester graduate), who had cut his teeth on the Africa desk. Agarwala had shown that "some doubts about the efficacy of adjustment in Africa began to emerge" in the late 1980s. "It was becoming clear that 'prices and markets could not deliver' without a solid domestic institutional base for governance and development management."[45] These reconstructed neoliberal ideas (with more political than economic reform) did not leak into the work on the Pacific Rim. Africa had to be cordoned off. Thomas had directed the publication of the *World Development Report 1991*, whose subtitle teased the South Commission report (it was *The Challenge of Development*, as opposed to *The Challenge to the South*). Thomas took Larry Summers's phrase, "market-friendly," and proposed that the World Bank pursue "market-friendly" development. It was quite separate from the MITI framework. "Like the Vatican," Robert Wade notes wryly, "and for similar reasons, [the Bank] cannot afford to admit fallibility."[46]

Véronica Montecinos and John Markoff, eds, *Economists in the Americas*, Cheltenham: Edward Elgar, 2009.

43   Wade, "Japan, the World Bank, and the Art of Paradigm Maintenance," p. 15.

44   It was eventually published as Vinod Thomas and Ramgopal Agarwala, *Sustaining Rapid Growth in East Asia and the Pacific*, Washington, DC: World Bank, 1993.

45   Ramgopal Agarwala and Pushpa Schwartz, "Sub-Saharan Africa: A Long-Term Perspective Study," paper for the World Bank Workshop on Participatory Development, May 17–20, 1994, pp. 13, 26. The next year, the World Bank published *Adjustment in Africa: Reforms, Results and the Road Ahead*, which provided a reconstructed neoliberalism, now more concerned with governance than money supply. For a critique of the turn to governance, see Susanne Soederberg, *Global Governance in Question*, London: Pluto Press, 2006.

46   Wade, "Japan, the World Bank, and the Art of Paradigm Maintenance," p. 35.

John Page, a Stanford student of the former Bank chief economist Anne Krueger, led the team tasked with producing the Japanese-pushed report. They found a "middle road": "it is possible that some of these non-orthodox policies helped some of the time, but, with some exceptions, we can't show it."[47] In 1993, the Bank published *The East Asian Miracle*, the fruit of this process. "Our evidence leads us to conclude that credit programmes directed at exports yielded high social returns and, in the cases of Japan and Korea, other directed-credit programmes also may have increased investment and generated important spill-overs."[48] Such tentative language was sufficient for the MITI, who saw this report as an opening salvo. They did not mind World Bank president Lewis Preston's anemic preface, in which he caviled, "The authors conclude that rapid growth in each economy was primarily due to the application of a set of common, market-friendly economic policies."[49] Preston came to the Bank from J. P. Morgan, and brought all the prejudices associated with the barons of Wall Street.

A World Bank–Japanese government seminar in Tokyo in early December 1993 raked the report over the coals. Masaki Shiratori argued that the theory of comparative advantage must not be seen outside history: "Many developing countries desperately need to get rid of the monoculture in such commodities as coffee, cocoa, copper and tin, which resulted in static comparative advantage."[50] Shiratori further noted, "A latecomer to industrialization cannot afford to leave everything to the market mechanism. The trial and error inherent in market-driven industrialization is too risky and expensive considering the scarcity of resources." Toru Yanagihara, a Yale graduate who had authored the October 1991 critique of Bank policy, was blunter. "Where's the beef?" he asked, before launching into a critique of the "black box" methodology behind the report.[51] Shiratori had also gone after the technical problems with the report.[52]

---

47   Ibid., p. 19.

48   *The East Asian Miracle: Economic Growth and Public Policy*, Washington, DC: World Bank, 1993, p. 356.

49   Ibid., p. vi.

50   Wade, "Japan, the World Bank, and the Art of Paradigm Maintenance," p. 29. Shiratori's presentation is "The Role of Government in Economic Development: Comments on 'East Asian Miracle' Study," paper presented at Overseas Economic Cooperation Fund conference on *The East Asian Miracle*, December 3, 1993.

51   For his full analysis, see Toru Yanagihara, "Anything New in the Miracle Report? Yes and No," *World Development* 22: 4 (April 1994). See also, "Pacific Basin Economic Relations: Japan's New Role?" *Developing Economies* 25: 4 (December 1987). Toru Yanagihara's presentation at the 1993 conference is "Framework Approach and 'Ingredients Approach.'"

52   The critique is along the lines of several of the essays in Albert Fishlow, Catherine Gwin, Stephan Haggard, Dani Rodrik, and Robert Wade, eds, *Miracle or*

He was particularly incensed by the disregard shown to the "infant industry" thesis—that the Japanese government had harnessed its resources to promote the creation of Japanese industry: "The government actively intervened to develop specific industries with high growth potential. We picked winners such as steel, shipbuilding, synthetic fiber, petrochemicals, automobiles, machinery and parts, electric appliances and electronics, and so forth, most of which were infant industries in Japan at that time. I totally disagree with the report's statement that 'many infant industries have never grown up.'"[53]

Shiratori's justified anger aligned with the historical record. Japan and Northwest Asia did not follow the kind of foreign direct investment- and multinational corporation–driven development that was more commonplace in Hong Kong and Singapore. Instead, land reforms in the 1940s and 1950s had been accompanied by state protection of crucial infant industries that were geared towards export. The experts called this formula "effective protection conditional on export promotion" (EPconEP). Such a strategy, as the Malaysian economist K. S. Jomo puts it, "can hardly be equated with trade liberalization."[54] A fantasy history had been grafted onto the Japanese story, and it was being sold to the rest of the South as reality. This irked Shiratori.

Isao Kubota agreed with his colleagues but was more optimistic: "Perhaps the best lesson could be that policy makers and policy advisers, including those in the World Bank, should not be dogmatic but be pragmatic. For that purpose *modesty, not arrogance, and a sincere attitude* toward finding the right policy measures, are essential."[55] Japan's $1.2 million grant for this study paid very limited dividends.

The contest between neoliberalism and MITI took place as Japan's own model began to unravel. A mini earthquake struck Kabutocho when the stock market–induced bubble burst in 1990; it was followed the next year by the bursting of the real-estate bubble. The yen was a compromised currency, chained to the dollar. The Plaza Accord (1985) allowed the dollar to devalue against the yen (to cut the US current account deficit), and then in 1995 Washington pushed Japan to devalue the yen. The Japanese economy went into free-fall, with ordinary people taking their earnings and burying them in their mattresses (the savings rate rose to 32 percent). Japanese banks re-inflated new asset bubbles along the Pacific Rim.[56] This was the prelude to the Asian

---

Design? Lessons from the East Asian Experience, Washington, DC: Overseas Development Council, 1994.

53   Shiratori, "Role of Government."

54   K. S. Jomo, "Introduction," in Jomo, ed., *South East Asian Paper Tigers? From Miracle to Debacle and Beyond*, London: Routledge, 2003, p. 13.

55   Wade, "Japan, the World Bank, and the Art of Paradigm Maintenance," p. 29.

56   Ronald McKinnon and Kenichi Ohno, *Dollar and Yen: Resolving the Conflict between the United States and Japan*, Cambridge: MIT Press, 1997.

Crisis of 1997–98, which finally buried Tokyo's confidence. It did not matter that the latter crisis could not be laid fully at the door of the MITI; deregulation of financial markets in the early 1990s was at the root of the credit crunch. Financial deregulation drew in hot money to the bourses of Indonesia, South Korea, and Thailand, but when the US Federal Reserve raised interest rates in the late 1990s to circumvent inflation, capital fled the Pacific Rim for the dollar.[57] The IMF ducked culpability, as did the US Federal Reserve. Unable to convert its reserves and power into an ideological and institutional alternative to the United States, Japan had to revert to its subordinate position.

The crisis that struck Japan hard in the late 1990s drew swift reprisals from neoliberal economists within the country who had derided the view that state intervention was a good idea. Noguchi Yukio called for the market to be freed from the developmental state. His was the more commonplace version of neoliberalism, with no cultural characteristics attached to economics. Ishihara Shintaro, meanwhile, also called for the retreat of the state, but this time from the standpoint of cultural nationalism: foreign interference had to end, and Japan needed to assert a manly ruggedness in its economic policy and towards its Asian neighbors. Ishihara's views governed the administrations of the two Japanese prime ministers—Junichiro Koizumi (2001–06) and Shinzo Abe (2006–07)—who drew Japan firmly towards a neoliberal foundation for what they thought would be growth, but which turned out to be long-term stagnation.[58]

East Asian intellectuals outside Japan went into a kind of cultural hibernation. A reconstructed Confucianism invigorated intellectuals and politicians from Singapore (Kishore Mahbubani and Lee Kuan Yew) and Beijing (Tu Weiming and Ye Xuanping Li). It was less an offensive display of an alternative path than a defensive protection of how the Pacific Rim had operated, trying to keep out the full influence of the Washington Consensus.[59] Neo-Confucianism

---

57   Robert Wade, "The Asian Debt-and-Development Crisis of 1997–?: Causes and Consequences," *World Development* 26: 8 (August 1998); and the essays in Jomo, *South East Asian Paper Tigers?* Yoshio Suzuki, the shadow minister of economy and finance, accepted this version of events, but suggested that, rather than protecting currencies, what was required was protecting the safety net for the payment system—maintaining financial deregulation, but ensuring these protections. Yoshio Suzuki, "What Lessons Can Be Learned from the Recent Financial Crises? The Japanese Experience," paper delivered at the "Maintaining Financial Stability in a Global Economy" symposium of the Federal Reserve Bank of Kansas City, Jackson Hole, Wyoming, August 28–30, 1997.

58   Laura Hein, "The Cultural Career of the Japanese Economy: Development and Cultural Nationalism in Historical Perspective," *Third World Quarterly* 29: 3 (2008), pp. 460–2.

59   Prashad, *Darker Nations*, p. 256. See also Kishore Mahbubani, "The United

explained the Rim's growth as a consequence of cultural factors. The switch by Japan to neoliberal policy eclipsed its ability to make a bid for an alternative path to development. Either there was a cultural component to Japan, Inc.—in which case it could not be exported beyond the borders of Confucianism—or there was no real Japan, Inc.—in which case the point was moot. In either case, it marked the end of the Tokyo Road.[60]

A RAILING AT THE ABYSS

By 1989, when Manmohan Singh delivered his lecture at the Bank, the South Commission and the NAM knew not to look to the North for inspiration and leadership. A brief interlude of hope in Japan had also faded by the early 1990s. The NAM states had to look elsewhere. They turned to the largest countries among them—those with the greatest confidence to find a solution to their economic and political challenges to become the leading engines of their regions. The NICs, such as the Four Tigers (Hong Kong, Singapore, South Korea, and Taiwan), had moved their societies from absolute poverty to relative prosperity. The poverty rate in South Korea, for instance, had fallen from 23.4 percent in 1970 to 4.5 percent in 1998. But South Korea's example, like that of the other NICs, was not replicable. Much of the groundwork for the take-off in the 1970s and 1980s was rooted in the social reforms of a generation earlier (land reforms, redistribution, and education provision). In 1989, South Korea's population was only 42.4 million, far smaller than the giants of the South.[61] Its unique development history and small size suggested that its path could not be followed schematically, and that it would not have the capacity to pull the rest of the South out of penury. Moreover, NICs like South Korea did not have the political stomach to act as the locomotives of the South; they looked to the North for markets and for financial stability, without so much as a backward glance at the other nations of the South. The NICs also relied upon the North for their military security. What was needed was for intellectuals to consider the potential of their large states (India, Brazil, China, Indonesia) that had the population and resources to become regional dynamos.

States: Go East, Young Man," *Washington Quarterly* 17: 2 (Spring 1994); and for a strong critical voice, Khoo Boo Teik, "The value(s) of a miracle: Malaysian and Singaporean elite constructions of Asia," *Asian Studies Review* 23:2, 1999.

60   Of course, Japan's economic strength has not been entirely whittled away. For the past fifteen years, "a very minor but nagging deflation has set in, and the economy's growth rate slowed to a crawl." Jon Hilsenrath and Megumi Fujikawa, "Japan's Bernanke Hits Out at His Critics in the West," *Wall Street Journal*, March 1, 2011, p. A12.

61   All the South Korean numbers, and more figures on the NICs, are in K. S. Jomo, "Growth With Equity in East Asia?" DESA Working Paper no. 33, New York: Department of Economic and Social Affairs, United Nations, September 2006.

At the 1989 NAM Summit in Belgrade, the Peruvian president, Alan Garcia, invited to breakfast representatives from the two formations that had begun to meet independently at the NAM: the Paris Initiative (Egypt, India, Senegal, and Venezuela) and the Peru Group (Algeria, Argentina, Indonesia, Jamaica, Malaysia, Nigeria, Peru, Yugoslavia, and Zimbabwe). Two non-NAM members (Brazil and Mexico) were invited to join the group.[62] Garcia proposed that they create a summit group of the South, a counterpart to the G7. This group would interact and negotiate with the G7 on behalf of the South. India's Rajiv Gandhi had proposed to create a summit group as well, but had intended that, rather than turn its eyes to the North, it should be a platform for South-South cooperation. It has often been said that Gandhi took this position to neutralize the efforts of Alan Garcia, which were more confrontational. At any rate, the small group agreed to establish the Group of Fifteen (G15). A statement was drafted, and Nyerere, in his capacity as chair of the South Commission, read it out at a press conference.

These leaders recognized that the formations they had inherited had run their course. UNCTAD had been constrained by pressure from the G7. Only two people staffed the G77's secretariat, while the ramshackle NAM had been unable to produce a coherent policy.[63] The UN had been substantially overrun by the P5. In February 1993, the UN secretary-general, Boutros Boutros-Ghali, had lunch with the US secretary of state, Warren Christopher, and the US ambassador to the UN, Madeleine Albright. Boutros-Ghali asked them to give the UN some latitude: "Please allow me from time to time to differ publicly from US policy." He recalls that Christopher and Albright "looked at each other as though the fish I had served was rotten." They said nothing. Boutros-Ghali recalled the statement by the Israeli prime minister, Golda Meir: "If you are with me 99 percent, you are not with me."[64] If the UN secretary-general felt under the thumb, it was hopeless for the G77 and the NAM—for the South in general. Those countries with some measure of economic and political confidence decided to put themselves forward as the unelected executive of the South. Before the South lay the abyss; the G15 was the railing that prevented free-fall.[65]

---

62 My narrative relies upon Kripa Sridharan, "G-15 and South-South Cooperation: Promise and Performance," *Third World Quarterly* 19: 3 (September 1998); the materials of the G15; interviews with people who have been involved with the G15 process; and, most importantly, Branislav Gosovic, "The South in the World Arena: Sufficient Institutional Support, the Missing Link," manuscript (contribution to a festschrift for Muchkund Dubey, 2010).

63 Fawzy Mansour, "A Second Wave of National Liberation?" *Monthly Review* 50: 9 (February 1999).

64 Boutros-Ghali, *Unvanquished*, p. 198.

65 This is a more generous interpretation than my first crack at it: Prashad, *Darker Nations*, pp. 280–1. There I treated the G15 almost as a commercial marketplace for the

Dr. Mahathir Mohamad of Malaysia embraced the idea of the G15 during the NAM meeting in Kuala Lumpur in 1989. It was not clear that the fifteen countries would be the engines for the NAM states, but they had the boldness to think that they might. Prime minister of Malaysia since 1981, Mahathir had vast ambition for his country. For the first few years, Mahathir pursued "Nicdom," to follow the example of the Four Tigers (Hong Kong, Singapore, South Korea, and Taiwan), whose state-directed capitalism came encased in the rhetoric of "Asian values," which appealed to the Malaysian elites. Mahathir pushed a cultural change in his country that would go along with the economic reforms he had announced. Islamism was accompanied by a call for Malaysians to become "a nation of workaholics."[66] A massive expansion of state investment, financed by Asian Rim capital and the Malaysian exchequer, was combined with a vast privatization program to encourage that capital to come to Malaysia. By the late 1980s, the dreams of the NIC road and of Japan Inc. had faltered. A decline in commodity prices showed up the fact that the Malaysian effort had been paid for by the export of raw materials. The financial turbulence increased the burden of an intractable foreign debt and stemmed the tide of financial investment. Mahathir recalibrated, moving towards a more state-authoritarian model, with no room for dissent and a greater push for industrialization (to cut back on Malaysia's reliance upon raw-material exports and component manufacturing). Consistent with his "Look East" policy, Mahathir adopted the idea of South-South cooperation. Much the same kind of thinking went on in Lima and Delhi, in Lagos and Algiers.

The North-South dialogue ended at Cancún, and there was no hope of any further openings. Mahathir expected that the Canadians or the French might pick up the baton, but neither seemed interested. Canada was not a good option. The United States had corralled both Canada and Mexico into discussions on the North American Free Trade Agreement (NAFTA), culminating in its passage in 1994. France was a better bet, except that François Mitterrand's government had more interest in the "southern wind" blowing from Francophone Africa than in the global South as a whole.[67] The Paris Conference of the 1970s had burned France's hand; it did not want to extend it again. Besides, Europe's attentions were diverted to the East. The Berlin Wall

fifteen countries to broadcast their various opportunities for transnational capital. My reading of the South Commission process has led me to alter my analytical assessment.

66   I draw from the remarkable work of Khoo Boo Teik, "Economic Vision and Political Opposition in Malaysia, 1981–96: The Politics of the Mahathir Era," *Copenhagen Journal of Asian Studies* 12 (1997), p. 12; and from his full study, *Paradoxes of Mahathirism: An Intellectual Biography of Mahathir Mohamad*, Kuala Lumpur: Oxford University Press, 1995.

67   Guy Martin, "Continuity and Change in Franco-African Relations," *Journal of Modern African Studies* 33: 1 (1995).

fell in August 1989, and the unification of Germany would take place within months. Jeffrey Sachs of Harvard packed his bags in Bolivia and set off for Poland, where he injected a strong dose of "shock therapy" into the already tired country, setting in motion a fire-sale of assets across eastern Europe and into Russia. Sachs and his colleague David Lipton portrayed the story as the East's "intense desire to rejoin the economies of Western Europe."[68] The anxiety over Europe's involvement in the European Union process and in the outreach towards the heartlands of fallen Communism was quite real. The South rightly worried that the already exhausted North-South dialogue would be sacrificed to the East-West communion.

At the first G15 meeting in Kuala Lumpur, in June 1990, the communiqué optimistically hoped that the East-West rapprochement would create "opportunities for a renewed thrust to international cooperation for development."[69] The next month, at a seminar of the ambassadors of the South in Geneva, Manmohan Singh worried that the entry of eastern Europe into the capitalistic bloc would hurt the "export interests of the Third World." Fierce competition for the Western markets would pick up, while the preferential trade agreements with the Eastern countries had already begun to unravel. "If the interests of the Third World are not to be hurt," Singh said, "both OECD countries and the USSR and Eastern Europe will need to devise effective mechanisms to ensure that the access of developing countries to their markets is progressively improved."[70] These hopes were soon dashed. By the second meeting of the G15 in Caracas, in November 1991, the "opportunities" became "challenges for international economic and political stability."[71] Public aid had already declined to historic lows, and private foreign direct investment was chary of going south in the throes of the debt crisis, and without proper guarantees on its investment. The G15 correctly forecast the total cessation of the global North's interest in development for the South.

The large countries, on which the hopes of the South rested, were not in any condition to exert themselves. Brazil had only recently been wrested from

---

68   David Lipton and Jeffrey Sachs, "Creating a Market Economy in Eastern Europe: The Case of Poland," *Brookings Papers on Economic Activity*: 1 (1990), p. 76. The facts of the "piratization" are assembled in Marshall Goldman, *The Piratization of Russia: Russian Reform Gone Awry*, New York: Routledge, 2003.

69   Group of Fifteen, "First Meeting of the Summit Level Group for South-South Consultation and Cooperation," June 1–3, 1990, Kuala Lumpur, p. 1.

70   Manmohan Singh, "The Impact of the Recent Evolution of East-West Relations on the Growth of the World Economy, in Particular, on the Economic Growth and Development of the Developing Countries, as well as on International Economic Cooperation," July 17, 1990, p. 5, SCA.

71   Group of Fifteen, "Second Meeting of the Summit Level Group for South-South Consultation and Cooperation," Caracas, November 27–29, 1991, p. 1.

dictatorship, but its government, under President José Sarney, plunged Brazil into the cauldron of IMF-style austerity. The fiscal situation in India, alongside various political trials, had the country in a kind of stasis, with little indication that it could break out in any direction. Indonesia festered under the authoritarian ineptitude of the Suharto regime, and South Africa remained under a racist apartheid government. It was unthinkable that any or all of these would break out of their institutional paralysis and forge a new path outside the constraints imposed on them by the North.

With no Soviet bloc, the US had begun to plot its "full-spectrum dominance" of the planet. The first demonstration of its armed might came in Panama (1989), and then against Iraq (1991). The US had long treated Central America as its backyard, and military interventions in the region had become commonplace. The assault on Iraq was of a different magnitude. Armed and funded by both the US and Saudi Arabia, Iraq had been the bulwark during the 1980s against Iran's attempt to revise the power equation in the Middle East.[72] Economically bankrupt and socially exhausted by the long war against Iran, Iraq in 1990 sought to revise the price of oil upwards to prevent a collapse into chaos. Kuwait refused, then demanded payment of its loans and, according to Iraq, began to drill into the Iraqi oilfields of Rumaila. Ambiguous remarks by the US ambassador to Baghdad allowed Saddam Hussein the illusion that he would be allowed to punish his neighbor (the ambassador had said, "We want oil to flow without hindrance, but we have never taken substantive positions on intra-OPEC or Arab border disputes").[73] After Saddam invaded Kuwait on August 2, the US went ballistic. US troops entered Saudi Arabia, US diplomats prowled the halls of the UN seeking a resolution against Iraq's action, and war drums sounded without respite. Saddam Hussein's war cabinet fretted. The US air war began in January, while Baghdad hoped for Soviet diplomatic intervention to stop a land war. It was in one of the all-night sessions in Baghdad that Saddam's culture minister, Hamid Hammadi, identified the real issue at stake. It was not Iraq's 1990 aggression, however egregious that was; nor was it Iraq's role in the Middle East (a problem that did exercise the various Gulf sheikhs). The rush to war was about something else: "All these developments intend not only to destroy Iraq, but to eliminate the role of the Soviet Union so the United States can control the fate of all humanity."[74]

---

72   For the war and its entangled alliances, see Dilip Hiro, *The Longest War: The Iran-Iraq Military Conflict*, New York: Routledge, 1990; and Joost Hiltermann, *A Poisonous Affair: America, Iraq and the Gassing of Halabja*, Cambridge: Cambridge University Press, 2007.

73   "President Bush's Response to Saddam's Message—Next Steps," Cable from US Ambassador April Glaspie to the State Department, July 27, 1990, Bush Library.

74   Conflict Records Research Center, Record no. SH-SHTP-A-000-931. Transcript of conversation between Saddam Hussein and his inner circle, February 24,

By the end of 1989, it was clear that the USSR was in serious decline. When German unification came onto the agenda, the Soviets tried to slow things down, at the very least preventing the united Germany from being part of NATO. Bush reacted in February 1990: "To hell with that! We prevailed, they didn't. We can't let the Soviets clutch victory from the jaws of defeat."[75] The US no longer needed to be politic. The cowboy was unleashed. As Boutros-Ghali and Gosovic argued, "This was an imperial version of global leadership, spearheaded by a single superpower and amply backed by legions of followers worldwide. It was guided by its geopolitical goals, underlying national objectives, domestic and interest group politics, and corporate agendas, and it drew inspiration and intellectual guidance from a specific school of political and economic thought"—namely, neoliberalism.[76]

It was no surprise, then, that the G15 suffered from very poor morale. Attendance at its annual summits was abysmal. The 1993 summit in New Delhi had to be cancelled for lack of a quorum (only three heads of government attended—from Indonesia, Malaysia, and Zimbabwe). The postponed summit, in March 1994, fared little better—only six of fifteen heads of government arrived. The G15 had created a set of useful programs, such as the South Investment, Trade and Technology Data Exchange Centre (SITTDEC) and the Gene Banks for Medicinal and Aromatic Plants (GEBMAP). These were flayed for lack of funds. The most remarkable failure came at Marrakesh, where the Uruguay Round of the GATT came to a close. At their Dakar summit in 1992, the G15 had suggested that a common stand would be an important step towards "the successful and balanced conclusion of the Uruguay Round."[77] The G15 did not produce such a position (partly because of the failed meeting in Delhi, which meant that the G15 met in March, only weeks before the April 1994 signatures on the GATT agreement in Marrakesh).

Debt remained on the agenda, and so too did intellectual property. The total debt was now $1,320 billion, and the G15 states themselves owed half of that amount. They were the bigger countries, but they remained as vulnerable as the LDCs. All this united them—but what divided them, and therefore resulted

---

1991, p. 13. These records were captured by the United States military and are now housed in the Institute for National Strategic Studies, National Defense University, Washington, DC. For the broader context, see my "Baghdad and the Emergence of the New World Order, 1990–2003," *Naked Punch*, 2012.

75 Mary Elise Sarotte, *1989: The Struggle to Create Post–Cold War Europe*, Princeton: Princeton University Press, 2009, p. 128.

76 Boutros Boutros-Ghali and Branislav Gosovic, *Global Leadership and Global Systemic Issues: South, North and the United Nations in a 21st Century World*, Versonnex: Transcend University Press, 2011, p. 28.

77 Group of Fifteen, "Third Meeting of the Summit Level Group for South-South Consultation and Cooperation," Dakar, November 21–23, 1992, p. 8.

in a lack of incentive and low morale, were their disagreements on international politics. The Latin American states led the way towards conciliation, if not utter subservience, to the North Atlantic states. Mexico was compromised by the ongoing NAFTA negotiations; its president, Carlos Salinas de Gortari had taken power after an unresolved election in 1988, and thereafter governed Mexico from the right (he reversed the 1982 bank nationalization, embraced the United States, and conducted a fire-sale of state assets, many of them to his associate Carlos Slim).[78] Argentina and Chile were petrified into quiescence by their fragile economic situation. To combat hyperinflation, the Argentine peso was pegged to the dollar, so the old Peronist fighter Carlos Menem had no space for maneuver. In Chile the government was in the hands of the Christian Democrats, whose leader, Eduardo Frei, told the 5th Summit of the G15 in Buenos Aires, in 1995, that they must produce a "viable and credible" proposal for the North Atlantic states. "All spirit of confrontation must be overcome and a climate of trust and solidarity generated."[79] By solidarity, Frei meant amicability with the North. Given the track record of Washington and other Northern capitals, this meant that the South had to be on its knees.

Such a posture did not appeal to others in the G15. Certainly the erratic leader of Malaysia could not stomach it; nor could Zimbabwe's combative Robert Mugabe. Both Mahathir and Mugabe were unlikely champions of the Third World's standard. Mahathir pulled himself up from the ranks of the lower middle class to become a doctor, and then entered politics through the United Malays National Organisation (his father, as it happens, is not Malay, but of Indian origin). A fierce determination to turn around Malaysia's subordination drove his entire political career. This was also what drove Mugabe, who had a similar class background to Mahathir (his father, a carpenter, abandoned the family early on). Both Mugabe and Mahathir were lucky that their keen intelligence and ambition were identified by benevolent adults; they left their native countries to study in different political cauldrons, one in Fort Hare (South Africa) and the other in King Edward VII Medical School (Singapore). Mugabe, unlike Mahathir, went into the rough and tumble of the guerrilla struggle against the racist regime of Ian Smith. Both Mahathir and Mugabe strengthened their positions as authoritarian leaders of their political parties, and neither had a strong affinity for democracy. They saw themselves as liberation leaders whose leadership should not be questioned. It was this authoritarian power that allowed them to buck the trend in the world and stand against the North Atlantic; they were already reviled, and they had little to lose. But that does not mean that they did not have to accept all manner of

---

78   Rafael Montesinos and Griselsa Martinez V, "Empresarios, Neoliberalismo y Las Miserias de la Transición," *El Cotidiano* 16: 100 (March–April 2000).

79   Sridharan, "G-15 and South-South Cooperation," p. 369.

compromises: in 1980 Mugabe went hat-in-hand to the IMF. Mahathir, on the other hand, refused an IMF package in 1997.[80]

Mahathir and Mugabe were pariahs in the eyes of the North Atlantic. This had little to do with their domestic authoritarianism, although that provided the G7 with fodder for mockery. Others with even more authoritarian tendencies (such as the Saudi royal family or Mubarak's neoliberal authoritarianism in Egypt) were given a free pass. What incensed Washington—and London—was the refusal of states like Malaysia and Zimbabwe to accede to the new geometry of power. From Washington came the idea of the "rogue state"—describing places such as Cuba, Iran, Iraq, Libya, and North Korea (with Malaysia and Zimbabwe not far behind) that, as US Secretary of State Madeleine Albright put it, "do not have a part in the international system, but whose very being involves being outside of it and throwing, literally, hand grenades inside in order to destroy it."[81] In this hyperbolic analysis, the rogue states posed an existential threat to US primacy. The rhetoric from Washington heated up as the 1990s unfolded, with William Perry, Clinton's secretary of defense, calling for an end to deterrence. The "rogue states," Perry argued in 1996, are "undeterrables ... madder than MAD [Mutually Assured Destruction]."[82] Military force was the only option against them. No wonder Mahathir and Mugabe were obdurate: they had nothing to lose. They wanted the G15 to have a much more ambitious role, to provide a countervailing force to Washington's dominance.

Mahathir and Mugabe had a surprising ally in India's P. V. Narasimha Rao, who told the 5th Summit, in 1995, that the North would not help the South, but on the contrary would burden them with "ill-concealed conditionalities based on some lofty-sounding principles such as the so-called social clause."[83] Under Rao, India had begun to liberalize its economy and turn its back on the older social contracts that came from the kind of heritage championed by Mugabe and Mahathir. It was a curious collaboration, but it also made sense. What

---

80   On Mahathir, see Khoo Boo Teik's two books, *Paradoxes of Mahathirism: An Intellectual Biography of Mahathir Mohamad*, Kuala Lumpur: Oxford University Press, 1996; and *Beyond Mahathir: Malaysian Politics and Its Discontents*, London: Zed Books, 2003. On Mugabe, see Horace Campbell's *Reclaiming Zimbabwe: The Exhaustion of the Patriarchal Model of Liberation*, Cape Town: David Philip, 2003. For the details of their lives, though both books are rather tendentious, see Barry Wain, *Malaysian Maverick: Mahathir Mohamad in Turbulent Times*, New York: Palgrave, 2010; and Andrew Norman, *Robert Mugabe and the Betrayal of Zimbabwe*, Jefferson: McFarland, 2004.

81   US Secretary of State Madeleine Albright gave this speech in February 1998. It is quoted in K. P. O'Reilly, "Perceiving Rogue States: The Use of the 'Rogue State' Concept by US Foreign Policy Elites," *Foreign Policy Analysis* 3 (2007), p. 298.

82   Ibid., p. 208; and Michael Klare, *Rogue States and Nuclear Outlaws: America's Search for a New Foreign Policy*, New York: Hill & Wang, 1995.

83   Sridharan, "G-15 and South-South Cooperation," p. 365.

united them was the simple problem of how to deal with the debt crisis, and the humiliation of the conditions that were placed by the North on the South for the meager funds to cover the deficits. In the 1990s, the Latin American states did not want to confront the North, whereas the Africans and Asians had more stomach for a fight. That would change in a few years, when a new political wave in Latin America overturned the older regimes and punctured the caution of the ruling elites.

The fissures in the G15 rendered it largely irrelevant. One part of it remains dynamic, however. From its first meetings, at the margins, business leaders from the South took their place. A Business and Investment Forum was formed, and these "leading entrepreneurs" became the conduit for South-South cooperation.[84] It was their interests that had become paramount. When talk of a planetary minimum wage came onto the agenda in 1994, Mahathir beat it down. Low labor costs in the tropical states allowed them a comparative advantage against the temperate states. The working class and poor of their own societies had become externalities.

NEOLIBERALISM WITH SOUTHERN CHARACTERISTICS

Then there are the Third World giants—India, Indonesia, and Brazil. If these three countries, representing about 900 million people, were to separate themselves from other Third World countries and speak as one, they would still not be able to escape the reality of domination by the developed countries—at best, they could get marginal and temporary concessions. For the reality is that the unity of even the most powerful of the subgroups within the Third World is not sufficient to allow its members to become full actors, rather than reactors, in the world economic system.

Julius Nyerere, 1979[85]

In December 1990 the beleaguered Indian government of Chandra Shekhar invited Manmohan Singh to leave the South Commission and return to India as a senior advisor.[86] Singh left the South Commission and came to India. Bad news awaited him. The macroeconomic picture was ugly: not only was the inflation rate at 17 percent, but also the debt-service ratio had increased to 32 percent of the GDP. For every rupee earned by the exchequer, a third would go off to pay for the external debt (which was at $70 billion). The government collapsed, and an election was called. During the campaign, the Congress candidate, Rajiv Gandhi, was assassinated. In a sympathetic landslide the Congress took the election of 1991 under its caretaker elder, P. V. Narasimha Rao. Rao

---

84   Group of Fifteen, "Second Meeting," p. 8.
85   Nyerere, "Unity for a New Order," p. 6.
86   Amir Habib Jamal to Manmohan Singh, December 11, 1990, SCA.

turned to Singh to take over the finance ministry.[87] The fiscal situation spiraled downward—reserves fell to $1.2 billion, which only amounted to two weeks of imports. India seemed poised to fall like Mexico in 1982. It was a treacherous situation.

The Indian government airlifted forty-seven tons of gold to London as security against a short-term loan of $400 million from the Bank of London. India turned to the IMF. In November 1991 Manmohan Singh said, "Negotiations with the IMF were difficult because the world has changed. India is not immune. India has to survive and flourish in a world we cannot change in our own image. Economic relations are power relations. We are not living in a morality play."[88] The IMF later claimed that India had not been forced into any conditions. There were many options on the table, and the reforms enacted by the Rao government, under the stewardship of Singh, were its own.[89] The World Bank advised the government of its choices: "The only real options are whether the adjustment is made in the context of an orderly, growth-oriented adjustment program with external financial support, or through a disorderly and painful process that will leave the country cut off from international capital markets for years to come and significantly reduce its growth."[90] If this was the reality, then Singh had only one choice, which was to begin a program of directed austerity. Ideology was hastily buried beneath arithmetic. Reform was not an answer to budgetary woes; it came from deeper ideological sources and political commitments, fears and hopes rooted elsewhere than in crisis management.[91]

---

87 The first choice had been I. G. Patel, the veteran economist who, like Singh, had run the Reserve Bank of India but, unlike Singh, had been instrumental in the passage of fourteen federal budgets in his long tenure at the Finance Ministry, 1953–72.

88 Jeremy Seabrook, "The Reconquest of India: The Victory of International Monetary Fundamentalism," *Race & Class* 34: 1 (1992), p. 10.

89 In Chennai, in 2009, IMF chief Camdessus said that India had recovered from its 1991 shock "at a lower cost" because it did not follow the Fund's Structural Adjustment Program to the letter. "The decision was with [the Indian government] to save itself from the mess." The reform conditions enacted were "yours," he said, referring to the budgetary austerity. G. Srinivasan, "When India Approached IMF in 1991," *Business Line*, March 22, 2009. Other options are laid out in C. P. Chandrasekhar and Jayati Ghosh, *The Market That Failed: A Decade of Neo-liberal Economic Reforms in India*, New Delhi: LeftWord Books, 2002, p. 31.

90 World Bank, *India: 1991 Country Economic Memorandum (in two volumes). Volume 1: Policies for Adjustment and Growth*, Report no. 9412-IN, August 23, 1991, p. i, World Bank Archives.

91 The crisis had its roots less in the import-substitution regime and mild socialism of the previous governments than in the reckless management of the import policy in the aftermath of the oil shocks. Rather than properly servicing the energy needs and finding a way to cover the imports with a prudent industrial policy, the governments

The rupee was devalued against the dollar by 22 percent, and the currency was brought somewhat in line with the dollar–Wall Street regime. The public sector was starved of funds, and a fifth of public enterprises were to be sold off to the private sector. Subsidies for the farm sector (fertilizers and sugar) took a fall, with licensing for the industrial sector withdrawn in all but eighteen core sectors. Imports became freer, and foreign investors were allowed to acquire a 51 percent majority share in Indian ventures. Singh's mantra was to seek trade, not aid—and to trade, he needed to expand the export sector. Cautious of these ideas when he ran the Reserve Bank of India and was on the Planning Commission, he had been changed by events in the 1980s. As the *Financial Times* put it, "What really seems to have changed his outlook, however, was his becoming secretary-general of the South Commission in 1987, when he visited South Korea and Taiwan. He was much struck by the pace of economic growth under export-oriented policies. Though he now has a clear vision himself of where he wants India to go, he is also a pragmatist in adapting to the political pressures of the moment."[92] The goal was Nicdom, with the state being put into motion to construct enclaves of industry geared toward export.

Singh was aware of the history of the Pacific Rim's expansion. Without the land reforms, partial redistribution, and expenditure on education and infrastructure, the Pacific Rim's successes would have been naught. India's ruling coalition did not have the mandate for this kind of expenditure: its landlord base militated against land reforms (indeed wanted, and won, the roll-back of the very mild reforms in North India), and its urban base was wary of any welfare payments to the countryside, where the bulk of social spending would have to go to mimic the NIC experiment. The IMF had no will for such spending, and there was otherwise nothing in the exchequer that allowed the

---

of the 1970s and 1980s went on a buying spree, largely in pursuit of military expansion. Between 1986 and 1988, the Indian government imported arms close to the total figure of arms purchases by Iran and Iraq combined, when those countries were in the midst of a gruesome war. For more on this line of enquiry, see Mrinal Datta-Chaudhuri, "The Background to the Current Debate on Economic Reform: Oil-Shocks, Recession in World Trade and Adjustment Problems in the Indian Economy," in Ashok Guha, ed., *Economic Liberalisation, Industrial Structure and Growth in India*, Delhi: Oxford University Press, 1990; and, curiously, Ranjit S. Teja, "IMF-Supported Program Helps India Emerge from Crisis," *IMF Survey*, September 21, 1992, p. 285. This position is challenged by the orthodoxy, led by Manmohan Singh and Montek Singh Ahluwalia. Ahluwalia, speaking for this orthodoxy, argued that India was a "growth laggard" that needed to be pushed into dynamism. M. S. Ahluwalia, "Lessons from India's Economic Reforms," in Timothy Besley and Roberto Zagha, eds, *Development Challenges in the 1990s: Leading Policymakers Speak from Experience*, Washington, DC: World Bank, 2005.

92   David Housego and Alexander Nicoll, "India's Financial Architect," *Financial Times*, September 2, 1991, p. 32.

government to follow this policy independently. Instead, there was an urge to take the post–Soviet Russian route—to liquidate the profitable and unprofitable parts of the public sector to raise funds. The Communist bloc in the parliament joined with an assortment of socialists (some from the Congress party) to hold back the pace of the divestment (and prevent a Russian-style fire-sale of productive assets). They also prevented a wholesale disembowelment of the pension and insurance funds. The financial sector was eager to get its hands on these funds, to convert them into securities and trade them not only in Mumbai's stock exchange but, if the parliament would go along with it, in the bourses of the North. The Left prevented these extreme steps. The "slow pace" of reforms upset the IMF, whose head, Michel Camdessus remarked that if the government did not slow down its spending, inflation would rise. India needed "tighter financial control," which meant lower interest rates and less social welfare payments (the IMF did not point out that Indian military spending had risen by 20 percent in the 1994–95 budget). But Camdessus recognized the democracy quotient: "India is a big democracy in the world, and in a democracy, you must devote time to carrying people with you. The government is currently in that business."[93] Lobbying to break the "distribution coalition" and to strengthen the "growth coalition" had become one of the government's main agendas.[94] Over the course of the 1990s, most of the socialist bloc would lose its will, leaving the Communists in the parliament alone in their fight to maintain the "distribution coalition."

Much the same process was going on in Brazil and South Africa. Each emerged from its particular type of dictatorship into the arms of a range of nationalists (from liberals to leftists). The governments faced acute financial challenges, not the least of which were fire-breathing international financial organizations eager to step in and offer the harshest medicine. The textbooks read in Brasília and Pretoria were not from the Third World project; they came from the World Bank and the IMF, as well as from their peers in the G15 orbit. The leaders did not talk about "neoliberalism," but about "modernization." Men such as Marcílio Marques Moreira (finance minister, Brazil), Fernando Henrique Cardoso (finance minister, Brazil), Pedro Malan (finance minister, Brazil), Henrique Meirelles (chairman, Banco Central do Brasil), Trevor Manuel (finance minister, South Africa), Alec Erwin (trade and industry

---

93 Vasantha Arora, "IMF Chief Defends Indian Reforms Despite Deficits," *India West*, April 29, 1994, p. 2.

94 The terms "distribution coalition" and "growth coalition" come from Mancur Olson's *The Rise and Decline of Nations: Economic Growth, Stagflation and Social Rigidities*, New Haven: Yale University Press, 1982. I borrow them without endorsing the implication in Olson that the "distribution coalition" is anti-technology. That is not necessarily the case. Nor is this coalition necessarily a narrow lobby (sugar farmers, for instance).

minister, South Africa), and Tito Mboweni (governor, Reserve Bank of South Africa) were cautious in their tone, but not in their policies. They used whatever political leverage they could gain to push through "reforms" that pleased the bond markets and the North Atlantic institutions. The financial sector had them under control. When the trade union leader Luiz Inácio Lula da Silva ran in the Brazilian election in 2002, the bankers went on strike through the stock market. This forced Lula to write a "Letter to the Brazilian People" (derided as a "Letter to Calm the Bankers") in June, in which he said that his government would continue to service the debt and enforce the IMF program (which he would renew in 2003). Lula won the election, but "his concessions imposed narrow limits for the new administration."[95]

Liberation and democracy struggles in Brazil and South Africa held political assets in hand. They had examples of failure before them: the countries of the Third World Project that had squandered their assets over the course of the previous generation. It was not necessary to repeat those mistakes. New trade unions, new agricultural workers' movements, new slum movements: these were on the doorstop, ready to be harnessed as partners in a political formation to stand fast against international finance, willing to mobilize internal resources towards genuine social development. What the governments did was not its only pathway. It could have turned towards the organized left-wing that was sympathetic, in South Africa, to the African National Congress (ANC), and, in Brazil, to the Workers Party (PT). During the long struggle against authoritarianism in these countries, a broad coalition was formed that included the Communist parties, the trade unions, the peasant organization, and the new social movements. Unity of this kind had not been enabled in India, for instance, where the Left flank was fractured. The Brazilian and South African left did not have unreasonable expectations. They recognized that the pace of change would be slow, but that the needle of public policy should remain towards the left and not drift rightward. That was the bare minimum that they required. For that reason, the South African Communist Party and the Coalition of South African Trade Unions went into alliance with the ANC, and the Movimento dos Trabalhadores Sem Terra (MST) and its allies followed Lula to Brasília.[96]

---

95   Lecio Morais and Alfredo Saad-Filho, "Lula and the Continuity of Neoliberalism in Brazil: Strategic Choice, Economic Imperative or Political Schizophrenia," *Historical Materialism* 13: 1, p. 10. The joke about the Letter (originally called *Carta ao Povo Brasileiro* and derided as *Carta para Acalmar Banqueiro*) is from Benjamin Goldfrank and Brian Wampler, "From Petista Way to Brazilian Way: How the PT Changes in the Road," *Revista Debates* 2: 2 (July–December 2008), p. 259.

96   For a sense of the close relationship between the PT and the MST, see an interview with the MST's leader João Pedro Stedile, "Landless Battalions," *New Left Review* II/15 (May–June 2002).

Neither the South African nor the Brazilian government would go down the path of their left-wing allies. Instead, they took them for granted, and, with no other options, these allies nevertheless remained yoked to the ANC and the PT. The correct *position* for the left was certainly clear (to broaden the distribution coalition, and to push for the working class and the peasantry to be at the forefront of policymaking). But the correct *strategy* to attain this objective was much less clear: Was the alliance with the government able to stave off the right, protect sections of society from the full thrust of the North, and build a few rafts for the growth of the distribution coalition? Few in the left labored under the illusion that the PT or the ANC were driving their societies towards socialism. For example, two years into the new South Africa, the SACP began to talk of the "1996 Class Project"—the modernization of South Africa on behalf of the über-elites and the upper echelon of the middle class. The Class Project of the government was not only economic, the SACP argued, but also "a deliberate strategy to marginalize the SACP and COSATU and perhaps even provoke a walk-out [by the SACP and the COSATU] from the alliance." Four years later, COSATU worried that the ANC's corporate style of governance would lead to a "low intensity democracy, where the people are reduced to electing leaders every five years or so."[97] The ghoulish international environment, with the US pushing ravenously for primacy, and the suffocating domestic terrain, with the ANC and the PT offering the rhetorical gestures of left-liberalism, paralyzed the left.

The concessions of the PT, the ANC, and the Indian National Congress produced a fundamental departure from the stated objectives of the regimes in Brazil, India, and South Africa. The leaderships in each of these countries pushed a set of policies with three basic orientations:

1. To please the bond market and international financial interests by cleaning up fiscal and monetary policy. Deficits had to be cut savagely, currency had to be re-evaluated within the dollar regime, and financial rules had to be aligned to allow confidence among international financiers that if they invested in the country their returns would neither be delayed nor confiscated (lower taxes, then, were the rule). Private foreign direct investment, not public concessionary aid, was the policy objective for these reforms. Banks urged the IMF and the World Bank not to fund the public sector—they directed those investment-starved states towards the privatization of state-run enterprises.

---

97 William Gumede, *Thabo Mbeki and the Battle for the Soul of the ANC*, Cape Town: Zebra Press, 2007, p. 159; and Blade Nzimande, "The Class Question as the 'Fault-Line' in Consolidating the National Democratic Revolution," *Umsebenzi* 5: 57 (June 7, 2006).

2. To please the Multinational Corporations, it was essential to accede fully to the new intellectual property regimes, as well as to reduce the tax burden on MNC operations in the country. Since the North Atlantic refused to engage in any discussion of science or technology transfer, the instinct among the new regimes was to seek technology through the MNCs. As India's Singh put it in 1991, "The modern technology we want is not with the government, but with multinational corporations."[98] South Africa's Manuel agreed with this view, and extended it to service delivery, insisting that "foreign investment in state-owned enterprises allows for access to cutting-edge technologies and increases the effectiveness with which these entities can deliver on the rollout of essential services."[99]

3. To discipline workers into the new regime of "just-in-time" production and export-oriented work habits, they slashed public-sector expenditure and the social net. If money was to be spent on the workers, it should go towards education and job training, not social welfare and "iron rice bowls." As Brazil's Cardoso put it, "Cheap labor and abundant natural resources no longer constitute comparative advantages in the new international production model." What was needed was not only better-trained workers, but "flexible labor-management relations" (weaker unions) and less "social levies" (such as pension payments) on small firms.[100] The banks required "fiscal equilibrium," which was a polite way of saying austerity conditions for the people.

Pliant legislatures offered no resistance to these changes. The siren song of the age was "the end of history," and, but for hardened social democrats and communists, few held fast to any alternatives other than liberal democracy. The God of Growth trumped all else.

In 1991, the World Bank warned the Indian government: "Stabilization necessarily will be painful, even if the costs can be contained and the poor protected. Reforms will affect the fortunes of various groups in the society, some of them politically powerful. Successful implementation of an appropriate program of stabilization and reform will require adept political as well as technocratic management."[101] The private industrialists were the first to get frisky. Vijay Kalantri, president of the All-India Manufacturers' Organisation, felt that the red carpet being offered to MNCs represented "exploitation. We

---

98   James Walsh, "A Cloudburst of Reforms," *Time*, August 5, 1991, p. 29.

99   Patrick Bond, *Against Global Apartheid*, London: Zed Books, 2003, p. 126.

100   Amaury de Souza, "Redressing Inequalities: Brazil's Social Agenda at Century's End," in Susan Kaufman Purcell and Riordan Roett, eds, *Brazil Under Cardoso*, Boulder: Lynne Rienner, 1997, pp. 78–9.

101   World Bank, *India: 1991 Country Economic Memorandum*, pp. 38–9.

don't need Coca-Cola, popcorn and chewing gum," he said in August 1993.[102] A year later, South Africa's finance minister spoke for his country's industrialists: "The worst case for this economy is to throw our industries to the vagaries of international competition rapidly and so destroy investment and jobs."[103] Many of the larger, more confident indigenous capitalists, however, quickly saw the advantages for themselves in the longer term, and came on board. In 1993, S. K. Birla, elder of India's Birla Group, urged the government on: "We must follow the success stories of other Asian countries and invite foreign investment to set up additional ports and improve other infrastructure facilities in the country." Trevor Manuel presided over a new strategy in 1996, the "central thrust of [whose] trade and industrial policy" was the "pursuit of employment creating international competitiveness."

The MNCs were eager to enter what a Wall Street financier initially dubbed "emerging markets."[104] Northern capital was unwilling to invest in the North Atlantic manufacturing sector, which was being quite dramatically undone. It sought new harbors in financial instruments devised by Wall Street and the City of London, mainly by selling securities on a cascade of asset bubbles. The "surplus" capital also sought havens in selective countries of the South. This foreign direct investment (FDI) provided very selective liquidity, choosing its countries based on the guarantees they were willing to provide for rates

---

102   The quotes from the Indian business leaders and politicians in the period 1991–95 come from a diary I kept, Eliot Weinberger style.

103   Hein Marais, *South Africa: Limits to Change*, London: Zed Books, 2001, p. 115.

104   The term was coined in 1981 by Antoine van Agtmael, a Dutch banker who had worked in the private sector and in the World Bank's International Finance Corporation (van Agtmael studied with the development economist Jan Tinbergen, the first winner of the Nobel Prize in economics). In 1987, van Agtmael founded Emerging Markets Management and, with David Fisher and Walter Stern (Capital), Mark Mobius (Templeton), and Nick Bratt (Scudder) brought portfolio capital into selected countries of the South. Antoine van Agtmael, *The Emerging Markets Century*, New York: Free Press, 2007, p. 6. In 1994 the US Commerce Department made the term official when it identified ten "big emerging markets": Argentina, Brazil, China, India, Indonesia, Mexico, Poland, South Africa, South Korea, and Turkey. Several traits united these countries:

> They are all physically large. They have significant populations and represent considerable markets for a wide range of products. Virtually all have strong rates of growth, or clearly hold out the promise of economic expansion in the future. Virtually all have undertaken some significant program of economic reforms and seem likely to expand on those programs in the future. Virtually all are of major political importance within their regions; moreover, they are "regional economic drivers"—their growth will engender further expansion in neighboring markets.
>
> US Department of Commerce, "The Big Emerging Markets," *Business America* 115: 3 (1994).

of return and for safety (they did not want any untoward confiscation due to political considerations). By the late 1990s, three-quarters of FDI went towards East Asia and Latin America (mainly Brazil).[105] Portfolio capital came into the stock markets, eager for short-term returns ("hot money").

Some of the FDI went towards capital-intensive but highly profitable sectors (such as to extract subterranean riches like oil and precious metals). This sector is lucrative, but typically distorts general social development. Being capital-intensive, it attracts foreign investment, which can raise the exchange rate of the host country, leading to contraction in the domestic economy (the proverbial Dutch Disease). The "resource curse" allows the country to earn foreign exchange, but at the expense of forgoing development. These sectors are typically not labor-intensive, so there are few jobs created. Dominated as they are by MNCs, there is little in the way of diversification of the production line: oil is pumped and leaves the country to be refined elsewhere. It is the great tragedy of resource wealth.[106]

Capital with longer-term commitments also made its entry into East Asia and parts of Latin America. The fragmentation of production chains made the "emergent" spaces increasingly attractive. Homes were needed for specific parts of the production chain. MNCs had feared entry into the space of the Third World Project, afraid that their long-term investment would become trapped by governments that might turn against them (nationalization was always a fear). With the disarticulation of production, this fear evaporated. Investment was spread across a number of countries, across the production chain; it was not trapped in one state. Each state had to concentrate on its core business and was therefore forced to interact with a group of other states along the production chain. For light industry and for service provision, the MNCs did not even have to invest very much, reliant as they became on local subcontracted firms that bore the brunt of the economic and political risks. The MNCs controlled the design of products and their branding—investments protected by the intellectual property regimes negotiated through the GATT. This process did not promote a general or horizontal development within a state-governed territory, but represented a specific and vertical advancement for some sections along the production chain.

The reasons for the "rise of the South" were many, and interlinked.[107] A

---

105 For the numbers, see *Global Development Finance: Financing the Poorest Countries*, Washington, DC: World Bank, 2002.

106 Terry Lynn Karl, *The Paradox of Plenty: Oil Booms and Petro-States*, Berkeley: University of California Press, 1997; and Jeffrey D. Sachs and Andrew Warner, "Natural Resource Abundance and Economic Growth," Development Discussion Paper no. 517a, Cambridge: Harvard Institute for International Development, 1995.

107 I am guided here by Yilmaz Akyüz, "The Staggering Rise of the South," Research Papers, no. 44, South Centre, March 2012.

commodity boom driven by massive buying on the part of China helped push the growth rates of much of the South higher.[108] Improvements in the debt situation in Latin America through restructured portfolios and the crafty use of commodity profits to write down debt reduced the debt overhang from 50 percent of GDP in 2000 to 35 percent of GDP in 2007. Low interest rates and lax rules on leveraging finance in the North Atlantic allowed financial institutions to produce huge sums of money that went in two directions, both instrumental in lifting growth rates in certain parts of the South: first, they inflated credit, consumption, and property bubbles in the United States and Europe that had to be fed by imports of manufactured goods produced in the South (mainly in East Asia); and second, they enabled large sums in FDI to traverse the increasingly liberalized planet in search of investment opportunities. It was this untethered Northern demand that fueled the massive and unsustainable growth rates of sections of the South. This was growth that was not autarkic, but reliant upon the debt-driven consumerism of the North.

Growth rates rose, budget deficits fell. Reform, it seemed, had worked. Domestic industries appeared to flourish, and the new service sector also blossomed. It was unthinkable that Brazil, India, and South Africa would be able to export services, but that is precisely what has occurred. But reforms had uneven effects in two different ways: a small section, the rich, benefited much more than the vast mass, and those who benefited did so *at the expense of the poor*.[109] In the case of the growth in these three countries, the areas that did grow did so because of the penalties imposed on the rest, whose livelihoods became much more precarious. Overall growth came not only from dynamic sectors such as information technology (a very small percentage of GDP), but significantly from cannibalistic economic activity (privatization, land grabs for real estate speculation).[110] Growth also came from high global commodity prices in the decade of the reforms and the construction of a robust domestic market (tailored to the emergent middle class). The ravenous Chinese economy absorbed primary commodities from across the planet, thereby inflating the prices of commodities. This was essential to the growth rates of countries like Brazil, India, and South Africa.[111]

---

108   Masuma Farooki and Raphael Kaplinsky, *The Impact of China on Global Commodity Prices: The Disruption of the World's Resource Sector*, London: Routledge, 2011.

109   This is the assessment of Prabhat Patnaik, "The Performance of the Indian Economy in the 1990s," in Patnaik, *The Retreat to Unfreedom*, New Delhi: Tulika, 2003; of Emir Sader, "Taking Lula's Measure," *New Left Review* II/33 (May–June 2005); of Marais, *South Africa*; and of Bond, *Against Global Apartheid*.

110   On the limits of the software sector, see Jyoti Saraswati, *Dot.Compradors: Power and Policy in the Development of the Indian Software Industry*, London: Pluto Press, 2012.

111   For Brazil, see Daniela Magalhães Prates, "A inserção externa da economia

A common strategy to enhance export-driven industrialization was to create economic enclaves such as export processing zones (EPZs). Writing for the World Bank's Foreign Investment Advisory Service, Xiaolun Sun noted that these enclaves pose serious problems:

> With the wide range of exemptions and special privileges granted to investments located in the EPZs, they exhibit very limited linkage with the local economies at large. In particular, low labor costs and avoidance of normal rules and regulations are often the main advantages sought by the FDI in such locations, who also tend to be footloose and have little incentive to transfer skills or technologies. Consequently, even though the immediate export and employment benefits are undeniable, the long-term sustainability and economic impacts of these zones are less certain.[112]

The nature of the growth rate freed up and expanded the middle class, but at the same time it *increased* the rate of inequality within society. The trajectory was not hopeful.[113]

Inequality increased between classes and within regions. Agricultural wages stagnated or fell. In 1993 the Reserve Bank of India merged the government-run Regional Rural Banks with commercial banks. Later, when elections loomed, the Indian government would offer rural credit as patronage, through schemes such as the Kisan Credit Cards, or through micro-credit schemes—all of which bound farmers to private entities that did not want to share the immense risk of farming.[114] This set the conditions for the epidemic of farmers' suicides across India since the 1990s. Urban unemployment rose among the working class, and absolute poverty increased. Labor unions and labor protections were almost

---

brasileira no governo Lula," *Política Econômica em Foco* 7 (November 2005–April 2006), p. 142.

112   Xiaolun Sun, "Foreign Direct Investment and Economic Development: What do the States Need to Do?" paper prepared for the Foreign Investment Advisory Service for the "Capacity Development Workshops and Global Forum on Reinventing Government on Globalization, Role of the State and Enabling Environment," sponsored by the United Nations, Marrakesh, Morocco, December 10–13, 2002, p. 15.

113   The World Bank's lead economist in the Research Department, Branko Milanovic has written very useful studies reporting the data on inequality and its effects. For example, see his *True World Income Distribution, 1988 and 1993: First Calculation Based on Household Surveys Alone*, Policy Research Working Paper no. 2,244, World Bank: Poverty and Human Resources, Development Economics Research Group, 1999; *Worlds Apart: Measuring International and Global Inequality*, Princeton: Princeton University Press, 2005; and *The Haves and the Have-Nots: A Brief and Idiosyncratic History of Global Inequality*, New York: Basic Books, 2011.

114   For an excellent critique of micro-credit, see Heloise Weber, "The Imposition of a Global Development Architecture: The Example of Microcredit," *Review of International Studies* 28 (2002).

gutted. Weakened labor and demands for a flexible workforce led to a dramatic increase in the "informal" sector in these countries. Statistics on informal work are hard to come by. Anything from about one-fifth (Brazil, South Africa) to close to 90 percent (India) of the workforce works in the informal sector.[115] The vast social divides in the three countries grew large on account of increased inequality—regions condemned to desolation (Bihar in India and Bahia in Brazil) had no hope of becoming like the shining global cities (Mumbai in India and Rio in Brazil), and within these shining cities the grave divides closed off opportunities for the majority of the population. Older axes of social division deepened—caste and race foremost among them.[116] The growth that emerged did not generate sufficient employment in the formal sector. It was the classic instance of jobless growth for the multitude.

The poverty and disparities were not outside the radar of the policymakers. They might not agree that the increased inequality was a consequence of their high-growth policies, but they did not always deny its existence.[117] In 1994, at the Davos World Economic Forum, India's Prime Minister Rao told the business community, "In the newfound enthusiasm for change, governments should not go overboard and plunge large chunks of their people into mass misery. They have no right to do so. I have no right to bring in mass misery to what is there. That is why the whole program in India is one with a human face." Greeted by unemployment numbers and labor protests earlier that year, India's Singh expressed his commitment to the old ideas in February 1994: "The philosophy that had dominated the lives of our leaders at that time was deep-rooted in both liberalism and Fabian socialism. These basic objectives continue

115   Ajaya Kumar Naik, "Informal Sector and Informal Workers in India," International Association for Research in Income and Wealth conference on "Measuring the Informal Economy in Developing Countries," Kathmandu, Nepal, September 24, 2009.

116   As the Congress of South African Trade Unions (COSATU) put it in 2002, "The main reason for this jobs carnage is that after ten years of liberation, our economy remains largely unrestructured with the structural problems we inherited from apartheid mismanagement still in place. The economy remains firmly in white hands, dominated by the few companies operating in the mining and financial sector." Patrick Bond, *Talk Left, Walk Right*, Scottsville: University of Kwa-Zulu Natal, 2005, p. 16. The statistical evidence for racial disparities is remarkable. See United Nations Development Programme, *South Africa: Transformation for Human Development*, Pretoria: UNDP, 2000, pp. 62–3. On the question of caste, see K. S. Chalam, *Economic Reforms and Social Exclusion: Impact of Liberalization on Marginalized Groups in India*, New Delhi: Sage, 2011.

117   Over the past two decades, there have been numerous attempts at the national and international (World Bank) level to change the methodology for the poverty line. In each case, there has been an attempt to shrink poverty arithmetically. For India, see Himanshu, "Counting the Poor: A Poverty of Statistics," *Live Mint*, September 9, 2008. For the World Bank, see Sanjay G. Reddy, "Counting the Poor: The Trust About World Poverty Statistics," *Socialist Register* 2006.

to guide our policies." Across the Indian Ocean, the new post-apartheid government in South Africa promised to govern according to a framework laid out as its Reconstruction and Development Programme (RDP). Homes needed to be built for the poor; electricity, water, and sanitation needed to be provided; healthcare and childcare had to be established as rights; free and compulsory education was imperative. This was the "human face" of development. The RDP lasted only two years. It was dismantled in 1996, and in its place came the Growth, Employment and Redistribution Programme (GEAR)—with growth in the driver's seat, and no human face in sight.[118] Indeed, impatience with social welfare had driven the process. In 1992 Rao complained that "India is not a *dharamshala* [holy place] in which people can eat for free."[119]

When growth rates did pick up and revenues began to expand, the exchequers initially seemed constipated. In Brazil, for instance, the surplus rose above the IMF fixed surplus target, and calls began to be made of the government that it "must learn to spend money." In India, foreign exchange reserves rose to double the minimum "norm."[120] Electoral and political pressure had more impact than the requests to spend money from international and domestic economists. Modest social relief programs did emerge slowly, in Brazil through the Fome Zero ("Zero Hunger") program as well as the Bolsa Familia ("Family Purse") program, and in India through the National Rural Employment Guarantee Act (2005). Food relief is essential, but it is a band-aid; development does not emerge from it.

The tendency towards social programs worried the leaders of the World Bank. It wanted schemes that properly regulated and disciplined labor; no more "hand-outs" to the poor. In a May 1990 memorandum, the Bank cautioned the Indian government and offered its own vision:

> The massiveness of India's poverty problem and the urgency of dealing with it make quick-fixes such as debt forgiveness, expanded public expenditures and guaranteed employment tempting. However, both the changing character of poverty (which is increasingly associated with landlessness and wage dependency in unirrigated rural areas, especially in the Eastern region of the country) and the fiscal constraints faced by government suggest that more efficient and effective means will have to be found to address the problems of poverty directly. Broad-based, target-driven, non-selective approaches are expensive and ineffective. Programs designed to increase the ability of the poor to participate in the growth process by improving their physical and educational status will have to be more precisely targeted, simplified

118   Stephen Gelb, "The RDP, GEAR and All That: Reflections 10 years later," *Transformation* 62, Johannesburg: Edge Institute, 2006.

119   *Indian Express*, February 10, 1992.

120   Morais and Saad-Filho, "Lula and the Continuity of Neoliberalism," p. 18; and Patnaik, "Performance of the Indian Economy," p. 185.

administratively and more closely attuned to community needs. Service delivery should focus on the most vulnerable, lowest income groups and regions.[121]

No more general welfare—only some modest provisions to keep the very poor alive. A decade later, in 2000, the World Bank's William Easterly (senior advisor in the Macroeconomics and Growth Division) made it clear at an IMF conference that, if a country ignored IMF and Bank advice, its poor would be better off. "A lot of countries that have gotten a lot of lending from the IMF and World Bank are worse off," he noted, with the Philippines and Zambia in mind. "I don't think the record is real encouraging." Easterly argued that the economy in places like Zambia was divided into two sectors—the formal and the informal: "The World Bank and IMF affect the modern, formal economy, but the poor are not in the modern, formal sector. The poor live in the margins."[122] The poor might not be as marginal to the formal sector as it seems. Their labor is linked to it in remarkable ways, but often indirectly. EPZ workers, for instance, often supplement their salary with food brought to them by their smallholder families; e-waste recyclers often collect the precious metals that are then brought to the smelters to re-enter the formal system. But the point Easterly makes is still sound: whatever modest advantages accrue to the population from EPZs or the "modern, formal sector" certainly do not trickle down to the vast mass of the population.

It was this reality that moved South Africa's Manuel, never averse to the IMF line, to tell the business press grudgingly in 2002, "Developing countries have undertaken many reforms, but the benefits are slim. We have undertaken a policy of very substantial macroeconomic reform. But the rewards are few."[123] The IMF's Michel Camdessus conceded the problem, urging the Bank and the IMF to be more careful with the "human cost" of poverty. Nonetheless, the doctor wrote out the same prescription: "The best route out of poverty is strong, sustainable high-quality growth."[124]

Research from the World Bank showed that there was a strong relationship between infrastructural development and income growth. From the provision of clean water and sanitation, transportation to work, and electrification as in East Asia, the welfare gains are discernible. A Bank study showed that

---

121   World Bank, *India: Trends, Issues and Options* (2 vols), *Volume 1: Executive Summary and Main Report*, Report no. 8360-IN, May 1, 1990, p. 34, World Bank Archives.

122   Mark Drajem, "IMF, World Bank Leave Poor Behind, Bank Economist Finds," *Bloomberg News*, November 7, 2000.

123   Bond, *Talk Left*, p. 221.

124   "Address by Michel Camdessus, Chairman of the Executive Board and Managing Director of the International Monetary Fund to the Board of Governors of the Fund," Washington, DC, September 28, 1999.

people wanted just these social goods.[125] The problem was that the Bank and the IMF were ambivalent about who should provide them—the government or the private sector. They favored the latter.[126] They thus became a boondoggle for private venture capitalists, most of whom saw these areas as new arenas to make quick profits. The IMF and Bank continued to champion the need for unfettered growth, while recognizing the need for modest social welfare and private sector–led infrastructure development. This was no longer the fundamentalism of monetary conditions alone; by the early 2000s the IMF and Bank were advocating a sophisticated development path that was already underway in countries like Brazil, India, and South Africa.[127]

The North-South dialogue had effectively ended. The markets of the North beckoned, but, saturated with East Asian goods and protected by subsidy and tariff barriers, they seemed out of reach. Far better for the countries of the South to seek markets in each other's societies; and far better to trade cheaper, but often still high-quality goods across the South rather than to buy from the expensive North. The asymmetries between North and South that drove the Uruguay Round of the GATT (preserving the high rents on patents for the North) were precisely what priced out Northern goods from Southern markets. This was the objective basis for the market-friendly "South-South cooperation," or what UNCTAD's senior economic affairs officer, Charles Gore, called the Southern Consensus.[128]

THE NEW INTERNATIONAL TRADE ORDER

Good foreign policy requires prudence. But it also requires boldness. It should not be shy or based on an inferiority complex. It is usual to hear that countries should act in accordance with their means, which is almost too obvious, but the greatest mistake one could make is to underestimate them.

Celso Amorim, minister of external relations, Brazil[129]

125   Deepa Narayan-Parker, Raj Patel, Kai Schafft, Anne Rademacher, and Sarah Koch-Schulte, *Voices of the Poor: Can Anyone Hear Us?*, vol. 1, Washington, DC: World Bank, 2000.

126   Antonio Estache, Sergio Perelman, and Lourdes Trujillo, "Infrastructure Performance and Reform in Developing and Transition Economies: From a Survey of Productivity Measures," World Bank Policy Research Working Paper no. 3514, February 2005.

127   The confusion in the Bank is explored in Dani Rodrik, "Goodbye Washington Consensus, Hello Washington Confusion? A Review of the World Bank's *Economic Growth in the 1990s: Learning from a Decade of Reform*," *Journal of Economic Literature* 45 (December 2006).

128   Charles Gore, "The Rise and Fall of the Washington Consensus as a Paradigm for Developing Countries," *World Development* 28: 5 (2000).

129   Celso Amorim, "A New World Map and Brazil's Foreign Policy," *The Hindu*, August 27, 2010.

By the 1990s the AIDS epidemic had reached catastrophic levels.[130] There is no adequate count of AIDS-related deaths in many parts of Africa, Asia, and Latin America. In some parts of Africa, mortuaries record "Slim Disease" as the cause of death.[131] It was a catastrophe. Doctors found that antiretroviral drugs worked to stem the passage of HIV towards full-blown AIDS. Pharmaceutical conglomerates based in the North sold these drugs at astronomical prices and were uneasy about reduced-cost provision of the drugs. GlaxoSmithKlein's treatment plan cost $12,000. The International Federation of Pharmaceutical Manufacturers Associations did not bat an eyelid. Its chief, Harvey Bale, told the *Guardian*, "For people with no income or little income, price is a barrier. I mean I can't afford certainly a car of my dreams, you know, which might be a Jaguar XJE or something like that."[132] Essential drugs had become about consumer choice, with only those able to afford them granted the right to them. "Africa," in the 1990s, had become the repository of all the bad dreams and garbage of the North: paternalistic philanthropy after the famines of the 1980s in the Horn morphed into disregard for the people; garbage, toxic waste, and illegal drug trials had catastrophic effects.[133]

Such a vision did not sit well in Brazil and South Africa.[134] The Brazilian government passed a patent law in 1997 with a provision (Article 68) allowing the government to declare a health emergency and circumvent

---

130   For an excellent overview, see Anne-Christine D'Adesky, *Moving Mountains: The Race to Treat Global AIDS*, London: Verso, 2004.

131   Scientists also called it the Slim Disease. D. Serwadda, R. D. Mugerwa, N. K. Sewankambo, A. Lwegaba, J. W. Carswell, G. B. Kirya, A. C. Bayley, R. G. Downing, R. S. Tedder, S. A. Clayden, R. A. Weiss, and A. G. Dalgleish, "Slim Disease: A New Disease in Uganda and Its Association with HTLV-III Infection," *Lancet*, October 19, 1985.

132   Sarah Boseley, "Harvey Bale Jnr, Drug Firms' Federation," *Guardian*, February 18, 2003.

133   On the aid machine and Ethiopia, see Vijay Prashad, "Bad Aid: Throw Your Arms Around the World," *Counterpunch*, March 29, 2010. I highly recommend Lawrence Summers's memo as World Bank chief economist (December 12, 1991) that opens, "'Dirty' Industries: Just between you and me, shouldn't the World Bank be encouraging MORE migration of the dirty industries to the LDCs?" One might also take a look at a US State Department cable on the details of Pfizer's payment to the Nigerian government against a lawsuit charging that it had conducted illegal medical trials for Trovan on children. Robert Tansey (Economic Counselor, Embassy Abuja), "Nigeria: Pfizer Reaches Preliminary Agreement for a $75 million Settlement," April 20, 2009 (09ABUJA671), Wikileaks Archive.

134   Marcelo Fernandes de Oliveira, "Estratégias internacionais e diálogo Sul-Sul no governo Lula: alianças duradouras ou coalizões efêmeras?"; and Gilberto Dupas, "África do Sul, Brasil e Índia: divergencias, convergencias e perspectivas," in Fábio Villares, ed., *Índia, Brasil e África do Sul: Perspectivas e Alianças*, São Paulo: UNESP, 2006. Thanks to Fábio Villares for the translation.

intellectual property strictures. South Africa's government, also in 1997, passed the Medicines Amendment Act, which allowed it to import cheaper AIDS medicines from places like India. The Indian drug companies took refuge behind a "transition rule" that allowed it to follow its older Patents Act rather than the World Trade Organization's much stricter rules (the Indian Patents Act only protected the process, not the product, whereas the rules of the World Trade Organization [WTO] protected the product itself, and so made reverse-engineering impossible). Indian firms such as Cipla and Ranbaxy were able to sell the AIDS drugs at a fraction of the costs claimed by Northern pharmaceutical firms.

In 1997 the US government put pressure on South Africa to revoke its law. Two years later, in April 1999, the US threatened to withdraw aid to South Africa and placed the country on its Special 301 watch list. Pressure from within the Democratic Party and from the global AIDS movement pushed President Bill Clinton to sign an Executive Order (no. 13155) in May 2000 that removed South Africa from the watch list. The pharmaceutical companies were outraged. When George W. Bush came into the White House in early 2001, they did not have to work too hard. Bush had the interests of the corporations close to his heart. Bush went after Brazil's Article 68—but the worldwide pressure was simply too great. In April 2001, the UN Human Rights Commission came on the side of Brazil and urged that its unique policy (making health a right, specifically for HIV/AIDS patients) should be the global norm. In June 2001, the UN held a special session of the General Assembly on AIDS. Its declaration called for a moderation of prices by pharmaceutical corporations and for allowances towards other firms that could produce the drugs by reverse-engineering. Article 55 of the UN's Declaration of Commitment on HIV/AIDS, however, did not take a strong position against the WTO. It simply asked the countries "to cooperate constructively in strengthening pharmaceutical policies and practices, including those applicable to generic drugs and intellectual property regimes, in order further to promote innovation and development of domestic industries consistent with international law."[135] India drafted a proposal to the WTO signed by forty-six other countries, including Brazil and South Africa, on "TRIPS and Public Health."[136] The Bush administration backed down.[137] On December 6, 2005, the WTO approved a change in the

---

135   "Declaration of Commitment on HIV/AIDS," UN General Assembly Special Session on HIV/AIDS, June 25–27, 2001, Article 55, p. 27.

136   India to WTO, June 29, 2001, no. IP/C/W/296.

137   "White House Drops WTO Claim Against Brazilian Patent Law," *Wall Street Journal*, June 26, 2001. The Bush team was also hypocritical. After 9/11, it violated all manner of intellectual property regimes when it authorized the production of ciprofloxacin (on which Bayer held the patent) to thwart anthrax.

TRIPS regime in the arena of public health. It was the first such amendment to the core WTO agreement.[138]

The fight against the US government and pharmaceutical companies demonstrated two points. Firstly, that if the larger countries of the South stood united and made a connection with global non-governmental organizations such as Médecins sans Frontières, they could get the US and large corporations to back down, or at least make some concessions. Power did not always reside in the North Atlantic. Secondly, countries like Brazil, India, and South Africa had objective interests in common. In this instance, both Brazil and South Africa required cheaper drugs, which were being produced by India's highly competent pharmaceutical industry. If Brazil, India, and South Africa could find such productive collaboration here, then why not elsewhere?[139]

The Bush administration went into the corner on this issue, but that was not its nature. The US government mocked the Kyoto protocol on climate change. It was dismissive of the International Criminal Court, established on the basis of the Rome Statute in 2002. The US withdrew from the 1972 Anti-Ballistic Missile Treaty, to the dismay of those who hoped for nuclear disarmament in the aftermath of the Cold War. All of these signals went directly to the heart of 760 United Nations Plaza, where a beleaguered Kofi Annan had his phone bugged by the US National Security Agency.[140] To the UN, Bush sent John Negroponte, who was known around the building for his infamous work as the legman for the US-supported wars of counter-revolution in Central America. A US State Department official translated the appointment in this way: "Negroponte is known as a guy who is devoted to *realpolitik*, which is in many ways the opposite of what the UN stands for. Giving him this job is a way of telling the UN: 'We hate you.'"[141]

---

138 "Members OK Amendment to Make Health Flexibility Permanent," WTO press release, December 6, 2005.

139 Earlier attempts, such as the Zone of Peace and Cooperation of the South Atlantic (1986–1994) and the Indian Ocean Rim Association for Regional Cooperation (1995–96), had proved only somewhat useful.

140 James Bamford, *The Shadow Factory*, New York: Anchor Books, 2008, pp. 140–1.

141 Stephen Kinzer, "Our Man in Honduras," *New York Review of Books*, August 21, 2001. Negroponte is only one in a series of despicable people sent to this post. Reagan dispatched Jeane Kirkpatrick to the UN early in his tenure. Later, Kirkpatrick wrote, "The enterprise more closely resembles a mugging than either a political debate or an effort at problem solving." Her view of the UN's members is characteristic: "The losers in this unconventional United Nations drama were those who seek to use United Nations arenas and procedures to polarize nations, spread hostility and exacerbate conflict for short-range political advantage." Hardly the basis for productive dialogue, which is not what Negroponte brought—nor did the man who came after him (John Bolton,

The hostility towards the UN intensified from 2002, when the US began its inexorable journey towards the complete strangulation of Iraq. The Gulf War of 1991 had been settled largely in the interests of the United States. The elder Bush declined to send troops to Baghdad; it was far easier to bleed Iraq through a brutal sanctions regime. The war was now fought by other means, including the occasional aerial sortie into Iraqi airspace. George W. Bush was eager to conclude this war from his first days in office.[142] South Africa's Thabo Mbeki was chair of the NAM from 1999 to 2003, thus during the period of the US attempt to push the war. He worked closely with Kofi Annan and put South Africa's Foreign Ministry to work trying to bridge the gap between the Iraqis and the United Nations. Iraq's foreign minister, Tariz Aziz, visited South Africa, and South Africa's deputy foreign minister, Aziz Pahad, visited Iraq. The NAM pushed back against the view that Iraq should be invaded because of its weapons of mass destruction; it pushed for more inspections, together with the majority in the United Nations. The US wanted South Africa to expel the Iraqi ambassador, Zuhair al-Omar, but Pretoria refused. At the same time, Brazil and India walked the halls of the UN trying to calm things down and prevent the US rush to war. Apart from the Germans, the main European G7 members planned to march in lockstep with the United States. Nelson Mandela put down a marker in 2002:

> If you look at those matters, you will come to the conclusion that the attitude of the United States of America is a threat to world peace. Because what [America] is saying is that if you are afraid of a veto in the Security Council, you can go outside and take action and violate the sovereignty of other countries. That is the message they are sending to the world. That must be condemned in the strongest terms.[143]

In March 2003, as war loomed, Brazil, India, and South Africa persisted in their diplomacy. When the US began its bombardment of Iraq on March 18, all three countries released strong statements in condemnation. Lula said that the war "disrespects the United Nations" and was not legitimate. The Indian External Affairs Ministry also held fast with the UN, worrying too about "the precarious humanitarian situation of the Iraqi people which war would only aggravate."

AIDS and the Iraq War brought the three countries together. In June 2003, at the margins of the G8 meeting in Evian, France, the foreign ministers of

---

who famously said of the UN, "There's no such thing as the United Nations. If the UN Secretary building in New York lost ten stories, it wouldn't make a bit of difference"). Jeane Kirkpatrick, *Legitimacy and Force: Political and Moral Dimensions*, vol. 1, Brunswick, NJ: Transaction, 1988, pp. 229–31.

142   Ron Suskind, *The Price of Loyalty: George W. Bush, the White House and the Education of Paul O'Neill*, New York: Simon & Schuster, 2004, p. 96.

143   Tom Masland, "Nelson Mandela: The USA is a Threat to World Peace," *Newsweek*, September 10, 2002.

Brazil, India, and South Africa went into a huddle. Celso Amorim (Brazil), Yashwant Sinha (India), and Nkosazana Dlamini-Zuma (South Africa) formulated a protocol for the creation of a new organization. These three had little in common. Sinha represented the hard-right Hindu nationalists, although he had come to them late in his career (after long tenure as a diplomat and politician in the socialist Janata Dal party). Dlamini-Zuma had been a student leader, part of the ANC underground, and then a doctor in neighboring Swaziland, before returning to South Africa to join Mandela's government. She had taken on the pharmaceutical companies as her first act of business. She came to the meeting with a good sense of the importance of that issue.[144] Amorim had waited his whole career for such a gathering. As the US ambassador to Brazil put it in his assessment of Amorim, his "leftist views tend to be held in check by traditional Itamaraty [Brazilian foreign service] care for diplomatic niceties and an almost reverential respect for reciprocity and multilateralism."[145] Nothing too radical was to emerge from these discussions. It was the foreign policy cognate of Southern neoliberalism.

The three met again in Brazil, where they released the Brasília Declaration. Out of these discussions emerged the India–Brazil–South Africa Dialogue (IBSA), which has since held annual meetings, as well as sponsoring a host of working groups. The Brasília Declaration is modest—a summary of the kinds of initiatives backed by the three countries over the years. The idea of the new union had been proposed earlier, as a kind of G7 of the South—or, as a South African trade document from 2001 put it, a G-South.[146] Nothing in the manner or the words of the newly created IBSA hinted at a revision of the world order. IBSA began cautiously, upholding the principles of the world order as it was,

---

144   Gumede, *Thabo Mbeki*, p. 423.

145   Ambassador Clifford M. Sobel, "Understanding Brazil's Foreign Ministry, Part 1: Ideological Forces," February 11, 2009 (09BRASILIA177), Wikileaks Archive.

146   Department of Trade and Industry, Republic of South Africa, "Driving Competitiveness: An Integrated Industrial Strategy for Sustainable Employment and Growth," May 21, 2001, p. 15. My analysis of IBSA draws from a number of essays, including Glady Lechini, "Middle Powers: IBSA and the New South-South Cooperation," *NACLA*, September–October 2007 (she mentions the "G7 of the South" quote, and attributes it to South African industries minister Alec Elwin, on p. 28); Chris Alden and Marco Antonio Vieira, "The New Diplomacy of the South: South Africa, Brazil, India and Trilateralism," *Third World Quarterly* 26: 7 (2005); Darlene Miller, "South Africa and the IBSA Initiative: Constraints and Challenges," *African Insight* 35: 1 (2005); Daniel Flemes, "Emerging Middle Powers' Soft Balancing Strategy: State and Perspectives of the IBSA Dialogue Forum" *GIGA Working Papers* 57 (2007); and Lakshmi Puri, "IBSA: An Emerging Trinity in the New Geography of International Trade," *Policy Issues in International Trade and Commodities*, Study Series no. 35, New York and Geneva: UNCTAD, 2007.

and only asking for it to be widened to allow the three countries entry into the leadership. Given the context of the Iraq War and of the emergence of Washington's testosterone primacy, it is no wonder that IBSA's most prominent principle was for the world to uphold the rule of law. Early in their communiqué, the foreign ministers stressed "the importance of respecting the rule of International Law, strengthening the United Nations and the Security Council and prioritizing the exercise of diplomacy as a means to maintain international peace and security."[147] Rather than arguing for a reconstruction of the international institutions, IBSA wanted to see them widened to allow for more democratic functioning. In concrete terms, this meant that IBSA members wanted to have permanent seats on the UN Security Council and a greater voice in the IMF and the World Bank.

The second major principle of IBSA was to "maximize the benefits of globalization and to ensure that it becomes a positive force for sustained economic growth in all developing countries."[148] IBSA took its marching orders from the International Labour Organization's World Commission on the Social Dimension of Globalisation (2004): "We wish to make globalization a means to expand human well-being and freedom, and to bring democracy and development to local communities where people live. Our aim is to build a consensus for common action to realize this vision, and to foster a process of sustained engagement to this end by the actors themselves, including States, international organizations, business, labour and civil society."[149] The World Commission was not so taken with the magic of neoliberal strategies to accelerate growth, seeing them often as a lever for increased inequality. Nevertheless, its idea of the "social dimension" of globalization was not absent from IBSA. It also intersected with the Millennium Development Goals (MDGs) agreed upon by the member-states of the UN in September 2000.[150] These in turn draw from the

---

147   IBSA, "Brasília Declaration," June 6, 2003, para. 3.

148   IBSA, "Agenda for Cooperation," New Delhi, March 5, 2004, para. 12. See also Lula's speech to UNCTAD XI, 2004, in São Paulo.

149   World Commission on the Social Dimension of Globalisation, *A Fair Globalisation: Creating Opportunities for All*, Geneva: ILO, 2004, p. 2.

150   The first seven of the eight MDGs (on poverty, education, gender equality, child mortality, maternal health, HIV/AIDS and other diseases, environment) are not controversial. The eighth (global partnership) was initially rejected by the North, which only accepted it when it came without a timetable, and without accountability. This point refers to the need for the North to restructure aid, and to provide debt relief and technology transfer. The rest did not pose a threat, and are largely seen as symbolic (there are many who also see problems in them: they might distort priorities, create reporting burdens on already overstretched state apparatuses, and provide the threat of further bases for loan conditions by finance providers). Sakiko Fukuda-Parr, "Millennium Development Goals: Why They Matter," *Global Governance* 10 (2004), p. 397–9.

Human Development Index, devised by the UN Development Programme in 1990. The social costs of globalization had to remain on the table, even as the IBSA states typically denied that the policies of export-driven growth ("globalization") were themselves responsible for the social crises inflaming the planet.

"We are not identified by a language, a culture, a single race, but we are defined perhaps by an ideology, and an ideology in the best sense of the word— an ideology of democracy, diversity, tolerance, a search for cooperation," said Amorim at a press conference in South Africa. IBSA, he noted, "is a very tender plant that needs to be watered every day."[151] Three countries, however significant, cannot make an impact on a world constrained by the power of the North Atlantic powers. It is perhaps for this reason that IBSA often speaks as the conscience of the South. At the September 2006 NAM meeting in Havana, Mbeki pointed out that the "masses of people always urge us to speak with a unified voice," and that therefore "the strengthening of South-South cooperation has helped create a stronger voice for the developing countries in multilateral forums."[152]

To speak for the South, Brazil, India, and South Africa took advantage of their political and economic importance in their respective regions. Brazil and South Africa are the largest economies in their regions, and both play a significant role in the political work of their continent.[153] India is dwarfed by the Chinese economy, but is nonetheless an important actor in South Asia, and in Asia generally. Their regional centrality was amplified by the IBSA states' attempt to project their influence across the planet. Lula traversed the continents, cementing alliances and friendships. He took Brazil into the Arab League, and held a Brasília summit of Latin American and Arab countries. Celso Amorim called this "an alliance of civilizations" (in opposition to Samuel Huntington's "clash of civilizations"). It was not as well attended by heads of state; nevertheless, as one commentator put it, "No wonder Washington hawks are uneasy. There's an emerging geopolitical axis on the map—Arab–South

---

151 "Remarks by Ministers Nkosazana Dlamini-Zuma, Pranab Mukherjee and Celso Amorim during the 5th India–Brazil–South Africa Ministerial Meeting," May 11, 2008.

152 "Address by the President of the Republic of South Africa, Mr Thabo Mbeki, Chairperson of the Group of 77, at the XIV Summit Conference of the Non-Aligned Movement," Havana, Cuba, September 15, 2006.

153 Much of this projection is articulated through the regional economic alliances, such as MERCOSUR, SADC, and so on. These were accelerated in response to the NAFTA dynamic. Jaime Serra, Guillermo Aguilar, José Córdoba, Gene Grossman, Carla Hills, John Jackson, Julius Katz, Pedro Noyola, and Michael Wilson, *Reflections on Regionalism: Report of the Study Group on International Trade*, Washington, DC: Carnegie Endowment for International Peace, 1997; and Richard Baldwin, "The Causes of Regionalism," *World Economy* 20: 7 (1997), pp. 870–1.

American. It's non-aligned. And it's swimming in oil."[154] The countries in Brasília for the conference were responsible for a third of global oil output. Going south from the Arab world, Lula's Brazil forged deep ties with African states. The Fortaleza Brazil-Africa Summit of 2003 was followed by Lula's first of four trips across Africa. Senegal's Aboulaye Wade called him "the first black president of Brazil." Brazil opened up its pharmaceutical formulas so that African countries could make their own AIDS drugs, and its trade with Africa was set to expand from a modest $5 billion in 2002 to $12.6 billion in 2005 (it rose to $20.6 billion by 2011). A foundation for the new geopolitical framework was hardening.

Meeting on the fringes of the G8 (the G7 plus Russia), the IBSA leadership pushed for its own political agenda. At Okinawa in 2000, the three countries had already reiterated the G8's failure to live up to its own commitment (made at the G8 Cologne summit in 1999) for unconditional debt relief for the most indebted states. At Hokkaido in 2008, the IBSA states joined with Mexico and China to produce their own "Political Declaration," bemoaning the lack of movement by the G8 on debt relief, on concessionary aid, on new trade rules— and of course on climate change. On the margins of the G8, asking for entry into the UN Security Council and wanting to get its hands on the levers of the World Bank and the IMF, the IBSA states displayed no ambitions to revise the world order. No New International Economic Order for the new mandarins of the South. They simply requested more room in the system.

But that very request could not be easily accommodated within the old order. In the kinds of claims it made on the system, the IBSA states did call for some changes. The MDGs could not be attained without reform to the system, notably in what is known as "global partnership"—increases of financial resources available to the South through debt relief and foreign aid. IBSA revised the idea of "security." The Bush administration restricted the definition of "security" to include only issues around terrorism, drugs, organized crime, and (eccentrically) intellectual piracy. The IBSA states agreed, but then added "HIV/AIDS, natural disasters, and the maritime transit of toxic chemicals and radioactive waste."[155] The idea of security was more broadly defined, noting that the "primary focus on human development, the fight against poverty, and measures to promote a better quality of life, should underpin and provide for greater guarantees for international peace and security."[156] Forgotten UN conferences, abandoned by the wayside by the Bush administration, returned to the agenda. IBSA picked up two in particular: the 1995 Beijing Conference on women's rights and the 2001 Durban Conference on anti-racism: "Social

---

154   Pepe Escobar, "From Baghdad to Brasilia," *Asia Times*, May 11, 2005.
155   IBSA, "Agenda for Cooperation," New Delhi, March 5, 2004, para. 5.
156   Ibid., para. 7.

empowerment makes better use of human potential, contributing to economic development in a significant manner."[157] The mention of economic development was standard fare in this neoliberal worldview, which cannot stomach any argument that does not propose some kind of tangible economic benefit.

This, indeed, is why most of the agenda of IBSA was about the economy—notably trade, technology, and finance.

Trade

The WTO hit the ground running in 1995. At its first ministerial meeting, in Singapore in 1996, problems arose between North and South over market access on both sides. The South had some extant tariff barriers against industrial goods from the North, but the main issue was its barriers to the free flow of finance. On behalf of Northern interests, the OECD created a Multilateral Agreement on Investments in 1995, which would have broken down these walls to "liberalized" finance. When a draft of the OECD agreement was leaked in March 1997, protests across the world halted what seemed to the bureaucrats in the North to be an inexorable process to streamline finance. The North's own barriers to trade were very rarely the subject of discussion, but they included—and still include—a slew of complex maneuvers such as anti-dumping actions, quotas, tariff peaks, and high rates of tariff escalation—as well as labor and environment regulations that are more often used in trade negotiations than to protect the environment or raise labor standards.[158] Various "Singapore Issues" (such as customs clearance) scuttled the work of the WTO from 1996 onwards. The third WTO conference, in Seattle in 2000, had to be hastily closed when protestors from around the world shut down the city, and when the Southern politicians within the Washington State Convention and Trade Center refused to back down on the Singapore Issues.[159] Seattle's cordite did not prevent the WTO from convening its next meeting, in November 2001, at a remote location in the oil state of Qatar. The WTO inaugurated the Doha Development

---

157   Ibid., para. 6.

158   Michael Finger and Ludger Schuknecht, "Market Access Advances and Retreats: The Uruguay Round and Beyond," Working Paper no. 2232, Washington, DC: World Bank, 1999; Michael Finger and Julio Nogues, "The Unbalanced Uruguay Round Outcome: The New Areas in WTO Negotiations," World Bank Policy Research Working Paper no. 2732, Washington, DC: World Bank, 2001; and Richard Kozul-Wright and Paul Rayment, "Globalization Reloaded: An UNCTAD Perspective," UNCTAD Discussion Papers no. 167, Geneva: UNCTAD, 2004.

159   On the protests, see Alexander Cockburn and Jeffrey St. Clair, *5 Days That Shook the World: Seattle and Beyond*, London: Verso, 2000. On the business conducted within, see Peter Bleyer, "The Other Battle in Seattle," *Studies in Political Economy* 62 (Summer 2000); and Jeffrey J. Schott, "The WTO after Seattle," in Schott, ed., *The WTO After Seattle*, Washington, DC: Institute for International Economics, 2000, p. 5.

Round with every expectation that it would be completed when the ministers met next, at the ill-fated Cancún meeting of 2003. A month before the WTO was slated to meet in Mexico, the Europeans and the US released their common proposal on agriculture.[160] The Quad zone (the US, Europe, Canada, and Japan) insisted that its agricultural subsidies (which the arcane language of the WTO called Producer Support Estimates) were not going anywhere, unsurprisingly raising the hackles of the South.

Twenty countries from the South, anchored by IBSA, produced a rival document. They stood toe-to-toe against the North. Cancún 2003 looked like 1981, except this time the South was not as despondent.[161] "The majority of the WTO members are developing countries," they noted. The heart and guts of the WTO rules should reflect the interests of these countries. They formed themselves as the G20.[162] The G20 brought Cancún to a halt because the North would not move on agricultural subsidies.[163] "Talks have collapsed and there is no agreement," announced Kenya's George Ongwen, and Malaysia's trade minister, Rafidah Aziz, blamed the failure on the North. "They kept demanding things that we couldn't deliver," she said.[164]

The South did most of its trade with the North—which is why the question of the high tariffs across the North Atlantic made such a difference. The total exports from the South in 2005 amounted to $3.7 trillion, up by three times in a decade. The "new geography of trade" drove the increase in exports.[165]

---

160   The "Derbez Draft" is document no. JOB (03)/156/Rev. 2, September 13, 2003.

161   Even the generally rather bilious Indian commerce minister, Arun Jaitley (of the BJP) stood firm for the South. Arun Jaitley, "There's a Road From Cancún," *Indian Express*, October 13, 2003.

162   Since its establishment, the group's membership has fluctuated, largely as Latin American countries went overboard in response to US pressure. Gilberto Dupas, *Atores e poderes na nova ordem global. Assimetrias, instabilidades e imperativos legitimação*, São Paulo: UNESP, 2005, Chapter 5.

163   Amrita Narlikar and Diana Tussie, "The G20 at the Cancún Ministerial: Developing Countries and Their Evolving Coalitions in the WTO," *World Economy* 27: 7 (2004), p. 951.

164   The US embassy in Brasília felt that the game was not up:

One positive aspect to underline is that, despite what we do see as tinges of 1970s ideological antipathy amongst the professional castes of Itamaraty, GoB actions are not being propelled by anti-US antagonism. On the contrary: the GoB is unrealistically counting on being able to both have its cake and eat it—to stand up to the rich nations with developing country demands, while paying little or no price in terms either of the WTO's future effectiveness or of overall bilateral relations with the US.

"Brazil: No Post-Cancún Regrets or Second Thoughts," September 26, 2003 (03BRASILIA3124), Wikileaks Archive.

165   UNCTAD, "Strengthening Participation of Developing Countries in Dynamic and New Sectors of World Trade: Trends, Issues and Policies," TD/396, May 17, 2004.

The ineffectual head of the WTO, Pascal Lamy, tried to push for the completion of the Doha Round, but it was not to be. Neither the United States nor Europe would allow their agricultural subsidies to be cut. The G20, with the firm support of IBSA, did not back down. No meaningful progress could occur without a discussion of these subsidies being on the table.[166] Instead, in the margins, the South tried to revive old models, such as the idea of the cartel. Led by Thailand, countries in Southeast Asia created the Organization of Rice Exporting Countries (OREC). One cartel might face off against another.

Technology

Northern growth over the past few decades has been built upon the control of intellectual property. Jobless growth and debt-fueled consumerism in the United States, in particular, rely upon rents from the designs and brands devised in the scattered enclaves of dynamism (from Silicon Valley to Silicon Alley). Therefore, the North has refused to budge on intellectual property.

The South's position since the discussions began in 1986 was well articulated in a formula proposed by UNCTAD: "Liberalization without technological learning will result, in the end, in increased marginalization."[167] Locking a society off from scientific and technical knowledge is a surefire way of locking it out of development—and indeed an effective way of breeding resentment and antirational ideas. Culture without scientific development would ossify. The "contribution of culture to a country's economy" is essential, the IBSA ministers argued. There was also a business side to this because of "the potential of creative industries to alleviate poverty and generate income."[168]

Unable to move an agenda for science and technology transfer from the standpoint of cultural development, the IBSA minister took another tack. Northern-based MNCs had acquired much of the cultural wisdom of the South. These MNCs were intent not only on protecting their own technological devices and formulae by law, but also on snatching new ones from outside their laboratories and fields. W. R. Grace's celebrated attempt to patent the neem tree between 1996 and 2005 provides one example. The South would now like to claim that if the North could for very little have access to these treasures, then why couldn't the South get access to the scientific and technological knowledge protected by the intellectual property strictures? The standpoint of cultural heritage was a profitable direction to continue the debate around the inequities of access to science and technology. In 2002, IBSA countries had led

---

166 The stagnation is well depicted in Chakravarti Raghavan, "Round No One Wanted Now Proving Difficult to End," *TWN Briefing Paper*, no. 53, March 2009.

167 UNCTAD, *Least Developed Countries Report 2007: Knowledge, Technological Learning and Innovation for Development*, Geneva: UNCTAD, 2007, p. i.

168 IBSA, "Cape Town Ministerial Communiqué," March 11, 2005, para. 55.

the creation of the Group of Like-Minded Megadiverse Countries. The intention of the Group was to create "an international regime to effectively promote and safeguard the fair and equitable sharing of benefits arising from the use of biodiversity and its components."[169] The Group took refuge in the Convention on Biological Diversity (enforced from 1993), which emerged in 1988 out of the Uruguay Round debate, but in effect was toothless.

Unable to gain any traction, the IBSA states and their allies latched on to the United Nations Framework Convention on Climate Change to make the case for technology transfer. One of the South's great victories was to add the following sentiment into the *Rio Declaration* (1992): "In view of the different contributions to global environmental degradations, States have common but differentiated responsibilities. The developed countries acknowledge the responsibility that they bear in the international pursuit of sustainable development in view of the pressures their societies place on the global environment and of the technologies and financial resources they command" (Principle 7). It was the phrase "common and differentiated responsibilities" that would be the key to opening up the debate.[170] The IBSA states, with China and the G77, pushed the North to accept the fact that its states and industries had been and continued to be the world's leading polluters. Given this, it was imperative from the South's point of view that the North bear the lion's share of the burden of ecological adjustment. In 2007, IBSA told the G8 at Heiligendamm that reductions in greenhouse-gas emissions "are an exclusive task" of the North—which should slow down emissions, but also share green technology with the South to allow it to "leap-frog" the greenhouse-gas-emitting phase of industrial development.

As the discussion on technology transfer took place at Bali in December 2007, pencils were being sharpened and new agreements set to paper in Europe. The South had pushed the UN World Intellectual Property Organization (WIPO) to take up the issue of a "development agenda" for intellectual property. The IBSA agenda was finally finding a home inside the one UN body tasked with the management of intellectual property. In its customary way, the North decided to go around the WIPO. It sought shelter in the World Customs Organisation (WCO), the union of customs administrations. The discussion here was led by the Northern Corporate Rightholders, who bargained alongside and as equal partners with the various member-states. The North moved its intellectual property agenda into the WCO, where the South remained at a

---

169   "Cancún Declaration of Like-Minded Megadiversity Countries," Cancún, Mexico, February 18, 2002, para. h.

170   The idea of "common responsibilities" goes back to the origins of the UN, but that of "differentiated responsibilities" has a much more recent provenance. It emerged, after much drama, in two conventions regarding the oceans: the 1972 Convention on the Prevention of Marine Pollution by Dumping of Wastes and Other Matter (the London Convention), and the 1982 United Nations Convention on the Law of the Sea.

disadvantage (its delegates are mainly customs officials who do not have any training in matters of intellectual property). The sting was discovered by accident by the South Centre—the intergovernmental agency that emerged out of the South Commission's work.[171] It was a vivid example of how the North deliberately tries to undermine the South—even, as in this case, when the IBSA agenda was remarkable for its lack of revolutionary fervor. No crumbs are allowed to fall from the North's plate; its desire is to eat more than its fill.

Finance

By the late 1990s, in the capitals of the North Atlantic, the language of humanitarian intervention had eclipsed the old-fashioned language of benevolent aid. F16s revved their engines, ready to bomb Belgrade and Baghdad, Kabul and Abidjan. NATO was better known than the European Community Humanitarian Aid Office (created in 1992) and the Development Assistance Committee. None of the G7 states lived up to their quite modest commitment to offer 0.7 percent of their national income as overseas aid (the figure comes from a 1970 UN resolution). What aid did come had to bear the imprimatur of the Paris Declaration of Aid Effectiveness—the North's surveillance unit to invigilate how the money was spent.[172]

Dramatic noises about aid, particularly to Africa, emanated from the G7 meetings at Gleneagles (2006) and Heiligendamm (2007). Even the editors of the *Economist* punctured the hypocrisy: "If saying the right thing were all that mattered, this year of 'making poverty history' could already be declared a triumph. The corporate bosses, political leaders and assorted celebrity do-gooders gathered last month in Davos talked of little else but their ideas to help the poor. Yet what really matters is not words but action."[173] By 2010, Bono's ONE Campaign concluded that a bit more than half the Gleneagles pledges had been honored: "The G7 have failed on trade and have been slow on aid quality, but have delivered on debt cancellation—though a new debt crisis threatens if donor practices are not altered to preserve the gains made to date."[174] With over $300 billion in liabilities, the African continent is on *debt row*. The modest reductions for the most highly indebted countries have not made a significant dent in the problem.

---

171   Yash Tandon, "WIPO, WCO, Intellectual Property and Border Guards," *South Bulletin* 15 (May 16, 2008). For an analysis of the WCO proposal, see Xuan Li, "SECURE: A Critical Analysis and Call for Action," *South Bulletin* 15 (May 16, 2008).

172   Yash Tandon, "Role of Civil Society in National Space," *South Bulletin* 21 (August 16, 2008), p. 9. See also his *Ending Aid Dependence*, Nairobi: Fahamu, 2008.

173   "Show Us the Money," *Economist*, February 10, 2005.

174   ONE, *The Data Report 2010: Monitoring the G8 Promises to Africa*, Washington, DC: ONE, 2010, p. 9.

Private finance, in the form of FDI, was no more reliable. Of the $1,306 billion in global FDI flows, only 29 percent ($379 billion) went south. Most of this was absorbed by the Pacific Rim and by the larger states. A minuscule amount went to the highly indebted countries. Of the global total, 16 percent, or $193 billion, left the South for other venues; finance capital in the South had become aggressive, seeking greener pastures in New York, London, and Frankfurt; it was no longer trapped by national boundaries. Money was hot, and unstable stock markets and currency prices allowed the financiers to seek profits in the short run based on minuscule price differentials. With liberalized finance, surplus capital sloshed around in search of very short-term returns, tipping over the applecart of planned development.

The IBSA ministers looked elsewhere. The North's credibility on debt relief was in question; it was better to seek finances from other sources. Manmohan Singh's mantra ("better trade than aid") was the dominant signpost, providing Southern neoliberalism with a justification for its turn to export-oriented production and trade. This was to be a route out of poverty: fluctuations in volatile commodity prices had to be controlled by a mechanism that had been on the table for a generation—a Commodity Stabilization Fund.[175] Discussion of "innovative finance" for development had been ongoing in Scandinavia, in darkened corridors of the UN world, and in the IBSA capitals. The Leading Group on Innovative Financing for Development, and its offshoot the Leading Group on Solidarity Levies, went to work in Paris (2006) and Oslo (2007) to discuss levies on air travel, tobacco sales, currency transactions fees, and remittances, as well as to discuss closing tax havens, preventing capital flight, expanding access to microfinance, and establishing advanced market commitments (AMC—a guarantee from donors that if a vaccine is developed by a pharmaceutical company it will be purchased). IBSA backed these idiosyncratic and weak efforts.[176]

In March 2002 the UN called a conference on Financing for Development in Monterrey, Mexico.[177] Delegates filed into the conference rooms whispering about the chaos that had so quickly overtaken Argentina, although there was no formal conversation about it. In 2001, Argentina had been pitched by the vicious orthodoxy of the IMF into financial free-fall. Presidents did not stay long in office (Adolfo Rodríguez Saá governed for a week), protests filled the cities (with the *piqueteros* banging their pots and pans, and the Moviemientos de Trabajadores Desocupados—the unemployed—seeking a solution to their hunger near the old Casa Rosadas). Riot police fired at the crowd, as the

175   IBSA, "Cape Town Ministerial Communiqué," March 11, 2005.

176   IBSA, "Rio de Janeiro Ministerial Communiqué," March 30, 2006, para. 6.

177   I am guided by the excellent analytical work of Susanne Soederberg, "Recasting Neoliberal Dominance in the Global South? A Critique of the Monterrey Consensus," *Alternatives* 30 (2005).

established political class wrung their hands in search of an exit. Argentina's crisis should have spelled doom for neoliberalism, but it did not.[178] The delegates at Monterrey arrived confident of their virtues and verities. Little had to be rethought.

A week before the conference opened, the World Bank released *Financing the Poorest Countries*. "The crisis in Argentina," the Bank argued, "illustrates how open capital accounts can compound the effects of unsustainable macroeconomic policies and high public sector debt, thus seriously complicating stabilization efforts." The root problem remained macroeconomic policies and public-sector debt—the government was spending too much and had not taken the peso in hand. Setting aside these problems of economic governance, the Bank warned of the dangers of capital mobility. Capital's lack of loyalty had to be guarded against. Restrictions on capital account transactions, according to the Bank, "have had only limited success in controlling capital outflows in the context of a weak investment climate, where domestic investment opportunities are limited and fears of confiscation or reduction in the value of assets provide considerable incentive to put money abroad."[179] One way to trap investment was to provide a productive sector for it to work upon. That could not occur, the Bank argued, if investment opportunities were being constrained by Northern tariffs.[180]

The Bank's mild caution did nothing to deflate the Monterrey consensus, which pushed for development funds from volatile private capital markets; and to secure those funds, it urged more trade and financial liberalization. Couched in the language of equity was a push for more of the same. "The Monterrey 'consensus,'" wrote the South Centre's Yash Tandon, "was, in fact, on the financialisation of development, instead of on the developmentalisation of finance."[181] Finance was firmly in the driver's seat.

With aid drying up, IBSA decided to get in on the act. The modestly financed IBSA Fund made its first grants to Guinea-Bissau (for agriculture and livestock development), Burundi (for infrastructure and HIV/AIDS prevention), Laos (for irrigation and water management), Cape Verde (for refurbishment of healthcare infrastructure), and Palestine (for a sports facility and towards youth engagement). It was not much compared to the problem before the South.

Trade, technology, and finance were the three prongs of IBSA's effort, but

---

178   Andrés Gaudin, "The Kirchner Factor," in Teo Ballvé and Vijay Prashad, eds, *Dispatches from Latin America*, New Delhi: LeftWord Books, 2006.

179   World Bank, *Global Development Finance: Financing the Poorest Countries*, Washington, DC: World Bank, 2002, p. 2—and on Argentina, p. 44.

180   Ibid., p. xii.

181   Yash Tandon, "Time for a New Bretton Woods Conference," *South Bulletin* 25 (October 16, 2008), p. 2.

each was constrained in one way or another by the asymmetries of power. The instrument for IBSA's effectiveness was not to be its own ambassadors at the Conferences and in the UN. It was to be the growing authority of the Southern MNCs. The IBSA Business Council and a Trade and Investment Forum set the terms for IBSA's work.[182] Associations of Commerce from one country met in another, making deals under the watchful and friendly eyes of commerce ministers.[183] The Tatas and Mahindras set up shop in South Africa, while the Airport Company of South Africa went to work at the Mumbai airport, Ranbaxy created Brazilian subsidiaries, and Petrobras sharpened its drills off the Indian coastline. These companies were part of a new set of Southern MNCs, employing 6 million people, whose total sales in 2005 reached an estimated $1.9 trillion. While certainly regulated, these firms are nonetheless given immense latitude by their governments, who see them as the main engines of growth. Scandals appear every other day on the front pages of newspapers but disappear in a day or so; their appearance is noted, and then dismissed. Nothing the MNCs do can be wrong.[184]

Business leaders were not the only ones lurking about at the IBSA summits. "Civil society" was also represented by artists and academics, and of course defense chiefs. In 2008, alongside a meeting in Cape Town, IBSA conducted a joint naval exercise (IBSAMAR I). India's foreign minister, Pranab Mukherjee,

---

182   IBSA, "Rio de Janeiro Ministerial Communiqué," March 30, 2006, para. 66.

183   For details, see Puri, "IBSA: An Emerging Trinity"; Marco Fuggaza and David Vanzetti, "A South-South Survival Strategy: The Potential for Trade among Developing Countries," *Policy Issues in International Trade and Commodities*, Study Series no. 35, Geneva: UNCTAD, 2006; and Ron Sandrey and Hans Jensen, "Examining the India, Brazil, and South Africa (IBSA) Triangular Trading Relationship," *tralac* Working Paper no. 1 (2007).

184   In the 1970s, the United Nations set up a UN Centre on Transnational Corporations. Its aim was to create a code of conduct for MNCs. Nothing of the sort emerged. In 1993 the UN merged the Centre into UNCTAD, killed the proposal for the code, and put it to work for the promotion of FDI. In 1999 Kofi Annan, UN secretary-general, revived the idea of the code as the UN Global Compact Program. At Davos, during the World Economic Forum, Annan announced, "I want to challenge you to join me in taking our relationship to a still higher level. I propose that you, the business leaders gathered in Davos, and we, the United Nations, initiate a global compact of shared values and principles, which will give a human face to the global market." In 2003 the UN published "Draft Norms on the Responsibilities of Transnational Corporations and Other Business Enterprises," but it took much of its "values and principles" from the rather lukewarm 2000 OECD "Revised Global Codes of Conduct for MNCs." The main point is that the UN would cease to be an independent arbiter of international rules crafted by the UN General Assembly, but that it would become a "partner" with global conglomerates to "work together" to create a "platform" for "a human face to the global market." All this relies upon bonhomie and good intentions. For that reason, the UNCTC's code of conduct is dead. What we have is something quite different.

hastened to note that these exercises "are not aimed at entering some kind of military alliance." A Joint Working Group on Defense worked on mutual consideration within the group for its burgeoning arms industries. The flurry in the press moved Celso Amorim to remark: "I don't think that a group of sociologists meeting in a room causes such attention, but a group of boats assembling with their flags causes attention."[185] "Civil society" was the domain of business and defense leaders. The others were on the margins, unable to move the dynamic of the IBSA. "Civil society" was largely decorative, cultural festivals for entertainment. All the real discussions took place in the boardrooms, the barracks, and the presidential palace.[186]

At Cancún and Copenhagen, the Chinese entered the conversation, providing heft to IBSA and its Southern constellation. It was a unique occurrence. At the Hong Kong ministerial meeting of the WTO in 2005, China had been cautious.[187] China's diplomatic instinct since it joined the WTO in 2001 was to "help to balance the dominance" of the United States, Japan, the European Union, and Canada.[188] A few years into the twenty-first century, matters changed a little. The vast Chinese trade surplus with the Europeans and the United States, as well as China's emergence as the second-largest economy in the world (after the United States), gave it considerable confidence that it could act to shape international relations in its interests. No longer was China's foreign policy trapped around the question of Taiwan's role in the world. Beijing now began to act in these world forums as a modest leader of the South. An enervated NAM had tried to push itself forward through the G15, whose failure engendered IBSA. China had begun to work with the G77 in 1981, but it was only in the past two decades that the G77 plus China has begun to coordinate policy properly—and, as we shall see, it was not till 2012 that they began to have an impact on international debates. It became apparent that IBSA's principal successes took place when it was backed by China. "China is the muscle of the group," as one analyst put it. "They are the ones with the big reserves. They are the biggest potential market."[189] China was the main locomotive for the South.

185   "Remarks by Ministers Nkosazana Dlamini-Zuma, Pranab Mukherjee and Celso Amorim, during the 5th India–Brazil–South Africa Ministerial Meeting," May 11, 2008.

186   This is all in spite of the rhetoric from the IBSA, with leaders urging "civil societies in India, Brazil and South Africa to enhance mutual contact and cooperation." IBSA, "1st IBSA Summit Meeting, Joint Declaration," Brasília, September 13, 2006. See also Khatchik Derghougassian, "IBSA No-Gubernamental: Movilización social, diplomacía ciudadana y governabilidad de seguiridad en la integración Sur-Sur," Working Paper, Universidad de San Andres, 2006.

187   Bibek Debroy, "WTO Ministerial: Deal Yet No Deal," *Business World*, January 2, 2006.

188   Supachai Panitchpakdi and Mark Clifford, *China and the WTO: Changing China, Changing World Trade*, Singapore: John Wiley, 2002, p. 192.

189   David Rothkopf, "The BRICs and What the BRICs Would Be without China,"

CHINESE HAMMER, SOUTHERN ANVIL

Between April 1987 and September 1993, Nyerere visited China five times. Each time he met either Deng Xiaoping or other senior members of the Communist Party or of the national or state-level leadership. In November 1989 the Chinese government took Nyerere to visit Shenzhen, the city at the heart of Guangdong's economic transformation. The immense weight of the Chinese experiment in "modernization" fell on this small fishing village, which had been chosen by Deng in 1979 as the first special economic zone (SEZ). Deng chose it for its proximity to Hong Kong, and within a decade it had become the anchor in the incredible social transformation that took place in the Pearl River Delta of South China. When Nyerere visited it ten years after its inauguration as an SEZ, he was flummoxed. Trips to China since the 1960s and close interaction with Chinese social developments had not prepared him for what he saw in this visit. He returned to Geneva entranced. Could China's success in Shenzhen be replicated elsewhere in the South?

Two questions preoccupied him, though he did not pursue them in the South Commission:

1. How had China been able to move from an agricultural country devastated by the Japanese occupation and war to a country with a much more resilient social basis than elsewhere in the South, and with an emergent industrial base that rivaled those in the North?
2. Would China be able to export its approach to other parts of the South, thereby becoming its engine?

Answers to these questions could not come from the one South Commission member from China. Qian Jiadong's interests were on the political rather than the economic side of things. A close associate of Zhou Enlai, Qian spent the rest of his career in the Ministry of Foreign Affairs, where he was highly respected and very effective (India's ambassador to GATT, S. P. Shukla, notes that Qian's "low-key defense was his wan smile").[190] Qian's son-in-law, Wang Yi, was at the time deputed to Japan as counselor in the Chinese embassy (he is currently a member of the Central Committee of the CPC). Debates over Japan's attempt to offer an alternative on the world stage were not unfamiliar; nor of course were the power-plays by Washington regarding debt and intellectual property. Qian was China's man at the GATT negotiations. But on the

---

Foreign Policy, June 15, 2009.

190   Email to author from S. P. Shukla, January 19, 2011. I am also grateful to Jiangyu Wang of the National University of Singapore for information on Qian. Most of my information on Nyerere's visit comes from letters written by Joan Wicken, Nyerere's secretary, SCA.

Shenzhen developments, he remained cautious. Nyerere's enthusiasm stayed at Qian's level. He did not pursue his questions further, and it shows in the deliberations and final report of the South Commission.

During the 1980s and into the 1990s, China dramatically altered its role in the world. A long period of decline and despondency, from the 1820s to the 1940s, came to a close when Mao led his armies into Beijing in 1949. Wracked by alarming rates of poverty and near famine, the realm of necessity inherited by the Communist regime was perhaps more in need of the restoration of normal life than of socialism. Two paths lay before the leadership. The first emphasized cooperative activity, and might be called the Yenan Way in homage to the Communist-led region of Shaan-Gan-Ning during the early 1940s.[191] Actual experience in Yenan relied upon top-down leadership, much as it tried to emphasize dispersed collective economic activity. Nevertheless, the principle of the Yenan approach was to promote the means to a democratic society. The second path emphasized heavy industrial development, and might be called the Soviet Way, since it was the general trend of Soviet development in the USSR after the Great Turn of 1928–29. The overlaps between the two paths are considerable, but there are a few differences. For one thing, the Yenan Way had a tendency to avoid or obscure the need to produce capital goods in an industrial sector, whereas the Soviet Way tended to assume that the social benefits of heavy industrial development in an enclave would eventually spill out into the agrarian sector. Typically, in the Chinese story, the "radicals" wanted to adopt the Yenan Way, while the "conservatives" wanted the Soviet Way.

In 1950 the beleaguered new government enacted an Agrarian Reform Law, on the assumption that the agricultural sector had to be the lead in the creation of a socialist society. Modest financial aid and crucial technological support from the Soviet Union (the 1950 Sino-Soviet Treaty of Assistance) provided a foundation for rebuilding infrastructure and moving towards the Soviet model of industry-led development. This did not please the "radicals" among the Chinese Communists, who were not disposed to enclave-like industrial development (such as that of Manchuria). The Chinese turned away from this kind of model in 1952, towards the collectivization of agriculture. A combination of natural disasters (1960–62), an end to Soviet support (1960), and an ill-conceived attempt to bring small-scale industry to rural areas (the Great Leap Forward, 1958) beset the Maoist leadership. Too many people died for too little gain. The egalitarian Yenan Way had to go into retreat before the Soviet Way, as heavy industry and technological expertise won out against horizontal development in the rural areas. Vice Premier Chen Yi took the lead in arguing

---

191   The classic work on this is Mark Selden, *The Yenan Way in Revolutionary China*, Cambridge: Cambridge University Press, 1971; for an elaboration, with an auto-critique, see Mark Selden, "Yan'an Communism Reconsidered," *Modern Chinese Studies* IV (January 1995).

that "[s]pecialized schools should not spend much time on politics and manual labor to the neglect of specialized studies." To be "red and expert" was not as important as to be an expert.[192]

The Cultural Revolution (1966–76) attempted to revive the Yenan Way, to make sure that socialism was built not only within isolated sections of the industrial heartland, but in the countryside in general. Most accounts of the excesses of the Cultural Revolution spend time on the cities, with stories of the rough removal of intellectuals into the countryside; few look to the countryside itself to understand its effects. Driven by the ethos of the Yenan Way, the government built hospitals, dispensaries, and schools in the countryside, and pressed for the construction of medium-scale industrial units attached to rural communes. Educational and industrial training alongside the social infrastructure of the new Chinese state produced healthy bodies with experience of factory work.[193]

The grand visions of the Cultural Revolution drove China's society into turmoil; towards its end, in 1976, both Mao Zedong and Zhou Enlai died. The death of the Great Helmsman left the ship of state in some disarray. The Cultural Revolution had come like a whirlwind. Inadequate political preparation among the masses and the suffering of large sections of the intelligentsia provided easy fodder for the more conservative elements in the leadership. Deng Xiaoping returned from exile, joining hands with acting premier Hua Guofeng to outmaneuver the redoubts of the Cultural Revolution (such as the Gang of Four), and take control of the Party and the state. Hua and Deng strengthened their hand by playing on the cult of Mao (Hua pushed the Two Whatevers policy—uphold whatever policies Mao encouraged and follow whatever Mao said). Deng used Hua to consolidate the power of his modernizers. By the early 1980s, with Deng and his group in charge, the Two Whatevers vanished. A new direction emerged driven by Deng's pragmatism (in 1961, Deng offered a slogan that would define his career: "It doesn't matter whether it's a white or a black cat, I think; a cat that catches mice is a good cat." Mao's reported retort was, "If it is all the same to them whether it is a white cat or a red cat, they will not mind if it is imperialism or Marxism-Leninism").[194]

192   W. A. C. Adie, "Political Aspects of the National People's Congress," *China Quarterly* 11 (July–September 1962), p. 80; and Feng Ting, "Concerning Redness and Vocational Proficiency," *Survey of the China Mainland Press* 2,776 (1962).

193   Barry Richman, *Industrial Society in Communist China*, New York: Random House, 1969 is a crucial source; and for a good summary of the situation by the 1970s, see Alexander Eckstein, *China's Economic Revolution*, Cambridge: Cambridge University Press, 1977. See also Carl Riskin, "Maoism and Motivation: A Discussion of Work Incentives in China," in Victor Nee and Jakes Peck, eds, *China's Uninterrupted Revolution*, New York: Pantheon, 1975.

194   Robert Weil, *Red Cat, White Cat: China and the Contradictions of "Market*

The mechanism for Deng's ascent was the combination of disparagement of the 1949–76 period with the canonization of Mao himself. But what Deng would be able to achieve in the period that followed relied almost entirely on the Maoist fruits—namely, the production of a healthy, literate and able population. These were China's greatest asset.

Quotations from Chairman Mao was not Deng's manual; he looked to Tokyo and Singapore. MITI's seventeen-volume official history was hastily translated into Chinese, and 800 Chinese government officials traveled to the Nomura Research Institute for various training programs.[195] Japan and China suffered from too much history. Protests broke out inside the government and in the streets, denouncing the "second occupation" of the country by the Japanese.[196] The adoption of the Japanese Way was less talked about but more emulated. The name for Deng's theory of the enhancement of the private sector was *wenzhu yitou, fangkai yipian*—"anchor at one end and let the other end be free." The anchor was the state, which would provide the financial and infrastructural backing for the free end, namely private enterprise.[197]

Singapore was an easier destination than Tokyo. In November 1978 Deng traveled to meet Lee Kuan Yew, putatively to discuss the Vietnamese war against the Khmer Rouge, but more pointedly to talk about economic reforms and overseas Chinese investment.[198] If Japan was a historical liability, overseas Chinese investment and the *guanxi* ("connections") of Chinese cultural

---

Socialism," New York: Monthly Review Press, 1996, p. 269.

195   In the autumn of 1992, Emperor Akihito made an important symbolic visit to China, and two years later Vice Premier Zhu Rongji went to Japan. Zhu told his hosts that he wanted China to follow Japan's cautious liberalization of equity markets, and its *keiretsu* system that integrated industry and banks with government. It was in this context that Chinese officials came to Japan to be schooled. For more of the contentiousness, see Linus Hagström, *Japan's China Policy*, London: Routledge, 2005.

196   Margaret Pearson, *Joint Ventures in the People's Republic of China*, Princeton: Princeton University Press, 1991, p. 50.

197   The state continues to play a very strong role in economic activity, even as the provinces are urged to let slip the anarchy of competition. For the timid role of business in state affairs, see Scott Kennedy, *The Business of Lobbying in China*, Cambridge: Harvard University Press, 2006.

198   Lee Kuan Yew, *From Third World to First: The Singapore Story, 1965–2000*, Singapore: Straits Times Press, 2001, Chapter 37. In 1978 Vietnam crossed the Mekong River to try and eject the Khmer Rouge from Southeast Asia. The Khmer Rouge had embarked on a genocidal policy that was anathema to the kind of socialism envisioned by the Vietnamese. The Chinese had backed the Khmer Rouge not out of any kind of fealty but because of the confounding logic of the Cold War (Vietnam's ally was the USSR, and because of the Sino-Soviet split in the late 1950s, China took the Khmer Rouge under its wing). Deng went to Singapore in November 1978 to secure ASEAN support against the Vietnamese.

familiarity would become the coin for the new manufacturing enclaves that Deng wished to build.

Returning from Singapore, Deng pushed the process that led, in April 1979, to the creation of the SEZ in Shenzhen. The government decentralized decision-making to the provinces, and allowed them to compete with each other for revenues and investment. Guangdong's advantage was its proximity to Hong Kong and to overseas Chinese capital and technical knowhow.[199] Deng's Shenzhen did not define the CCP's growth model in the 1980s. Cautious about the restoration of capitalism, the CCP crafted measures to prevent the emergence of large-scale private ventures. Instead, in the 1980s, small rural enterprises began to engage in small-scale businesses. These rural household and collective enterprises (including township and village enterprises) produced goods for the Chinese market. The subsidization of subsistence farming allowed the rural firms an advantage over urban state-owned enterprises, which had to provide welfare benefits and guaranteed employment to their workers.[200] This short burst of rural dynamism was brought to an end in the 1990s. Deng's political ascent was complete after 1989, when those who did not adopt his own position vanished into obscurity. The 1989 protests by industrial workers of the Soviet Way and students with an affinity for the Yenan Way or US-style liberalism were struck down, leading to international condemnation.[201] Northern investment in China's SEZ sector dried up. The Chinese leadership turned much more aggressively to overseas Chinese capital, including the enclave economies of Hong Kong, Singapore, and Taiwan. Deng visited Shenzhen in his celebrated Southern Tour of January 1992, and exhorted the local government to continue its exertions: "The 'four small dragons' [Hong Kong, Singapore, South Korea, and Taiwan] in Asia have developed very rapidly, so has your development. Guangdong should strive to catch up with them in twenty years' time."[202] China had to emulate both the direction and speed of this development.

Two years later, in 1994, China passed a new Company Law to open the door to the private corporate sector—including the privatization of state-owned enterprises and ending of welfare programs—and to relax the barriers against FDI. Jiang Zemin and Zhu Rongji expressed their preference for the "corporate

199   My analysis of the transition in China is guided in large measure by Ho-fung Hung, "Rise of China and the Global Overaccumulation Crisis," *Review of International Political Economy* 15: 2 (May 2008). For the point about decentralization and overseas capital, see pp. 154–5.

200   Joel Andreas, "A Shanghai Model?" *New Left Review* II/65 (September–October 2010), pp. 66–7.

201   Hui Wang, *China's New Order*, Cambridge: Harvard University Press, 2003.

202   "Records of Comrade Deng Xiaoping's Shenzhen Tour," *People's Daily*, January 18, 2002.

capitalism of the West, and they favoured supermarkets over farmers' markets, department stores over street vendors, large factories over small ones, and corporate chains over mom-and-pop businesses."[203] Rural China suffered deeply. The number of rural enterprises declined from 24.9 million in 1994 to 20 million in 1998.[204] A credit squeeze, combined with a drop in grain prices in 1996, put a nail in the coffin of rural China. The advantages accrued by the peasantry were transferred to the factory; new taxation of agriculture and higher costs for agricultural inputs reduced the agricultural surplus, which was transferred by the enlarged bureaucracy into the export-oriented industrial sector on the Pacific Rim. The "burden of this massive project fell on the shoulders of the peasants," reported Chen Guidi and Wu Chuntao.[205] Rural incomes dropped quite dramatically. The peasantry was not helped when the government began to curtail the "iron rice bowl" of the Maoist era. Social goods such as medical treatment and education soon came at a price.

Distress in the countryside pushed young workers towards the newly created SEZs, where manufacturing jobs provided cash wages. "An army of peasants turned their backs on the soil and marched into the city," wrote Chen and Wu. "The peasants do all they can to leave: smart young people apply for college or get jobs through connections; at worst they flood into the city as migrants." This process depleted the countryside: "The dwindling human resources soon usher in a decline in material resources, and the spirit of creativity is exhausted."[206] By the late 1990s, China's SEZ production had taken charge of its growth dynamic. Both the Yenan and Soviet Ways fell by the wayside, as the SEZ Way came to dominate. By the time Nyerere visited Shenzhen on behalf of the South Commission, state expenditure on infrastructure and the SEZ promotion of manufacturing had changed the landscape entirely. Farms were vanishing under the weight of industrial development, and farmers had either fled into the interior or been transformed into industrial workers. The *gongren* (industrial proletariat) became the *dagongmei* (those who work for the SEZ bosses). Growth rates skyrocketed (8.5 percent growth in per capita GDP on average between 1999 and 2003). This growth was anchored in high investment rates that facilitated a ceaseless expansion in exports of goods of ever higher value.

SEZ production was predicated upon FDI investment and low wages for migrant workers. Earlier fears that FDI would constrain Chinese sovereignty and return China to the semi-colonial period were cast aside by Deng in the

203   Andreas, "Shanghai Model," p. 70.

204   Yasheng Huang, *Capitalism with Chinese Characteristics: Entrepreneurship and the State*, Cambridge: Harvard University Press, 2008, p. 79.

205   Chen Guidi and Wu Chuntao, *Will the Boat Sink the Water? The Life of Chinese Peasants*, New York: PublicAffairs, 2006, p. 149.

206   Ibid., p. 206.

late 1980s. Early studies by the Chinese leadership on the role of FDI found that it "had not caused major disasters: PRC sovereignty was intact." FDI poured in ($60 billion flowed into China's Pacific Rim in 2002, and by 2011 the annual figure rose to $116 billion). FDI was central, but so too was China's low effective wage rate. Migrants appreciated the fact that urban (including SEZ) rates were more than three times as much as rural wage rates.[207] Nonetheless, the Chinese urban wage rate was lower than that in the Atlantic states, which meant that as Northern wages stagnated, so too did wages in China.

In the early years, the CCP leadership was unhappy with SEZ efforts in Guangdong and Fujian, even though Guangdong was on its way to being the leading province for exports. What worried them was the lack of skilled Chinese labor in the SEZ firms, the large outlay of state funds for infrastructure, and, most of all, the corruption and crime that resulted from fast money.[208] They pushed the provincial governments to move to import technology. Deng sold the CCP the promise of FDI with the pledge that it would not come without technology transfer—the bugbear of the South Commission. In 1987, Deng noted that the PRC had to be bolder in "absorbing foreign investment and technology." "To settle the problem" of laggard FDI, Deng said in 1987, "we should open the door still wider to the outside world, create a more favorable environment for investment and be bold in using foreign capital; on the other hand it is hoped that foreign parties would be more open-minded in technology transfer."[209] This was the crucial dyad: the point was not just to attract *investment* that retained China's position as a provider of raw materials or cheap labor; China also had to make sure that FDI would come into the country with *technology*. This was by far the most contentious issue in the Uruguay Round, but the sheer size and promise of the Chinese labor force and its putative market, as well as the obstinacy of the PRC leadership, allowed it to force MNCs to transfer technology to Chinese companies. SEZs were enhanced by the creation of open port cities and economic and trade development zones (1984–85), free trade zones (1992), and high-technology development zones (1995). These zones would house factories, research centers, and innovation centers—with the research and innovation centers acting as funnels for new technologies out of the foreign firms into the Chinese firms.

The push for technology transfer came in what China's Ninth Five-Year Plan (1996–2000) called "pillar industries"—namely automobiles, construction, electronics, heavy machinery, and petrochemicals: "In developing pillar industries, the initial technology must be relatively advanced. While importing

207   Huang, *Capitalism with Chinese Characteristics*, p. 157.
208   Jonathan Spence, *The Search for Modern China*, New York: Norton, 1990, pp. 673–5.
209   Pearson, *Joint Ventures*, pp. 67–8.

advanced technologies, we should boost our own technological development and renovation capabilities, build up the scale of economies and pay attention to economic returns."[210] Of the Chinese government, Rhett Dawson, president of the Information Technology Industry Council (an American high-tech trade association), pointed out, "They are fairly unabashedly trying to grow their industry on the technology we've developed. They have a deliberate policy."[211] "You cannot survive in China," Yun Yong of Samsung said, "without becoming a Chinese company. That includes local technology development, product design, procurement, manufacturing and sales."[212]

During his tour of South China in 1992, Deng addressed anger that his SEZ strategy would compromise Chinese socialism. "There is no cause for alarm when a greater number of foreign-funded enterprises are established," he noted. "The advantages are on our side; we have large and medium-sized State-owned enterprises, we have rural enterprises, and most importantly, the political power is in our hands."[213] These advantages might have been there, but the problem was that China had begun to produce *too much*. Beijing allowed provinces to compete against each other. There was little overarching regulation for the new SEZ sector. The rush to build more factories that produced similar goods led to a situation of overcapacity. Three-quarters of Chinese industries faced the problem of overcapacity by 2006, before the credit crunch that began the next year.[214] This was a vast manufacturing bubble that was waiting to explode.

The massive Chinese industrial machine churned out goods in all sectors through the 1990s. Low wages and industrial technology made it virtually impossible for the workers themselves to buy the immense amount of goods that poured off the conveyor belts. Besides, these belts were directed into containers that boarded ships heading off to the ports of Los Angeles and San Francisco, where trains took them to Wal-Mart and other retail giants, where the now largely underemployed US consumers drew upon personal credit lines to pacify their advertising-driven desires. A satanic symbiosis grew between the hardworking but underpaid Chinese workers and the underemployed but over-credited US consumers. This relationship was turbulent. In 2005, the

---

210   Li Peng, "Report on the Outline of the Ninth Five-Year Plan for National Economic and Social Development and the Long-Range Objectives to the Year 2010," 4th Session of the 8th National People's Congress, March 5, 1996.

211   Jerry Harris, "Emerging Third World Powers: China, India and Brazil," *Race & Class* 46: 3 (2005), p. 14.

212   Ibid., p. 10; Yifei Sun, "What Matters for Industrial Innovation in China: R&D, Technology Transfer or Spillover Impacts from Foreign Investment?" *International Journal of Business and Systems Research* 4: 5–6 (2010).

213   Weil, *Red Cat, White Cat*, p. 227.

214   Hung, "Rise of China," pp. 158–9.

IMF's chief economist, Raghuram Rajan, pointed to various troubling factors in the world economy. "These include the excessive dependence of global growth on unsustainable processes in the United States and to a lesser extent in China, the elevated level of asset prices, particularly housing, and the high and volatile price of oil. The downside risks to our forecast are thus considerable." The United States worried the IMF because of its vastly troubled imbalance between robust consumption patterns and anemic effective demand. China, on the other hand, worried Rajan because of its "overdependence on demand from other countries," namely the United States. Rajan hoped that "a growing China that consumes more will benefit not only itself but also the world."[215] The idea that the Chinese market would absorb the imbalances and save the system started us on the path towards the idea that "locomotives" (led by China) are no longer needed for the South, but might perhaps be needed for the North. It is a remarkable shift of emphasis.

In late 2005, the vice chair of the China WTO Research Center, Wu Jia-Huang, gave a talk at the Industrial Development Forum of the UN Industrial Development Organisation (UNIDO). After a long career at UNCTAD and as the Chinese Foreign Ministry's GATT director, Wu was fully aware of the intricacies of international trade and the vicissitudes of international finance. By 2005 China had become the "workshop of the world." Wu acknowledged that at the opening of his talk, noting dryly, "Industry plays a very important role in China's economy." By 2005 it had become clear to a section within the CCP leadership that all was not well with the Chinese experiment. President Hu Jintao and Premier Wen Jiabao spoke for the vast Chinese interior, which was where their political roots lay. Both Hu and Wen spent their early political years in the province of Gansu, in the northwest of the country—far from Shanghai and Shenzhen, the political base of their predecessors Jiang Zemin and Zhu Rongji. Early in their tenure, both Hu and Wen toured the interior and spoke openly about the absolute poverty and rising inequality in the country. The Gini coefficient for China went from a position of reasonable equality (0.29 in 1981) to less equal (0.39 in 1995) to very unequal (0.41 in 2007) by the time

---

215   Raghuram Rajan, "Global Imbalances: An Assessment," IMF Research Department, Conference at the Ronald Reagan International Conference Center, Washington, DC, October 25, 2005. Rajan's talk is also used in Hung, "Rise of China," p. 151. Rajan (with Luigi Zingales) is the author of *Saving Capitalism from the Capitalists*, New York: Crown Business, 2003, which provided a salutary critique of unstable capitalism (they nonetheless hold that "free markets are perhaps the most important tools for lifting the huddled masses out of poverty"). After his tenure at the IMF, Rajan returned to the University of Chicago, from where he advised the Indian prime minister, Manmohan Singh, on financial matters. In September 2008, Rajan's Committee on Financial Sector Reforms for the government of India provided some recommendations to protect India from the credit crunch and the financial crisis.

Hu entered his post. This certainly put down a cautionary marker. So too did the rise in public protests (what the government calls "mass incidents").[216] In 2005 the Ministry of Public Security reported 87,000 such "incidents," up by almost 7 percent from the previous year.[217] Hu spoke of the need to create a "harmonious society" (*hexie shehui*). In the context of this openness, Wu Jia-Huang spoke of the "60 million poverty-stricken Chinese today." He hastened to add that "China has 87,000 welfare institutions and enterprises together with their 2 million staff members engaged in welfare and relief activities. Last year more than 26 million poor people benefited from various relief programs. Another 17 million people received temporary assistance." This was of course important—and to the people in distress, essential.

The choice before Wu, as before Hu and Wen, was simple. The government could push for a "Maoist" solution to the increased inequality, or it could push for a social-democratic resolution within the confines of the present arrangements. The former way would have meant that the Chinese surplus would no longer go in such vast amounts into the Northern banks and into Northern treasury bills (and in turn to Northern consumers as unsecured credit). Instead, these monies could go to the Chinese population either through transfer payments (redistribution of income) so as to increase their consumption base (and quality of life), or to public investment not only to improve the infrastructure for the export-oriented society (roads for private cars and high-rise buildings for businesses), but to enhance the social wage. Both the transfer payments and the increase in the social wage would revive the quality of life of the people and transform the basis of Chinese society. Such "Maoist" ideas are not without a base in contemporary China. As Qian Liqun put it, Mao's legacy is "a fruit hard to consume, but impossible to discard."[218]

But China's export model made it difficult to pivot from the trap of feeding its consumers in the US (China held $906.8 billion of US treasury securities in October 2010) to building the capacity of its own population. That is the catch of the export-oriented model. Wu was ensnared by the lure of growth: "I believe that economic growth and trade expansion are preconditions for effective poverty alleviation," he said in 2005, with the "precondition" now becoming the eternal constraint.

Rather than turn towards a social justice agenda ("growth with equity," the South Commission's formula, had also been recited by Hu and Wen), the Chinese authorities went South. "In recent years," Wu told the UNIDO conference, "a good number of Chinese enterprises are prepared to invest their

---

216   Ching Kwan Lee, *Against the Law: Labor Protests in China's Rustbelt and Sunbelt*, Berkeley: University of California Press, 2007.

217   "China to 'Strike Hard' against Rising Unrest," *Reuters*, January 26, 2006.

218   Qian Liqun, "Refusing to Forget," in Chaohua Wang, ed., *One China, Many Paths*, London: Verso, 2003, p. 305.

money overseas. They are looking for suitable sectors in suitable countries. There are many opportunities for South-South cooperation in the field of industrial development."²¹⁹ "South-South Cooperation," a term out of the South Commission, refers to the broad universe of Chinese economic and political relations with the three continents of Africa, Asia, and Latin America—some of this for reasons of raw-material needs (particularly energy and metals), but also to build up new markets for the Chinese goods that cannot be absorbed in the North. South-South Cooperation also refers to the world of diplomacy, with the IBSA states and China on a rampage through the various forums to try and shift the legal boundaries of international relations.

The term "industrial development" was crucial, and was not used only because Wu was speaking at UNIDO. This is particularly so for Africa. Outside "aid" for African development in the twentieth century has not been focused on industrial growth or even social development. The main parameter of such growth in the recent past (from 1973) was for African states to undergo structural adjustment, to tear down whatever modest social-welfare provisions they had created after independence, and to erect much more robust security apparatuses to protect the interests of the resource-extractors. Whatever "aid" came into the country had so many strings attached that the independent governments had to question their own supposed freedom. No wonder that by the early twenty-first century, writers of socialist (Yash Tandon) and neoliberal (Dambisa Moyo) persuasions equally denounced the aid-driven and structural-adjustment strategies of the North.²²⁰ Even though the colonial and IMF legacies are bitterest in the African context, they are no less despised in South America and the Arab world. As Anouar Abdel-Malek put it, the Chinese have no "legacy of harsh colonial governance and foreign interference in local and regional affairs."²²¹ It helps as well that China canceled $10 billion in debt held

219   Wu Jia-Huang, "China in the Same Boat with the South for Industrial Development," Industrial Development Forum, 11th General Conference of UNIDO, Vienna, Austria, December 3, 2005.

220   Yash Tandon, *Ending Aid Dependence*, Cape Town: Fahamu, 2008; and Dambisa Moyo, *Dead Aid: Why Aid is Not Working and How There is Another Way for Africa*, New York: Farrar, Straus & Giroux, 2009. At the Forum on China-Africa Co-Operation in Cairo, on November 8, 2009, Wen Jiabao said, "I have read a book titled *Dead Aid* written by Dambisa Moyo. The author talks about her personal experiences and draws the conclusion that China's assistance to Africa is sincere, credible, practical and efficient and is welcomed by the African people. I am confident that time will prove that friendship and cooperation between the Chinese and African people has a bright future."

221   Anouar Abdel-Malik, "China's Message to the Arabs," *Al-Ahram* 708 (September 16–22, 2004); Chris Zambelis and Brandon Gentry, "China Through Arab Eyes: American Influence in the Middle East," *Parameters*, Spring 2008. On Latin

by various African states to China in 2003, and has since then been generous with its debt relief (unlike the North).[222] The Chinese look back to Bandung for their lineage, rather than to colonialism or structural adjustment, and from there they are able to avoid seeming patronizing thanks to the "trade not aid" ethos of the South Commission, and now of the Chinese leadership.

For the tired-out Southern leadership, China's "success" is a beacon. Donald Kaberuka, a former minister of finance in Rwanda and now president of the African Development Bank, is a representative figure: "We can learn from [the Chinese] how to organize our trade policy, to move from low to middle income status, to educate our children in skills and areas that pay off in just a couple of years."[223] The limitations of the Chinese model, in terms of its capacity to generate mass employment and to find markets for its vast quantities of goods, does not dampen the hope that the tarnished faith in Americanism might now be redirected into a relatively unblemished Sinoism. "The Chinese are investing in Africa and are seeing results," said Sahar Jolly, Sierra Leone's ambassador to China, "while the G8 countries are putting in huge sums of money and they don't see very much."[224]

Certainly the Chinese thrust into the South is not motivated by any attempt to establish a model of development. There is reticence about considering a *zhongguo moshi*—a China Model. There are no institutional alternatives being proposed, and there is no drive to supplant the intellectual thrust of the World Bank and IMF. "The reluctance of Chinese intellectuals to speak on general world issues," Arif Dirlik argues, "even as the PRC is headed for world power

---

America, see Hernán Gutiérrez, "Oportunidades e desafíos de los vinculos económicos de China e América Latina y el Caribe," *CEPAL Serie Comercio Internacional*, no. 42, Santiago, CEPAL, 2003.

222   Chris Melville and Olly Owen, "China and Africa: A New Era of 'South-South Cooperation,'" *Open Democracy*, July 8, 2005, p. 2.

223   Godwin Nnanna, "Beyond China's Year in Africa," *China Dialogue*, January 19, 2007.

224   Barry Sautman and Yan Hairong, "Friends and Interests: China's Distinctive Links with Africa," in Dorothy Grace Guerrero and Firoze Manji, eds, *China's New Role in Africa and the South*, Cape Town: Fahamu, 2008, p. 106. A view of China in Africa in the 1990s and in the decade that followed is provided in Ian Taylor, "China's Foreign Policy Toward Africa in the 1990s," *Journal of Modern African Studies* 36: 2 (1998); and Serge Michel and Michel Beuret, *China Safari: On the Trail of Beijing's Expansion in Africa*, New York: Nation Books, 2010. There are some distinctions, as the Chinese have now deepened their interest in the creation of infrastructure and have loosened their general policy of silence on the internal character of the African states with which they deal (the test case here is Sudan, where it is widely believed that, as a consequence of mainly Atlantic pressure, the Chinese have urged the Sudanese government to less violent policies in Darfur).

status, is a striking characteristic of most of their writing."[225] What motivates it, on the surface, is a search for raw materials and for markets, with the magnanimous development agenda alongside but not driving these efforts. From Brazil came soy, soy oil, iron ore, and ethanol, at the same time as Chinese-made shoes, textiles, clothing, and toys flooded the Brazilian market. To circumvent tension (such as the standoff over Brazilian soybeans in 2003), the Chinese and Brazilians have proceeded to create joint ventures with the purpose of moving the Brazilian economy along the value chain, into automobiles, aircraft, and electronics. Embraer's collaboration with the Harbin Aircraft Industry and with Hafei Aviation is one example of this, as is the joint venture between Compania Vale do Rio Doce and Baosteel to build a $2.5 billion steel complex in Maranhão state.[226]

The IBSA states are at the center of this South-South Cooperation, with China as the "leading goose" and the IBSA states flying in its wake. China's rapid urbanization and substantial surplus enthrall the elites of the IBSA states and others in the South, many of whom believe that this is a reproducible pathway. The Chinese investment in the South, however, is itself not necessarily a sign of strength; it might as well be a sign of weakness—of an export-oriented industrial giant gradually shut out from the saturated consumer-driven debt economies of the North (mainly the United States), and therefore now eager to create and cultivate new markets in the South. At the UNIDO meeting, Wu noted that "China feels in the same boat with the developing members of the WTO." China positions itself as a Southern state, and by most measures that is precisely what it is. Of course there are major differences between, say, China and Lesotho, the former being a Permanent Member of the Security Council and holder of a large surplus capital pool. It is this heft that powered the South in its WTO challenges at Doha, Cancún, and Copenhagen.

LOCOMOTIVES OF THE NORTH?

Speaking of the growth of India and China, along with the other challenges confronting both of us, he said, "We need a vehicle where we can find solutions for these challenges together—so when these monsters arrive in 10 years, we will be able to deal with them."

US Ambassador Craig R. Stapleton, recounting a conversation with former French Prime Minister Michel Rocard, October 2010[227]

---

225   Arif Dirlik, "China's Critical Intelligentsia," *New Left Review* II/28 (July–August 2004), p. 137.

226   Such shifts are also at work in some African states, as is evidenced in Michel and Beuret, *China Safari*; and in David Barboza, "Some Assembly Needed: China as Asia Factory," *New York Times*, February 9, 2006, p. B1.

227   Ambassador Craig R. Stapleton, "Ambassador's Meeting with Michel Rocard," October 27, 2010 (05PARIS7360), Wikileaks Archive.

By the early 2000s, the research analysts at Goldman Sachs, the major investment bank, began to pay attention to the new Southern bloc. One of its leading
analysts, Jim O'Neill, coined the term BRIC: Brazil, Russia, India, China.[228]
O'Neill had no sense of the politics; he was invested in the economics. To
Goldman's analysts, size mattered: the BRIC states covered vast amounts of territory on which lived very large populations, and these people had now begun
to produce enormous amounts of goods and services. Brazil and Russia supplied raw materials to India and China, who in turn supplied manufactured
goods and services in trade to the North Atlantic. The transactions between
these giants had the potential to take place without Europe, Japan, and the
United States, which had hitherto been the broker for most of world trade.
Not only would the BRICs emerge as major entities on the planet, but the analysts felt that the BRICs had the potential to supplant the North. The BRICs
will become the main "engine of new demand growth and spending power,"
which could "offset the impact of graying populations and slower growth in the
advanced industrial economies."[229] Goldman Sachs hoped that the potential of
the BRIC states would rescue the North from the crises of deindustrialization
and financial instability. Finally, a zone of the world had appeared to absorb the
excess finance and buy the large volume of commodities.

For Goldman Sachs, the BRIC states had only an economic role. This
was to utterly miss the dynamic that stretches from the G15 to IBSA to IBSA-
plus-China (also called BASIC). These groupings have as much political will
as economic potential. But the growing economic size of these countries had
not resulted in comparable political heft. The IBSA states joined Japan in its
long quest for political authority in a world where it had already attained economic prosperity and power. Since the 1990s, Japan and Germany had been
promised a permanent seat on the UN Security Council. In 2004, Japan and
Germany joined Brazil and India in their bid to enlarge the Council's permanent membership.[230] South Africa joined its IBSA colleagues in a call for
regional representation—another Asian state, a South American one, and an
African one. Under the leadership of the UN General Assembly's president,
Miguel d'Escoto Brockmann (Nicaragua), in 2008, the UN took up the issue
of its reform. "We support early reform of the Security Council—an essential
element of an overall effort to reform the United Nations—in order to make
it more broadly representative, efficient and transparent," d'Escoto wrote in a
letter to the member-states. The call has fallen on deaf years.

---

228   Goldman Sachs, *The World Needs Better Economic BRICs*, Global Economics
Paper no. 66, 2001.
229   Goldman Sachs, *Dreaming with BRICs: The Path to 2050*, Global Economics
Paper no. 99, October 1, 2003, p. 2.
230   Aziz Haniffa, "Group of Four aggressively push Security Council Bids," *India
Abroad*, October 1, 2004, p. A6.

The other important demand for political assertion has been to bring democracy to the IMF and the World Bank—the two institutions dominated by Europe and the United States. Between the Asian financial crisis of 1997–98 and the credit crunch of 2007, the IMF had become subdued. The aggressive days of Jacques de Larosière and Michel Camdessus had given way to the anodyne leadership of Horst Köhler and Rodrigo de Rato. Unraveling faith in the Structural Adjustment Program and in the Washington Consensus undermined the legitimacy of the IMF and the World Bank, particularly as middle-income states turned to private capital flows for finance (in 2005, the private flows to developing countries totaled $491 billion—whereas the IMF lent just over $1 billion).[231] The New York Times let slip in 1998 that the IMF might be directed by a European and staffed by economists from every continent (but only a few graduate schools in the Atlantic world); but in the end "it acts as the lapdog of the US Treasury."[232]

As the country with vast surpluses, China made the loudest noises, in the most genial way, for greater voting power in the IMF. "The voices of those countries is under-represented, and their economies are developing very rapidly," said Sadakazu Tanigaki, the Japanese finance minister, in 2006. "If those facts are not adequately reflected, the IMF will not be able to maintain its credibility and legitimacy."[233] Entry into the Executive Committee of the IMF by Brazil and India (joining China and Russia), which is what was gained by 2009, is of little value, since it takes very few decisions: it is a sleepy sinecure for Central Bank officials who are near retirement. The IMF's Independent Evaluation Office report from 2008 acknowledges this. In 2007, the German minister of finance, Peter Steinbruck, told the International Monetary and Financial Committee that Germany would press for "fair representation" based on "relative weight in the global economy." The problem is how one calculates that. The Indian finance minister, P. Chidambaram, felt that if GDP was the gold standard, then it must be converted using purchasing-power parities—or, in other words, the standard of living and population in a country must be taken into consideration when one measures the size of its economy. Such a measure would give India and China control over the IMF and the World Bank. It was not to be permitted.

With little political power, the South's locomotives remained unable to push their main issues onto the agenda: debt and technology transfer. On debt, the locomotives no longer proposed to gain investment through aid. What they

---

231   Eric Helleiner and Bessma Momani, "Slipping into Obscurity? Crisis and Reform at the IMF," Working Paper no. 16, Centre for International Governance Innovation, University of Waterloo, February 2007, p. 3.

232   David Sanger, "As Economies Fail, the IMF is Rife with Recriminations," *New York Times*, October 2, 1998.

233   "Newly Emerging Economic Powers Force IMF to Rethink its Structure and Operations," *Universia Knowledge*, Wharton Business School, September 6, 2006.

required was FDI from private capital, and they wanted to use their comparative advantage of lower subsistence levels to produce goods at a lower cost than in the North. Trade in these goods would increase the surplus of the states, which could then invest this surplus towards further development. That was the way to get out of the shadow of debt. However, agricultural subsidies in the North and the variously designed techniques to shut off access to Northern markets compromised this strategy. The call for laissez-faire principles came only from the mouths of ideologues—it did not reflect the orientation of the economic borders. It was this standoff that blocked the WTO round that began in Doha and foundered in Cancún. Without political power, it was unlikely that the locomotives extract any progress from the European Union and the United States.

On technology transfer, the locomotives hoped to use the debates around public health and climate change to make progress. The WTO had allowed an amendment to its rules on public health, but this did not significantly change the overall architecture of the intellectual property regime. But IBSA and China did make a dent in the climate round. At Copenhagen, for instance, these states pushed the more carbon-guilty North to pay a tax for its carbon-emitting past to finance a global investment fund in green technology. This fund would supplement the development of technology for solar energy, wind energy, biofuels, and nuclear energy. It helps that China is one of the world leaders in solar technology (Suntech, the Chinese firm, is one of the largest). But the mechanism for technology transfer has not been developed beyond the level of principles, and barriers to technology transfer, in TRIPS for instance, militate against these developments.

Unable to be fully servile, the South's locomotives have tried to make the most of differences within the G8 to edge their way into its decision-making. The weak link was France's Nicolas Sarkozy. In 2003, the French had already invited the Plus 5 countries (Brazil, China, India, Mexico, and South Africa) to the Evian Summit of the G8. At the next two summits (Gleneagles, 2005, and Heiligendamm, 2007) the G8 leaders spoke timidly of trying to "institutionalize the dialogue" with the locomotives. Chancellor Angela Merkel wanted the G8 and the Plus 5 to establish the "conditions of stability and confidence for the global economy." "It is clear," she said in 2007, "that this responsibility must be shared by the main emerging economies, such as China, India and Brazil, and that, as globalization advances, the G8 becomes less and less capable of shouldering all its load on its own."[234] The G8 had no joint communiqué with the five guests; they were left on the margins. It was worse at the Hokkaido G8 meeting in 2008. No one seemed to pay much heed to the interlopers; it was as if they had simply come for the photographs.

---

234 "Focus of the German G8 Presidency," G8 Summit, Heiligendamm, 2007.

By early 2008, the financial crisis had set in. A contraction in the credit markets followed the bankruptcy of Lehman Brothers and the merger of the major investment banks in the United States and Europe. Treasury departments and Central Banks rushed to provide stimulus programs to prevent the stalled economies from going into financial cardiac arrest. The seven sick men propped each other up as best as they could. Gathering in Hokkaido in July 2008 to stiffen their resolve against their own electorates, they tried their best to find an alternative to austerity, whose political implications were horrendous. During the 1991 recession in the North, exports to the South helped save the North's manufacturing sector from disaster.[235] They hoped for a repeat. "Emerging markets' economies are still growing stronger though our growth has moderated," the G8 said in its final statement. To escape the turbulence and uncertainty, the G8 pointed its finger where it did not belong, at "elevated commodity prices, especially of oil and food," and at "growing current account surpluses." In other words, the "emerging economies and the oil producing countries" needed to conduct a "smooth adjustment of global imbalances," namely by buying more from the North and bringing oil prices down. "In some emerging economies with large and growing current account surpluses"— namely, China—"it is crucial that their effective exchange rates move so that necessary adjustment will occur."

The South had had to wallow in its debt crisis through the 1980s and into the 1990s; there had been no talk of exchange-rate adjustment to benefit the South, only fiscal discipline resulting in social austerity. A minuscule percentage of the surpluses that went to the stock exchanges came to the South, but nothing in the kind of volume that might have balanced the enormous inequities of global finance. An act of social cannibalism allowed the countries of the South to survive, and then, barely, recover. Now, with the North in distress caused by the engineered financial casinos, talk began of the need to manage the imbalance through the political manipulation of exchange rates. But what few managed to articulate was that, when the US and Japan played this game with the Plaza Accord and the reverse Plaza Accord, it did not kick-start manufacturing in the US—exchange rate manipulation simply accorded strength to the dollar, rather than getting the workers in Detroit back into their factories.[236] Political currency manipulation was favored over an old policy that had been rejected by the US over the years within the IMF, what the economist Yanis Varoufakis calls a "surplus recycling mechanism."[237] Unlike debt-recycling,

235   IMF, *World Economic Outlook: Spillovers and Cycles in the Global Economy*, Washington, DC: IMF, 2007, p. 125.

236   Aaron E. Cobet and Gregory A. Wilson, "Comparing 50 Years of Labor Productivity in US and Foreign Manufacturing," *Labor Monthly Review* 51, June 2002.

237   Yanis Varoufakis, *The Global Minotaur: America, the True Origins of the*

which is punitive and only deals with the symptoms of problems, surplus-recycling would enjoin a mediating body (such as the IMF or World Bank) to transfer surplus finance from the surplus side of the balance of payments to the deficit side. No such common-sense solution was permitted, since that would create a mechanism that did not privilege Atlantic primacy.

Heads held high, the G8 leaders placed responsibility for the disaster on the South (and eventually Southern Europe, where Italy, Greece, and Spain were spoken of with the kind of cultural disdain normally reserved for the Global South). Not a word of the role of high finance in the creation of opaque asset bubbles, whose lifespan had run their course; not even a word of censure for the deregulation of high finance. In October 2008, the former Federal Reserve chair Alan Greenspan told a Congressional committee, "Those of us who have looked to the self-interest of lending institutions to protect shareholders' equity, myself included, are in a state of shocked disbelief."[238] Greenspan's mea culpa seemed utterly self-serving, particularly in light of the literature that had warned of the grave dangers to society posed by the inordinate power of finance. In 2005, popular *New York Times* commentator Paul Krugman inveighed against Greenspan: "He's like a man who suggests leaving the barn door ajar, and then—after the horse is gone—delivers a lecture on the importance of keeping your animals properly locked up."[239] The IMF also fell on its knees, later saying that it had been blinded by the "Greenspan Put"—the claim that the Federal Reserve would continue to protect asset prices by injecting liquidity into the system. The IMF's study of its own role in the debacle found that it had "praised the United States for its light-touch regulation and supervision that permitted the rapid financial innovation that ultimately contributed to the problems in the financial system." Mirroring Greenspan, the IMF had "recommended to other advanced countries to follow the US/UK approaches to the financial sector," and remarkably, "did not sufficiently analyze what was driving the housing bubble or what roles monetary

---

Financial Crisis, and the Future of the World Economy, London: Zed Books, 2011, Chapter 3.

238 Edmund Andrews, "Greenspan Concedes Error on Regulation," *New York Times*, October 23, 2008. Other apologies also came in from the stalwarts of the financial press and the economics professions. For example, Paul Samuelson, "Balancing Market Freedoms," *New York Times*, November 19, 2007; and Martin Wolf, "Why Financial Regulation is Both Difficult and Essential," *Financial Times*, April 15, 2008.

239 Paul Krugman, "Greenspan and the Bubble," *New York Times*, August 29, 2005. Krugman continued, "One way or another, the economy will eventually eliminate both imbalances [the housing bubble and the trade deficit with China]. But if the process doesn't go smoothly—if, in particular, the housing bubble bursts before the trade deficit shrinks—we're going to have an economic slowdown, and possibly a recession. In fact, a growing number of economists are using the 'R' word for 2006."

and financial policies might have played in the process."[240] Neither the IMF nor the Federal Reserve warned against inadequate leverage limits and risk management. Few complained about Greenspan's dangerous inflation of the asset bubbles. High rates of inequality in the United States had combined with high rates of financial manipulation by the banks to create a toxic environment that would inevitably lead to collapse. In addition, half a trillion dollars of hard-earned reserves were transferred from the South to the North between 1997 and 2005 (as debt-servicing and as reserve accumulation).[241] This money helped fuel the Greenspan Put; but the reserves dwindled as the stock markets hemorrhaged.

Just before the credit crunch, the Europeans sent a former finance minister of France to run the IMF. In Lionel Jospin's government, Dominique Strauss-Kahn organized French CEOs into the Cercle de l'Industrie (1993) to campaign in Brussels for a better deal for French business. He had intimate ties to corporations, but he did differ slightly from what he considered the "Anglo-Saxon model"—that is, the turn to prioritizing short-term profit over the long-term interests of firm and nation. It was on this topic that Strauss-Kahn commissioned François Morin to write a report on this short-term thinking inside corporate governance—a report that was hastily buried in the archives. This said something of Strauss-Kahn's ideological compass: his rhetorical needle oscillated towards Atlantic liberalism, but it would always settle on the orthodoxy of Atlantic policy. The credit crunch threw any attempt at reform of the IMF to the winds, but it provided Strauss-Kahn with the opportunity to sail the IMF ship into the center of the storm. The IMF put itself forward as an important agency to help guide the world economy out of crisis. If this was an opportunity for the IMF to emerge from obscurity, it was also an opportunity for the Southern locomotives. They needed each other. Hoping to buy their way into leadership of the IMF, the locomotives put some of their reserves into the IMF's dwindled holdings and tried to influence the policy discussion inside the Fund.

Strauss-Kahn did not sound like Camdessus, who was a ventriloquist for the Washington Consensus. The IMF research section under Strauss-Kahn advanced some views that appeared unorthodox to the unschooled ear. For instance, the IMF now suggested that capital controls were not perhaps such a bad idea—particularly to hold down finance capital's huge incentives to make rapid profits regardless of any social good ("hot money"). Other studies

---

240   Independent Evaluation Office of the International Monetary Fund, *IMF Performance in the Run-up to the Financial and Economic Crisis, 2004–07*, Washington, DC: IEO of the IMF, January 10, 2011, p. 6.

241   United Nations, *World Economic and Social Survey, 2008: Overcoming Economic Insecurity*, New York: UN, 2008, p. 12.

seemed to retreat from harsh talk of "labor market flexibility" that had previously characterized the literature, which referred to the removal of distortions such as labor unions and wage protections. The new Fund suggested that too much "flexibility" resulted in high levels of inequality, and thus very high levels of personal indebtedness. Strauss-Kahn started to quote John Maynard Keynes, and to suggest that the goal of economic management should no longer be growth but "jobs, jobs, jobs."[242] Even the World Bank's Robert Zoellick concurred, speaking more cryptically of "inclusive growth." In early 2011, before the exposure of Strauss-Kahn's disgraceful behavior against a hotel maid, he had visited George Washington University. "The pendulum will swing from the market to the state," he said. "Globalization has delivered a lot … but it also has a dark side, a large and growing chasm between the rich and the poor. Clearly we need a new form of globalization" to prevent the "invisible hand" of loosely regulated markets from becoming "an invisible fist."[243]

Behind the rhetoric lay a more prosaic reality. The capital controls that the IMF validated were to be used only in certain circumstances, and even then only temporarily. In fact they had already been used to good effect in Brazil and Chile, whose currencies had been protected during the credit crunch. As economist Jayati Ghosh pointed out, "Once again the IMF is behind the policy curve, struggling to remain relevant by belatedly justifying policies that have already been put in place."[244] When the IMF led the charge into southern Europe to help stave off a meltdown of capitalism, it did not defend the rights of labor, but once more championed "labor market flexibility" and austerity. It took the "creditor's point of view," and encouraged high unemployment rates as a means to save the bond ratings of Greece, Ireland, and Portugal.[245]

Fears of financial meltdown threw the G8 into frenzy. After the Asian financial crisis of 1997–98, the finance ministers of the North had called on certain key countries to join them in a new grouping, the G20. The G8 joined with key Pacific Rim states (Australia, China, Indonesia, South Korea), central states of the Middle East (Saudi Arabia and Turkey), the IBSA states (India, Brazil, South Africa), and Mexico. This G20 met briefly, and then went on hiatus after the Asian flu had settled down. During the 2000s, its main task was to talk

242   Binyamin Applebaum, "At Meeting of World Financial Bodies, a Sharper Focus on Middle East Inequalities," *New York Times*, April 15, 2011, p. B3.

243   Howard Schneider, "IMF Chief Sees Larger State Role in Economy," *Washington Post*, April 11, 2011.

244   Jayati Ghosh, "To Make the IMF Relevant Will Take More than a New Leader," *Guardian*, April 20, 2011.

245   Mark Weisbrot, "Emerging Out of the IMF's Shadow," *Guardian*, April 18, 2011. Much more sympathetic to the new IMF is Joseph Stiglitz, "The IMF's Switch in Time," *Time*, May 5, 2011.

about tax evasion. There were no discussions that ran parallel to the agenda of the IBSA and the South. When the financial crisis of 2007–08 broke out, the G20 was awakened. Sarkozy went to Delhi in January 2008 and told business leaders, "At the G8 summit, eight countries meet for two and a half days and on the third day invite five developing nations—Brazil, China, India, Mexico and South Africa—for discussions over lunch. This is injustice to 2.5 billion inhabitants of these nations. Why this third grade treatment to them? I want that the next G8 summit be converted into a G13 summit." This was Sarkozy's Gaullist moment, intended to put some daylight between the Anglo-Saxon attack on Iraq and France's "benign" colonial history. Sarkozy's indignation ended at his borders. The third-grade treatment remained acceptable for the *racaille* in the *banlieues*, but not for the leadership of their homelands. Under pressure from his economic advisors and people like Sarkozy, Bush revived the G20. Five summits were organized in quick succession: Washington (2008), London and Pittsburgh (2009), and Toronto and Seoul (2010). No new measures emerged from these gatherings. They allowed the IMF to take charge of the recovery, with India and China putting additional reserves into the Fund; but there was no ideological soul-searching. The communiqué from the London summit in April 2009 could have been written ten years earlier: "We believe that the only sure foundation for sustainable globalization and rising prosperity for all is an open world economy based on market principles, effective regulation, and strong global institutions." The G20 adopted wholesale the New International Financial Architecture (1999) that, as Susanne Soederberg puts it, "sought to facilitate market transparency without imposing state-led regulations."[246]

The G20 met in Pittsburgh in 2009, when it appeared possible that global capitalism might implode. Talk of global Keynesianism was in the air, and it looked as if neoliberalism was on its knees. The final communiqué from Pittsburgh did not disguise its true intentions—to use government stimulus packages to get over the slump, and then return to business as usual. "We will avoid any premature withdrawal of surplus," the eminences wrote, "at the same time, we will prepare our exit strategies and, when the time is right, withdraw our extraordinary policy support in a cooperative and coordinated way, maintaining our commitment to fiscal responsibility." There was nothing here to indicate a fundamental course correction, no indictment of the "finance coalition"—the bloc formed when the politicians and the state bureaucrats "as if by osmosis" adopted "the objectives, interests and perceptions of reality of the private vested interests that they are meant to regulate and survey in the

---

246   Susanne Soederberg, "The Politics of Smoke and Mirrors: The G-20 London Summit and the Restoration of Neoliberal Development," in Konings, *Great Credit Crash*, p. 225.

public interest."[247] No concern for the "total malfunction of the genome of finance."[248]

The G20 finance ministers, who called themselves the "Sherpas," met in Busan, South Korea, in June 2010 to create the agenda and draft documents for the 2010 Toronto G20 summit. The ministers met in the lush Paradise Hotel. They told the press that it was time for austerity. Yoon Jeung-Hyun, South Korea's minister for strategy and finance, led the charge. In 1992 he had pushed South Korea's capital market liberalization, watched it go into crisis, and was then the one tasked with crisis management (in an epic meeting with the IMF in the J. P. Morgan building in 1997). The Busan text was interpreted by Yoon as follows: "The recent events highlight the importance of sustainable public finances and the need for our countries to put in place credible, growth-friendly measures, to deliver fiscal sustainability, differentiated for and tailored to national circumstances. Those countries with serious fiscal challenges need to accelerate the pace of consolidation." The keyword here was "consolidation," which in the argot of the financiers meant the reduction of government deficits and indebtedness. Or, in almost popular language: the Pusan Sherpas called for austerity.

The Greek financial meltdown provided the lesson. That Goldman Sachs had colluded with the Greek ruling elite to enable and mask its debt was not the issue: the lesson from the Greek debacle was that European countries had to hastily bring down their deficits. These deficits now had to be paid for not by higher taxes on the rich (or even more effective tax collection on extant rates), but by cuts in government social spending and by effective taxation of all kinds on the working class and the precariat. The consumption of the elite could not be touched, but the consumption of the poor, low as it was, was going to be curtailed.[249] In the UK, the newly elected Conservatives hastened to slash government spending, with the Conservative leader, David Cameron, telling his fellows to change their "whole way of life." Angela Merkel's German conservatives were not far behind with their cuts—this after Merkel had forced the Greeks to wield their own hatchet. An 80-billion-euro cut was to start the process, with more in the wings. "The direction is the right one," said an editorial in *Bild*. "The government is saving money on items it no longer wants to pay for that can only be financed through debt. Every private individual should do the same with his finances. The program isn't heartless." Spain's Zapatero

---

247 Willen Buiter, "Central Banks and Financial Crises," paper presented at "Maintaining Stability in a Changing Financial Situation," Federal Reserve Bank of Kansas City symposium, Jackson Hole, Wyoming, August 21–23, 2008, p. 106.

248 Henri Bourguinat and Éric Briys, *L'Arrogance de la Finance. Comment le Théorie Financière a Produit la Krach*, Paris: La Découverte, 2009, p. 45.

249 Stathis Kouvelakis, "The Greek Cauldron," *New Left Review* II/72 (November–December 2011).

cut 15 billion euros from his budget. Spain was "moving in absolutely the right direction," declared the IMF's chief. The new policies were a "shot in the arm." Even Merkel expressed her "full confidence in Spain." Not so the workers, who mimicked their Greek comrades on the Spanish streets.[250] The cuts were the down payment for the modest debt-recycling enjoined on central banks and on the exchequers of the surplus-bearing economies (in Europe, this meant Germany).

Obama sent his encyclical to the G20, cautioning that Europe was being too hasty in its turn to austerity. Obama could not follow them, having neither the political capital nor the political will. In the past, he wrote, the stimulus was "too quickly withdrawn and resulted in renewed hardships and recession." He wanted "credible plans," which meant the appearance of another route. He could not afford to be outside what David Cameron called "the international mainstream" of debt management; it would look awkward. The main difference between the forces of growth (Obama) and of austerity (Merkel) was not strategic, but tactical. Obama had the US economy in mind, not the Greek people, when he promoted growth in Europe. The US was worried that a collapse of the European banking system would threaten US banking institutions. US banks had already reduced their exposure to the Greek financial system; a Greek exit from the Eurozone might infect the rest of southern Europe (Italy and Spain), in whose financial markets the US banks were more heavily leveraged, both directly and indirectly. A Europe-wide collapse would devastate US financial firms. To prevent this outcome, Obama was insistent that the European Central Bank create a cushion for a credit crunch and provide "confidence" to investors to prevent them from abandoning the euro. Twenty-first-century Keynesianism apparently has less to do with creating jobs than with using public money to create a financial firewall to protect the banks.

A less awkward option for Obama was to blame China—now an established art in Washington. The current refrain from Washington is to demand that China devalue its currency, thereby reducing its surplus dollars. There is a demand that the Chinese government needs to push polices that increase domestic consumption and reduce its domestic saving rate: the Chinese need to be made into consumers. Currently the personal consumption of the vast Chinese population is only 16 percent of that of the US population. If the Chinese were to adopt American consumption habits, imagine the ecological stress. But the real demand was for the Chinese to drop all their currency and capital controls, eviscerate their already threadbare regulatory institutions, and—as it was put in a joint report from the World Bank and the PRC's Development

Research Center of the State Council in February 2012—"embrace the market economy."[251]

Austerity for the working class and the poor in the North was combined with a demand that the South pay up to save the financial system that had tormented it for a generation. Alongside the G20 process, the heads of government of China, Brazil, India, and Russia began a new series of meetings (known, bizarrely, as the BRIC summits). The first was in Yekaterinburg, Russia, in June 2009, where they produced a much stronger statement than was available from either the G20 or the IBSA group. Their countries "must have a greater voice and representation in international financial institutions, whose heads and executives should be appointed through an open, transparent and merit-based selection process." The demand for democracy in the IMF and World Bank was now couched in the language of reconstructed neoliberalism (good governance, transparency). It was a clever gesture. Whereas the G20 had sidestepped the urgent need for finance in the bulk of the South, where poverty and inequality had increased within a year of the credit crunch, the BRIC summit called upon the powers to "step up efforts to provide liquid financial resources" to the poorest. Most chillingly for the North, the BRIC states wanted to sidestep dollar seigniorage and create a new global currency that was "diversified, stable and predictable." This urge for a new global currency made its appearance inside the G20 when Christine Lagarde, France's finance minister, called for a new global monetary system "founded on several international currencies."[252] The initial move was to increase the supply of IMF Standard Drawing Rights as a way to infuse liquidity into a paralyzed system (though, as long as the Chinese yuan was outside the SDR basket, which included the dollar, the yen, the euro, and the pound, the SDR was not representative of the current monetary landscape).

In April 2010, the second BRIC summit was held in Brasília, on the same day as the IBSA summit. The two had partly harmonized, although at the 5th IBSA summit, in South Africa, Manmohan Singh said that IBSA should remain intact, since it was "unique" with the three countries drawing their "strength and global influence from their common political model of being major

---

251   Luke Deer and Ligang Song, "China's Approach to Rebalancing: A Conceptual and Policy Framework," *China & World Economy* 20: 1 (2012); Yu Yongding, "The Impact of the Global Financial Crisis on the Chinese Economy and China's Policy Responses," TWN Global Economy Series, no. 25, Penang: Third World Network, 2010; World Bank and the Development Research Center of the State Council, People's Republic of China, *China 2030: Building a Modern, Harmonious and Creative High-Society*, Washington, DC: World Bank, 2012.

252   Liz Alderman, "Trade and Monetary Issues Top Agenda at G-20 Meeting," *New York Times*, February 15, 2011, p. B2.

developing democracies geographically located over three continents."[253] South Africa applied to join the BRIC group, and the third BRIC summit in Sanya, China, became the first BRICS summit. The group is extraordinary in its scale: it accounts for 40 percent of the world's population, a quarter of the world's land mass, and a fifth of the world's GDP. Its agenda drew from that of the BRIC and IBSA, but it had much greater geopolitical weight.

The BRIC-IBSA union into BRICS was a high point for the locomotives' international strategy. However, it did not yet offer the three necessary components of a genuine challenge to Northern dominance. First, there was no *military* platform for the alliance, and so no threat to the overwhelming power of the US military and NATO. Indeed, in 1998 the Russian foreign minister, Yevgeny Primakov, suggested a military bloc between Russia, India, and China, but this was rejected by China, and later India.[254] The Shanghai Cooperative Organization (SCO)—formed in April 1996 between China, Russia, Kazakstan, Kyrgyzstan, and Tajikstan, with India as an observer—had a very limited agenda. The three main powers spend modest amounts on their military compared to the United States (of total global military expenditure in 2009, Brazil commanded 1.7 percent, India 2.4 percent, and China 6.6 percent). The test case for the failure of the BRICS to move an agenda that differed from that of the G7 was Libya, where the G7's military arm, NATO, was able to fill the vacuum left open by UN Security Council Resolution 1973; when it called upon "member states" to use "all necessary means," the only ones who had the military clout to act were the United States (by itself) or the United States (through NATO). The BRICS attempt to push an agenda of negotiation through the African Union had failed.[255]

Second, the BRICS alliance has failed to create an *institutional* basis for its challenge to the North. The alliance seeks entry into the very institutions that are controlled by the North. The BRICS states have increased their position in the IMF and have tried to secure more authority in the United Nations. The South failed to rally around a candidate to replace Strauss-Kahn, making it easy for the Europeans to install their candidate (Christine Lagarde) into the office at 19th Street in Washington, DC. When it came time to back a new secretary-general of the International Labour Organization, the South once more settled early on the preferred North Atlantic candidate, Guy Ryder, instead of the various African candidates and the Malaysian economist K. S. Jomo.[256] These elections led up to the selection of the new WTO head in 2013. It is unlikely that

253   Sandeep Dikshit, "IBSA Must Remain Restricted to 3 Countries: Manmohan," *The Hindu*, October 19, 2011.

254   "China Cautious on Primakov Plan," *The Hindu*, December 23, 1998.

255   Vijay Prashad, *Arab Spring, Libyan Winter*, Baltimore: AK Press, 2012.

256   Vijay Prashad, "Labour Needs a Fresh Leader," *The Hindu*, May 11, 2012.

the candidate will stray from the orthodoxy maintained by the organization's current head, Pascal Lamy. No Southern flavor will be added to these institutions that have for so long been encrusted with neoliberal ideas.

Third, the BRICS group has not endorsed an *ideological* alternative to neoliberalism. What it has advanced is a set of proposals that are gentler than Northern neoliberalism, with a modest challenge to US hegemony (in the form of the displacement of the dollar as a core currency). The UN General Assembly's president, Miguel d'Escoto Brockmann, established a UN Conference at the Highest Level on the World Financial and Economic Crisis and Its Impact on Development (June 1–3, 2009). Organized by the former World Bank economist and Nobel laureate Joseph Stiglitz, the panel failed to produce an ideological alternative. It called for the same kind of colonoscopy of the financial system as had the G20 at its November 2008 Washington meeting: a critique of the jargon-laden financial system that essentially offloaded risks to consumers and arrogated vast amounts of power and wealth to the banking system. The Stiglitz report called for a more robust regulatory system to govern the financial sector, but it did not challenge the massive power of the oligopolies or the institutional control of the global economy by the IMF, the World Bank, the bond markets of the North, and the ratings agencies. There was no fundamental challenge to the neoliberal assault.

A critical voice on the panel, Pedro Páez of Ecuador, proposed to decouple the world's economies "from the dollar's crisis logic." The "commercial dependency (and intra-firm trade) with the North is sky high," Páez noted. He proposed a series of regional monetary arrangements and regional currencies. If these came into effect, the South could reduce "the artificial need for dollars in the regional trade, financial markets, and therefore, the technical need for reserves through the deployment of the intra-continental system of settlements." Such a project would bring countries within regions closer together and protect remote nations from complete capitulation to the wiles of the US Federal Reserve Bank and the gargantuan banks of Wall Street, the City of London, and the Finanzplatz. Páez's idea resembled initiatives taken at the Banco del Sur, but these were at a very elementary stage—and no one, not even the Banco del Sur, dared move away from dollar seigniorage. One small experiment began in 2010 within the Bolivarian Alliance for the Americas (ALBA), when these Latin American states began to use a virtual currency for commercial exchanges within the bloc. The introduction of the "sucre" (Sistema Único de Compensacíon Regional, or Unified System for Regional Compensation) resembled that of the euro in 1999. The timing has been bad for the sucre. As the euro implodes, anxiety has set in among the ALBA members about the long-term viability of this currency. For the time being, it does not act as a replacement currency but as a way to denominate trade across borders within the ALBA bloc. A small interruption in dollar dependence did emerge, however, when the Chinese began to offer $95 billion yuan swaps to developing countries. The head of the China Investment Corporation (one of the largest sovereign funds in China), Gao Xiqing, pointed out that China would not indefinitely park its surplus assets in the United States, particularly if the now relatively predictable were to become increasingly unsustainable.[257]

The project of the South languished from 2008 onward. The locomotives prepared themselves, but found—perhaps to their surprise—that the wrong bogies had been attached to them. By early 2011 it had become clear that the US economy had come to rely upon exports to China, India, Latin America, and the Middle East.[258] At the same time, World Bank head Robert Zoellick pointed out before his visit to India that "India's return to high levels of growth is helping the global economy recover from the crisis."[259] Fundamental change in the planet's political economy was off the cards. The locomotives of the South, which had bailed themselves out of the debt crisis, were now being called upon to rescue the North. Of such painful ironies is contemporary history made.

THE SOUTH PROPOSES

In late March 2012, the BRICS group met in New Delhi for their fourth summit. Most of what was said at the summit, and in its Delhi Declaration, was pabulum, as one has come to expect of such meetings. However, there were at least two significant developments that set this summit apart.

First, the BRICS states not only restated their critique of the world economic order and North Atlantic financial hegemony, but offered new policy guidelines and institutions as a remedy. "It is critical for advanced economies to adopt responsible macroeconomic and financial policies," the Delhi Declaration scolded the North, "avoid creating excessive global liquidity and undertake structural reforms to lift growth that create [sic] jobs." A majority of the world's workers were vulnerable in their jobs. In May 2012, an International Labour Organization report found that 75 million young people were unable to find work—4 million more than in 2007. "Discouraged by high youth unemployment rates," the ILO notes, "many young people have given up the job search altogether, or decided to postpone it and continue their stay in the education system."[260] More than 6 million young people withdraw from the labor force

---

257   James Fallows, "Be Nice to the Countries that Lend You Money," *Atlantic*, December 2008.

258   This is the judgment of Robert Hormats, under-secretary of economic affairs, State Department. Eric Lipton, Nicola Clark, and Andrew Lehren, "Hidden Hand of Diplomats in Jet Deals," *New York Times*, January 3, 2011, pp. A1, A6.

259   "India's Growth Helps Global Economic Recovery: World Bank," *The Hindu*, January 9, 2011.

260   ILO, *Global Employment Trends for Youth 2012*, Geneva: ILO, 2012, p. 7.

every year. Where they have been able to find jobs, they are predominantly in the temporary labor market. Austerity programs make life harder for these workers, who often have to support family members who have lost formal employment. Austerity might improve GDP, but it will not create jobs.

Brazil's Dilma Rousseff told the press that the monetary policy of the North "brings enormous trade advantages to developed countries, and results in unfair obstacles to other countries." As an alternative to the dollar-denominated financial system, the BRICS states created a modest new credit facility in local currencies, so that BRICS states and others could now trade with each other without recourse to the dollar or other such "international" currencies, reducing the transaction costs for intra-BRICS trade as well as threatening to remove the dollar from its pedestal as the main currency of international trade. In addition, the BRICS states directed their finance ministries to research the possibility of the creation of a new development bank, a Bank of the South (a BRICS version of the South American Banco Sur, founded in 2009 with an initial capital outlay of $20 billion, to supplant the hegemony of the World Bank and the IMF). The leadership hoped that the new BRICS bank would mobilize resources for infrastructure and development in the BRICS states and in other developing countries. If it were influenced by the Banco Sur, the BRICS bank could be a practical venue for the creation of a new institutional foundation outside neoliberalism.

The second development to emerge from the Delhi summit was that the BRICS states would take some more steps towards a retreat from full subservience to the North Atlantic's political leadership. It remained unclear where the BRICS states proposed to plant their flag, but what was increasingly clear was that there is frustration with the cynicism and hypocrisy of the NATO agenda in North Africa and West Asia, in the encirclement of Eurasia with a missile shield and military bases, and in the trade debates. There was little that the BRICS states could do in the area of foreign policy, having such limited means to counter the alliances set in place by the NATO states in the Arab world, for instance. It was much easier to exert themselves in the trade arena.

Evidence for this exertion was in the margins. The key is to be found in paragraph 17 of the Delhi Declaration, which considers "UNCTAD to be the focal point in the UN system for the treatment of trade and development issues." The Declaration also "reiterates our willingness to actively contribute to the achievement of a successful UNCTAD XIII, in April 2012." Sustained attack on UNCTAD by the Atlantic powers since the 1980s pushed it into a corner, and made it largely irrelevant as the Atlantic world took its business into forums such as the World Trade Organization, where it was able to rule the day. Slowly, the South has tried to revive UNCTAD, whose policy framers have become a bit more aggressive in their defense of an alternative to neoliberalism. One example of this new motivation is in UNCTAD's 2011 report, which is a carefully argued assault on the power and influence of finance capital. In Chapter 5, on commodity markets, UNCTAD argues that the commodity boom cannot be explained by rising demand from the BRICS states. Instead, the culprit can be found among the index investors—the speculators whose commodity trades are motivated by "factors totally unrelated to commodity price fundamentals." What explains the rise in commodity prices, including food and oil, is

> the greater presence of financial investors, who consider commodity futures as an alternative to financial assets in their portfolio management decisions. While these market participants have no interest in the physical commodity, and do not trade on the basis of fundamental supply and demand relationships, they may hold—individually or as a group—very large positions in commodity markets, and can thereby exert considerable influence on the functioning of these markets.[261]

Reining in finance capital from commodity markets will do a whole lot more for food and fuel prices than aggressive exploration for energy sources in vulnerable shorelines and arctic icecaps, or through the subsidies given to vast agricultural conglomerates.

UNCTAD's studied criticism of finance capital and insistence on the reform of the financial sector has earned it the ire of the global North's mandarins. In the negotiations towards a consensus document for the UNCTAD's April 2012 meeting, the North put up as many obstacles as possible. Its seasoned negotiators fought to remove all reference to the financial crisis from the document and to insist that UNCTAD deal only with its core mandate. The draft text was expanded from 24,000 to 30,000 words with issues having to do with the World Bank's favorite idea, "good governance," and with matters of freedom and democracy—all, incidentally, outside the UNCTAD mandate. Each paragraph had to be scrupulously parsed by the North's negotiators, slowing down the process and thereby making a mockery of it. On March 19, the Swiss ambassador to UNCTAD, Luzius Wasescha, pointed out gleefully that, at the current rate of progress (three hours per paragraph), it would take 487.5 negotiation days to get through the draft. This was the strategy of what he called "creating chaos."[262] The US statement on March 19 was just as irritable: "The [UNCTAD] Secretariat should not pursue issues outside UNCTAD's mandate—such as the reform of global financial systems. Not only does this particular issue stray far beyond UNCTAD's mandate and its expertise, it also faces strong opposition by many members," namely the United States. How finance can be seen as "far" from issues of trade and development boggles the mind.

---

261   UNCTAD, *Trade and Development Report 2011: Post-Crisis Policy Challenges in the World Economy*, Geneva: UNCTAD, 2011, p. 114.

262   The section on UNCTAD XIII is based on my reporting for *Asia Times* and *Frontline*.

The North's position rankled former staff members of UNCTAD, who released a statement on April 10 entitled "Silencing the message or the messenger ... or both?" The signatories had once held senior UNCTAD posts, and included a former secretary-general, Rubens Ricupero. "When I arrived at UNCTAD in 1995," Ricupero told IPS, "there was already a conspiracy afoot by the 'usual suspects,' the rich countries—not to change the mandate as they want to now, but to simply suppress the organization that they have never accepted since its inception." Three days later, the negotiating bloc of the South (the G77 plus China) released a very strong statement. Pisnau Chanvitan, the Thai head of the bloc, noted that the North had "regressed to behavior perhaps more appropriate to the founding days of UNCTAD, when Countries of the North felt they could dictate and marginalize developing countries from informed decision-making." The North's behavior, Chanvitan noted in a leaked draft of the statement, "seems to indicate a desire for the dawn of a new neo-colonialism."

UNCTAD XII, in 2008, produced the Accra Accord, in which was buried the philosophical difference between North and South on state policy and development. The North preferred the "market" as the conductor of social affairs, while UNCTAD indicated that "developing countries should pursue development strategies that are compatible with their specific conditions within the framework of an enabling State." This "enabling State" was to deploy "its administrative and political means for the task of economic development, efficiently focusing human and financial resources." The financial crisis struck after UNCTAD XII. As the delegates left Accra and went off to digest their compromises, the toxic banking sector reared its head. UNCTAD had warned about toxic finance for about a generation, but few had listened to its Cassandra-like persistence. In 2009, the North made at least two important concessions to the South in exchange for Indian and Chinese financial contributions to the IMF and other multilateral agencies: first, that the G8 would be wound up in favor of the G20; and second, that the international financial architecture would be reformed. As confidence has returned to the North, however, it has reneged on both these promises. It was in this context that UNCTAD's work became much bolder on the role of finance in social life.

At Doha in 2012, the global North went at UNCTAD from many directions. It tried to use the question of internal reform of the organization as a threat against the staff. Complaints about duplication in the UN system go back to the 1960s, when the US tried to prevent UNCTAD from being born. The North suggested that UNCTAD's budget could be trimmed so that it might return to work on its mandate and not to take up issues already dealt with in other UN organizations. Here the global North neglected to note that the "other" UN organizations, such as the International Monetary Fund and the World Bank, are closely aligned to the US and Europe, and are not beholden to the South. Such a pushback against UNCTAD had not been seen since at least the 1970s.

Unfortunately for the North, the main countries of the South gathered together to defend UNCTAD. The most important outcome of Doha was not the final document, but the emergence of the South as a potent force.

The negotiations on the final document continued until 5 p.m. on the last day, holding up the closing ceremony as the text had to be translated. The final document, the "Doha Mandate," was optimistically named. Coming out of such a contentious process, with the North smarting, the Doha Mandate was nonetheless quite an achievement. All the sections that the North attempted to strike down (on hunger and food security) made their way into the final document. The North wanted to walk away from one particular paragraph that was in the final document of the 2008 UNCTAD XII:

> Developing countries should pursue development strategies that are compatible with their specific conditions within the framework of an enabling State, which is a State that deploys its administrative and political means for the task of economic development, efficiently focusing human and financial resources. Such a State should also provide for the positive interaction between the public and private sectors. (Paragraph 115, Accra Accord)

Part of the fight at Doha was over the ratification of the Accra Accord—and, centrally, whether this philosophical attitude to the "enabling State" should be accepted. In line with dominant neoliberal thinking, the North wanted to substitute this interventionist idea for a more laissez-faire notion of the state. The North's draft suggested that, rather than an "enabling State," UNCTAD should be tasked with the promotion of "an effective State, working with private, non-profit and other stakeholders" to "help forge a coherent development strategy and provide the right enabling environment for productive economic activity." The debate between the "effective" state and the "enabling" state fractured along North-South lines. The final text was a compromise, with neither side entirely able to have their way:

> Each country has the primary responsibility for its own economic and social development, and national development efforts need to be supported by an enabling international economic environment. The State, having an important role to play, working with private, non-profit and other stakeholders, can help forge a coherent development strategy and provide an enabling environment for productive economic activity. (Paragraph 12, Doha Mandate)

Fragments from each draft entered the paragraph, leaving the argument unsettled. Given the poor negotiating position of the G77 plus China—the main negotiating arm of the South—this was nonetheless quite a feat. As I was told by Norman Girvan, former board member of the South Centre and former secretary-general of the Association of Caribbean States, "In the context of the sustained efforts of the North in the run-up to the Conference to emasculate UNCTAD's mandate, and taking into account the formidable political and economic resources at their disposal to divide the South, I share the view of those who judge it to be a victory for the South. It only goes to show that maintaining a firm, united position by the South is the only way to win even modest gains in global forums. Division is fatal." The G77 was able to stave off the strong-arm tactics of the North and leave intact UNCTAD's original mandate, including its ability to conduct research that would "enable" a better understanding of the financial crisis and provide policy tools for states to intervene in favor of people-centered development rather than finance-centered globalization.

"The highlight of the Conference," Heiner Flassbeck, director of UNCTAD's Division on Globalization and Development Strategies, told me, "was the fiercely contested negotiation of the Doha Mandate. Regardless of the specifics of the text as adopted, for me the process that created it was more significant." The specifics were not so central because the real debate was not on practical policy matters. It was on the broader principle of how to understand the international framework for economic policy, and what UNCTAD should be permitted to do to make that framework amenable to genuine people-centered development. "The attempt that was mounted to exclude UNCTAD from working on global macroeconomic, financial and monetary issues was not new," Flassbeck said, "but its advocates came out much more aggressive than ever before. I cannot but conclude that UNCTAD's work, and here mainly the work of my division, has been perceived as professionally strong, but too critical to be allowed in the international chorus of Washington Consensus–like voices." The North's cavil about UNCTAD's duplication of the work of the WTO or the IMF was specious. Unlike the WTO and the IMF, sections within UNCTAD, such as Flassbeck's Division on Globalization, produce high-level empirical work that is grounded in a theoretical framework unwilling to cheerlead for neoliberal policymaking and finance-driven globalization. The North had a political objection to UNCTAD, not a bureaucratic one.

During the debt crisis of the 1980s, a weakened global South saw UNCTAD's secretariat partly sequestered to the interests of the North. From 1974, the UN Centre on Transnational Corporations (UNCTC) had been hard at work building up a database on transnational corporations and setting up a code of conduct for such firms. In 1992 the UNCTC was brought into UNCTAD, where its mandate was radically transformed. Instead of being a watchdog of transnational firms, the UNCTC put its resources towards helping them to enter the South. It was in this period that large sections of UNCTAD became invested in channeling foreign direct investment into the South. At Doha, many of the seminars were precisely on this theme—providing technical and political support for transnational firms and for FDI into the countries of the South. Some of this work is done by the International Trade Centre, a joint project of the WTO and UNCTAD. In the 1990s and early 2000s, UNCTAD's core positions were whittled down as it absorbed the general neoliberal orientation. It was no surprise when Dr. Supachai left the directorship of the World Trade Organization in 2005 that he came to head UNCTAD.

While the Doha Mandate strengthened Flassbeck's Division on Globalization, it did not weaken the general thrust of this other side of UNCTAD. Flassbeck told me that the difficult negotiations at Doha might be seen by "responsible people in UNCTAD as an opportunity for renewing UNCTAD and indeed for revitalizing the G77, which has rediscovered the value of UNCTAD as a source of second opinions on global economic issues, or a 'think-tank for developing countries,' as one delegate put it in the closing ceremony." If Flassbeck is correct, then the larger countries of the South—namely India, China, Brazil, and South Africa—might bring this new political will to bear on other aspects of the North's policy agenda, as well as on a rehabilitation of the critical work on transnational corporations and FDI. None of these states have demonstrated an appetite to challenge the neoliberal policy agenda of the North. What they have done, however, is to resist the North's attempt to shape the trade environment more fundamentally to the advantage of transnational firms than to those of farmers and miners of raw materials and primary commodities in the South. UNCTAD XIII was memorable for a revitalized G77 and for the growing confidence of Brazil, India, China, and South Africa to stand up for a Southern consensus.

On March 19, 2012, the US delegates to UNCTAD told a meeting that the UN organization must "move past tired old debates from another era." But these debates, such as that over financial-system reform and social development, have returned in the deliberations of the locomotives of the South. Whatever the limitations of the regimes in Brazil, Russia, India, China, and South Africa—and there are many, as we have seen—it is undeniable that they are forcing open a new debate in such forums as the UNCTAD meetings. There is no indication that neoliberalism will fall to its knees on its own. There is only slightly more evidence that the BRICS states have had enough of the arrogance of the North in the policy debates that encage the world's peoples in poverty and despair.

CHAPTER FOUR

A Dream History of the Global South

Tomorrow, perhaps, the future.

W. H. Auden

In 1989, the hillside settlements around Caracas, Venezuela, rose up in revolt against the rise in bus fares, spurred on by an increase in petroleum prices. The *Caracazo* stunned the Venezuelan elite, who had been comfortable in their assumption that the firm hand of the state and the analgesic transfer payments to the population had contained the social consequences of inequality. The uprising was the most spectacular demonstration of a series of "IMF riots," or "bread riots," of the 1980s and early 1990s. It was not repeated elsewhere on the same scale, but it represented the density of anger shared across the global South.

The conditions against which this bitterness festered and these rebellions developed were well recognized by the UN's family of organizations. By late 1992, the World Health Organization (WHO) and the Food and Agriculture Organization (FAO) had found that "over 780 million people, mainly in Africa, South Asia and Latin America, do not have enough food to meet their basic daily needs for energy and protein." Even more startling, the WHO and FAO noted, "More than two billion people subsist on diets that lack the essential vitamins and minerals required for normal growth and development and for the prevention of premature death and disabilities such as blindness and mental retardation."[1] Inside the FAO, it had become clear that hunger was not a neutral category, since women, as bearers of so much of the domestic space, gave up their own nutritional necessity and their own health for the betterment of their families.[2] It was women who were often the leading force in these "IMF riots," which were really protests against the catastrophic situation for the vast mass.

A series of revolts spread across the global South and, strikingly, into the heartlands of the global North (of which the most remarked upon was the 1992 Los Angeles uprising). The decade of the 1990s was filled with relatively

---

1 International Conference on Nutrition, *Final Report of the Conference, Rome, December 1992*, Geneva: World Health Organization and Food and Agriculture Organization, 1992, p. 15.

2 Alain Marcoux, "The 'Feminization of Hunger'—What do the Surveys Tell Us?" *SD—Dimensions*, October 2001. Marcoux finds that the bias is strongest in North India and China, but that it is not absent elsewhere.

spontaneous actions across the planet. Much of it was a result of at least five processes:

1. The enforced austerity that threatened the survival of large numbers of people. Pushed by governments in thrall to the "business civilization" of the Washington Consensus, and egged on by transnational corporations and the international finance institutions, these policies cut back both the delivery of social goods and the subsidies ameliorating the prices of necessary goods (fuel and water, in particular). The media generally called these protests "bread riots" or "IMF riots," which correctly located them in terms of the distress they expressed over the procurement of everyday items (bread, water) whose availability and affordability had been made harder by the IMF's Structural Adjustment Programs and the austerity harakiri of the state authorities.

2. The increasing unemployment resulting from the transfer of work from people to technology (in industry certainly, but most sharply in agriculture), from the addition of millions of new and highly disciplined workers from the enclaves of the Eastern bloc and China to the workshops of transnational enterprise, and from the deflationary policies of the G7 states. In Western Europe itself, there were 8 million registered unemployed people in 1970, but by 1994 that number had risen sharply to 35 million.[3] The US maintained lower rates of unemployment, but this was largely a function of a vastly different jobs landscape—with high rates of incarceration and of poor-quality service jobs producing a population more *disposable* than unemployed.[4] UN data from the International Labour Organization showed rising rates of unemployment, although even these figures are modest if we recognize the "disguised unemployment" due to the poor collection of information and the callous definition of what counts as "employment."[5] Fights against the introduction of technology and the shuttering of workplaces, as well as for employment (often led by students), marked the urban landscape in the late 1990s.

3. Neoliberalism's growth strategy is premised upon the sectors of finance, insurance, and real estate (FIRE), as well as on the fire-sale of public assets to private corporations. The latter result more often than not in massive firings of workers, and occasionally in asset-stripping or the dismantling of the productive sector for immediate profit rather than

---

3   OECD, *Jobs Study*, Paris: OECD, 1994.

4   Vijay Prashad, *Keeping Up with the Dow Joneses: Debt, Prison, Workfare*, Boston: South End Press, 2003.

5   Joan Robinson, "Disguised Unemployment," *Economic Journal* 46: 182 (June 1936).

long-term returns. FIRE tends to seize assets (such as land for real estate development or for mineral extraction) to undercut the livelihood of the mass of the people, which is why so many protests in this period were to protect land in the public domain. The formula is simple: if a firm cuts jobs, its shares rise on the stock market. In the world of FIRE, this perversion is normal.

4. By the late 2000s the global hunger rate rose to close to 1 billion. It was a consequence of the displacement of large numbers of people from family farms and agricultural work. In their stead came the agricultural industry, or agribusiness, swept into the lands on the coat-tails of neoliberal reforms that enabled them to consolidate vast holdings, gain privileged access to precious water, plough the land with expensive inputs (fertilizers and pesticides), use machines and monoculture to produce high yields—and at the same time displace farmers, undermine soil and plant diversity, pollute water, and leave many people unable to buy expensive processed industrial food (often tasteless, as a powerful book on the tomato demonstrates).[6] Governments, following the rules of neoliberal policy, withdrew from any attempt to offer subsidies and price supports to farmers, or to maintain schemes for the provision of necessities at fair prices. From Haiti to Egypt, farmers have tried to assert themselves against engineered processes that leave them unable to make a livelihood and remain on the soil. In the 1990s, US industrial chicken manufacturers dumped their less popular "dark meat" into the Haitian market and crushed the island's domestic poultry businesses, leading to the collapse of one of the few dynamic sectors in the rural economy.[7] Farm suicides in India are now at catastrophic levels; journalist P. Sainath shows that, since 1995, a quarter of a million farmers have taken their own lives, and the numbers have continued to rise. What is most distressing about this utter collapse of agricultural life, and its social consequences, has been its predictability: in 1997, the FAO published a study on neoliberal policies in Latin America cataloguing their dangerous political and social consequences.[8]

---

6   Barry Estabrook, *Tomatoland: How Modern Industrial Agriculture Destroyed Our Most Alluring Fruit*, Kansas City: Andrew McMeel, 2011. For a broad study of the shift, see Raj Patel, *Stuffed and Starved: The Hidden Battle for the World Food System*, Brooklyn: Melville House, 2007.

7   Noam Chomsky, "The 'Noble Phase' and 'Saintly Glow' of US Foreign Policy," in Noam Chomsky, Paul Farmer, and Amy Goodman, eds, *Getting Haiti Right This Time*, Monroe: Common Courage Press, 2004, p. 7.

8   Alain de Janvry, Nigel Key, and Elisabeth Sadoulet, *Agricultural and Rural Development Policy in Latin America: New Directions and New Challenges (FAO Agricultural Policy and Economic Development Series—2)*, Rome: FAO, 1997.

5. Hunger, unemployment, agricultural destruction, and asset theft are bad enough, but they feel worse if they increase alongside the aggrandizement of a minority of the population. Those who controlled property and power seemed to benefit greatly in the 1990s, borne aloft by the various asset bubbles in the global stock exchanges. As the 1999 Human Development Report put it, "Gaps in income between the poorest and the richest people and countries have continued to widen. In 1960, 20% of the world's people in the richest countries had 36 times the income of the poorest 20%—in 1997, 74 times as much." These gaps had regional dimensions. The sharpest rise in inequality, according to the Human Development Report, was in the former Eastern bloc, with Russia in the lead, followed outside the bloc by China, Thailand, Indonesia, and the OECD countries. "The net worth of the world's 200 richest people increased from $440 billion to more than $1 trillion in just the four years from 1994 to 1998. The assets of the three richest people were more than the combined GNP of the 48 least developed countries."[9] "Some have predicted convergence," the Report concluded, "but the past decade has shown increasing concentration of income among people, corporations and countries."

A decade of national struggles after 1989 erupted onto the global stage in the late 1990s and into the 2000s, when protestors disrupted the meetings of the international finance institutions in Madrid (1994), Seattle (1999), Washington, DC (2000), Genoa (2001), Gothenburg (2001), and Barcelona (2002).[10] Each of these protests was met with fierce resistance from police and security services. This counter-reaction demonstrated that it was not that the state had been weakened by the pressure from transnational capital and international finance institutions, but that the state had transferred its allegiance from a nominal concern for the vast mass to the full-throated defense of the rights of the propertied. In 1999, Dr. Makanjuola Arigbede of the Nigeria Poverty Eradication Forum noted drily, "We are on a mission to rescue [president Olusegun Obasanjo,] who has been hijacked by the IMF and the World Bank. This country belongs to Nigerians." More accurately, Obasanjo had succumbed to the Stockholm Syndrome—he was not only willing to enforce the Washington Consensus, but equally happy to mobilize the full force of the state to crush any dissent, whether it was regional disgruntlement or anger on the coastline against the free ride given to the Shell corporation. Obasanjo's

9   UNDP, *Human Development Report 1999: Globalization with a Human Face*, New York: UNDP, 1999, pp. 36–7.

10   Jessica Woodroffe and Mark Ellis-Jones, *States of Unrest: Resistance to IMF Policies in Poor Countries*, London: World Development Movement, 2000.

reaction to the protests had become typical on both sides of the North-South divide.

Some basic principles gave coherence to the idea of the global South—a term that properly refers not to geographical space, but to a concatenation of protests against neoliberalism:

- fairer distribution
- autonomy from private capital
- right to well-being
- social justice

These principles are at a high level of generality—and, as we shall see, there is little ability at this level of the struggle to formulate a more precise set of global demands or a global political program. Some movements emphasize one aspect of this list, others another. They come from many traditions, some intuitive, others ideological. Attempts at unity between these movements and protests are frequently called for, and just as often seen to fail. The failures are certainly a function of a subjective lack of trust or common experience, but also of more objective factors—particularly the antagonistic interests of different groups, across national or class lines, and equally across lines of social oppression.

The protests of the new epoch push against neoliberalism, sometimes motivated by a desire to retreat to the past, sometimes by a desire to seek a future social order moored in human history but not imprisoned by it. There is no obvious single pathway. Few have the answers, although many are asking the right questions. We are at a moment of transition, where openness to experiment and a willingness to learn from and to teach each other is paramount. A call for such a conversation is not an endorsement of pluralism. It is, instead, a recognition that none of the established political traditions has a monopoly on the truth. Those who seek the future are few, and weak. In the explosion of creative activity against neoliberalism, there is always the possibility of a breakthrough to something different.

TWENTY-FIRST-CENTURY INTERNATIONALISM

I consider the concept of utopia worse than useless. What has transformed the world is not utopia but need. The only time and place where our work can have impact—where we can see it, and evaluate it—is tomorrow. Let's not wait for utopia.

José Saramago, World Social Forum, Porto Alegre, 2005

By the early 1990s, the only internationalism that seemed realistic was Americanism.[11] The Eastern bloc had gone by the end of 1991, and Boris Yeltsin had adopted a stringent policy of privatization under the name of "reform." The utopian dream of socialism shuddered to a standstill, as Russians seemed more enamored by US-inspired commodities than by the promises of a Communist future. By 1992, China had adopted a new economic agenda that suggested that it too had abandoned the formal aspects of socialist construction. With the Third World Project already in tatters, and the South Commission report already shelved without having been carefully read, it was quite correct for the Hegelian ideologue of Americanism Francis Fukuyama to declare that history had ended—that there was no longer any substantive alternative to liberal capitalism.[12] Fukuyama recognized, in the spirit of Milton Friedman's "natural rate of unemployment," that inequalities would not disappear. It was the duty of *liberal* capitalism to ensure the widening of equality. History would continue, but dramatic social transformations (such as the socialist break) would not occur. The American Century (inaugurated in the late 1920s) would get a second chance.

Bill Clinton played the lead role in the drama of Americanism. He genially sold "America" as the planet's future, with "free trade" agreements the counterpart of older economic and political arrangements. Clinton pushed the North American Free Trade Agreement (NAFTA) as an object lesson for the future. If it worked, then it would be followed by free trade agreements between the United States and other countries: there would be no need for a multilateral trade regime if bilateral treaties could tie the US to those who wanted to emulate it. At the signing ceremony for NAFTA, on December 8, 1993, Clinton was mindful of the historic moment: "We have the opportunity to remake the world." "We cannot stop global change," he pleaded with those who were unsure about the impact of open borders for business. "We cannot repeal the international economic competition that is everywhere. We can only harness the energy to our benefit. Now we must recognize that the only way for a wealthy nation to grow richer is to export, to simply find new customers for the products and services it makes." Mexicans and Canadians would be the first in line to buy US products, but they were not to be alone for long: "We are now

11   Cf. "Internationalism … is no longer coordination of the major capitalist powers under American dominance against a common enemy, the negative task of the Cold War, but an affirmative ideal—the reconstruction of the globe in the American image, *sans phrases*." Perry Anderson, "Internationalism: A Breviary," *New Left Review* II/14 (March–April 2002), p. 24.

12   Francis Fukuyama, "The End of History?" *National Interest* 16 (Summer 1989)—elaborated into *The End of History and the Last Man*, Harmondsworth: Penguin, 1992. For a critique, see Perry Anderson, "The Ends of History?" *A Zone of Engagement*, London: Verso, 1992.

making real progress toward a worldwide trade agreement so significant that it could make the material gains of NAFTA for our country look small by comparison." This was the agreement that created the World Trade Organization in 1995. It was the dawn of a new "American Century," with the Cold War over and "free trade" dominating the future.

As the ink dried on NAFTA on the first day of 1994, the ghost of Zapata rose in the southern regions of Mexico. The Zapatista National Liberation Army (EZLN) entered the town of San Cristóbal, Chiapas, and its leader, Subcomandante Marcos, announced to the startled tourists: "We apologize for the inconveniences, but this is a revolution." ¡Ya Basta! proclaimed the EZLN in its communiqué: "Enough is Enough!"[13] For the EZLN, their revolt was not simply against the Mexican government, but against NAFTA, which it called a "death sentence," and against the entire epoch of neoliberalism. In an early message, Marcos's alter-ego, the philosopher-beetle Durito, noted, "Neoliberalism is not in crisis, neoliberalism is a crisis!" During the 1980s, the Mexican government had undermined domestic maize production (as the giant conglomerate Bimbo pushed sales of its bread at the expense of tortillas), sending *campesinos* and their daughters into the factories along the US-Mexican border, and across the border into undocumented work in the United States.[14] The EZLN carried the burdens of those whose life-chances had been reduced by the portent of the "American Century."

The EZLN's warnings bore fruit. As a result of NAFTA, the peso collapsed in December 1994, and 1995 GDP went into negative territory (–8.7 percent). The Mexican state had already registered warnings of the unrest in Chiapas, having sent 3,000 soldiers of its army into the jungles in May 1993. At first the EZLN looked like a conventional guerrilla army, but it had no stomach for a fight: Marcos was quick to sue for peace, wanting to use the surprise of January 1 to the advantage of the indigenous communities of the region. The government had other ideas, covertly and overtly sending in its armed might to crush the rebellion. After the first anniversary of the rebellion, with the EZLN still in the saddle, Chase Manhattan Bank's Emerging Markets Group prepared a memorandum on Mexico that candidly stated its interests in the nation: "While Chiapas, in our opinion, does not pose a fundamental threat to Mexican political stability, it is perceived to be so by many in the investment community.

13   I rely for my narrative on the superb work by Bill Weinberg, *Homage to Chiapas: The New Indigenous Struggles in Mexico*, London: Verso, 2000; on the collection of writings of Marcos, ¡Ya Basta! Ten Years of the Zapatista Uprising, ed. Ziga Vodovnik, Oakland: AK Press, 2004; the lovely essay by Alma Guillermoprieto, "Zapata's Heirs," in her *Looking for History: Dispatches from Latin America*, New York: Vintage, 2001; and Paul Farmer, "Lessons from Chiapas," in his *Pathologies of Power*, Berkeley: University of California Press, 2005.

14   Weinberg, *Homage to Chiapas*, pp. 66–7.

The Government will need to eliminate the Zapatistas to demonstrate their effective control of the national territory and security policy."[15] Precisely to do this, a month later, the Mexican government launched a major offensive led by Enrique Cervantes Aguirre (he had been chief of staff of the 27th Military Zone in Guerrero when the state crushed the leftist uprising in the 1970s).[16] Protests in Mexico City and elsewhere after massacres of Indians in the jungles (notably in Chenalho in 1998) pressured the government into a military stalemate, and allowed the EZLN to set up its base areas in the heart of Chiapas.[17] Here the EZLN built institutions to govern the countryside and the towns—a parallel state that owed much to the traditions of the various indigenous communities that inhabited the region.

The EZLN stuck its foot in the door of history with its combination of indigenous notions of autonomy and revolutionary humor (in the communiqués of Marcos and the panache of the dot-comrades that he spawned). "Learn to put the date to your letters," Marcos wrote. "History is moving so fast, it might even be good to put the time of day."[18] The entry of the EZLN into San Cristóbal reminded North America of the presence of misery, and of the institutional roots of another vision. It did not matter that Marcos himself refused to provide a firm alternative ("Zapatismo is not an ideology, it is not a bought and paid for doctrine. It is an intuition").[19] The Zapatistas' historical role was to rebuke Clinton and NAFTA. A part of the EZLN's destiny was that its presence undercut the philosophical foundation of neoliberalism and Fukuyama's end-of-history thesis. By donning ski masks and taking up their low-caliber (sometimes wooden) rifles, the members of the EZLN suggested that other opinions has as much authority as Americanism to speak for the present and the future.

In 1996, the EZLN hosted an *encuentro* in their base area of Chiapas, which brought hitherto unconnected activists into what seemed like a new historical time, with a new horizon opening up against neoliberalism. Journalist John Ross called it a "monumentally eclectic gathering of young European

15   Ken Silverstein and Alexander Cockburn, "Major US Bank Urges Zapatista Wipe-Out: 'A Litmus Test for Mexico's Stability,'" *Counterpunch* 2: 3 (February 1, 1995).

16   I reported on these developments at that time, talking to many EZLN people as well as a few in the military; see, for example, "The Struggles of Chiapas," *Frontline* 15: 18 (August 29–September 11, 1998). During the decade I wrote several times on Chiapas and Mexico for *Frontline*.

17   Vijay Prashad, "Massacre at Chenalho: Erasing the Chiapas Uprising," *Economic and Political Weekly*, January 10, 1998.

18   Subcomandante Marcos, *Shadows of Tender Fury*, New York: Monthly Review Press, 1995, p. 112.

19   Subcomandante Insurgente Marcos, *Our Word Is Our Weapon*, ed. Juana Ponce de León, New York: Seven Stories Press, 2002, p. 440.

anarchists, aging Latin American guerrilleros, US cybernauts and the *indigenas* of Mexico Profundo."[20] The gathering was called the Intergalactic Encounter for Humanity and Against Neoliberalism. When did the *encuentro* begin? asked Marcos, obscured beneath in his ski mask. "We don't know. But we do know who initiated it. All the rebels around the world started it." The *encuentro* formed the basis for the creation of the International Network Against Neoliberalism, which pledged to propagate the principles of the Intergalactic Encounter in "every continent, in every country, in every countryside and city, in every home, school or workplace where human beings want a better world." Zapatismo revived militancy in the Americas and Europe, with word of its energy spreading to Africa and Asia. People's Global Action, which would have an influence in the Seattle protests of 1999, was formed after the 1996 *encuentro*.[21] That the EZLN would later settle into a regional formation and prove unable to influence the tide of Mexican politics is not relevant.[22] What it did do was revive a moribund indigenous movement and even the left movement in Mexico, and played its part in revitalizing internationalism for the twenty-first century.

Equally as important as the Zapatistas were the outgrowths of two different key political developments that eventually gave rise to two major UN meetings. The first was what came to be called the international environmental movement, but which was as often as not the indigenous rights movement, and the movements for control over common property and for less harmful uses of nature (including the uses of very large dams which would displace untold numbers and ruin agricultural life for many others). A hunger for resources unleashed firms in search of minerals and fuels, regardless of the misgivings of indigenous communities who held land in trust and, even when they did not live in harmony with the land, at least did not tear it to shreds. In the Americas, the indigenous movement prepared to mourn the 500th anniversary, in 1992, of the arrival of Christopher Columbus in his New World, forming the Continental Campaign for 500 years of Resistance. In Africa and Asia, indigenous campaigns grew out of local resistance to transnational firms and their local agents. The Ogoni in Nigeria, for instance, formed the Movement for the Survival of Ogoni People in 1992, under the leadership of the writer Ken Saro-Wiwa, to confront the destruction wrought on their homeland by the Shell corporation's

---

20   Weinberg, *Homage to Chiapas*, p. 161.

21   David Graeber, "The New Anarchists," *New Left Review* II/13 (January–February 2003), p. 63.

22   It did, however, have an impact on the growth of popular movements, as shown by Richard Stahler-Sholk, "Autonomy and Resistance in Chiapas"; and Aída Hernández Castillo, "Zapatismo and the Emergence of Indigenous Feminism," in Vijay Prashad and Teo Ballvé, eds, *Dispatches from Latin America*, New Delhi: LeftWord Books, 2006.

oil operations.[23] In 1989 the people who lived along the Narmada River formed the Narmada Bachao Andolan (Save the Narmada Movement) to fight against the creation of the mammoth Sardar Sarovar Dam.[24] Such movements became the backbone of the local and transnational emergence of the "environmental" movement, which was as much about the rights of communities as about the inviolability of nature. At the UN World Conference on Environment and Development, held in Rio de Janeiro in 1992, there was an attempt to suborn these myriad needs and demands to the politics of carbon and climate change.[25] But the Earth Conference could not absorb all the energy from this "environmental" movement, which was to have an impact at the 1993 Vienna World Conference on Human Rights, at the 2001 Durban World Conference Against Racism, Xenophobia and Other Forms of Intolerance, the 2002 Johannesburg World Summit on Sustainable Development, and in the growth of twenty-first-century radical internationalism.

The second development was the growth of the international women's movement, which had already been given a strong boost in the UN process (with women's conferences in Mexico City in 1975, Copenhagen in 1980, Nairobi in 1985, and Beijing in 1995), driven by the grassroots emergence of new women's movements as a consequence of the neoliberal processes of the feminization of poverty and hunger, and the reinscription of conservative gender norms in the landscape of consumer-driven desire. At Beijing, the UN conference was split between an official ministerial conference and an NGO–social movement conclave. The latter was by far the more vital, with groups from all over the world pushing hard against the neoliberal thrust: from indigenous women in the Centre for International Cooperation to Indian women in the All-India Democratic Women's Association; from the World International Democratic Federation to Botswana's Emang Basadi Women's Association. In anticipation of the Beijing Conference, the UNDP produced its *Human Development Report* on gender and human development. The report created a new Gender-related Development Index, which showed how poorly most of the world was doing in terms of gender equity (only the Nordic countries came out reasonably well). It also showed that "[w]omen work longer hours than men in nearly every country," and yet women were paid for only one-third of the work they did (the rest being "invisible work"), and that those being paid earned only a fraction of what men earned. "Since status in contemporary society is often equated with

23   Ike Okonta and Oronto Douglas, *Where Vultures Feast: Shell, Human Rights and Oil*, London: Verso, 2003.

24   Amita Baviskar, *In the Belly of the River: Tribal Conflicts over Development in the Narmada Valley*, New Delhi: Oxford University Press, 1995; and Judith Whitehead, *Development and Dispossession in the Narmada Valley*, Delhi: Pearson, 2010.

25   Ken Conca, "Greening the United Nations: Environmental Organisations and the UN System," *Third World Quarterly* 16: 3 (1995).

income-earning power," the report noted, "women suffer a major undervaluation of their economic status."[26] The women at Beijing and elsewhere pointed out that the problem was not their status alone, but also their lack of power in society and their lack of control over cultural, economic, political, and social institutions. The forceful critique of neoliberalism expressed at Beijing's non-ministerial forum moved the women's movements, the indigenous movements, and the other new social movements into close affinity with one another as twenty-first-century internationalism blossomed.

By the mid 1990s, the Non-Aligned Movement was struggling to find its own footing. It had never been at the center of debates around economic policy, having left them to the G77. NAM did not have a New York office and did not make any attempt to lobby the international finance institutions in Washington. The G15 was rendered marginal to international policymaking in the newly created World Trade Organization (1995). The G77 plus China had a small office on the thirty-ninth floor of the UN building (with two staff members). It had only a modest role. The institutional might of the South had been weakened.[27] Its demographic majority in the UN General Assembly came to naught before the drive from the G7 to turn over important decisions to the UN Security Council.

A drive to "reform" the UN further undermined the South. In the 1990s, the UN set up a Commission on Global Governance, co-chaired by the Swedish prime minister, Ingvar Carlsson, and Shridath Ramphal (formerly of the South Commission and a former head of the Commonwealth). Their 1995 report, *Our Global Neighborhood*, recommended the closing down of the two important secretariats of the South on economic matters—UNCTAD and UNIDO. It held that the regional economic bodies (the Economic Commissions for Latin America, Africa, and Asia) could also be wound up.[28] The Commission on Global Governance proposed the creation of an Economic Security Council to "bridge the gap between the various international economic institutions."[29] It was swatted down by the Atlantic powers on procedural grounds (it would have required a change to the UN Charter). The institutional imbalance between the South and the G7 prevented the South from pursuing its agenda at all. The site of opposition was no longer in the halls of the UN. Resistance to the WTO and

---

26 UNDP, *Human Development Report: Gender and Human Development*, New York: Oxford University Press, 1995, p. 6.

27 To get a sense of the North's shenanigans in the WTO, see Fatoumata Jawara and Aileen Kwa, *Behind the Scenes at the WTO: The Real World of International Trade Negotiations*, London: Zed Books, 2011.

28 Walden Bello, *Deglobalization: Ideas for a New World Economy*, London: Zed Books, 2004, p. 92.

29 Mahbub ul Haq, "An Economic Security Council," *IDS Bulletin* 26: 4 (October 1995).

the G7 now came less from the sidestepped Southern institutions than from militancy on the streets.

Decision-making withdrew into the forums controlled by the G7, and the broader policy discussions between government and business took place in private venues such as the World Economic Forum (WEF), held in Davos, Switzerland. The WEF was recast in 1987 to keep pace with the growth of a seemingly transnational capitalist class whose tentacles touched all manner of accumulation activities, as well as to governance. It remained the case that three-quarters of the participants at the WEF came from the United States and Europe (in 2002), yet it also hosted powerful people from Africa, Asia, and Latin America.[30] In 2000 the World Women March, the Brazilian Movement of the Landless, and the French forum ATTAC, among others, held a counter-event in Zurich and proceeded to march towards Davos. The physical isolation of the WEF and the security around it made such a protest futile. It was simply one more illustration of the sequestration of the elite.

Those who participated in the 2000 march decided to form an annual event somewhere in the global South as a counterpoint to Davos. While Davos hosted the World Economic Forum, this group would host a World Social Forum.[31] Rather than create an alternative institutional platform to the Atlantic-dominated organizations such as the IMF and the WTO, as well as other public institutions, the counter-event was formed as a mirror against a private forum—the WEF. The Workers' Party (PT) in Brazil held power in the state of Rio Grande do Sul and in the city of Porto Alegre, which was chosen as the site for this protest-gathering to be held in 2001.[32] The World Social Forum (WSF) was organized by a council whose leadership was largely drawn from European organizations (such as ATTAC and the newspaper *Le Monde Diplomatique*). Within a year, that is, by 2002, the WSF had become an important venue for activists from all over the world. The WSF remained in Porto Alegre for three years before it went to other parts of the world: Mumbai (2004), Bamako, Caracas, and Karachi (2006), Nairobi (2007), Belém (2009),

---

30   Katherine Fawcett, "It's a Small World After All … At the Top: The View from Davos," senior thesis, International Studies Program, Trinity College, Hartford, CT, May 2011.

31   The literature is vast, but for a useful synthesis see Heather Gautney, *Protest and Organization in the Alternative Globalization Era*, New York: Palgrave, 2010; Teivo Teivainen, "World Social Forum and Global Democratization: Learning from Porto Alegre," *Third World Quarterly* 23: 4 (2002); Jai Sen and Peter Waterman, eds, *World Social Forum: Challenging Empires*, New Delhi: Viveka Foundation, 2004; and *Hacia el Partido de Oposición: Foro Social Mundial, Porto Alegre 2002*, España: El Viejo Topo, 2002.

32   Emir Sader, "Beyond Civil Society: The Left After Porto Alegre," *New Left Review* II/17 (September–October 2002), pp. 90–1.

and Dakar (2011). It returned to Porto Alegre in 2012. The Forum was, as Michael Hardt put it, "unknowable, chaotic, dispersive. And that overabundance created an exhilaration in everyone, at being lost in a sea of people from so many parts of the world who are working similarly against the present form of capitalist globalization."[33] The WSF's internationalism was rooted in opposition to IMF Structural Adjustment and undemocratic state intervention. It represented a unity *against*. The social base of this internationalism was varied, from landless peasants in Brazil to the socially marginal Roma, from those fighting to preserve rights to land and minerals to those fighting for regulations over transnational corporations. Class interests were differentiated, even as their horizon of *opposition* was similar.

Many WSF participants wanted to formulate a concrete program to anchor the work being done, in preparation for inheriting the world once the neoliberal project had fully unraveled or been defeated. To articulate this horizon of opposition, various sections of the WSF tried to formulate a more comprehensive document than the overall WSF Charter of Demands. The Porto Alegre Consensus (2005) and the Bamako Appeal (2006) drew together the totality of the demands of the anti-globalization or alternative globalization (*outra globalizaçao*) movements, from debt relief to fair trade. The main commitments of the Bamako Appeal were:

- Construct an internationalism joining the peoples of the South and the North who suffer the ravages engendered by the dictatorship of financial markets and by the uncontrolled global deployment of the transnational firms.
- Construct the solidarity of the peoples of Asia, Africa, Europe, and the Americas confronted with challenges of development in the twenty-first century.
- Construct a political, economic and cultural consensus that is an alternative to militarized and neoliberal globalization and to the hegemony of the United States and its allies.

By 2011, at the Dakar Forum, these principles had been reframed as "axes":

Axis 1: Deepen our critical analysis of capitalism.
Axis 2: Strengthen the struggles and resistance against capitalism, imperialism and oppression.
Axis 3: Build democratic and popular alternatives.

---

33 Michael Hardt, "Today's Bandung?" *New Left Review* II/14 (March–April 2002), p. 113.

Neither the Consensus nor the Appeal went very far. Two major differences of opinion among the participants prevented any progress on making the WSF into a political actor. The first hesitation came over the question of political parties. It was of course the case that the very space for the WSF was provided by the institutionalized work of the political parties. Porto Alegre was chosen because it had become the hub of the PT.[34] Nevertheless, there was a great deal of anxiety over allowing the political parties to co-opt the energy of the social movements. Dispersion of political energy was not, therefore, an accidental byproduct of bad organization, but, for some, the precise gain of a new way of thinking. The gap between the organized forces (whether in political parties or in other hierarchically organized forms) and the networked forces (whether in small affinity group structures or in highly dispersed nodes) was formidable. It is remarkable that these two discordant forms of political organization have been able even to remain allied in the WSF process over this past decade. A general tendency of the network forces that abjure hierarchy is that they often fall into the trap of covert leadership, with the most charismatic or hardworking people allowed to shape the direction of the seemingly unstructured forum.[35] At the same time, the political parties are often guilty of being far too hierarchical, with few avenues for the vast mass of their membership to shape the program that is forged from the top. Rather than allowing for a genuine dialogue on the organizational forms privileged by one or the other pole, seeing that each had much to gain from the other, disagreement was set aside in favor of "unity."

The second disagreement was on the problem of ideological unity itself. Is it useful for the divergent groups to forge some kind of unity, whether programmatic or pragmatic? This divide maps almost perfectly onto the previous one, with those who favor political organization also in favor of programmatic ideological unity, and those who favor dispersed nodes more inclined to open-ended action. Walden Bello, who had helped author both the Consensus and Appeal, wrote a long note of dissatisfaction with the WSF. "The WSF as an institution is unanchored in actual global political struggles, and this is turning it into an annual festival with limited social impact."[36] Bello, who had run the Bangkok-based Focus on the Global South, worried that the WSF had not "fulfilled its historic function aggregating and linking the diverse counter-movements spawned by global capitalism." But others worried precisely

---

34   Sader, "Beyond Civil Society," p. 92.

35   This debate about de-centered networks takes place in a context in which the US government aggressively promotes "democracy," which can mean the creation of a "civil society" that enables the Atlantic powers and the transnational corporations to "control the governments of those countries." William Robinson, *Polyarchy*, Cambridge: Cambridge University Press, 1996, p. 69.

36   Gautney, *Protest and Organization*, p. 86.

about this form of aggregation. David Graeber pointed to the "networks based on principles of decentralized, non-hierarchical consensus democracy," and argued that these "new forms of organization *are* its ideology."[37] Graeber's illustrations of this claim relate more to how to organize a protest in a democratic manner than to how to bring democracy into everyday life. It is reasonable to assert that the networks and affinity groups are a productive way to engage the relations of domination at protests, but what is the strategy by which one hopes to negate those very relations? As University of São Paolo professor Emir Sader notes, this approach "distances itself from the themes of power, the state, the public sphere, political leadership and even, in a sense, from ideological struggle."[38]

Despite the frequent invocation of the idea of unity, there seems to have been little attempt to offer a theory of what this might resemble. Would unity mean subsuming the variety of political views and institutions into one international, or would it mean that the various groups and tendencies would work together in action around a common set of themes? Would unity be restricted to working-class groups (a united front), or would it include all classes and all social formations (a popular front)? Would it be more useful to allow for a diversity of views and approaches, or to try to forge a united platform around which groups had to operate together? These questions were raised in the margins of the WSF, but there was no institutional space to hash them out, though they are fundamental to any dialogue around the desire for unity. Instead, the idea of unity remained a talisman for those dismayed at the festival character of the WSF, and did not itself become part of a conversation among groups and individuals considering the question of strategy and the institutional forms necessary for social transformation.

No debate of this scale took place inside the WSF. Rather, the debate devolved into one of internal process: questions were raised, such as who gets to speak, why celebrity intellectuals got the big stage, and who made the decisions. Since the WSF organizing committee was an ad hoc body, questions were raised about its right to represent the world's movements, and its inability to create a representative format for those who came to the meetings. This debate over process would consume a great deal of time within the WSF.

---

37 Graeber, "New Anarchists," p. 70. For an ethnography sympathetic to this diversity, and which values the networks as "fluid processes, not rigid structures," see Jeffrey S. Juris, *Networking Futures: The Movements Against Corporate Globalization*, Durham: Duke University Press, 2008, p. 5. See also Naomi Klein, "Farewell to 'End of History': Organization and Vision in Anti-Corporate Movements," in Leo Panitch and Colin Leys, eds, *Socialist Register 2002: A World of Contradictions*, New Delhi: LeftWord Books, 2001.

38 Sader, "Beyond Civil Society," p. 92.

Emir Sader regarded the rejection of parties and governments as a serious matter because "it would severely limit the formulation of any alternatives to neoliberalism, confining such aspirations to a local or sectoral context—the NGOs' mantra, 'Think global, act local'; proposals for fair trade; 'ecologically sustainable development'—while giving up any attempt to build an alternative hegemony, or any global proposals to counter and defeat world capitalism's current neoliberal project."[39] Sader's harsh assessment was directed as much against anarchist-inspired groups as it was against the increasing presence of NGOs. It is not as if anarchist-inspired groups had no alternative project, but that their project was not against market and state; increasingly it was to abjure the market and state and create autonomous domains of self-regulated activity. This was a perfectly reasonable approach in localities of the North, but it was hard to imagine how this could be "scaled up" for the entirety of society—or how such a project might work in the South, where it remained unfamiliar.

The real problem was not the anarchist-inspired groups, whose own bravery at the counter-protests had provided the necessary basis for strengthening resistance within the North; it was the role of the "democracy industry" and the World Bank that has pushed for the growth of "civil society"—in fact, code for foundation-funded NGOs delivering services, or using micro-investment schemes to build capacity among the people. These micro-projects have their place. But like reforms in general, micro-projects produce what one might unkindly call charity in the countryside and in the slums. They often conform to the neoliberal demand that the state abdicate many of its social justice functions in favor of NGOs. Many NGOs end up acting as contractors in areas vacated by the state (healthcare and education, for example), as part of the neoliberal project of the international financiers. The problem with the micro-sector is that it claims to be locally based (close to the grassroots) and at a distance from state power. Disdain for state power and a concentration on the local severs the link between local struggles and national or regional movements. NGOs, in these cases, depoliticize their "target" populations by concentrating on the delivery of goods rather than on social transformation.[40] In the name of empowerment, many of these agencies preach the gospel of "enterprise" and "private initiative"—precisely the neoliberal ideas that reproduce the dereliction of the countryside and the proliferation of slums. Issues were thus taken up in a piecemeal fashion, rather than in a framework that would implicate the powerful—who routinely held the checkbooks for many of the organizations involved. Most alarmingly, some of the most powerful NGOs

---

39   Ibid., p. 92.

40   John Harriss, *Depoliticizing Development: The World Bank and Social Capital*, New Delhi: LeftWord Books, 2001.

are far from grassroots-based, relying for their survival upon large foundations. Their access to money allows them to siphon off the most talented people, who are then lost to the mass movements committed to social transformation. Local agendas are driven by the NGO, rather than by the genuine needs of the people.[41]

The 2011 WSF took place in Dakar, Senegal, at around the same time as the Arab Spring was attempting to create a rupture with neoliberalism and authoritarianism in the Middle East and North Africa. The energy from Cairo's Tahrir Square made its way to the University of Dakar campus. Once more, however, the debate broke out over whether the WSF was a "political *space*" or a "political *actor*." The mass movements at Dakar and the enthusiasm of Cairo could not ultimately be aggregated by the WSF process towards the production of a sharp final communiqué. After much deliberation, the WSF "adopted a document as its final declaration that seemed somewhat helpless, lost in commonplaces, and was strategically quite useless."[42] The significance of the WSF is not in either its process debates or in its communiqués or its strategic vision, but in its very existence. While the people of Caracas were sitting down in front of buses and beginning their march into the city center in 1989, the Socialist Utopia was unraveling across Eurasia. A straight line runs from the *Caracazo* uprising in 1989 to the counter-events against the meetings of the IMF, the World Bank, the WTO, and the G7, and from the EZLN's *encuentro* in 1996 to the WSF: all these events signaled that the global South might indeed have regained the initiative in the streets. The events of 9/11 and the War on Terror seemed to dampen the momentum, but it recovered in February 2003 as about 10 million people gathered in over sixty countries to try to put a stop to the rush for war against Iraq. Quite rightly, Patrick Tyler wrote in the *New York Times*, "There may still be in our planet two super-powers: the United States and world public opinion"—though this was not "world public opinion" alone, but the will that had emerged out of the twenty-first century's internationalism.[43]

The WSF is a utopian space, unable because of its shallow social roots to provide the basis for a robust internationalism. This is not to say that it has no value; quite the opposite. If we see the WSF as a process and not as an event or even a party, it becomes clear that it is incubating a future platform for

---

41   The literature on the NGOs is vast. I rely here upon Jude Fernando, *The Political Economy of NGOs*, London: Pluto Press, 2011; Elisabeth Armstrong, "Globalization from Below: AIDWA, Foreign Funding and Gendering Anti-Violence Campaigns," *Journal of Developing Societies* 20: 1 (June 2004); and Tessa Morris-Suzuki, "For and Against NGOs: The Politics of the Lived World," *New Left Review* II/2 (March–April 2000).

42   Ulrich Brand, "From Dakar to Egypt and Back Again: The 2011 World Social Forum and its Future," Center for the Study of Social and Global Justice, University of Nottingham, February 2011, p. 8.

43   Patrick Tyler, "A New Power in the Streets," *New York Times*, February 17, 2003.

internationalism.[44] The First International was grounded in mainly European trade unions, the Second International in mainly European social-democratic parties, and the Third International in nation-based communist parties (the Fourth International was in many ways an offshoot of the Third, since it was an international clearinghouse of left-wing parties that followed Trotsky's critique of the Soviet-led International. There was no difference in the social basis of its unity). Today there is no clear social force that could yet form the basis for the twenty-first century's international. No wonder that Ulrich Brand of ATTAC concluded his reflections on the limitations of the WSF with the comment that "the last few years have shown that points of leverage or indeed practical political breaks with neoliberal imperial or even capitalist logics occur rather at the local and national level (see for example the Latin American examples), or within specific fields of conflict" rather than at the international level.[45] The most effective zones for building that social basis remain national and regional. Examples of these national and regional breakthroughs can be found in Latin America, which we will go into below, and in the Arab Spring.

THE AGONIES OF INTERNATIONAL SOLIDARITY

At the 2006 WSF in Caracas, Hugo Chávez took the stage at the main plenary session to offer a modified version of the choice posed to humanity by Rosa Luxemburg: socialism or death. "Capitalism has destroyed the ecological equilibrium of the earth," he argued. "Time is short. If we do not change the world now, there may be no twenty-second century for humanity." This was a conclusion that was widely accepted at the WSF and among those who had only known capitalism's negatives. The problem was not the diagnosis, but the way out: How to proceed to socialism? Chávez had been to the WSF in 2005, and now reported that "many talks took place, without conclusion. We are not here to waste our time. We must urgently build a new socialist movement. We should go toward setting up a worldwide anti-imperialist movement."

An organized social force of this kind did not emerge out of the WSF dynamic. What happened instead was that the WSF fragmented into regional and continental units, such as the Asia Social Forums, the Senegal Social Forums, the US Social Forum, and the Durban Social Forum. Even the principal WSF gathering had become regional: the Mumbai event drew mostly participants from India, the Nairobi event from East Africa, and the Belém event largely from Latin America. The tendency to the regional and the national

---

44   Jacklyn Cock, "A Better or Worse World? The Third *World Social Forum*, Porto Alegre 2003," Centre for Civil Society, Research Report no. 5, University of Kwa-Zulu Natal, April 2003, p. 11.

45   Brand, "From Dakar to Egypt," p. 9.

remained very strong. The regional WSFs were the chosen venue for organizations and activists to join forces to build and strengthen localized movements. The "social forum" became a coordination space for organizations busy in parochial struggles to find linkages between their own campaigns and those of others, and thereby lift those struggles onto a wider political arena. But why have the regional forums been more successful than the worldwide WSF? And why has the creation of a new International failed to take off? Heather Gautney ends her useful survey of this blockage with her assessment that the WSF "has failed to address the controversial problem of agency."[46] But can the problem of agency—in other words, of who is the subject of this new dynamic and what it should look like—be addressed in our time? Is it perhaps utopian to attempt to create a planetary political platform that is considerably out of step with the concrete divisions that shatter the fragile dream of internationalism?

In our time, capital appears fully integrated. It does seem to operate, most of the time, in harmony between its various fractions.[47] Tensions among capitalists certainly exist, and these are sometimes manifested through their national governments. Scaremongering about Chinese or Gulf capital buying assets in the United States accompanies anger on the part of Boeing or Airbus if one of them wins a massive contract at the other's expense. These disputes persist, and at a much more grassroots level they may even devolve into active warfare (as in the Great Lakes region of Africa, home to what some call the ongoing Fourth World War).[48] But given the transnational reach of the very largest corporations, and the difficulty of identifying whose finance capital is lodged in which assets or banks, it is hard to map out decisively the social dimensions of inter-capitalist conflicts: it is not as if English firms are in competition with Chinese firms, since those very English firms may be manufacturing their products in China, just as the Chinese firms may be highly integrated into the City of London's financial markets. This relative integration of capital makes the World Economic Forum a realistic venture, although most of its participants are from the Atlantic world.

Even on the plane of capital, there are some voices that are uncertain about the scale of globalization. Pankaj Ghemawat's *World 3.0* points out that the champions of globalization (Thomas Friedman in *The World Is Flat*, for instance) promote a "chimera, dangerously exaggerating actual flows across

---

46   Gautney, *Protest and Organization*, p. 180.

47   The strongest position that resembles Karl Kautsky's ultra-imperialism thesis is taken by William I. Robinson, "Global Capitalism Theory and the Emergence of Transnational Elites," UNU Wider Working Paper no. 2010/02 (January 2010). It is also the view of Lionel Jospin, *Le Monde comme je le vois*, Paris: Gallimard, 2005.

48   Gérard Prunier, *Africa's World War: Congo, the Rwandan Genocide, and the Making of a Continental Catastrophe*, London: Oxford University Press, 2009.

borders."[49] The data show that 80 percent of global stock-market investment takes place in companies that are based in the nation-state of the investor, and that exports make up only a quarter of the world's economy. More dramatically, less than one-fifth of Internet activity takes place across national borders, and only 2 percent of students leave their home country for university. What we have, Ghemawat argues, is a form of *semi-globalization*, in which the nation-state or regional containers remain fundamentally important as zones of economic and political activity. The WEF's claims of unity are exaggerated—the facsimile of the self-image of the transnational corporations (whose own board members are often sourced from the country whose flag the corporation flies).

Such claims of unity are not possible in the world of labor, in the world of everyday life, in the harmed lives of people across the planet. Reflecting on thirty years of writing about women in the *maquiladoras* and on the mediocre attempts at international solidarity, Patricia Fernandez-Kelly notes how disconcerting it is that "at both ends of the geopolitical spectrum," in Mexico and in the United States, there "has been the absence of viable workers' movements aimed at curtailing some of the noxious effects of economic internationalization."[50] This absence cannot be simply dismissed as the result of a lack of effort; it must be explained despite the enormous efforts that have been made.

There are of course cultural barriers, since people who do not share a bourgeois cosmopolitan framework—the English language and MBAs, for example, in the case of the capitalist layer—do not have a broad cultural framework for communication. Exchange of information is impeded not only by language differences, but by the difficulty of bringing the views of, say, Oriya farmers fighting against a steel plant to coca farmers in Bolivia—Internet access is minimal, theoretical frameworks of distress and resistance are different, and the time spent bridging the gap is not available to people knee-deep in the politics of survival and struggle. Representatives of these struggles benefit from trips to other lands, since it widens the horizon of everyone; but such trips are not always possible, and do not always result in long-term connections.

The main problem with unity in the global South is not subjective, or simply a function of a failure to bring people together effectively.[51] The divides

---

49   Pankaj Ghemawat, *World 3.0: Global Prosperity and How to Achieve It*, Cambridge, MA: Harvard Business Press, 2011, p. 16.

50   Patricia Fernandez-Kelly, "The Global Assembly Line in the New Millennium: A Review Essay," *Signs* 32: 2 (2007), p. 510.

51   Åke Wedin's study of union solidarity points us towards an additional problem, which is the tendency to arrogance among some unions in the global North towards unions in the South. The union solidarity movement must work, he notes, to build on "common interests," and "one of those interests which they have in common, beyond the national frontiers, is to fortify the weak parts of the common world front of

at this time are resoundingly *objective*, and it is to such barriers that we need to attend more closely. The theorist who has provided the clearest assessment of these barriers is the Indian Marxist Prabhat Patnaik, and what I present below is an elaboration of his ideas.[52]

The force of transnational capital acts in a similar way against states—in each case, it adopts a neoliberal attitude, pushing for minimum state regulation of capital and its business enterprises, and uncomfortable with demand management (stimulus spending, for instance) unless it directly benefits capital itself.[53] States around the world, whether in the advanced industrial zone or not, are forced—on pain of expulsion from the "international community"—to act on behalf of capital and against the interests of the vast masses of the people. Some states are protected from the wiles of transnational capital: the United States, for instance, can rely upon the dollar's use as the global reserve currency to run deficits, although even in the US's debt problem is not without political ramifications.[54]

If we look beyond the impact of transnational capital on the apparatus of the state and see its impact on classes, an altogether different story appears. Given the problems of excess capacity, unemployment and the growth of a *disposable* class in the advanced industrial states, the central force for the fight-back has been composed of white-collar workers, potential white-collar students, and public service employees—this pattern has been consistent from the *indignados* to Occupy. Typically urban, these protests target the austerity regime and its social consequences.[55]

There is a marked tendency in these struggles to oscillate between demands for social democracy and demands for social fascism—from the protests calling for an expansion of the social wage (as in the mass demonstrations of southern Europe) to those calling for it to be slashed (the Tea Party and the growth of Euro-fascism). In the United States, the Tea Party movement seeks the restoration of an older racist bargain—one that the white working class and white-collar middle class have lost as a result of the social processes of

---

workers against employers." Åke Wedin, *La "Solidaridad" Sindical Internacional y Sus Victimas*, Stockholm: Instituto de Estudios Latinoamericanos de Estocolmo, 1991, p. 162.

52   I am most reliant here upon Prabhat Patnaik, "A Marxist Perspective on the World Economy," in his *Re-Envisioning Socialism*, Delhi: Tulika Books, 2011; and a longer version of the same paper, "Notes on Contemporary Imperialism," n. d., draft manuscript in author's possession.

53   Harvey, *Brief History of Neoliberalism*, pp. 70–1.

54   Gowan, *Global Gamble*.

55   Antonis Vradis and Dimitris Dalakoglou, eds, *Revolt and Crisis in Greece: Between a Present Yet to Pass and a Future Still to Come*, Oakland: AK Press, 2011; and Clare Solomon and Tania Palmieri, eds, *Springtime: The New Student Rebellions*, London: Verso, 2011.

globalization. To finance the US imperial adventures it supports, it is willing to put up with only a livable wage even if the bloodhounds of money capture the bulk of the social wealth for themselves. Such a dream is anachronistic. The Tea Party represents the patriotism of fools, but it is also accurate: their jobs *have* gone overseas to places such as China and India, although that is not the fault of Chinese and Indian workers.[56] Euro-fascism of this kind cannot see beyond the loss of its own aristocratic place in the world of labor, but it does see that. It has more solidarity with what it perceives as its national corporate class than with workers overseas who are exploited by that very class. The mass basis for internationalism does not rest in these quarters.

In Latin America, the economy is largely urban, and largely industrial and semi-industrial. It was the long period of dictatorship in the 1980s, and then of neoliberal social democracy in the 1990s, that sharpened the ideological basis of the white-collar middle class and rooted parts of it in the camp of anti-imperialism, at least in so far as it did not maintain its allegiance with the status quo. It was this transfer of allegiance to parties that favored the working class and the indigenous (chiefly in Venezuela and Bolivia, but also in Argentina, Chile, Paraguay, Uruguay, and Peru) that enabled the "pink tide" to sweep Latin America in the 2000s.[57] The campaigns against neoliberalism that produced the "pink tide" isolated the oligarchies, who then (as in Venezuela in 2002) sought refuge in the United States for help in coups or other such political machinations.

One of the distinctive aspects of Latin American politics has been the emergence of the indigenous movements, whose own questions are rooted in matters of social dignity and in the destruction of their livelihood by what Patnaik calls "accumulation through encroachment"—threats to land and to what lies beneath the land (mainly oil and natural gas) from transnational corporations and the sufficiently bribed neoliberal regimes of the 1990s. What the indigenous communities of Latin America face is precisely the kind of assault faced by tribal communities in India, which is not far from the offensive against landless farm-workers, smallholder farmers, petty producers in rural and urban areas, and the working class in much of both Africa and Asia. According to the UN's Population Division, there are now about 3.3 billion rural-dwellers, 3 billion of whom are in the "less developed regions" (0.8 billion in India, 0.8 billion in China, and 0.1 billion in Indonesia, followed by Pakistan, Bangladesh, Nigeria, Ethiopia, and Vietnam). Of all rural-dwellers, 71 percent live in

---

56 Paul Craig Roberts, *How the Economy Was Lost: The War of the Worlds*, Oakland: AK Press/Counterpunch, 2010, pp. 11–14.

57 For example, see Andrés Gaudin, "The Kirchner Factor"; and Raúl Zibechi, "The Uruguayan Left and the Construction of Hegemony"—both in Ballve and Prashad, eds., *Dispatches from Latin America*.

Asia.[58] Resistance against neoliberal policies in Africa and Asia will come largely from these social classes, and not from white-collar workers, who have so far continued to benefit from the transfer of jobs from the advanced industrial world. These white-collar workers have not tasted the bitter pill of neoliberal collapse like their counterparts in Latin America. It is the peasantry, in alliance with public-sector workers and the industrial working class in much of Africa and Asia, that now provides the most concerted resistance to the current dispensation. There are no precise equivalents or allies for the African and Asian peasantry in the advanced industrial states, where it is feelings of emotional solidarity that typically provide the linkage and not the tempered chain of experience.

Having laid out these empirical snapshots of the different leading classes in the struggles over the past decade, one can see the wisdom of Patnaik's contention that "a coordinated global resistance is not on the horizon."[59] Instead, he emphasizes the centrality of building resistance within the nation-state, and his analysis can easily be extended to regions (he writes mainly of India, but the analysis he provides is equally applicable to the Bolivarian experiments in Latin America).[60] For Patnaik, there are two reasons why the national or regional container is the forum for resistance and transformation. The first has to do with the peasant question, which is formatively about land and rights— both of which are framed around national laws. Transnational agribusiness and the food industry certainly command the center of attention in the fight for justice on farmland. The coordination of struggles against vast corporate ensembles is essential, but also difficult ("one cannot help feeling that those who insist on such international coordination are altogether oblivious of the peasant question"). Cargill might quit one field for another, and in its place will come the Charoen Pokphand Group. The economic elements of rural society remain untouched by the storm-clouds in the agribusiness sky. To get to the fundamental problem—the lack of power of the peasantry in our societies and the reliance of the peasantry on petty production—it is the peasantry that has to organize itself to transform the states that frame laws on land and agricultural policy.[61]

Distress in the countryside is hard to discount. For that reason, the international foundations and the World Bank promote micro-reforms through

58   Department of Economic and Social Affairs, Population Division, *World Urbanization Prospects: The 2005 Revision*, New York: United Nations, 2006, pp. 3, 18.

59   Patnaik, "Notes on Contemporary Imperialism."

60   The empirical evidence for Patnaik's theoretical claim is assembled in Sam Moyo and Paris Yeros, eds, *Reclaiming the Nation: The Return of the National Question in Africa, Asia and Latin America*, London: Pluto Press, 2011.

61   Prabhat Patnaik, "Socialism and the Peasantry," in his *Re-Envisioning Socialism*.

NGOs and various para-statal organizations. These micro-reforms target parts of the problem, whether it is a lack of access to irrigation or to small funds on the part of petty producers. Across Africa and Asia, these developments have drawn potentially militant peasants into government or NGO employment, working to provide relief in an otherwise parched political landscape.[62] If governments offer more systematic agricultural support, it is often directed at the dominant classes in the countryside. These "farmers" have encouraged an agrarian populism that has allowed them to procure the bulk of the state's resources and protect their own large holdings against the aspirations of the landless. In return, they have promised the politicians their electoral and political support, as long as the state does not open up questions of land reform.[63] Over the course of the past thirty years, this sort of agrarian populism has masqueraded as "land reform." The constitutional fight to distribute land among the population has now largely lapsed for want of political will among the ruling classes in the global South. What we have instead are sporadic attempts at land seizure, whether organized by the MST in Brazil or the war veterans in Zimbabwe—or, in a less organized way, in the regions that ring urban areas and in slumlands within them.[64]

As the Uruguay Round unfolded, and the rules of trade worked against farmers and peasants, farm organizations in the Americas gathered in April 1992 at the second congress of the Unión Nacional de Agricultores y Ganaderos (National Union of Farmers and Ranchers) in Managua, Nicaragua. They considered forming some kind of coordination body for rural workers, to "find the means to have our voice and our propositions heard by those who would usurp our right to cultivate the land and assure our families' dignity."[65] A year later, forty-six farm leaders, largely from the Americas and Europe, met in Mons, Belgium, to form La Vía Campesina (Road of the Peasant). The raison d'être of LVC was to bring the peasants' rejection of neoliberal agricultural policies to international deliberations (such as the GATT Round and in the various agricultural conferences held by the FAO). The main idea that developed out of the LVC was "food sovereignty," or "the right to produce food on our own territory."[66] At the World Food Summit in Rome, LVC challenged the FAO to recognize that food was first a basic need, and only then a commodity for

---

62   James Petras and Henry Veltmeyer, "Age of Reverse Aid: Neo-Liberalism as Catalyst of Regression," *Development and Change* 33: 2 (2002).

63   Tom Brass, *Peasants, Populism and Postmodernism: The Return of the Agrarian Myth*, London: Frank Cass, 2000.

64   There are many case studies in Moyo and Yeros, *Reclaiming the Land*.

65   Annette Aurélie Desmarais, "The Vía Campesina: Consolidating an International Peasant and Farm Movement," *Journal of Peasant Studies* 29: 2 (January 2002), p. 95.

66   Ibid., p. 100.

trade. The WTO's "right to export" came under fire for its blindness to the way in which the export of food grains often led to undernourishment and starvation among those who worked the land, and to hoarding among traders in search of better prices. In 1999 LVC joined with the Food and Information Action Network to create the Global Campaign for Agrarian Reform. The new Campaign sought to provide support to national struggles for land reform and land occupations.[67]

LVC provides a platform for regional and national peasant organizations to fight against their common enemy: neoliberal policies that include the evisceration of farm subsidies to the small and landless peasantry, the bolstering of transnational agribusiness firms, and the entry of more sophisticated and ecologically damaging Green Technologies (including genetically modified seeds). As the main scholar of LVC, Annette Aurélie Desmarais, argues, "the international work of farm organizations is possible only if and when the organizations are strong and consolidated at the local and national levels."[68] LVC is made up of hundreds of organizations that represent about 150 million people. Some of these are very small, while others are rather large (the Karnataka Rajya Raitha Sangha by itself counts about 10 million, while the Korea Women's Farmers Association has 8,000 members). Of those in LVC, Raj Patel writes, "It's a mixed bag of movements. Some of its members are landless, some own land and hire the landless; some are small producers, some are medium-sized. What counts as a small farm in Canada is an estate in India. Clearly not all farmers are equal, and neither are their social organizations."[69] This is precisely why LVC decided to forge its strength through first five and then eight regional units. "National organizations within the region are expected to work well together," Desmarais notes, "and regions will find resources to strengthen the work at the regional level."[70] The strongest regional unit is in Latin America, and indeed "the Vía Campesina's positions and actions reflect more of the Latin American experience and perspective."[71] This is a good development for Latin America, with powerful peasant organizations such as the Brazilian MST and the Coordinador de Organizaciones del Campo (a regional forum of farm-workers set up in Lima, Peru, in 1994 to represent Bolivian coca growers

67   Ibid., p. 108. David Featherstone, "Spatialities of Transnational Resistance to Globalization: The Maps of Grievance of the Inter-Continental Caravan"; and Paul Routledge, "Convergence Space: Process Geographies of Grassroots Globalization Networks"—both in *Transactions of the Institute of British Geographers*, new series 28 (2003).

68   Desmarais, "Vía Campesina," p. 109.

69   Patel, *Stuffed and Starved*, p. 16.

70   Annette Aurélie Desmarais, "The Power of Peasants: Reflections on the Meanings of La Vía Campesina," *Journal of Rural Studies* 24 (2008), p. 142.

71   Ibid., p. 143.

and land-reform advocates in Guatemala). LVC was first based in Belgium, and then moved for eight years to Tegucigalpa, Honduras, before it shifted to Jakarta, Indonesia.

The experience of LVC reaffirms Patnaik's broad point, which is that the politics of the peasantry must first be rooted in national and regional containers. As Desmarais notes, "The base, articulated through the national and the regional, is the heart and driving force of the Vía Campesina: local issues and local activism drive the Vía Campesina's global interventions."[72]

The second reason why Patnaik favors the national or regional container is that the immediate struggles of the people cluster around the improvement of their living and working conditions. "The workers who struggle for such an improvement cannot possibly be asked to wait until a new World State has come into being that is favorably disposed to the interests of workers and peasants," he argues.[73] These tangible demands must be framed in terms of the agencies that manage the public treasury (the state) and regulate the expropriation of the economic surplus (the state). Of course, control over policy in these agencies is not entirely within the sovereignty of nation-states. International finance, international organizations (WTO, IMF, World Bank), and transnational corporations frame the limits of state intervention on behalf of the vast mass.

Simply putting pressure on national governments to change their budgetary policies is not going to be sufficient, since these governments are either wittingly or unwittingly under the influence of larger forces. It is to combat those larger forces that a few international platforms did arise, such as the Comité pour l'annulation de la dette du Tiers Monde in Belgium, in 1990, and then, in 1994, the 50 Years Is Enough network. CADTM includes such groups as the Union Nationale des Syndicats Autonomes du Sénégal and the Ivory Coast's Forum National sur la Dette et la Paureaté. The 50 Years Is Enough network comprises groups such as the Development Group for Alternative Policies, Friends of the Earth, Global Exchange, Greenpeace, International Rivers Network, and Oxfam America. These groups are based mainly in the Atlantic world, although they have connections with activists and organizations in the South. These organizations produced a great deal of useful material on the deleterious impact of the World Bank and the IMF, and on the structural nature of the massive debt. Given the enormous power of the IMF and the World Bank and their authority over governments, and given also the lack of mass campaigns to bolster the work of these transnational groups, it is no wonder that their agenda stalled. Moral suasion went only so far, and in times of acute crisis (such as during the earthquake in Haiti) a rush to cancel debts

---

72   Ibid., p. 109.
73   Patnaik, "Notes on Contemporary Imperialism."

and appear humanitarian on the part of the Atlantic powers annulled the force of their critics.

The other set of transnational agencies that have made an important impact in the realm of livelihood delivery are the international NGOs, some of which have led campaigns against the international finance organizations in alliance with the UN agencies. Groups like ActionAid, Oxfam, and Action Against Hunger double as relief organizations and as lobbyists inside the UN system, where they have often stiffened the spines of unsteady national governments of the South. It was because of their presence and the frustration among the member-states of the South that the FAO seeded the Alliance Against Hunger and Malnutrition in 2001. But even here, the Alliance relied upon national initiatives and regional partnerships, most of which emerged from states that had been forced to be accountable on issues of hunger by popular movements and political parties inside their borders. In Brazil, a combination of social Catholic agitation against hunger, the creation of Citizenship Action Against Hunger and Misery and for Life, and the victory of the PT in 2002 pushed the government to create the Brazil Fome Zero (Zero Hunger) set of policies, which included the creation of a proper social wage (*bolsa familia*). In India, one of the crucial elements of the Common Minimum Programme of the United Progressive Alliance government was designed to tackle the problems of rural unemployment and hunger. The core part of the alliance was formed by the neoliberal-oriented Congress Party and the Communists; and it was the latter, in association with a vibrant array of social movements committed to these issues, that pushed hard for the passage of the National Rural Employment Guarantee Act (2005). These national policies are now reflected in regional blocs, such as the Hunger-Free Latin America and Caribbean Initiative (founded in 2005 by Brazil and Guatemala) and the Alliance Against Hunger in Western Africa (held together by Benin, Burkina Faso, and Mali). The liberal limit of social justice on the international stage is encapsulated by the UN Declaration of Human Rights (1948), and then narrowly reaffirmed in the Millennium Development Goals (2000). It was only when the class basis of the nation-state or the region was challenged by the struggles of the peasantry and the working class, with their various allies in the middle class, that such policies could be implemented. Pressure from organized and powerful mass movements helped to move the state away from the realm of repression to the realm of social democracy. The main vector for the delivery of social goods was the state, even as it was transnational pressure on international financial bodies and UN agencies that forced the financial bodies to lift their feet off the neck of the people, and the latter to provide technical support for designing mechanisms to widen the social wage.

Patnaik does not directly refer to a third problem for internationalism in this period: the vastly different subsistence levels that divide the Atlantic world

from the farmlands and slumlands of Africa and Asia. The costs of social repro-
duction are higher in Europe and North America, with workers in the latter
forced to earn substantially more since most social services are offered only for a
fee—healthcare being the most costly item. It would be impossible in the North
for workers to offer their labor for rates at all comparable to those offered by
workers in Africa and Asia, as well as large parts of Latin America. These disparities create an enormous gulf between the workers of the world. It is imperative
in the North that the massive surpluses (amounting to trillions of dollars)
stashed away by the well-heeled are mobilized towards the creation of a robust
social wage (healthcare, public transportation); this would enable people to earn
lower wages, which would no longer be sequestered to provide the essentials
of life (such as insurance premiums for healthcare and for automobiles). These
battles demanding austerity for the propertied and a social wage for the people
can only take place within the containers of Europe and North America. At the
same time, in Africa and Asia, workers will fight to benefit from the increase in
their productivity—gains so far swept up by transnational firms; and peasants
will build their resistance to neoliberal farming and increase their subsistence
needs. If successful, such struggles will provide a commonality of interest on the
objective basis of which deeper struggles for the planet can be waged.

If global resistance is not on the horizon, that does not mean that struggles must turn inwards. Precisely the opposite is necessary, which is to say that
national and regional struggles must be alert to the ideological importance of
internationalism, while also forging genuine institutional platforms that might
support it. If we are not alert to the objective limitations of internationalism in
the present, the failure of internationalist politics in this inhospitable present
will tarnish internationalism's importance in the future when the social conditions for it reappear. The difficulty of building proper international institutions
from below has everything to do with the absence of the social conditions for
internationalism. These must be crafted, and as our movements do so through
the building of regional and national power, they must incubate an internationalism that is not utopian, but real.

The assessments of the WSF, LVC, and the Alliance Against Hunger and
Malnutrition each turn their gaze longingly on Latin America, where one sees
the main breach with neoliberalism in the defeat of the Free Trade Area of the
Americas (FTAA) and the emergence of the Bolivarian dynamic in the ALBA
(Alianza Bolivariana para los Pueblos de Nuestra América), in Brazil's anti-
hunger policies, and in Venezuela's agrarian revitalization programs.

POR AHORA—FOR NOW

On February 27, 1989, the people of Caracas threw off the mask of consent.
When the *Caracazo* unfolded, a young radical was at home: Lieutenant Hugo

Chávez. Chávez, who was then head of the presidential guard at the Miraflores Palace, had contracted an illness and had been dismissed by the palace's doctor. From his bed, he heard reports about the uprising. For a decade, Chávez had been involved in a military officers' conspiracy called the Liberation Army of the Venezuelan People—a platform, he later told Gabriel García Márquez "to prepare ourselves in case something should happen."[74] On the day of the rebellion he was absent from his post, and his comrades found themselves more in the role of spectators than actors. Neither the civilian left groups nor the radical officers properly anticipated the social explosion. For the troops it was a moment of crisis, because they had been asked to shoot at their fellow citizens (the official death toll was 372, but that is probably an underestimate by a factor of ten). When Chávez returned to his post a few days after the smoke had cleared, one of his soldiers said to him, "Look here, major, is it true about the Bolivarian Movement? We'd like to hear more about it; we're not prepared to go on killing people."[75]

During the *Caracazo*, the feeble regime of Pérez, the South Commission member, signed a new agreement with the IMF—a package (*paquetazo*) characterized by severe neoliberal orthodoxy. It spelled more austerity for the people and more liberalization for business; pain for the many, gain for the few. By the end of the year, almost half of Venezuelan society had slipped below the official poverty line. The conditions for unrest not only remained—they festered.

Chávez and his officers did what they knew, which was take the path of conspiracy. An attempted coup d'état in 1992 failed. Chávez, unlike the entire political class of Venezuela, apologized on television for the error of his actions. "I alone shoulder the responsibility," he said—but only after the tantalizing statement, "unfortunately, for the moment, the objectives we had set ourselves have not been achieved in the capital." The phrase, "for the moment"—*por ahora*—struck a chord. It meant that, later, the movement might succeed. This phrase was the slogan of the Bolivarian movement through the 1990s, which led to the creation of the Fifth Republic Movement (MVR). As the election of 1998 approached, sections of the left and those who opposed what Chávez called "the pole of national destruction" joined forces with the MVR. This *Polo Patriótico* secured 56 percent of the vote. It was "the revenge of the dispossessed."[76] Chávez and his party took control of the government.

Within a decade, almost all of South America's countries elected governments of the left: Brazil (2002), Argentina (2003), Uruguay (2004), Bolivia

74   Richard Gott, *Hugo Chávez and the Bolivarian Revolution*, London: Verso, 2005, pp. 36–7.
75   Ibid., p. 47.
76   Tariq Ali, *Pirates of the Caribbean: Axis of Hope*, London: Verso, 2006, p. 26.

(2006), Chile (2006), Ecuador (2006), Paraguay (2008), and Peru (2011). Only the Guyanas and Colombia remained outside the trend. On the heels of the elections in Bolivia, Chile, and Ecuador, the Mexican intellectual and politician Jorge Casteñada conjured up a categorical divide between the "two lefts." The first left (Argentina, Brazil, Chile) was "modern, open-minded, reformist and internationalist, and it springs, paradoxically, from the hard-core left of the past." The second left (Venezuela, Bolivia, Ecuador) was "born of the great tradition of Latin American populism, is nationalist, strident, and close-minded." Such a division is attractive to those of a neoliberal persuasion because it allows them to peel away the former from the latter, demonize the "populists," and claim that there is no difference between the neoliberal agenda and that of the "modern" left.[77]

Such divides are not only unreasonable, but also singularly unhelpful. Every country gets the left political force that it deserves. Each social formation has a different class composition, a different relation of ethnic minorities to a majority population; each has a separate colonial history with differential capitalist development, and has its own distinctive progressive political traditions. A broth of anarchism, anarcho-syndicalism, Marxism, communism, agrarian populism, and social Catholicism, alongside the memory of messianic great leaders (from Bolívar to Perón) and indigenous communitarianism, has created a slew of ideas, traditions, and resources for the political struggles across the region. In 1959 Silvio Frondizi, who founded Argentina's Revolutionary Left Movement, put the notion of the "left" plainly: "Although the 'left' does not have much scientific value, its use has conferred on it the meaning of a critical revolutionary position vis-à-vis the current capitalist society, aiming at its transformation into a future socialist society." Frondizi's impatience with reform belied his own all-embracing understanding of the left tradition, whose parties had to tread a fine line between the alleviation of immediate grievances and the creation of a collective will decisive enough to risk total social transformation. In one place, revolutionary time moves faster than in another—but that does not mean that the leadership should be exculpated for its own failures.

Emir Sader takes the Castañeda line to task for failing to produce a proper distinction, not between the good and the bad left, but between "those countries that have signed free trade treaties with the United States, and those that prioritize processes of regional integration."[78] Steve Ellner elaborates on this fundamental distinction, identifying tempos of unity among the Latin American left regimes and the social movements that enfold them. Looking at Venezuela, Bolivia, and Ecuador, Ellner finds that they all sought to rewrite

---

77 Jorge Castañeda, "Latin America's Left Turn," *Foreign Affairs*, May/June 2006.

78 Emir Sader, *The New Mole: Paths of the Latin American Left*, London: Verso, 2011, p. 141.

their constitutions, all used the democratic majorities they had secured to push for far-reaching changes, and all emphasized "social participation and incorporation over considerations of economic productivity."[79]

The UN Economic Commission on Latin America and the Caribbean (CEPAL, in its Spanish initials) has shown that per capita income fell both in the 1980s (the "lost decade") and in the 1990s (the so-called "decade of recovery"). Reasonable studies indicate that between 1982 and 1993, the number of those living in poverty increased from 78 million to 150 million. CEPAL's document on this was aptly titled *La brecha de la equidad* ("The Equity Gap"). The objective collapse of social indicators in Latin America, and the creation of new economic spaces (the automobile industry in Brazil, computer assembly in Mexico), as well as a renewed assault on the raw material resources of the area, has produced re-engaged social movements. These include indigenous movements, workers' movements, socialist movements, women's movements—some organized on conventional party lines, others as autonomous spaces; some along hierarchies of traditionalism, others in sharp contradistinction to these inherited norms. What unites the dynamic of the "pink tide" in Latin America is the two decades of severe cataclysm for the continent, from the 1980s dictatorships to the neoliberal orthodoxy of the 1990s. It was during this period that the various left-wing political organizations and trade unions forged working relations with emergent social movements. They fought together to send the military back to the barracks, and they fought against the economic policies followed by the civilian heirs to the military regimes that then marked the social life of Latin America. It was this close alliance between the electorally oriented and state-oriented political parties and the issue-oriented and social-oriented movements that produced the PT in Brazil and the MAS in Bolivia (a similar process in the 1980s and 1990s forged the Tripartite Alliance in South Africa, which included the African National Congress, the South African Communist Party, and the Coalition of South African Trade Unions). This history of working closely together in the struggle, united in actions against both the dictatorships and the neoliberal social democrats, forged emotional and political ties between the two main strands of political activity.

When the political tide seemed to turn, this "alliance" moved to the electoral sphere, with the social movements willing to gamble (*aposta*, as they said in Brazil) on the link to yield dividends. The gamble paid off as the pink tide approached. The Washington Consensus had helped to equalize suffering for the lower ranks of Latin American society: 50 percent of the region's people lived in poverty by 2000, with a quarter in what is known as "extreme poverty." The situation was such that less than a third of the region's people believed that

---

79   Steve Ellner, "Distinguishing Features of Latin America's New Left: The Chávez, Morales and Correa Governments," *Marxist* XXVII: 4 (October–December 2011), p. 15.

privatization was good. The rest knew that its impact had been diabolical. The new regimes had to work in the context where the old social classes of property and power had not been fully vanquished. The negation of these struggles would have provoked not only a backlash from the masses, but a great sense of despair that the very agents that they had elected with such fanfare had let them down. At the same time, the new regimes had to work very prudently. They came to power by the ballot—in many cases holding together a broad and shallow coalition. This meant that very radical reforms could not be easily accomplished within the space afforded. The moves of the new governments were cautious: the reduction of public foreign debt (Argentina) and restrained disputes with big corporations to review their contracts for resource extraction and industrial production (for all its rhetoric, Bolivia's nationalization of gas fits this description).[80] Neither have the regimes acted to increase the minimum wage—instead they have worked hard to increase productivity by asking for more from workers, including greater use of technology. There have been some modest attempts to contain inflation: the Argentine government capped the prices of products like beef and set limits on utility rates. Funds from increased commodity prices went towards the creation of new housing schemes for the poor (in Bolivia) and anti-hunger programs (in Brazil). These regimes pushed their policies to the limits of the social-democratic consensus, and often no further. Hints of a new economic development agenda were stifled by the grotesque barriers placed on the regimes—the lingering power of the United States in the region; the overwhelming institutional power of the old social classes; the reluctance of the military to relieve itself of state power and its link to property; and, of course, the insecurity of the new social democrats, who were uncomfortable with a direct assault on international finance.[81]

Venezuela was an outlier. As oil prices remained high, the revenues from this sector enabled the Bolivarian Revolution to finance its social justice agenda. Given its reliance upon oil prices, the Venezuelan government has tried to move rapidly on its agenda of social transformation. "While it is perfectly true that during the first period in office, the Bolivarians remained prisoners of macroeconomic policies and were unable to bring immediate benefits to those who needed them the most," Tariq Ali observes, "the partial solutions that began to be implemented after 2002 were extremely important. They improved the lives of millions of poor people by providing them with education and better healthcare. These achievements cannot be measured simply in cash terms and those who dismiss or ridicule them have, in most cases, little awareness of the

---

80   On Bolivia's nationalization, see James Rochlin, "Latin America's Left Turn and the New Strategic Landscape: The Case of Bolivia," *Third World Quarterly* 28: 7 (2007).

81   Juan Carlos Moreno-Brid and Igor Paunovic, "What is New and What is Left of the Economic Policies of the New Left Governments of Latin America?" *International Journal of Political Economy* 37: 3 (September 2008).

social crisis that had gripped Venezuela or the reasons for the popularity of the process."[82] The ability of the state to move in the direction of the demands of the people was enhanced by oil revenues, but blocked by constitutional limits and the power of the old social elites (who attempted a coup d'état in 2002, with US backing). Both legal and the political barriers needed to be circumvented.

Chávez went several times to the ballot, using the electoral support he earned over the decade after 1998 to revise the Constitution along more popular lines (similar moves were made by Morales in Bolivia). It is senseless to live within the constitutional boundaries set by oligarchies or military dictatorships, neither of which had any regard for popular participation or social well-being. State power was the goal, but it had been clear to the Bolivarian movement that state power did not mean only control of the state apparatus; if it meant only this, then the Bolivarians would have to do the dirty work of the oligarchy's 1961 Constitution. To write the new Bolivarian Constitution (1999), the Venezuelan population voted in a Constituent Assembly, which drafted a Constitution that was then ratified in a popular vote. This had never happened before in the country's history. The Constitution draws from a variety of resources, including Latin America's revolutionary history (featuring the liberator Simón Bolívar and the Marxist José Carlos Mariátegui) and Marxist theory (notably the remarkable Soviet jurist Evgeny Pashukanis). It is an astounding document, with provisions for deeper democracy at one level, and another for the widest recognition of human rights. The Chávez government had already formed the Barrio Adentro program to provide government-sponsored healthcare for the population. But without the new Constitution this policy would simply have been at the mercy of the government. Now, the Constitution directed the government to provide healthcare, as it was now legally binding. All of this was funded, propitiously, by the oil revenues that flooded into Venezuela's state coffers.

One of the clearest illustrations of the power of constitutional change was the creation of Venezuela's Housewives' Union. Drawing on proposals from the Centro de Estudios de la Mujer (at the Universidad Central de Venezuela), the 1999 Constitution adopted Article 88, which recognized work in the home as having economic value and provided housewives with social security benefits.[83] A group of women took this article and formed the Union in 2003, building its membership to more than 100,000, using it as a space to educate women about their rights in the new Constitution, and offering them an avenue to exercise power in their society. "Many of our women are inside their homes all the time," Lizarde Prada, the general coordinator of the Union, told journalist

---

82   Ali, *Pirates of the Caribbean*, p. 59.
83   Interview with Alba Carosio in Carlos Martinez, Michael Fox, and JoJo Farrell, *Venezuela Speaks! Voices from the Grassroots*, Oakland: PM Press, 2010, p. 71.

Ben Dangl. "In the house they work as cooks, decorators, teachers, babysitters, and doctors—all of this in one person. Our union helps to empower the housewives. Many of them were stuck in their homes, they didn't have time to read or write, they were always cooking and cleaning, they weren't informed. Many of our women are opening their eyes now."[84] Alongside the Union emerged the Madres del Barrio Misión, a program to combat poverty from a gender perspective inside the slums. As Alba Carosio of the Centro de Estudios de la Mujer puts it, the Misión supports women in the slums "for a certain period of time so that they have a minimum income—a minimum income that allows them the opportunity to go about the process of acquiring a career while resolving the issue of how to feed their children." It needed a gendered approach because "we discovered that within poverty the most poor are women."[85] The Constitution also allowed for a much more directed approach to tackle the problems faced by women, particularly sexual and family violence (tackled in the 2006 Law on the Right of Women to a Life Free of Violence). The Bolivarian reforms have been conservative on issues of reproductive and sexual rights, held back mainly by strong opposition from the Catholic hierarchy and by patriarchal ideas of control over female bodies that are of course not absent from the Bolivarian parliamentarians.[86] "This culture must be challenged permanently," said Alba Carosio, "because centuries of patriarchy cannot be overcome within ten years. We have an open door with great possibilities. There exists a greater symbiosis than ever between feminist ideas and socialist ideas, but we still have a long road ahead of us."[87]

The "open door" Alba Carosio speaks of comes with the constitutional leeway. Having these new values enshrined in the Constitution lifts an enormous burden from the social movements, who now have to fight for implementation rather than for recognition of these values as important. A capacious agenda has emerged as a result of the new Constitution.[88] The regime established various programs designed to do more than provide services. Certainly Barrio Adentro provided healthcare, and the Banco de la Mujer provided credit

84   Benjamin Dangl, *Dancing with Dynamite: Social Movements and States in Latin America*, Oakland: AK Press, 2010, pp. 102–3.

85   Carosio interview in Martinez, et al., *Venezuela Speaks!*, p. 73.

86   Inés N. Rojas Avendaño, "Women and the Democratic State: Agents of Gender Policy Reform in the Context of Regime Transition in Venezuela, 1970–2007," PhD, Georgia State University, 2009, Chapter 4.

87   Carosio interview in Martinez, et al., *Venezuela Speaks!*, p. 77.

88   For details see Steve Ellner, "The Revolutionary and Non-Revolutionary Paths of Radical Populism: Directions of the Chavista Movement in Venezuela," *Science and Society* 69: 2 (April 2005); George Ciccariello-Maher, *We Created Him: A People's History of the Bolivarian Revolution*, Durham: Duke University Press, 2012; and Gott, *Hugo Chávez*, pp. 256–9.

for women, but most of the programs enabled ordinary people to command resources and take charge of their communities. The soup kitchens (*casas alimentarias*), for instance, enable women not only to be fed, but to run their own social service organizations. Literacy is necessary for these programs, so the regime has offered a vast array of popular programs for study, such as *Misión Ribas*, *Misión Robinson*, and *Misión Sucre*. In much of this sphere, women are in the vanguard, and with their increasing participation "in the framework of cohesive community networks, there is much more opportunity to build democratic and sustainable projects."[89]

Alba Carosio quite rightly underscores the permanent revolution in the domain of culture. Cultural change is the hardest kind: it is far easier to change governments and rewrite constitutions, or even to nationalize entire sectors of economic life. Changing habits and rituals—the capillaries of everyday life—is far more difficult, and made harder by the inherent conservatism of ordinary people in a fast-moving society where changes often produce more harm than good. One of the hallmarks of the Bolivarian process, despite the centrality of Chávez, is that it has brought about the creation of a new generation of leaders from the working class, the peasantry, and the slumlands. All speak for themselves, in their own tempo, and in the full realization that they must live with the day-to-day consequences of their demands. It is because cultural change from below is so slow-moving that there is a temptation towards impatience; many might want to be critical of the modesty of the demands by this or that emergent voice. But change does not happen by being right all the time; it comes from the creation of a new set of voices who are able to tackle social brutality and to articulate a path out of it.

In terms of this permanent revolution in culture, one of the most important dimensions in the Bolivarian project is in agriculture. If you go to a grocery store in Venezuela—not only in the well-appointed Caracas districts, but also in small towns and in the barrios—you will be surprised to see that most of the goods (70 percent of foodstuffs) are imported, largely from the United States.[90] The main staple for most people is wheat, often as pasta—in a country that grows almost no wheat. Venezuelans are second only to the Italians in consumption of pasta (thirty pounds per person annually). This consumption habit was financed by the oil economy, but it is not a sustainable way to live. After the discovery of oil, Venezuela's agricultural sector was eviscerated as food imports overwhelmed the peasantry and new habits—including the European-style consumption of pasta—broke down more traditional forms of

---

89 Sujatha Fernandes, "Barrio Women and Popular Politics in Chávez's Venezuela," *Latin American Politics and Society* 49: 3 (Fall 2007), p. 122.

90 For a good introduction to the attempt at endogenous agriculture, see Gott, *Hugo Chávez*, pp. 157–65.

sustenance. By 1960, 35 percent of the population lived in rural areas; but by 1998 that proportion had dropped to 12 percent. The bulk of the population gathered into overcrowded slums that ringed the cities—the areas from where the *Caracazo* began.[91] The land in the rural areas was concentrated in a few hands (5 percent of landowners held 75 percent of the land), and the prevalence of agricultural labor gave way to the lure of waged work in the oil industry and in its ancillary service sector.[92]

One of the least remarked aspects of the Bolivarian Revolution has been the attempt to produce real sovereignty for people, not only by enabling them to live where they wish (which is often in rural areas), but also by ending their dependence both on oil and on hostile governments (such as the United States). People have abandoned rural areas for three reasons: healthcare, education, and employment. The Bolivarian regime has sought to respond to the demand for healthcare and education through its various *Misiónes*. The third challenge—creating jobs in the countryside—is much harder. Agriculture is devastated, and the cultural practices that used to underpin it no longer survive. This is the reason for the mass migrations of the past half-century from the South to the North. "There are no great social movements," writes the Mexico-based scholar Guillermo Almeyra bitterly, "except that expressed through emigration."[93] To revive agriculture, the Bolivarian regime has taken its intellectual cue from the Vía Campesina's concept of "food sovereignty," and promoted a set of new laws and policies to facilitate this. The new Constitution deemed *latifundios* anti-social, and allowed idle land to be seized and farmed. Since 1998, 180,000 families have moved onto one-third of the *latifundios*. To enable them to break ground, the state has increased its credit scheme (from $164 million in 1999 to $7.6 billion in 2008), provided a debt-eradication program ("Plan Zero Debt"), and offered technical support through agronomists and cooperative planners (under a scheme named "Campo Adentro," or Into the Countryside).[94] The Bolivarian regime is not only faced with the task of building the capacity of the peasantry; it is also going to have to effect cultural change in eating habits, going back to grains that can be grown in the Amazon region, and see whether it can create a new appetite for them: rice, corn, cassava, and *quinchonocho*. To this end, the regime has created a network of feeding houses (*casas de aliment-ación*) to provide home-cooked meals to the most needy, using local products.

---

91   Gregory Wilpert, "Land for People Not for Profit in Venezuela," in Peter Rosset, Raj Patel, and Michael Courville, eds, *Promised Land: Competing Visions of Agrarian Reform*, New York: Food First Books, 2006, p. 250.

92   Ibid., p. 252.

93   Guillermo Almeyra, "Mexico is Becoming Latinamericanized," in François Polet, ed., *The State of Resistance*, London: Zed Books, 2007, p. 53.

94   Christina Schiavoni and William Camacaro, "The Venezuelan Effort to Build a New Food and Agriculture System," *Monthly Review*, July 1, 2009.

On a small-scale basis, the state has also opened low-cost restaurants known as the Arepera Socialista, which will experiment with new diets and new forms of communal eating.[95] The regime also provides free food to 4 million children through the School Feeding Program, and requires that workplaces with more than twenty people provide food or the opportunity to eat through the 2004 Law for Workers' Nutrition. These measures could all provide avenues for the cultivation of new diets, and of course for Venezuela to eradicate hunger and hopelessness (malnutrition-related deaths halved between 1998 and 2006).[96]

Venezuela's drive for food sovereignty is being emulated by Bolivia, which has passed a Law of Productive, Communal and Agricultural Revolution. The Bolivians make use of the idea of *Suma Qamaña* ("living well"), or of living well with Pachamama ("Mother Earth"). Ciro Kopp, an engineer at the National Council for Food and Nutrition, put the case for the new law along the lines of the Venezuelan example:

> About 20 to 25 years ago, 70 to 80 percent of what we ate was produced locally in Bolivia, but then we embraced the agro-industrial model and now 70 to 80 percent of what we eat comes from the agro-industry, which makes us dependent on technologies and price controls from abroad. So, in the same way that industrialists received support from the government in the past, now it's small farmers who need help ... Bolivia is a center of origin of several Andean crops such as potatoes, quinoa, chili and corn. It is essential to strengthen the systems of production, natural selection and exchange of seeds that farmers have been doing for centuries. Our focus should be first of all to feed the country. If our priority is to export, what are people going to eat?[97]

These discussions about the revitalization of local agriculture are not restricted to Venezuela, or to Latin America. They can be found across the South, and indeed increasingly in the North (notably in the campaigns to eat locally grown food in the cities of the North). These are not romantic gestures, but attempts to found new relationships to nature and to work, to break out of the thrall of

---

95 "Besides the price, [Minister of Commerce Eduardo Saman] highlighted another key difference between socialist and capitalist 'arepera': customers pay only after eating, while 'in fast food chains ... they only think about money.' In the Arepera Socialista, the cash register is in a corner of the room and customers pay only after eating, self-reporting how many of the arepas they ate." "Making Socialism Easier to Swallow," January 19, 2010, 10CARACAS43, Wikileaks Archive.

96 Mark Weisbrot, Rebecca Ray, and Luis Sandoval, *The Chávez Administration at 10 Years: The Economy and Social Indicators*, Washington, DC: Center for Economic and Policy Research, 2009; and Schiavano and Camacaro, "Venezuelan Effort."

97 Mattia Cabitza, "Will Bolivia Make a Breakthrough on Food Security and the Environment?" *Guardian*, June 20, 2011.

agribusinesses, which thrives on processed food and on its control over the transnational commodity chain. There are elements in these movements that make a fetish of the *local*, which has a tendency to produce parochialism. Trade across regions, even in foodstuffs, is essential for our cultural diversity and the enrichment of our diets. What is central here is not the local as such, but the capacity of people to control their environment and not to be subordinated by the immense power of transnational firms over the production and distribution of food.

From Venezuela to Argentina, the great diversity of the pink tide is apparent, as are the vast differences in the temperament of its leadership. Nevertheless, because of the relative fragmentation of the bloc of the left, the tendency in the electoral arena has been towards the centralization of power around the personality of the leaders (Chávez, Morales, Lula).[98] Some of the energy of social movements has been absorbed into the regimes of the tide (that of the *piquetero* leadership into the government of the Kirchners, for example). The leftist leader is not, however, without mechanisms of accountability. The rich terrain of social struggle remains intact, and it is occasionally able to wield authority when it needs to (what Benjamin Dangl calls the "dance with dynamite").[99] The problem is that the social movements are not always able to determine policy—although in Venezuela there is a strong sentiment among those in the barrios that they should continue to have a role in the creation and implementation of policy.[100] This is conceived as a process in which they dance with the Chavista structures, trying to influence and gain from them in the process. The Bolivarian state has tried to draw in these movements, and to create institutions to empower them more effectively—the Círculos Bolivarianos, the Unidades de Batalla Electoral, and the Unidades de Batalla Social; but these are often used instrumentally by the state, rather than allowed the kind of autonomy necessary to allow creative expression from below. But what is important is to recognize that there is no unitary process at work; things are fluid and contested, as they should be.

Though they deploy a variety of socialist policies, these are not socialist regimes in the full sense. Aijaz Ahmad notes that the Bolivarian dynamic in Latin America is more "capitalism with a human face" than "socialism of the

---

98   The debate around the personality of Morales is, then, a bit misplaced. The problem is not personality, but the limitations of the pink tide itself. Pablo Stefanoni and Hervé do Alto, *Evo Morales, de la coca al Palacio: Una oportunidad para la izquierda indigena*, La Paz: Editorial Malestra, 2006.

99   Benjamin Dangl, *Dancing with Dynamite: Social Movements and States in Latin America*, Oakland: AK Press, 2010.

100   Martinez, Fox, Farrell, *¡Venezuela Speaks!*, p. 8; Jonah Gindin, "Chavistas in the Halls of Power, Chavistas in the Streets," in Ballve and Prashad, eds., *Dispatches from Latin America*, p. 87.

twenty-first century."[101] The Bolivian vice president, Álvaro García Linera, points out that the struggle in Latin America is not fully developed. It begins with a crisis of the state that enables a "dissident social bloc" to mobilize the people into a political project. A "catastrophic stand-off" develops between the bloc of power and the bloc of the people, which in the case of Latin America was able to be resolved for the moment on the side of the people. The new government must then "convert opposition demands into acts of state," and build a deeper and broader hegemony by "combining the ideas of mobilized society with material resources provided by or via the state." The turning point ("point of bifurcation"), for García Linera, comes through a "series of confrontations" between the blocs that are resolved in unexpected ways, with either the consolidation of the new situation or the reconstitution of the old.[102] We are at or near the point of bifurcation. What will come next cannot be predicted. Be that as it may, the results of the Bolivarian experiment so far are impressive: a study by the UN Population Fund and CEPAL found that poverty in Venezuela had been cut almost in half (from 48.6 percent in 2002 to 27.6 percent in 2008), the country having the lowest inequality in income distribution in the region, and child malnutrition having been reduced by 58.5 percent over the past decade. This handful of figures demonstrates what has been achieved through the various experimental policies of the Bolivarian regime.

To defend the gains of the pink tide and to expand their scope of action, the regimes and social movements moved against the free trade agenda of the United States. In 2005 the Bush administration went eagerly to Mar Del Plata, Argentina, to push to establish the Free Trade Areas of the Americas. In an earlier epoch, the US government would have called on the military or the oligarchy to exercise dictatorial power against the social forces ranged against it. The Monroe Doctrine of 1823 had carved out the Americas as the zone of influence of the US, and it was on this assumption that the US government encouraged military coups and rigged elections. The Monroe Doctrine has now been invalidated by the rise of powerful social movements. In a real sense, the US has had to withdraw its influence north of the Amazon River. All that remains is a very close connection with the oligarchy that rules Colombia and with the aristocratic elites of Venezuela, who have tried ceaselessly to overthrow Chávez.

But the isolation of the US is a momentary phenomenon. The South American leaders did not invalidate FTAA; they simply asked to continue the dialogue elsewhere, for few of these regimes can afford to spurn entirely the

---

101   Aijaz Ahmad, "Imperial Sunset?" *Frontline* 24: 6 (March 24–April 6, 2007).

102   Álvaro García Linera, *La Potencia Plebeya: Acción colectiva e identidades indígenas, obreras y populares en Bolivia*, Buenos Aires: CLACSO/Prometeo Libros, 2008, pp. 394–5; and Sader, *New Mole*, pp. 136–7.

massive economic and military power of the United States. This ambiguity is well expressed by Brazil's foreign minister, Celso Amorim: "We don't want to bury the agreement, and we don't want to resuscitate it either." The dialogue moved in 2004 to Chávez's proposed Bolivarian Alliance for the Americas (ALBA). The discussion around ALB begins with the recognition of the disparity between the countries of the Americas, with some (such as Haiti) in the throes of chaos, while others are fairly stable. A singular achievement of progress would be to transfer resources to the vulnerable countries through a Compensatory Fund for Strategic Convergence. These funds would be used to create food self-sufficiency for each country, as well as regional markets for equitable trade. Further, while the FTAA privileges the intellectual property rights of technological and scientific conglomerates, ALBA is invested in the rights of genetic biodiversity and of indigenous knowledge. The new rent economy contributes greatly to the asymmetry between North and South, and ALBA's notion of intellectual property would foster mutual development. Finally, ALBA opposes the policies of privatization, deregulation, and fiscal liberalization. Its singular achievement has been to insist upon the well-being of people as its foundation.

Venezuela's foreign minister, Ali Rodriguez, explained that ALBA does not oppose integration between the nations of the region: "Two positions are facing each other," he said, "those who want to support integration on the basis of competition and the other that wants to promote integration on the basis of economic cooperation, solidarity and respect for sovereignty."[103] After negotiations failed to produce movement on either proposal, Chávez commented, "Yesterday was very interesting. Some defended free trade, while we proposed various alternatives beyond the mirages of a free trade agreement." As an alternative, Chávez and the Bolivarians proposed a series of initiatives that undermined neoliberal policy: the collective renegotiation of Latin American debt; the creation of an International Humanitarian Fund to provide resources for social development; the creation of a Bank of the South that would not pursue deflationary neoliberal policies; the de-dollarization of inter-state trade and of cash reserves, including petro-currency. These were all very innovative approaches that have begun to make an impact on the region.

The dynamic from ALBA has now entered the political sphere, with the creation in February 2010 in Cancún of the Community of Latin American and Caribbean States. What is remarkable about this CLACS is that, unlike the Organization of American States, it does not include the United States and Canada. "Whenever the United States is present," Morales said at the meeting, "democracy is not guaranteed, peace with social equity is not guaranteed."

---

103   I covered the event in "Mr. Danger in his Labyrinth," *Frontline* 22: 24 (November 19–December 2, 2005).

Chávez's Venezuela was selected to host the first organizational summit of CLACS in July 2011. CLACS is the final verdict on US hegemony in the region, and another sign that an alternative platform to neoliberalism is on the horizon.

SLUMLANDS

> El Pueblo tiene hambre.
> [The people are hungry.]
> Slogan during the Caracazo, 1989

The Caracazo began in the barrios of Caracas, from where people marched into the city center to loot from the rich and vent their anger. Rage was the dominant emotion.[104] Such frustration anchored the Bolivarian project, taking it to victory in 1998. Since then, the people of the Venezuelan slums have formed committees to manage their neighborhoods and to ensure that they bargain for their part of the social wealth. Dissatisfaction persists, and so does crime. The social goods from the new regime do not flow as quickly as it should and could. Older obligations to class and state prevent the slums from getting their due. That is what makes La Piedrita in the Caracas neighborhood of 23 de Enero so complex: one day this "gang" seems to be a Chavista brigade and the next day Chávez calls its leader a terrorist. Down the street are the Alexis Vive Collective and the Coordinadora Simón Bolívar, which are more reliably Chavista. In the full light of the Bolivarian project, the slumlands are no longer simply the badlands. They are also places of organization, with radio stations and food kitchens, community organizations, and health clinics. They teem with life, and, in the context of the Bolivarian project, are flourishing.

The name of the 23 de Enero neighborhood refers to January 23, 1958—the date when the president of Venezuela, Marcos Pérez Jiménez, was rousted from his seat by a popular rebellion. It is fitting that this restive area bears the name of that uprising. It is not uncommon in the large slumlands that dominate the great cities of the Third World Project for districts to adopt the names of monumental events. In Baghdad, after the coup that brought the Nasserite general Abdul Karim Qassim to power in 1958, the regime addressed the severe housing shortage by erecting housing in an area called al-Tharwa, "the Revolution." It became a bastion of the Iraqi Communist Party, just as Beirut's southern suburbs (dahiyeh) were home to workers who joined the Lebanese Communist Party, or Bombay's Girangaon ("mill village") contained the workers and families who belonged to the Communist Party of India and its mass organizations. Until the 1980s, residents in these working-class districts worked in industrial

---

104 The prehistory of rage is captured in Alejandro Velasco, "A Weapon as Powerful as the Vote: Urban Protest and Electoral Politics in Venezuela, 1978–1983," Hispanic American Historical Review 90: 4 (2010).

enterprises and belonged to trade unions that organized them at the point of production. Mass organizations and the Communist Parties then built political bases in the residential areas. The tidal wave of globalization swept away the older industrial forms—the factories that once employed the residents in these nationalist projects. With the factories went the unions, who tried to hold on in fierce fights against the closing down of their plants and the threatened loss of housing that followed. Obstinate traditions of protest won many of these communities the right to remain where they were, even as the upkeep of their neighborhoods was no longer the role of the old industries, but had not passed fully to the state.

As the crisis in agriculture struck the countries of the South, more and more people migrated into its major cities. Many came to work in the construction projects unleashed by neoliberalism: the shopping malls and freeways, the new luxury apartment complexes and international airports. There was little or no worker housing, so that such workers lived on the land they worked, or else built "temporary" homes on public land that became the slums abutting the shining cities they erected. Bombay's population grew from 4.4 million in 1950 to 19.9 million in 2004, while Mexico City grew from 2.9 million to 22.1 million in the same period. In 2003, the UN estimated that one in five billion people on the planet lived in slums. "Instead of being a focus for growth and prosperity," the UN's HABITAT report noted, "the cities have become a dumping ground for a surplus population working in unskilled, unprotected and low-wage informal service industries and trade." This informal sector, which with the agricultural crisis was the engine of slum growth, was "a direct result of liberalization."[105]

Informal work and informal housing had their own limitations. The former meant that politics in the realm of production was severely curtailed. Union efforts in the informal sector have been concerted but futile. The compulsions of bare life in the slums forced its residents into various forms of political action. They need to ensure a supply of water and electricity, some security of tenure in their homes, and even access to education and healthcare. The politics of consumption has emerged as the focus of a significant amount of slumland political activity. The main framework, from the shack dwellers' movement in South Africa to the Assembly of the Poor in Thailand, has been the idea of urban citizenship, or perhaps more properly rights to the urban slum.[106] The primary demand for urban citizenship can be gleaned in the demands for the redistribution of social goods and public space. This can be seen in the widespread

---

105   Mike Davis, *Planet of Slums*, London: Verso, 2006, p. 175, quoting the UN HABITAT's *The Challenge of Slums*, 2003.

106   James Holston, "Insurgent Citizenship in an Era of Global Urban Peripheries," *City & Society* 21: 2 (2009).

refusals to pay for city services: 40 percent of the residents in Beirut's Hayy-Assaloum have refused to pay their electrical bills, and large numbers of the residents of Accra's Sodom and Gomorrah slum have refused to pay their water bills. The secondary demand from the slums is to be left alone. Slum-dwellers frequently build their own homes (what in Brazil is called *autoconstrução*). State intrusion typically brings bulldozers and policemen in search of a bribe, and is thus best avoided. Well-conceived plans for development from the slum-dwellers are ignored—for example, sanitation plans developed by the Orangi slum-dwellers of Karachi. When the state intervenes to "better" the slumlands, it has often meant disaster for the already perilous existence of its residents.[107] "Modernity," as Asef Bayat puts it, "is a costly affair."[108]

The grammar of slum politics is not easy to decipher. Employed in the informal sector, residents of slums have few traditional political weapons at their disposal. It is not possible to strike against employers, since theirs is often a politics of consumption rather than of production. Looking at a range of examples from Africa and Asia, Bayat argues that the initial impulse of the slum-dwellers is not to carry out their "quiet encroachments" as "a deliberate political act." Rather, they are driven by the "necessity to survive and improve a dignified life," he argues. It is only when the quiet encroachments advances that one sees that "quietly, individually and gradually, the defense of their gains is often, although not always, collective and audible."[109] The "Operation Dead Towns" movement in Niger, Cameroon, and other parts of western Africa (from 1991 onwards), the Bolivian Water Wars (Cochabamba, 2000) and Gas Wars (2003), the Soweto Water Wars (2003), and so on, illustrate these audible protests that emerged out of the quiet encroachment that preceded them. The little protests accumulate into a social force capable of such outbursts. But these are rare, and rarer still are the victories, such as that of the residents of Cochabamba against the privatization of their water. In the maquiladoras and

---

107   Arif Hasan, *Understanding Karachi: Planning and Reform for the Future*, Karachi: City Press, 1999.

108   Asef Bayat, "From 'Dangerous Classes' to 'Quiet Rebels': Politics of the Urban Subaltern in the Global South," *International Sociology* 15: 3 (2000), p. 549. The literature on slums is vast, and crosses continents. For good introductions, see Robert Neuwirth, *Shadow Cities: A Billion Squatters, A New Urban World*, London: Routledge, 2004; Janice Perlman, *Favela: Four Decades of Living on the Edge in Rio de Janeiro*, New York: Oxford University Press, 2010; Garth Myers, *African Cities*, London: Zed Books, 2011; Asef Bayat, *Street Politics: Poor People's Movements in Iran*, New York: Columbia University Press, 1997; Ashwin Desai, *We Are the Poors: Community Struggles in Post-Apartheid South Africa*, New York: Monthly Review Press, 2002; and several essays in Mike Davis and Daniel Bertrand Monk, eds, *Evil Paradises: Dreamworlds of Neoliberalism*, New York: New Press, 2008.

109   Bayat, "From 'Dangerous Classes,'" p. 547.

in the EPZs, workers have fought hard to build up their unions. From Mexico's Sindicato de Jornaleros y Obreros Industriales y de la Industria Maquiladora to India's Maruti Suzuki Workers' Union, brave and important work has been ongoing to build up the capacity of the vulnerable and overworked labor force. Horrendous working conditions have produced such terrible events as the fire in the Karachi garment factory in September 2013, where more than three hundred workers burned to death. No corporate self-regulation or labor rights monitoring from afar can substitute for building worker power in their own work places. Older trade unions that painstakingly built their locals in the now shuttered factories have had to learn new skills to break through into the world of subcontracting and off-site production. The learning curve has been very steep, but over time some gains are apparent. A combination of active hostility from management and from the government's labor bureaucracy and violence from mafia-type gangs has made the terrain all the harder to build upon.

Older forms of political organization in the domain of the working class, such as trade unions, have a hard time catering to the needs of the slum-dwellers who do not work in identifiable factories. The growth of home-based work and of very small processing and manufacturing outfits inside the slums has mushroomed. It is hard for workers in such sites to form unions, and hard as well for the most well-meaning government bureaucracy to have oversight over their dispersed work places. A variety of political forms enter this arena. The first, which we have dealt with already, are the organizations that emerge out of the politics of quiet encroachment, the political forums of the slum-dwellers themselves (community organizations, platforms to fight for various social goods, defense committees to seek justice for those arrested or killed). In many cases, these organizations receive logistical support and advice from NGOs that base themselves on the outskirts of the slumlands—and in some cases, as Bayat says, the "professionalization of the NGOs tends to diminish the mobilization feature of grassroots activism."[110] The sheer concentration of people draws in the political parties, whose tentacles seek the vote banks they embody, in exchange for which they are willing to release parts of the social wage. Both NGO professionalism and political patronage combine to produce a relationship of clientelism, with the slum-dwellers as clients and the NGOs and political parties as patrons. Rights are set aside in favor of goods—which is why one of the most common "NGOs" in the slum is the gang, whose bosses provide social services and protection financed by illegal activities and sustained by severe violence.[111]

---

110   Ibid., p. 535. For more on this, see Asef Bayat, "Activism and Social Development in the Middle East," *International Journal of Middle East Studies* 34 (2002).

111   John Rapley, "The New Middle Ages," *Foreign Affairs* 85: 3 (May–June 2006), p. 102.

An early indication of slumland politics is the entry of patrons to manage the physical plant of these neighborhoods. Al-Tharwa, in Baghdad, would be renamed Saddam City, and later, after Saddam Hussein's fall, Sadr City—first in honor of the authoritarian populist who ran the Iraqi state, and later of the clerical populist family that took charge of the neighborhoods after his defeat. In southern Beirut, Hezbollah would insinuate itself into the slumlands, as would the Shiv Sena in Bombay. Mahmoud Ahmadinejad's election campaign in 2005 gave voice to sections of Iran previously excluded from the political process: slum-dwellers and rural workers (44 percent of urban Iranians live in slums). He was standing for them, and he knew it. At a public event in October 2006, Ahmadinejad announced the idea of the "Justice Share," whereby the state would distribute the shares of certain companies among 4.6 million of the poorest Iranians, who would automatically become stockholders of the nation's wealth. This was the kind of patronage that was familiar in Chávez's Venezuela and in Thaksin's Thailand. Rising economic inequality, awareness of the class-based sacrifices of the Iran-Iraq War of the 1980s, and a lack of meaningful secular alternatives probably played a significant role in the movement of the poor towards such characters as Ahmadinejad, who, in addition to his populism, displays a personal piety and antipathy to the nouveau riche that appeals both in the youth-depleted rural areas and in the youthful slums of the cities. Despite their political differences, there is a cord that binds the slumland bases of Chávez, Thaksin, and Ahmadinejad. These political heavyweights have relied upon the "floating population" of the slums, now untethered by the loss of jobs in the formal sector and the retreat of trade unions. Organizations for the working class dissolved and were replaced by more hierarchical organizations of clerisy or authority, either way with little popular backing. The working class lost its footing in the formal sector, slipping into the informal labor markets and the slumland politics of clientelism.

The political character of the slumland is not easily defined, but it does not derive from the people themselves. Rather, it comes from outside—from the interests of those who yoke slum-dwellers into a patron-client relationship. Sometimes clericalism might be pro-establishment (Shiv Sena), sometimes anti-imperialist (Sadr); sometimes it leans towards socialism (Bolivarianism), and sometimes it has no such pretensions (Hezbollah). The cast of slumland politics is indeterminate, as the actual views of slum-dwellers are not often elaborated into organizations that reflect their needs and views.

Whether in the miserable slums of Kibera outside Nairobi or Kabul's Chaman-e-Hazoori and Khoshal Khan Mina (which house half of Kabul's people), or the more developed slums of Istanbul's Sultanbeyli and Rio's Rochina, these habitats take on the appearance of permanence. The social goods released through patronage and the hard work of the people who live in them produce life-worlds that are no longer simply temporary. The Brazilians say it is inevitable (*asfaltização*) that these slums will harden their walls and attract shops and businesses. But such permanence is fragile: it is at the whim of a bourgeois state that oscillates between permissiveness and denial. The elite classes have seceded from their own worlds, preoccupied in the cycle of accumulation on a global or national scale. This "global class" is marooned in its prosperity, besieged by the angry hordes. Unsustainable capitalism produces a dispirited (if not angry) humanity and a ravaged environment. Rather than dealing substantively with nature and people, the new "global class" relies upon its military to bash the planet and its peoples into submission (a 2004 Pentagon report on climate change put it plainly: "Disruption and conflict will be endemic features of life. Once again, warfare would define human life").[112] "Night after night, hornet-like helicopter gunships stalk enigmatic enemies in the narrow streets of the slum districts, pouring hellfire into shanties or fleeing cars," writes Mike Davis.[113] The slum could be anywhere: South Central (Los Angeles), Tivoli Gardens (Kingston), Sadr City (Baghdad), Lyari (Karachi), or Clichy-sous-Bois [Paris]. Slum-dwellers have their own view of things, including of "security." Kalpana Sharma puts the case from Mumbai's millions:

> They will tell you that they are secure in their neighbourhood because everyone knows everyone else, no outsider can enter without someone noticing the person, and at times of need most people come out to help. Gadgets like CCTV cameras cannot enhance their sense of security. What they want is "secure" housing, a place where they do not need to worry about the municipality's demolition squads, or the designs of a builder wanting to redevelop the land on which they have lived for decades. No one speaks of that kind of "security." They want security from the people who set fire to a slum. That is also terror of a kind. People lose their lifetime of belongings. A builder steps in to redevelop the land. And those who lived there peaceably for generations are told they have to prove their "eligibility" by producing the very documents that have been destroyed. Can there be anything more terrifying than finding yourself homeless and document-less in a city like Mumbai? Everyday life is terrifying for the majority in the city. It is a terror to which you get inured; you do not even think of it as terror.[114]

The view from the slum is buried. The security of the "global class" and its corporate institutions are far more important than the security of nature and of humanity. For this reason the state garrisons and occasionally bulldozes the slums. But they are otherwise tolerated, as long as their patrons (politicians, NGOs, gangs) are able to maintain the semblance of order.

---

112   Mark Townsend and Paul Harris, "Now the Pentagon Tells Bush: Climate Change Will Destroy Us," *Guardian*, February 22, 2004.

113   Davis, *Planet of Slums*, p. 206.

114   Kalpana Sharma, "Wounded Mumbai," *Economic and Political Weekly* XLVI: 30 (July 23, 2011).

To be tolerated is not a sufficient political condition. As Mike Davis puts it, "the future of human solidarity depends upon the militant refusal of the new urban poor to accept their terminal marginality within global capitalism."[115] Anchored in local movements in India (Mahila Milan and the National Slum Dwellers Federation), in Thailand (the Asian Coalition for Housing Rights), and in South Africa (the South African Homeless People's Federation), Slum Dwellers International (SDI) was formed in 1996. It uses its bases to fight for more resources for slum-dwellers (both from national budgets and from private funds such as the Gates Foundation). It also facilitates the exchange of slum-dwellers from one city or one continent to another, to learn about the common experience shared across continents. SDI, which has a majority female membership, has been invited to provide input to policies being shaped by the United Nations—in particular its Habitat Program.[116] SDI, like the Self-Employed Women's Association (SEWA), does the reform work that often makes the difference between a bare existence and a fuller life. However, what such organizations do not provide the slum-dwellers with is an opportunity to elaborate their sense of the insufficiency of life as it is, or political alternatives that go beyond the current dispensation.

In the absence of this opportunity, well-meaning organizations in the slumlands may easily become shills for governments or for foundations. It was because it did not have a deeper political analysis that the SDI found itself unable to link with the shack-dwellers' group, Abahlali baseMjondolo (AbM), whose civil disobedience is not to the taste of the SDI, and whose fierce determination to defend the rights of its membership means that it must speak out against the international organizations that fête SDI. "It is clear to us that everyone wants to speak and act in the name of the poor," the AbM noted in 2007, "but that very, very few organisations are willing to speak to the poor."[117] AbM does not want to see the poor tolerated and offered marginally improved housing; it wants to produce a much broader human condition. The same is true of SEWA, whose work with self-employed women is commendable but whose limitation is a too-close alignment with the state. This meant that, after

---

115   Davis, *Planet of Slums*, p. 202.

116   Sheela Patel, Celine D'Cruz, and Sundar Burra, "Slum/Shack Dwellers International: From Foundations to Treetops," *Environment and Urbanization* 13: 2 (2001); Sheela Patel and Celine D'Cruz, "The Mahila Milan Crisis Credit Scheme," *Environment and Urbanization* 5: 1 (1993); Benjamin Bradlow, "Out of the Garden of Eden: Moving Beyond the Rights-Based Agenda in the Urban Sector," *Sustainable Development Law and Policy* 11: 1 (Fall 2010); and Srilatha Batliwala, "Grassroots Mobilization as Transnational Actors: Implications for Global Civil Society," *Voluntas: International Journal of Voluntary and Nonprofit Organization* 13: 4 (December 2002).

117   "Neither the March Nor the Money are Ours," www.abahlali.org, November 22, 2007.

the 2002 Gujarat pogrom against Muslims, SEWA could not openly censure the government of the Far Right that ran the state and directed the killing. It remained silent so as to win some relief for its membership, both Hindus and Muslims. In the words of one Muslim member of SEWA, Rahimaben: "Now so many women were bitter and accusing. They would see me and say, where is your unity now?"[118] On the other hand, the inter-sectoral organizing of the fifteen-million-strong All-Indian Democratic Women's Association (AIDWA), which like AbM puts its politics front and center, presses for both everyday reforms and revolutionary transformation.[119] Organizers who hail from the slumlands are frequently themselves impoverished, and sometimes barely able to lift their political horizon beyond the question of bare life; struggles for survival are essential, not a strategic choice. In such conditions, long-term strategy is a luxury—but a necessary one.

Organizations such as AIDWA and AbM, despite their different scales, provide a hint as to the potential for transformative work in the slumlands. From the standpoint of a government, the *Misíons* of the Bolivarian regime provide an example of what the forces of the left can accomplish in tackling the social basis of marginality that has fostered the slumlands. Between the *Misíons* and AIDWA, the only difference is that, in one case, state power has been wielded on behalf of the slum-dwellers. The Bolivarians could not ignore the slum-dwellers, because they constituted their initial and most enduring base of support. Left movements elsewhere need to apply that lesson in organization-building for reform and transformation into the domain of the slums—abandoned until now to the clerics and authoritarian populists, the NGOs and the gangs.

THE WORLD IN 2047

In 2047 the *Communist Manifesto* will be 200 years old. What will be redeemed from that far-seeing document of the nineteenth century? When Marx and Engels wrote the *Manifesto*, they speculated about the dynamic of the future: in essence, they saw the capitalist system break free of its European origins:

> The cheap prices of commodities are the heavy artillery with which it batters down all Chinese walls, with which it forces the barbarians' intensely obstinate hatred of

---

118   For a positive assessment of SEWA, see Michael Denning, "Wageless Life," *New Left Review* II/66 (November–December 2010); and for a report on SEWA's paralysis during the Gujarat pogrom, see Tony Vaux, "Experiences of Communal Violence," *Seminar* 619 (March 2011). SEWA's director writes of the pogrom, but avoids the issue of SEWA's hesitancy. Reema Nanavaty, "Doosri Azadi," *Seminar* 619 (March 2011).

119   Elisabeth B. Armstrong, *Gender and Neoliberalism in India: The All India Democratic Women's Association and Globalization Politics*, New York: Routledge, 2013.

foreigners to capitulate. It compels all nations, on pain of extinction, to adopt the bourgeois mode of production; it compels them to introduce what it calls civilization into their midst, i.e., to become bourgeois themselves. In one word, it creates a world after its own image.

In the course of the first century after that book was written, their prognosis proved only partly correct. Capitalist social relations certainly swept across parts of the globe, but various older forms of oppression (caste relations, racial apartheid, bondage, gender inequalities) remained as long as the social wealth produced as a consequence of these relations could be absorbed into the cycles of capitalist accumulation. When Marx first wrote about the idea of the proletariat in the early 1840s in his native Germany, the industrial sector barely existed. His friend Engels had more experience of industrial concerns in Britain. It was through their shared understanding of the restiveness of the industrial workers, and their theoretical extrapolation of the proletariat's role in concentrated factories, that Marx and Engels turned to the proletariat as the subject of history. Their expectation that the world would soon be divided into two classes—the bourgeoisie (who owned the means of production) and the proletariat (who had nothing to lose but their chains)—did not fully come to pass: it is true that a very narrow segment of the population agglomerated much of the world's property and capital, but it was also true that the remainder was divided into those who enjoyed some stability, and therefore access to the illusion of upward mobility, and the vast mass who relied upon their hard work and wits to survive an iniquitous social system.

One of Marx's great prophecies was that the remarkable advance in technology would not necessarily benefit humanity, particularly if it was controlled by those of property, who would use science and machines to protect their gains rather than for the social advancement of all of humanity. That has been the case, machines having been used to displace people into desperation rather than liberate them from work—and intellectual property rights protecting wealth rather than advancing scientific solutions to social and natural problems. Banks deployed their accumulated capital to perform financial wizardry. Mathematics is the lead science, not chemistry, physics, or biology. It is no longer necessary to make things in order for profits to be harnessed; it is enough to manipulate numbers. Finance makes its own maps; money takes wide detours around the human imagination. Disposable people are needed to sign the forms for attractively packaged credit that they cannot properly afford; and then they are needed to take the blame for the system's torments. Their hopes and dreams, their visions and needs, are not at the center of things.

Our story began with the death of Atlantic liberalism and the birth of neoliberalism, which went by the name of the Washington Consensus. The new ideology was not only the consensus between 15th Street (the US Treasury) and 19th Street (the IMF) in Washington's powerful geography. It soon became the ideology of the elites in the South, who were chastened by the collapse of the Third World Project in the maw of the debt crisis of the 1980s. Sustained pressure from the G7 destroyed the possibility of other futures, and tempered the policy space to mirror the ideology of neoliberalism. The end of history was accompanied by a claim to the end of geography, the world apparently having been rendered "flat." But these were illusions, as inequalities widened within both North and South, as well as between them. No more *dirigiste* intervention by the state, no more social wage, no more New International Economic Order: now everyone was expected to aspire to the impossible—the American Dream. The contradictions could not be suppressed, as new political forms rose in the barrios and the shacks, in the farms and the slums, and in the new governments that had a closer fealty to the disposable than did those who lived in Richistan. We are now at the point where these contradictions have begun to favor the bloc of the People.

> *Dekh raftaar-e inquilab, Firaq*
> *Kitni aahista aur kitna tez.*
>
> Witness the pace of revolution, Firaq
> How slow, and how swift.

Afterword: A New South Commission

I began to research *The Poorer Nations* as the age of US primacy (1990–2003) ended. I wrote it in the interregnum between that epoch and the one that has yet to be fully born. The book studied the entrails to be able to identify new directions, settling on two major concepts—regionalism and multipolarity—to order my thoughts. My interest is in the regional and multilateral projects—created out of the poorer nations—that act in the name of the South. These are regional projects such as Bolivarianism and multilateral projects such as the IBSA and the BRICS.

When the book was published, the UN's Human Development Report of 2013 arrived with the title *The Rise of the South: Human Progress in a Diverse World*.[1] This report made the case for diversity and democracy in inter-state relations, and it suggested, as I do, that the new conversation about multipolarity had something to do with the "rise of the South." "This growing diversity in voice and power is challenging the principles that have guided policymakers and driven the major post–Second World War institutions," say the authors of the UNDP report. "Stronger voices from the South are demanding more representative frameworks of international governance that embody the principles of democracy and equity."[2] The report seems to see this creature, the "South," sometimes as a homogeneous entity and sometimes as a moniker for a collection of unrelated states. In *The Poorer Nations*, my interest is in the way regional and multilateral projects emerge out of the states of the South.

The authors of the UN report celebrate the remarkable fortunes of what are called the emergent economies—mostly the BRICS states. As the Global North settled into stasis after 2007, these emergent countries registered a more gradual slowdown—with some even able to register modest gains in sections of their economies. That this growth was largely premised on high commodity prices and that its foundation was weakened by vulnerabilities—such as reliance upon anemic Northern demand—did not make an impact on the optimism of this UNDP report. Nor did the optimism register any worry about the danger posed to the South's powerhouses by "hot money" flows. Morgan Stanley considers five countries (Brazil, India, Indonesia, South Africa and Turkey) as part of its "fragile five"—currencies vulnerable to predatory hot

---

1 *Human Development Report 2013. The Rise of the South: Human Progress in a Diverse World*, New York: UNDP, 2013.

2 Ibid., p. 1.

money.[3] Morgan Stanley was referring to the way Northern currency speculators, armed with capital thanks to low-interest borrowing in the North, could swoop into Southern financial exchanges, extracting huge short-term profits and destabilizing the emergent economies. Growth in the emergent South remains premised on unsustainable and erratic high commodity prices and hot money. Combine that problem with a domestic growth model premised upon real estate, the service industry and low-wage manufacturing—a recipe for the development of enclaves of prosperity amid slums of deprivation[4]—and the UNDP's optimism should be more guarded.

The South has arrived. But it has not arrived without deep-set problems.[5] The diagnosis of its arrival needs to be tempered by the dangers that remain in place.

US PRIMACY

Signs of the demise of US primacy are legion. The invasion of Iraq drew the US into its second simultaneous land war (Afghanistan being the other). It was an adventure that cost an enormous amount in financial terms but also in military and diplomatic terms. Estimates vary widely: Joseph Stiglitz and Linda Bilmes suggest that the wars over the past decade cost somewhere between $4 and $6 trillion dollars.[6] Despite overwhelming power in the air, the US military on the ground was worn down by casualties and lack of morale. Generals cautioned about the extension of military use, which put a damper on the most important resource of US primacy.[7] As US military use extended beyond efficacy, US diplomatic power waned—despite the wishes of leading foreign policy analysts

3   Neil Dennis, "Volatility: Emerging Markets Sell-Off Abates After Summer Storms," *Financial Times*, October 6, 2013. For more on the "carry trade," see Massimiliano La Marca, "Carry Trade and Financial Fragility," *Coping with Globalized Finance: Recent Challenges and Long-Term Perspectives*, eds. Heiner Flassbeck and Massimiliano La Marca, Geneva: United Nations Conference on Trade and Development, 2007.

4   Vijay Prashad, "India: Slums, Students and Resistance," *Red Pepper*, August 2013.

5   Nor should one take an overly pessimistic approach because the arrival of the BRICS is not going to be hasty. It will take time. This is something not clear in much of the policy literature, which suffers from impatience and cynicism. For an example, see Ruchir Sharma, "Broken BRICS: Why the Rest Stopped Rising," *Foreign Affairs*, November–December 2012.

6   Joseph Stiglitz and Linda Bilmes, *The Three Trillion Dollar War: The True Cost of the Iraq Conflict*, New York: Norton, 2008. Linda Bilmes updates the information in her report "The Financial Legacy of Iraq and Afghanistan: How Wartime Spending Decisions Will Constrain Future National Security Budgets," Harvard Kennedy School Faculty Research Working Paper Series, RWP13-006, March 2013.

7   Andrew Bacevich, *Breach of Trust: How Americans Failed Their Soldiers and Their Country*, New York: Metropolitan, 2013

such as Richard Haass, president of the Council on Foreign Relations. Haass, in April 2013, called for an extension of the American Century for the simple reason that its alternative "is not an era dominated by China or anyone else, but rather a chaotic time in which regional and global problems overwhelm the world's collective will and ability to meet them."[8] Regionalism and multipolarity portends chaos for Haass, and for the Americans whose well-being he cares about more than that of anyone else. "Americans would not be safe or prosperous in such a world," he concludes in his plea for twenty-first-century US leadership. "One Dark Ages was one too many; the last thing we need is another."

The North, despite the protections of intellectual property rights, began to see that the export of jobs (outsourcing) had enriched its multinational corporations and very small numbers of its elite, but had hollowed out its own economies. Income inequality, driven by underemployment and by a structural jobs crisis, sat uneasily beside people's expectation in the North that they would be bathed in commodities. A loose credit regime enabled the population to continue to buy despite slack income. As we all know, this credit-induced consumerism was joined with real estate speculation as well as financial speculation on credit card debt, housing debt and pension plans to produce the "jobless growth" boom that crashed in 2007. Long before that crash, reports from the IMF warned about the "global imbalances" that threatened economic stability.[9] The imbalance had reached such a point that between 1996 and 2004, the US absorbed hundreds of billions of dollars from the Global South to cover its current account deficit—the poor financed the rich.[10] The credit crunch of 2007 had been portended years earlier as US fundamentals showed a shift from

---

8   Richard Haass, "How to Build a Second American Century," *Washington Post*, April 26, 2013; and Stephen Brooks and William C. Wohlforth, *World Out of Balance: International Relations and the Challenge of American Primacy*, Princeton: Princeton University Press, 2008. Haass's view enjoys a firm consensus among the US foreign policy elite. Former US national security advisor Zbigniew Brzezinski writes that there is unlikely to be the "coronation" of a successor to the US. Rather the world will enter a "protracted phase of rather inconclusive and somewhat chaotic realignments of both global and regional power, with no grand winners and many more losers." *Strategic Vision: America and the Crisis of Global Power*, New York: Basic Books, 2012.

9   Raghuram Rajan, "Global Imbalances: An Assessment," Washington, DC, October 25, 2005. For an assessment of the IMF's role in the inflation of the US bubble and its failure to blow the whistle loudly or clearly enough, see Sanjay Dhar, "IMF Performance in the Run-Up to the Financial and Economic Crisis: Bilateral Surveillance of the United States," Washington, DC: International Evaluation Office of the IMF, Background Paper 10/04, December 9, 2010.

10   C. P. Chandrasekhar and Jayati Ghosh, "The Myth of a Global Savings Glut," International Development Economics Associates (IDEAS), September 30, 2005.

a productive, jobs-rich economy to one of structural joblessness and vitiated social welfare provisions. The US increasingly relied on its rentier power. The tenuous hold of the dollar as the world's currency still allows the US to print its money at will without fear of inflation, but how long this privilege will remain is anyone's guess. The collection of rents on intellectual property is essential to US growth rates, although even here there is a great deal of unease around the world with the way in which rents on some essential goods—pharmaceuticals, for example—get priced out of the reach of ordinary people. The architecture of US economic power is founded on pillars (the dollar, intellectual property laws) that are already being challenged from the emerging states.

Evidence of the weakness of the United States is in the failure of its political elite to craft an agenda for a jobs program. Richard Haass proposes that "what stands in the way of the next American century is American politics … Partisanship can be healthy, but not when it leads to an inability to govern and to make." If the mess of American democracy would sort itself out, Hasss suggests, then it would—amazingly—follow policies that are supposedly already being pursued: "fixing broken public schools, repairing or replacing aged infrastructure, modernizing immigration policy, reforming health care, negotiating new trade accords, lowering corporate taxes, reining in spending on entitlements, and reducing debt as a share of GDP."[11] The lack of concern for the hemorrhaged jobs sector is stunning—between 2007 and 2011, the International Labour Organisation shows, the US unemployment rate rose by 4.3 percentage points. "This sharp increase in long-term unemployment," says its *Global Employment Trends* report from 2013, "is a sign of severe labour market distress, characterized by extremely weak job creation, an increase in persons receiving unemployment benefits, growing risks that the unemployed will slip through the cracks of the underlying social protection systems as benefits are exhausted, and a risk of long-term structural damage in the labour market due to growing skills mismatches."[12] Recovery in the US can only truly occur when the jobs crisis is taken seriously and job creation becomes more than electoral rhetoric. It is the collapse of the US jobs market that has been the asphyxiating canary in the coalmine. Solutions from the political class—such

---

11 Haass, "How to Build a Second American Century." For the full argument, Richard Haass, *Foreign Policy Begins at Home: The Case for Putting America's House in Order*, New York: Basic Books, 2013.

12 International Labour Organisation, *Global Employment Trends 2013: Recovering From a Second Jobs Dip*, Geneva: ILO, 2013, p. 35. The situation is as dire in Europe. The unemployment rate on the continent in early 2013 ran to 12 percentage points, whereas in Southern Europe it was over 25 percentage points (youth unemployment remains between 55 and 70 percentage points). Heiner Flassbeck and Costas Lapavitsas, "The Systematic Crisis of the Euro—True Causes and Effective Therapies," *Studien*, Berlin: Rosa Luxemburg Stiftung, 2013, p. 33.

as lowering corporate taxes and ensuring the soundness of the dollar—tend to strengthen the economic prospects of the propertied few over the disenfranchised many.

Rising unemployment and a switch in US capital from industry to finance indicates for writers such as Immanuel Wallerstein and Giovanni Arrighi that a "slow decline" of US power began in the 1970s after a "golden age of American capitalism" that ran from 1945 to the 1970s.[13] The exaggerations of US warfare of the 2000s sped up the process of decline, with the terminal point of US power within reach. *The Poorer Nations* shares the general tenor of this literature. However, it has not been my argument that US power will collapse any day soon: US imperial power remains since US and European control of the main international institutions (including the United Nations, the IMF, the World Bank, the ratings agencies, and so on) continues despite challenges from other powers, as I detail in the book. It has also not been my argument that the decline which is easily visible is directly related to the "golden age of American capitalism" that opened up in the 1940s. On the contrary, I argue that it is not US power that is in decline but the period of US primacy that has certainly ended. US uni-polarity slowly floundered for three reasons: (1) the US economy weakened through the normal course of capitalism's punishing drive toward joblessness; (2) US military authority could destroy a country but it could not form it in its image; and (3) social movements from below—of an entirely wide range of political and cultural commitments—emerged to challenge this decade of US primacy.

REGIONALISM

One indicator of the demise of US primacy was the declaration of independence from Latin America. Driven by struggles that span the entire continent of South America, into Central America and the Caribbean, new political platforms emerged—such as the Bolivarian Alliance for the Peoples of Our America (ALBA) and the Community of Latin American and Caribbean States (CELAC). These announced that they would now manage their region without US interference, and that they would craft policies to pursue new goals—full employment and universal health care, for instance, rather than a private-sector agenda of wealth preservation. When the US attempted to scuttle this process—most dramatically with the attempted coup in Venezuela in 2002—it failed. Whatever problems exist in the region, and there are many, the single most decisive contribution of South America that it has modeled is a form of

---

13 Immanuel Wallerstein, *The Decline of American Power: The US in a Chaotic World*, New York: The New Press, 2003; and Giovanni Arrighi, *Adam Smith in Beijing: Lineages of the Twenty-First Century*, London: Verso, 2009.

regional interaction absent Great Power intervention. It has, in other words, brought regionalism out of the arid international relations textbooks to life and clothed it with innovative policy initiatives. These were underwritten by the class configuration of Venezuela's governing bloc and its indigenous oil and gas industry—Venezuela could subsidize oil sales by 40 percent to fourteen Caribbean states, it could barter oil for Bolivian soybeans and it could exchange oil for Cuban medical personnel because of a sustained, but irregular, commodity price boom.

No such climate exists in other parts of the Global South—where, on the contrary, the apocalyptic horses of war, famine and social inequality stalk the land. Old social elites and notables in most of Africa and Asia prefer an entente with the United States and Europe—and its threadbare promise of a business civilization—to a challenge to world order. A potential opening in North Africa and West Asia was dampened by coups and civil wars, a process that is well known in Central and East Africa, where democracy movements are squandered before military officers and business interests. Tensions between India and Pakistan prevent a robust regionalism germinating in South Asia, while similar and more dangerous tensions between China and Japan and the two Koreas squander any possibility for a regional entente in East Asia.

MULTIPOLARITY

One of the most interesting admissions in the 2012 US National Intelligence Council's report is the view that "by 2030, no country—whether the US, China, or any other large country—will be a hegemonic power."[14] What the intelligence officials forecast is the "diffusion of power" among states and to individuals, with democracy as the vector for this transfusion. Fascinatingly, the report makes no mention of the BRICS bloc, whose role in this diffusion I have emphasized in the *The Poorer Nations*. From the US analysts' perspective, it is inter-state rivalry that continues to explain the world with no room for the kind of bloc that the BRICS represents. What the US National Intelligence Council cannot fathom is a world order premised not so much on chaotic diffusion as a new kind of multipolarity or multilateralism—with countries such as China and India, which they predict will be the most dynamic of states by 2030, collaborating through the BRICS formation to settle inter-state and to manage non-state problems.

The IMF and the OECD predict that China will have the world's largest economy by 2016 or shortly after.[15] This would have been impossible to gauge in

14   National Intelligence Council, *Global Trends 2030: Alternative Worlds*, Washington, DC: Office of the Director of National Intelligence, 2012, p. iii.
15   A. Johansson, et al. "Looking to 2060: Long-Term Global Growth Prospects.

1991, when a Second American Century was deemed inevitable. China began its market reform agenda in 1992, the year after the USSR collapsed, and it did not begin to register astronomic growth rates till the next decade. What is interesting about China is that despite its economic power, it seems unwilling to seek the mantle of something like Chinese primacy or to thrust upon the world a Beijing Consensus. Fears of China taking over the world are typically overblown, and often lead to prescriptions for a new Cold War between the US and China that would be, as Henry Kissinger puts it in *On China*, catastrophic. Far better, from his point of view, to have the US and China evolve a Pacific Community based on a "tradition of consultation and mutual respect" that enables "parallel national aspirations."[16] What Kissinger proposes is something that sections of the Chinese establishment would welcome, although there is an equally large section of the Chinese ruling bloc that is far more inclined to the logic of regionalism and multipolarity than to a joint partnership with the United States.[17]

In 1992, Deng Xiaoping envisioned the emergence of China in the near future, "We will only become a big political power if we keep a low profile [*tao guang yang hui*] and work hard for some years; and we will then have more weight in international affairs."[18] A debate over the need to continue the "low profile" strategy has taken hold in the Chinese international relations community, with some taking the view that it is time to set this aside and proclaim a "China Dream" (such as Liu Mingfu, a former leader in the People's Liberation Army) and others keen to retain the idea and allow Chinese power to help produce a new multilateral and regional order (such as Wang Jisi, the Dean of the School of International Studies, Beijing and Director of the Institute of International and Strategic Studies at the Party School of the Central Committee).[19] Since at least 2001, Wang Jisi has been putting forward the view

---

A Going for Growth Report," OECD Economic Policy Papers, no. 3, 2012. The Chinese Academy of Sciences picks the date 2019.

16   Henry Kissinger, *On China*, New York: Penguin, 2012.

17   For an excellent overview of the sweep of Chinese intellectual thought, see Enfu Cheng, "Seven Currents of Social Thoughts and Their Development in Contemporary China with a Focus on Innovative Marxism," *The Marxist*, vol. 28, no. 4, October–December 2012.

18   Leng Rong and Wang Zuoling, eds., *Deng Xiaoping Nianpu (1975–1997)*, Beijing: Central Party Literature Press, 2004, p. 1346 quoted in Dingding Chen and Jianwei Wang, "Lying Low No More? China's New Thinking on the Tao Guang Yang Hui Strategy," *China*, vol. 9, no. 2, September 2011, p. 197.

19   Liu Mingfu's *Zhongguo Meng (The China Dream)* was published in 2010. But it is Wang Jisi who is the more influential. See his "China's Grand Strategy: A Rising Power Finds Its Way," *Foreign Affairs*, vol. 90, no. 2, March–April 2011 and Mingjiang Li, "Rising from Within: China's Search for a Multilateral World and

that "the key notion and belief in China's conceptualization of international politics is multi-polarization." When Hu Jintao ascended to the leadership in 2001, one of his first speeches included the argument that "multipolarity [*duojihua*] constitutes an important base in Chinese foreign policy."[20] China seems eager to work through the BRICS, and to manage a system framed by multipolarity.

Does the idea of multipolarity have a concrete existence in the world, apart from the lexicon of Chinese diplomacy and increasingly the diplomacy of the BRICS states? The claustrophobic conflicts in West Asia and Central Asia appear doomed as regional or multilateral interventions fail to make any breakthrough. The African Union and the Arab League—two platforms that should be harnessed by their members to promote peace—are squandered, reduced to second-rank status, and the interventions of Europe and the United States (as well as Russia, acting less like a BRICS member and more like a Great Power) are welcomed by regional elites. Nevertheless, even here regional entities make their appearance—such as the Syria Contact Group (Egypt, Iran, Saudi Arabia and Turkey) in 2012 and the call for a regional conference to settle the dispute in the Great Lakes region of Africa. Slowly the BRICS states have moved from focus on trade relations to political matters; what we do not have as yet is evidence that the rhetoric at the BRICS summit on questions of Palestine and Syria has resulted in any genuine diplomatic initiatives to promote multipolarity and regionalism in both the United Nations and in the various peace conferences that are often called by the United States and Europe (as well as Russia in its Great Power garb).

The South from Above (BRICS) has the potential of putting an end to the era of US primacy. If it does not demonstrate the will to establish a new system, the BRICS will drift into irrelevance. In the conference halls of the United Nations and even in the IMF and the World Bank, new policy ideas are being bandied about—such as alternatives to the dollar as the main international currency, and ratings agencies to compete with Moody's and Standards & Poor's. But these new developments are slow. A shift can only occur if the regional developments such as those in Latin America are emulated elsewhere, and if these in concert are able to put pressure on the Global North and the Southern elites to surrender their neoliberal policy prescriptions. But to get there, the South from Below must be able to translate the million social mutinies into political power of some kind. False starts in the Arab world are a setback but not

Its Implications for Sino-US Relations," *Global Governance*, vol. 17, no. 3, July–September 2011.

20   David Scott, "Soft Language, Soft Imagery and Soft Power in China's Diplomatic Lexicon," *China's Soft Power and International Relations*, eds. Hongyi Li and Yiyi Lu, New York: Routledge, 2012, p. 41.

a defeat. Impossibly complex struggles in Eastern Europe and Southeast Asia indicate that the people are energetic, but the direction of their political formations and campaigns are unclear—sometimes egged on by toxic nationalism or by charismatic elite politicians who use popular energy for their own sectional gain. Confidence that these places will produce platforms of regionalism in the manner suggested by Bolivarianism is not high. Nevertheless, this is the way of the future—the possible history of the Global South—as regional entities under pressure from social movements fashion themselves for self-governance once US power begins to drift homewards.

None of this is by itself generative of a radical future. It is simply a more democratic one. But one of the arguments of *The Poorer Nations* is that even this democratic future is not possible without a shift in the class configurations in the Global South. Old elites are not prepared for this shift. They remain enamored of US power, and are unsure how to deal properly with the "rise of China." Such responses are rooted in an older paradigm of primacy, not able to grasp the shift to a world where multipolarity and regionalism will be the governing concepts. The only way for the transition to multipolar regionalism to occur is if the old elites are dethroned from political power by social movements that now take political power.

A NEW SOUTH COMMISSION?

The authors of the UNDP report *The Rise of the South* note that it would be a good idea to "establish a new South Commission to bring a fresh vision of how the South's diversity can be a force for solidarity."[21] If such a Commission were to be established, and if it were to have the full backing of the BRICS—as it should—what would it propose? Given the weaknesses I have pointed to and the BRICS's own hesitation to be a model for anyone, this is not an idle question. If the South does not want to produce an empty model, at the very least it has in its experiments around neoliberalism produced some new principles to anchor the kind of discussion that would happen at a new South Commission. What would these principles look like? Multilateralism and regionalism provide the scaffolding of a new order. What happens inside that skeleton is the real question, and it is to that which a new South Commission would have to attend.

Better ideas do not by themselves change the world. The suffocation of the dominant social forces precludes alternative ideas from being taken seriously. There are hundreds of designs in engineering labs for smokeless chimneys and waterless toilets, but their existence has not meant that they have been adopted for mass usage. It will require a shift in social power to allow new ideas and new technologies to become acceptable in our times. In the absence of such a

---

21 *Human Development Report 2013*, p. 119.

change, an "alternative" will simply mean a solution of a practical nature that is not capable of being fully embraced.

What is possible within the current dispensation is social welfare. Though this is not a systematic alternative, it is nothing to be scoffed at. When the social crisis is acute, as it is now, any form of relief is to be welcomed. Measures to bring down the prices of foodstuffs, provision of unemployment benefits or government employment schemes, and so on, are necessary, but they should not be confused with an alternative path. Does this mean that alternatives are impossible? Far from it. Popular struggles and innovative social incubators have given rise to several policy ideas. These ideas often emerge from the energy of mass social movements, but they are given short shrift by a media that does not or chooses not to understand its language.

Below are three broad principles that should be central to a Twenty-First-Century South Commission:

Universal Access—The idea of basic needs came out of the UN and then was impounded by the neoliberal framework of the Millennium Development Goals (MDG). What was lost in the MDG's accountancy was the principle of universal access by every person to certain basic needs—food, healthcare, employment, social security and so on. The core demand of the basic needs campaign, clear to the majority of the world, is that access must be institutionalized. Those in authority cannot discount these demands. What they do is to accept them in principle and then hollow them out in implementation. They say that universal access is too expensive. Well it is certainly expensive, but it is not beyond our means. Given the way the social surplus is appropriated by very few and is spent on wars and security, such demands are certainly impractical. But that is a political problem, not an economic one. Because it is a political problem, two elements have to considered—the growth of political movements to champion and defend universal access, and the role of UN agencies to monitor such access.

Economic Power—When economics became a technical science, it abjured considerations of economic power. It seems an embarrassment to talk about land reforms and trade unions. Control over land is crucial in Africa and Asia, where farmers continue to battle against all odds to maintain their sovereignty over their livelihood. Alongside this lingering and urgent demand for control over land, is that for control over industrial processes. The global commodity chain has annulled the policy of nationalization—rendering mute the ability of a state to take hold of its industrial plants. This means that those whose tentacles stretch across continents exercise power over industry. These multinational corporations had once been studied by the UN at the Centre for Transnational Corporations, set up in 1974, but Northern power closed down that office in 1993. It is hard for workers to build their own power against these firms, and it is hard for the UN to even study the way in which corporate power operates outside the purview of democratic accountability. If the UN cannot take hold of multinational companies, it certainly has no regulatory authority over money. Seemingly mysterious social forces, hidden behind ratings agencies and ideas such as "confidence of the markets," dampen the ability of states to widen their policy framework—if novel policy decisions are taken, money goes on strike. The price of borrowing is a form of power that is rarely understood in public, and the idea that economics is a kind of undecipherable hieroglyphic simply reinforces the undemocratic way in which money commands economic activity.

Social Wage—Any investigation of an alternative, in an age of ecological crisis and structural unemployment, has to take seriously the forgotten idea of the social wage. Better public goods, forged with the best of today's science, would not only reduce the burdens on individuals and families, it would enable societies to create socio-ecological solutions to problems. Rather than using private cars with high insurance premiums, people will use more public transport such as light rail. The focus should be on high-quality public rather than private healthcare. These are elementary policies burdened by the calculated failures of the public sector in an earlier era and overshadowed by the highly subsidized and malignant private sector of our times. Absent a discussion about the creation of public goods, it is doubtful if any solution to the climate catastrophe can be envisaged.

This is the framework of an alternative. These are the principles that should anchor the new thinking if there is to be a second South Commission, and certainly it should be a formulation that should be taken seriously by those of us who are interested in ideas of development and social justice. We now have new institutional platforms that could be shaped with a much more capacious imagination.[22]

January 2014
Beirut, Lebanon

---

22 Sections of this afterword were delivered as the keynote address at the UNCTAD Public Symposium, Geneva, June 2013; as a keynote presentation at the thirtieth anniversary conference of the Welfare Association, Ramallah, October 2013; and as an intervention at the European Center for Peace and Development, Belgrade, October 2013.

Acknowledgements

The seed for this book fell onto the ground as I finished writing *The Darker Nations*, whose story began in the 1920s and came to a close in the 1980s. It seemed to me that last section of the book—how the Third World Project was defeated and what emerged afterwards—lacked dimension. I had indicated that more would be found in the Brandt Commission and the South Commission, as well as in the emergence of the G7 from 1974, but I did not develop these ideas.

It took a push from Lisa Armstrong for me to head out to Geneva and see if the South Commission had any archives that might indicate a fuller story. I wrote to the South Centre, which is the heir to the Commission, and received a very gracious invitation from its director, Martin Khor. In Geneva, Xin Cui and Vasantha Pushparaj made me very welcome, and led me to the old bomb shelter in the basement—where I discovered the entire archive of the South Commission, untouched since it had been put there by Vasantha and others. With a key to the shelter and little else to do in Geneva, I basically lived there, coming up for air and to eat but for little else. At the Centre, I was lucky to meet Yash Tandon, the former director of the Centre, and several of the impressive and hard-working staff. Near the Gare Cornavin I met with Chakravarti Raghavan, who led me through the intricacies of the North-South Dialogue.

Over the years, I have benefited greatly from the wisdom of the Geneva set. R. Krishnamurti, the *chef de cabinet* to UNCTAD Secretary-General Raúl Prebisch, not only advised me throughout the process of my research, but also graciously sent me his own archive of letters and documents. I refer to these as the Krishnamurti Papers. Branislav Gosovic, who was the guts of the South Commission and the first director of the South Centre, not only granted me access to his memory, but he read the entire manuscript, pushed me into new places, and saved me from a great deal of embarrassment. He also invited me to address a Special Session of the United Nations in Geneva to commemorate the fiftieth anniversary of the Non-Aligned Movement, where I was able to meet with and learn from Benjamin Mkapa (former president of Tanzania and chairman of the board of the South Centre), Angélica Navarro Llanos (permanent representative of Bolivia to the UN in Geneva), Richard Kozul-Wright (UNCTAD), Raja Khalidi (UNCTAD), Nitin Desai (former UN under-secretary-general for economic and social affairs), and several others. I appreciate very much the memories and analyses of other Geneva hands, such as S. P. Shukla (particularly on GATT), Prakash Shah (particularly on oil diplomacy), and Thandika Mkandawire (at the time of UNRISD). Conversations with two of India's finest diplomats, both ambassadors to the UN—Nirupam Sen and Hardeep Singh Puri—helped me understand the intricacies of the UN's history over the past thirty years. Nirupam in particular gave me the confidence to tell the story of the paralysis in the UN through the visible hand of the G7. On this, Branislav's work with Boutros Boutros-Ghali has been an essential handbook. An early interview with Devaki Jain, one of the most innovative of the commissioners on the South Commission, and an enduring friendship with her, have provided me with the intellectual compass to orient myself in these debates and histories. I am grateful to Boutros Boutros-Ghali for his encouragement during the process of writing this book.

Having read the South Commission's papers and learned a great deal from its insight, I knew that I needed to pivot backwards to learn about the demise of Atlantic liberalism (through the Brandt Commission) and the rise of the G7. I was fortunate to learn as much as I could from the Willy Brandt papers at the Bibliothek der Friedrich-Ebert-Stiftung (Bonn). The G7 documents for the early years are tucked away in the Gerald Ford Presidential Library at the University of Texas (Austin), in the Margaret Thatcher Foundation, and in the Ronald Reagan Presidential Foundation and Library (Ventura, CA). I was also helped along by the G8 Information Centre at the University of Toronto.

Meeting the next generation of diplomatic historians in the United States and Western Europe helped me orient my analysis along the lines of their remarkable research. A conference at Williams College in 2010 allowed me to interact with Jeffrey Byrne, Paul Chamberlain, Piero Gleijeses, Ryan Irwin, Chris Lee, Erez Manela, and later, at Princeton in 2011, with some of the same but with the addition of Rinna Kullaa, Michele Louro, Bradley Simpson, and Jason Parker. At Williams, I met Shanti Singham, who is linked through her remarkable father Archie to this entire history. Later I met her brother Roy Singham, another member of the fellowship of the Third World, and Pernille Ironside, whose UNICEF work is part of the good side of history indicated in this book. James Parisot invited me to talk about these themes at Binghamton, where I was happy to see my friend and comrade Walden Bello, whose work is all over this book. Conversations and readings of the work of my friends Jayati Ghosh and K. S. Jomo have been essential to my formulations. They will see echoes of their own work here.

I delivered part of Chapter 4 as a lecture in Vienna—for which thanks to Berthold Unfried and Eva Himmelstoss, and my old comrade, Marcel van der Linden. Chatting with David Mayer, Raquel Varela, Ralf Hoffrogge, Janos Jemnitz, and others was a tonic. Alex Lubin invited me to Beirut to deliver what became the introduction to this book at the Prince Alwaleed Bin Talal Bin Abdulaziz Alsaud Center for American Studies and Research at the American

University of Beirut. Fawwaz Trabulsi published it in Arabic in *Bidayat*, and Magid Shahide did so in *InterFace*.

So much of what I write is guided by the friendship and encouragement of Sudhanva Deshpande. Prabir Purkayashta is not only a singular touchstone, but also a terrific resource. The encouragement and advice of Brinda Karat, Prakash Karat, and Aijaz Ahmad meant the world to this book. As I hope that Chapter 4 makes clear, I rely greatly on the political wisdom and the sheer intelligence of Prabhat Patnaik.

The planetary scope of the book was enriched by a project that I have been doing with LeftWord Books, the *Dispatches* series. With Teo Ballvé I edited *Dispatches from Latin America* (2006), learned a great deal from the hemisphere, and eventually got to meet many Latin Americanist intellectuals, such as Ben Dangl, Steve Ellner, Greg Wilpert, Joaquin Chavez, Carol Delgado, Pablo Morales, Christy Thornton, and Greg Grandin. I edited *Dispatches from Pakistan* with Qalandar Bux Memon and Madiha R. Tahir. Qalandar's enthusiasm and energy had an infectious role to play, pushing me to a more creative reading of Fanon, to take seriously the granite block. With Paul Amar, I edited *Dispatches from the Arab Spring*, a book that was produced alongside my own book on the Libyan War, *Arab Spring, Libyan Winter* (AK Press). We assembled some superb scholars to reflect on the contemporary events with an eye to history and sociology. While working on my book and the edited volume, I continued to learn so much from old and new friends—Pepe Escobar, Bassam Haddad, Toufic Haddad, Adam Hanieh, Sam Husseini, Karim Makdisi, Syed Mohammed Marandi, Magid Shihade, Mayssun Sukharieh, and Fawwaz Trabulsi. I look forward to the volume that shall come on Africa and on Southern Europe.

My editors Alexander Cockburn, Jeffrey St. Clair, and R. Vijayshankar at *Counterpunch* and *Frontline*, the team at *Asia Times*, and Siddharth Varadarajan at *The Hindu* provided me with a unique opportunity to try out my ideas. Alexander's departure as I was working on the final parts of this book was a blow; he taught me how to write. I am glad to have friends whose intellectual sustenance is essential, people such as Tariq Ali, Vivek Bald, Patrick Bond, Noam Chomsky, Jo Comerford, Omar Dahi, Junot Diaz, Ruthie Gilmore, Craig Gilmore, Doug Henwood, Sami Hermez, Robin Kelley, Bakari Kitwana, Amitava Kumar, Raza Mir, Jeff Napolitano, Sunaina Maira, P. Sainath, and Mayssun Sukharieh. I have come to rely on my Chicago Team: Bill Ayers, Martha Biondi, Bernardine Dohrn, Jesse Jackson, Santita Jackson, Alice Kim, Lisa Lee, Harish Patel, Barbara Ransby, James Thindwa, and Janette Wilson; my NYC friends (among others): Kazembe Balagun, Lisa Duggan, Johanna Fernandes, Ali Mir, Liz Mestres, Joan Morgan, Rupal Oza, Prachi Patankar, Ashwini Rao, Najla Said, Nikhil Singh, Teju, and Max Uhlenbeck; my colleagues at Trinity: Zayde Antrim, Raymond Baker, Davarian Baldwin, Janet Bauer, Kifah Hanna, Shafqat

Hussain, Seth Markle, Garth Myers, Maurice Wade, Johnny Williams, and Dean Rena Fraden.

I am grateful to Andy Hsiao at Verso and Sudhanva Deshpande at LeftWord, who edited *Darker Nations* and have been with me again as we worked on this "sequel."

I am grateful for the love and support of my vast family that stretches from Calcutta (Mummy, Rosy) to California (Leela, Jojo, Meera and the kids, and the Armstrongs), going through Delhi (my *mashis*, Atiya, Shonali, Tara, Mimi, Reeka, and more kids...) and Madras (Rani and Harish and even more kids), and so many points in between.

Zalia Maya and Rosa Maya are already aware of what these books are about. Zalia, at eleven, is a compassionate analyst of the social collapse in the US, having looked at foreclosures with empathy and dismay. Rosa, at six, is sitting beside me as I type this, pretending to read *Capital*, volume 2. Lisa, who read the entire manuscript, knows that large sections of it are simply the result of our twenty-five-year intellectual and political partnership. That is why this book is for her.

Index

On the Typeface

This book is set in Minion, a typeface designed by Robert Slimbach for Adobe Systems in 1990, which has become one of the few contemporary book faces to rival the classic types of Caslon, Bembo, and Garamond. Though it has no obvious precursor, it retains a calligraphic sentiment that Robert Bringhurst dubs "neohumanist" in his *Elements of Typographic Style*.

Telltale features of Minion include the subtle cant in the bar of the "e," the angular bowl of the "a," and the tapered bulbs that terminate the head of the "a" and the tails of the "y" and "j."

Minion's restrained personality and even color have made it a popular workhorse type, the narrow set width of which provides economy yet does not detract from its suitability for book settings.